# ADVANCED TEXTS IN ECONOMETRICS

**Other Advanced Texts in Econometrics**

*ARCH: Selected Readings*
Edited by Robert F. Engle

*Asymptotic Theory for Integrated Processes*
By H. Peter Boswijk

*Bayesian Inference in Dynamic Econometric Models*
By Luc Bauwens, Michel Lubrano, and Jean-François Richard

*Co-integration, Error Correction, and the Econometric Analysis of Non-Stationary Data*
By Anindya Banerjee, Juan J. Dolado, John W. Galbraith, and David Hendry

*Dynamic Econometrics*
By David F. Hendry

*Likelihood-Based Inference in Cointegrated Vector Autoregressive Models*
By Søren Johansen

*Long-Run Economic Relationships: Readings in Cointegration*
Edited by R. F. Engle and C. W. J. Granger

*Modelling Economic Series: Readings in Econometric Methodology*
Edited by C. W. J. Granger

*Modelling Non-Linear Economic Relationships*
By Clive W. J. Granger and Timo Teräsvirta

*Modelling Seasonality*
Edited by S. Hylleberg

*Non-Stationary Time Series Analysis and Cointegration*
Edited by Colin P. Hargreaves

*Outlier Robust Analysis of Economic Time Series*
By André Lucas, Philip H. Franses, and Dick van Dijk

*Panel Data Econometrics*
By Manuel Arellano

*Periodicity and Stochastic Trends in Economic Time Series*
By Philip Hans Franses

*Progressive Modelling: Non-nested Testing and Encompassing*
Edited by Massimiliano Marcellino and Grayham E. Mizon

*Stochastic Limit Theory: An Introduction for Econometricians*
By James Davidson

*Stochastic Volatility*
Edited by Neil Shephard

*Testing Exogeneity*
Edited by Neil R. Ericsson and John S. Irons

*Time Series with Long Memory*
Edited by Peter M. Robinson

*Time-Series-Based Econometrics: Unit Roots and Co-integrations*
By Michio Hatanaka

*Workbook on Cointegration*
By Peter Reinhard Hansen and Søren Johansen

# Finite Sample Econometrics

AMAN ULLAH

OXFORD
UNIVERSITY PRESS

# OXFORD

UNIVERSITY PRESS

Great Clarendon Street, Oxford OX2 6DP

Oxford University Press is a department of the University of Oxford.
It furthers the University's objective of excellence in research, scholarship,
and education by publishing worldwide in

Oxford New York

Auckland Bangkok Buenos Aires Cape Town Chennai
Dar es Salaam Delhi Hong Kong Istanbul Karachi Kolkata
Kuala Lumpur Madrid Melbourne Mexico City Mumbai Nairobi
São Paulo Shanghai Taipei Tokyo Toronto

Oxford is a registered trade mark of Oxford University Press
in the UK and in certain other countries

Published in the United States
by Oxford University Press Inc., New York

British Library Cataloguing in Publication Data
Data available

Library of Congress Cataloging in Publication Data
Data available

ISBN 0-19-877447-8 (hbk.)
ISBN 0-19-877448-6 (pbk.)

1 3 5 7 9 10 8 6 4 2

Typeset by Newgen Imaging Systems (P) Ltd., Chennai, India
Printed in Great Britain
on acid-free paper by
Biddles Ltd., King's Lynn, Norfolk

# Contents

To my daughter, Sushana Ullah

# Preface

Over the last five decades, significant advances in the estimation and inference of various econometric models have taken place. This includes the classical linear model where the explanatory variables are nonstochastic (fixed) and the error is normally distributed, and the non-classical models, where these classical assumptions are violated. These models are frequently used in applied work, such as the simultaneous equation models, models with heteroskedasticity and/or serial correlation, limited dependent variable models, panel data models, and a large class of time series models. Many of these models may also be nonlinear, explanatory variables can be stochastic and errors follow nonnormal distributions. While the classical linear model is often estimated by the ordinary least squares (LS) or generalized least squares (GLS) estimators, the non-classical models have largely used the maximum likelihood (ML), the method of moments, the instrumental variable, and the extremum estimation techniques. Within this setup, establishing the properties of estimators in the classical linear model are straightforward for samples of any size and they are well presented in econometrics textbooks. For the non-classical models, however, textbooks have mostly presented large sample theory results despite the existing finite sample analytical results. One explanation of this may be the technical difficulties in developing the existing finite sample results and the complexities of their expressions.

It is well known that the large sample theory properties may not imply the finite sample behavior of econometrics estimators and test statistics. In fact, the use of asymptotic theory results for small or even moderately large samples may give misleading results. The field of finite sample theory has been developing rapidly since the seminal contributions of Sir R. A. Fisher. Its applications in improving the inference for finite samples, the issues of bias-adjusted estimation, analyzing weak instruments, determining optimal instruments and bootstrapping have further enhanced the importance of the large existing literature on the finite sample.

This book is intended to provide a somewhat first comprehensive and unified treatment of finite sample theory and to apply the basic tools of this to various estimators and test statistics used in various econometric models. Both time series and cross section data models as well as panel data models are considered.

The results are explored for linear and nonlinear models as well as models with normal and nonnormal errors.

An aspect of the book is to use fairly unified approaches to develop the results in finite sample theory. Within this framework we also indicate, at appropriate places, the alternative methods developed by others and provide the results in a simpler way. In some cases we are able to establish more general results and sometimes we provide new results. Since we include some new results in addition to previously known ones we hope that this book may be helpful for further developments of the finite sample results in many other econometric situations.

The book contains seven chapters and an appendix. Chapter 1 gives the introduction to finite sample econometrics. Chapter 2 gives the methods of obtaining the moments of econometric statistics. The methods of analyzing distributions are given in Chapter 3. The finite sample results for various econometric models are then discussed in Chapters 4–7. Chapter 4 deals with the results in the classical regression model. Chapter 5 considers the analysis of models such as the heteroskedasticity model, the serial correlation model, the seemingly unrelated regressions model, the limited dependent variable model, and the panel data model. The time series models are analyzed in Chapter 6. Finally, Chapter 7 gives results for the simultaneous equations models. It is assumed that the reader is familiar with the basic concepts of calculus and statistics and has a good background in introductory econometrics.

This book is designed for graduate courses in econometrics and statistics. It can be used both as a textbook and as a reference for the graduate courses in econometrics and statistics. Since the focus of the book is on the finite sample results and not on details about econometric models, this book can also be supplemented by standard econometrics texts. Finally, the book may also be useful for students and researchers in other applied sciences, such as medicine, psychology, engineering, and sociology.

I want to express my deep appreciation to those who have helped and influenced the gradual development of this over the years work. In particular, I would like to thank R. A. L. Carter, D. E. A. Giles, D. Hendry, G. Hillier, G. Judge, J. Knight, E. Maasoumi, R. Mittelhammer, A. L. Nagar, G. D. A. Phillips, P. C. B. Phillips, B. Raj, H. D. Vinod, A. Zellner, and V. Zinde-Walsh. Clive Granger was especially encouraging regarding this project and provided useful comments. Yong Bao and Xiao Huang read the complete manuscript and provided helpful comments. I am deeply grateful to Carolina Stickley, who typed this challenging manuscript with remarkable skill and accuracy. Finally, the largest debt, of course, belongs to my wife Shobha and daughter Sushana for their patience and help in making this work a reality. I would especially like to acknowledge my great debt to my guru A. L. Nagar, and to my friend and co-author, the late Viren Srivastava.

# 1

# Introduction

An important tool of econometric inference for analyzing an economic phenomenon is the use of the asymptotic distribution theory of estimators and test statistics. One important reason for the popularity of the asymptotic theory results in econometric analysis is their ultimate simplicity. For example, using the central limit theorems, most of the estimators can be shown to follow normality, which can then be utilized to form confidence intervals. It is often observed, however, that asymptotic properties are commonly shared by several estimators of any specific parameter of interest. For example, the ordinary least squares (LS) estimator and the Stein-rule estimators (under certain conditions) for coefficient vectors in a linear regression model have the same asymptotic distribution. Similarly, for coefficients in an over-identified structural equation of a simultaneous equation model, the two-stage LS, and the limited information maximum likelihood (ML) are known to have identical asymptotic properties under some mild conditions. A similar result holds for the three-stage LS and for the full information maximum likelihood estimators too. In the context of seemingly unrelated regression equations, all feasible generalized LS estimators stemming from the consistent estimation of the variance–covariance matrix of disturbances have identical asymptotic distributions. Consequently, in such circumstances it is not possible to deduce any clear preference of one estimator over the other. Besides this, asymptotic properties hinge upon a crucial condition that the number of observations be infinitely large. This condition is generally not met in practice, although there are an increasing number of data sets in finance, development economics, and labor economics, which contain a large number of observations. Even if a large number of observations is available, it may not be desirable to use them because they may not satisfy some of the other conditions of the asymptotic theory results, which are often not verified by the practitioners. For instance, longer time series observations may tend to violate the assumption of constancy of parameters on which the asymptotic theory is based. Also the time series observations may follow random walks or some other kind of nonstationarity, which can violate the standard asymptotic normality results, a point first brought to attention by Granger and Newbold (1974) and developed by Phillips (1986). Moreover, the question relating to how "large" the number of observations should be to achieve the asymptotic properties results remains largely unanswered. Thus the basic requirement of the number of observations to be infinitely large for the asymptotic results to hold true may not be achieved in many practical applications and therefore the use of inference procedures based on the asymptotic distribution theory may cast doubts about their continued validity in finite samples since the asymptotic results need not carry over to finite samples, a point first brought to attention in the seminal work of Fisher (1921). For example, if the asymptotic distribution of an estimator has the smallest variability, its finite sample exact distribution may not continue to possess the property of smallest variability. To illustrate this point, let us consider a bivariate linear regression model:

$$y_i = \beta x_i + u_i, \quad i = 1, 2, \ldots, n, \tag{1.1}$$

where $y_i$ and $x_i$ denote the $i$th observation on the variable and the explanatory variable, $\beta$ is the unknown regression coefficient and $u_i$ is the error term with the following properties:

$$E(u_i) = 0 \quad \text{for all } i$$

$$E(u_i u_j) = \begin{cases} \sigma^2 & \text{for all } i = j \\ 0 & \text{for all } i \neq j \end{cases}$$

$\sigma^2$ being an unknown but finite quantity. Further, it is assumed that $1/n \sum_{i=1}^{n} x_i^2$ tends to a finite nonzero quantity $m_{xx}$ as $n$ approaches $\infty$. This assumption does not hold, for instance, in the presence of trend. For example, if $x_i = i$, we have

$$\frac{1}{n} \sum_{i=1}^{n} x_i^2 = \frac{n(n+1)(2n+1)}{6}$$

whose limiting value as $n \to \infty$ is obviously not finite.

The ordinary LS estimator of $\beta$ is given by

$$b = \frac{\sum_{i=1}^{n} x_i y_i}{\sum_{i=1}^{n} x_i^2}, \tag{1.2}$$

which is the best linear unbiased estimator with variance as

$$V(b) = E(b - \beta)^2 = \frac{\sigma^2}{\sum_{i=1}^{n} x_i^2}. \tag{1.3}$$

The asymptotic distribution of $n^{1/2}(b - \beta)$ is a normal distribution with mean 0 and variance $(\sigma^2/m_{xx})$.

Similarly, an unbiased estimator of $\sigma^2$ based on ordinary LS residuals is given by

$$s^2 = \frac{1}{(n-1)} \sum_{i=1}^{n} (y_i - bx_i)^2. \tag{1.4}$$

If the errors follow a normal probability law, it is well known that the exact distribution of $b$ is normal with mean $\beta$ and variance $(\sigma^2/\sum x_i^2)$ while the exact distribution of $(n-1)s^2/\sigma^2$ is the $\chi^2$ distribution with $(n-1)$ degrees of freedom (d.f.). Further, $b$ and $s^2$ are stochastically independent.

Now let us consider the following two estimators of $\theta = \beta^2$:

$$\hat{\theta}_0 = b^2$$

$$\hat{\theta}_1 = b^2 - \frac{s^2}{(\sum x_i^2)}. \tag{1.5}$$

If we define

$$e = (b - \beta)$$

$$\epsilon = (s^2 - \sigma^2) \tag{1.6}$$

it follows from the normality of disturbances that

$$E(e) = 0, \qquad E(e^2) = \frac{\sigma^2}{(\sum x_i^2)},$$

$$E(e^3) = 0, \qquad E(e^4) = \frac{3\sigma^4}{(\sum x_i^2)^2}, \tag{1.7}$$

$$E(\epsilon) = 0, \qquad E(\epsilon^2) = \frac{2\sigma^4}{(n-1)}.$$

Using these results, we observe that

$$E(b^2) = E(\beta + e)^2$$
$$= E(\beta^2 + 2\beta e + e^2)$$
$$= \beta^2 + \frac{\sigma^2}{(\sum x_i^2)}$$

so that the bias of $\hat{\theta}_0$ is

$$B(\hat{\theta}_0) = E(\hat{\theta}_0 - \theta) = \frac{\sigma^2}{(\sum x_i^2)}. \tag{1.8}$$

Similarly, the mean squared error (MSE) of $\hat{\theta}_0$ is

$$\text{MSE}(\hat{\theta}_0) = E(\hat{\theta}_0 - \theta)^2$$

$$= E(b^2 - \beta^2)^2$$

$$= E[(\beta + e)^2 - \beta^2]^2$$

$$= E(2\beta e + e^2)^2$$

$$= E(4\beta^2 e^2 + 4\beta e^3 + e^4)$$

$$= 4\beta^2 \frac{\sigma^2}{(\sum x_i^2)} + \frac{3\sigma^2}{(\sum x_i^2)^2}$$

$$= \frac{\sigma^2}{(\sum x_i^2)} \left[ 4\beta^2 + \frac{3\sigma^2}{(\sum x_i^2)} \right]. \tag{1.9}$$

For the estimator $\hat{\theta}_1$, we find that the bias and MSE are

$$B(\hat{\theta}_1) = E(\hat{\theta}_1 - \theta)$$

$$= E\left[ b^2 - \frac{s^2}{(\sum x_i^2)} - \beta^2 \right]$$

$$= E\left[ (\beta + e)^2 - \frac{\sigma^2 + \epsilon}{(\sum x_i^2)} - \beta^2 \right]$$

$$= E\left[ 2\beta e + e^2 - \frac{\sigma^2}{(\sum x_i^2)} - \frac{\epsilon}{(\sum x_i^2)} \right]$$

$$= 0. \tag{1.10}$$

$$\text{MSE}(\hat{\theta}_1) = V(\hat{\theta}_1) = E(\hat{\theta}_1 - \theta)^2$$

$$= E\left[ 2\beta e + e^2 - \frac{\sigma^2}{(\sum x_i^2)} - \frac{\epsilon}{(\sum x_i^2)} \right]^2$$

$$= \frac{\sigma^2}{(\sum x_i^2)} \left[ 4\beta^2 + 2\left(1 + \frac{1}{n-1}\right) \frac{\sigma^2}{(\sum x_i^2)} \right]. \tag{1.11}$$

Examining the expressions (1.8) and (1.10), we find that the estimator $\hat{\theta}_0$ is biased and the bias is positive while the estimator $\hat{\theta}_1$ is unbiased. Similarly, we observe from (1.9) and (1.11) that the MSE of $\hat{\theta}_0$ is larger than the variance of $\hat{\theta}_1$ when $n$ exceeds 3. These results are exact in nature. If we look at the asymptotic properties, it is easy to see that both the estimators $\hat{\theta}_0$ and $\hat{\theta}_1$ are consistent. Further, the asymptotic variances of $n^{1/2}(\hat{\theta}_0 - \theta)$ and $n^{1/2}(\hat{\theta}_1 - \theta)$ are identical and their expression is $(4\beta^2\sigma^2/m_{xx})$. It thus follows that both the estimators are asymptotically equivalent in the sense that they have the same asymptotic properties and therefore one cannot be preferred over the other. However, the corresponding results in finite samples clearly reveal that $\hat{\theta}_0$ and $\hat{\theta}_1$ have markedly different properties.

Next, let us consider the estimation of $\theta = (1/\beta)$, the inverse of the regression coefficient $\beta(\neq 0)$. It is customary to estimate it by $\hat{\theta} = (1/b)$. Now consider the $r$th $(r > 0)$ moment of it:

$$E(\hat{\theta}^r) = E\left(\frac{1}{b^r}\right)$$

$$= \left(\sum x_i^2 / 2\pi\sigma^2\right)^{1/2} \int_{-\infty}^{\infty} \frac{1}{b^r} \exp\left\{-\frac{1}{2\sigma^2}(b-\beta)^2\left(\sum x_i^2\right)\right\} db, \quad (1.12)$$

which is infinite. It thus follows that $\hat{\theta}$ has no finite moments. In other words, the exact distribution of $\hat{\theta}$ possesses no finite moments. However, it can easily be seen that the asymptotic distribution of $n^{1/2}(\hat{\theta} - \theta)$ is normal with mean 0 and variance $\sigma^2/\beta^4\left(\sum x_i^2\right)$. Thus the moments are finite for an infinitely large number of observations while they are infinite for a finite number of observations.

The results in (1.2) to (1.12) can also be verified for a special case where $x_i = 1$ for $i = 1, \ldots, n$. In this case, (1.1) becomes the population mean model $y_i = \beta + u_i$ and the estimator $b$ in (1.2) reduces to the sample mean $\bar{y} = \sum y_i/n$. To emphasize the above points further, consider $b_1 = nb/(n+1)$ to be an alternative estimator of the mean $\beta$. Then, one can easily show that both $b_1$ and $b$ are asymptotically unbiased and their asymptotic MSEs are equivalent, that is $n$ MSE $(b_1) = n$ MSE $(b) = \sigma^2$ as $n \to \infty$. However, their finite sample behaviors are different. While $b$ is unbiased, $b_1$ is biased; $E(b_1) - \beta = -\beta/(n+1)$. Further MSE$(b) = V(b) = \sigma^2/n$, but MSE$(b_1) = (n^2/(n+1)^2)V(b) + \beta^2/(n+1)^2$. Thus MSE$(b) <$ MSE$(b_1)$ so long as $\sigma^2/\beta^2 < n/(2n+1)$.

The above illustrations clearly demonstrate that the asymptotic distribution theory may lead to some results, which may significantly depart from those based on exact finite sample distribution theory. This is not to suggest that the asymptotic distributions should be outrightly discarded; they are valuable in their own right. They are not completely irrelevant from a practical point of view because generally when we estimate an unknown parameter, we want the estimator to be quite precise and in order to achieve this objective we have to have a large sample. The limitations of the asymptotic distribution theory with special reference to its failure to shed light on the performance of inference procedures in certain finite sample situations clearly sensitize as well as emphasize the need of an investigation of finite sample distribution theory to base our conclusions on it. Indeed the availability of both the finite sample and the asymptotic results is also useful for answering the questions as to how large the observations should be so that the asymptotic results hold.

Having discussed above the importance of finite sample econometrics we now turn to a brief description of the developments in this area and then indicate the methodologies to be used in this book. Fisher (1921, 1922, 1928, 1935), more than seven decades ago, laid the foundation of modern finite sample theory. Also, see the fundamental work of Cramér (1946) on the distribution theory. It was brought into econometrics by the seminal work of Haavelmo (1947), and Anderson and Rubin (1949) on the exact confidence regions of structural coefficients, and that of Hurwicz (1950) on the exact LS bias in an autoregressive model. This was followed by the important contributions of Basmann (1961), Bergstrom (1962), Kabe (1963, 1964), Richardson (1968), Sawa (1969), Anderson and Sawa (1973), Ullah and Nagar (1974), Hillier, Kinal, and Srivastava (1984), and Phillips (1983) on the exact density and moments of the estimators in the simultaneous equations model. All these important contributions were related to obtaining exact results, which hold for any size of the sample; small, moderately large, or very large. However, these results were often very complicated to draw meaningful inferences from them. A major development took place through the pioneering work of Nagar (1959) on obtaining the approximate moments of the $k$-class estimators in simultaneous equations. Sargan (1975, 1976, 1980), and Phillips (1977$b$, 1978, 1980) rigorously developed the theory and applications of Edgeworth expansions to derive the approximate distribution functions of econometric estimators. The idea of the Edgeworth expansions stems from the fundamental work of Edgeworth (1896, 1905)—see also Chebyshev (1890), Gram (1879), Charlier (1905), and Cramér (1928). More details on the Edgeworth expansion can be found in Wallace (1958), Chibishov (1972), Phillips (1980), and Rothenberg (1984$a$). The moments of the Edgeworth approximate distributions can be the same as Nagar's approximations of the moments (Rothenberg 1984$a$). These approximate distributions are also known as the asymptotic expansions or large sample approximations, and these provide the results which will tend to be between the exact and asymptotic results. Thus it can tell us how much we lose by using the asymptotic result and how far we are from the known exact results. The latter also measures the accuracy of the approximate results. A significant growth in the literature took place through the dedicated work of J. D. Sargan and his students at the London School of Economics, A. L. Nagar and his students at the Delhi School of Economics, R. L. Basmann and his students at Texas A&M, T. W. Anderson and his students at Stanford, and P. C. B. Phillips, among others. Most of the contributions of these schools were confined to the analytical derivations of the moments and distributions in the simultaneous equations model, the details of which can be found in the surveys by Basmann (1974), Anderson (1982), Mariano (1982), Phillips (1980, 1983), Taylor (1983), and Maasoumi (1988). These developments include the finite sample results by using the Monte Carlo methodology (see Hendry 1984). Recently, bootstrapping (resampling) techniques have become popular (see Hall 1992; Jeong and Maddala 1993; Li and Maddala 1996; Vinod 1993; Horowitz 2001). Both Monte

Carlo and bootstrapping will not be discussed in this book. The analytical results we develop here, however, are useful for both these simulation methods.

Despite the above research contributions, the discussion of analytical finite sample results in elementary as well as advanced text books is almost negligible. Usually a typical text book starts with analytical finite sample results (exact mean and variance, say, of the LS estimator) in the regression chapter and then continues using, instead, asymptotic theory in the remaining chapters.

There are perhaps several reasons for this. First, the derivations of finite sample results, especially exact results, are often demanding and require a knowledge of statistical distribution theory. Terms like Wishart distribution, zonal polynomials, manifolds, noncentral distributions, have undoubtedly kept economists away from this area of research. In addition, the results are often complicated and lengthy. Second, results are mainly available for estimators in static simultaneous equations but not as much for other models such as the heteroskedastic, dynamic regression, limited dependent variables, or rational expectations. Third, several different techniques have been developed to study the finite sample behavior of a given estimator or test statistic. For example, several papers (e.g. Sawa 1972; Nagar and Ullah 1973) exist on the exact moments of the two-stage least squares and, similarly, several papers on its exact density (see Richardson 1968; Anderson and Sawa 1979). Learning and mastering each and every technique is beyond the scope of most graduate students and researchers. No attempt is made in this book to present these various techniques and interested readers are referred for detailed references to Phillips (1983, 1987*d*), Mariano (1982), Taylor (1983), and Rothenberg (1984*a*).

In this book we attempt to provide unified approaches to study finite sample econometrics. Essentially we discuss a unified technique for obtaining the exact moments, and a technique for obtaining the exact distributions. This is based on the observations in Ullah (1990), Lye (1987, 1988), and Cribbett, Lye, and Ullah (1989) that a large class of econometric estimators and test statistics can be written as a ratio of quadratic forms, or in general a real valued function $h(y)$ of the vector $y$ of observations on the dependent variable of an econometric model. Basically, using Ullah (1990), the technique of obtaining the exact moments amounts to replacing the expectation of $h(y)$, $y \sim N(\mu, 1)$, by $h(d)$, where the operator $d = \mu + \partial/\partial\mu$. This is an extremely simplified generalization of the techniques used in Baranchik (1964), Ullah and Nagar (1974), and A. Ullah and S. Ullah (1978). To obtain the exact density functions, the use of Gurland (1948), Imhof (1961), Davies (1980), and Forchini (2002) evaluation of the distribution function of the ratio of quadratic forms is proposed. The alternative techniques of obtaining the exact moments and distributions are compared, discussed, or referred to at appropriate places.

The exact results are often complicated to analyze. In view of this, the approximate distributions based on the results for the Edgeworth expansion of distributions of a function $h(y)$ are presented. For obtaining the approximate Edgeworth type moments, Nagar (1959) large sample approximation and its generalization in Rilstone, Srivastava, and Ullah (1996), Bao and Ullah (2002), and Kadane (1971) small-$\sigma$ approximation and its generalization in Ullah, Srivastava, and Roy (1995) are considered in this book. In some special cases, these approximations are compared with the Laplace approximation in Lieberman (1994$a$).

The techniques of obtaining the exact and approximate moments described above are presented in Chapter 2 along with some examples. The techniques for the exact and approximate distributions are presented in Chapter 3. The applications of these techniques and other finite sample results for various econometric models are then presented in the remaining chapters. Essentially, Chapter 4 analyzes the finite sample analysis of the estimators and test statistics in the case of regression models with the scalar covariance matrix of the errors. Chapter 5 then considers the regression models with the nonscalar covariance matrix of the errors. This includes the estimators and test statistics in the context of linear regression with heteroskedasticity and serial correlation, seemingly unrelated regressions, limited dependent variables, and panel data models. In Chapter 6 we deal with the dynamic time series models. Finally, Chapter 7 considers the analysis of the simultaneous equations model. The important features of all these chapters can be summarized below: ($a$) focus of each chapter is on analyzing finite sample behavior of the econometric estimators and test statistics; ($b$) simpler and unified techniques are used for deriving exact and approximate results; ($c$) results are explored for both normal and nonnormal error; ($d$) finite sample results are presented and analyzed for different kinds of econometric models in cross section and time series cases.

# 2

# Finite Sample Moments

## 2.1 Introduction

It was discussed in Chapter 1 that there is a need for unified techniques to obtain the exact and approximate moments of econometric estimators and test statistics. The objective of this chapter is essentially to provide such techniques. These techniques will be supported by illustrative examples to help clear the basic ideas behind the main results.

## 2.2 Exact Moments: Normal Case

Let $y$ be a scalar random variable, which is distributed according to normal law with $\mu = Ey$ and $\sigma^2 = V(y)$. The density function of $y$ can be written as

$$f(y) = ((2\pi)(\sigma^2))^{-1/2} \exp\left\{-\frac{1}{2}\left(\frac{y-\mu}{\sigma}\right)^2\right\}, \quad -\infty < y < \infty. \qquad (2.1)$$

This is well known to be symmetric around $\mu$, its mean, median, and mode coincide, its kurtosis coefficient is 3, and its inflexion points occur at $\mu \pm \sigma$ where $\partial^2 f(y)/\partial y^2 = 0$. A feature of the normal density, which is not well known but plays an important role in developing our main results is that

$$\frac{\partial}{\partial \mu} f(y) = \frac{1}{\sigma^2}(y-\mu)f(y), \qquad (2.2)$$

which can be rewritten as

$$(y-d)f(y) = 0 \quad \text{or} \quad yf(y) = df(y), \qquad (2.3)$$

where $d$ is the derivative operator involving $\mu$ and $\sigma^2$

$$d = \mu + \sigma^2 \frac{\partial}{\partial \mu}. \qquad (2.4)$$

9

This feature of the first derivative of normal density in (2.3) can be generalized as

$$h(y)f(y) = h(d)f(y) \quad \text{or} \quad (h(y) - h(d))f(y) = 0, \tag{2.5}$$

where $h(y)$ is any real valued analytic function of $y$. The equality in (2.5) is obtained by first writing the Taylor series expansion of $h(y)$ around $d$ as

$$h(y) = h(d) + (y - d)h^{(1)}(d) + \frac{(y - d)^2}{2}h^{(2)}(d) + \cdots \tag{2.6}$$

and then noting that

$$h(y)f(y) = h(d)f(y) + (y - d)f(y)h^{(1)}(d) + \frac{(y - d)^2}{2}f(y)h^{(2)}(d) + \cdots$$
$$= h(d)f(y) \tag{2.7}$$

because $(y - d)^s f(y) = 0$ for $s = 1, 2, \ldots$, from (2.3); $h^{(s)}(d) = \partial^{(s)} h(y)/\partial y^s$ evaluated at $y = d$.

**Exercise 1**   Let $h(y)$ be a real valued scalar analytic function of an $n \times 1$ normal random vector $y$ with the $n \times 1$ mean vector $\mu$ and the $n \times n$ positive definite covariance matrix $\Sigma$, that is, $y \sim N(\mu, \Sigma)$. Show that

$$h(y)f(y) = h(d)f(y), \tag{2.8}$$

where

$$d = \mu + \Sigma \frac{\partial}{\partial \mu}. \tag{2.9}$$

*Solution*   The multivariate normal density of $y$ can be written as

$$f(y) = (2\pi)^{-n/2} |\Sigma|^{-1/2} \exp\left\{ -\tfrac{1}{2}(y - \mu)'\Sigma^{-1}(y - \mu) \right\}. \tag{2.10}$$

Then $\partial f(y)/\partial \mu = \Sigma^{-1}(y - \mu)f(y)$, or $yf(y) = (\mu + \Sigma(\partial/\partial \mu))f(y) = df(y)$, which gives $h(y)f(y) = h(d)f(y)$ by using the Taylor expansion of the function of a vector $y, h(y)$.

The feature of normal density in (2.5) and Exercise 1 shows that a normal density multiplied by a function $h(y)$ is identical to multiplying it by $h(d)$ where $d$ is nonstochastic. This fundamental feature of the normal density helps us to obtain the exact moments of the function of $y, h(y)$, in a straightforward way.

**Lemma 1**   *If $h(y) = (h_1(y), \ldots, h_m(y))'$ is an $m \times 1$ vector of real valued analytic functions of an $n \times 1$ normal random vector $y$ with the mean vector $\mu$ and variance covariance matrix $\Sigma$, that is, $y \sim N(\mu, \Sigma)$, and $Eh(y)$ exists, then*

$$Eh(y) = h(d) \cdot 1 = h(d), \tag{2.11}$$

*where $d = \mu + \Sigma(\partial/\partial\mu)$. Further, if $h(y)$ and $g(y)$ are two column vectors of real valued functions of $y$, and have finite expectations, then*

$$Eh(y)g(y) = h(d)Eg(y). \tag{2.12}$$

**Proof**   From Exercise 1, $h_j(y)f(y) = h_j(d)f(y)$ for $j = 1, \ldots, m$. Thus for the $m \times 1$ vector $h(y), h(y)f(y) = h(d)f(y)$. The result in (2.11) then follows by noting that

$$Eh(y) = \int_y h(y)f(y)\,dy = \int_y h(d)f(y)\,dy = h(d)\int_y f(y)\,dy = h(d)\cdot 1. \tag{2.13}$$

Similarly

$$Eh(y)g(y) = \int_y h(y)g(y)f(y)\,dy = \int_y h(d)g(y)f(y)\,dy$$

$$= h(d)\int_y g(y)f(y)\,dy = h(d)Eg(y). \tag{Q.E.D.}$$

In (2.13) we note that $f(y)$ is an exponential function and the fact that differentiation under the integral sign is permitted. Further in (2.11) $h(d)\cdot 1$ reminds us that the derivative operator $d$ is to be used on the constant 1.

The result in Lemma 1 provides a unified and simple technique for obtaining exact moments of various special cases of the function $h(y)$. Essentially, this technique transforms the problem of obtaining the expectation of complicated functions with the evaluation of their derivatives, which can be easily obtained and/or numerically calculated. Since most of the estimators and test statistics can be written in terms of the function of a data vector $y$, Lemma 1 provides a single method for obtaining their moments. We note, however, that for some econometric statistics (2.11) of Lemma 1 is useful, and for others (2.12) of Lemma 1 along with Lemma 2 below is useful. The results in both the lemmas are simple and do not require any extensive knowledge of statistical distribution theory.

Another important point is that Lemma 1 provides a recurrence relationship among the higher order moments of $h(y)$. For example, if we consider $h(y)$ to be a scalar function

$$Eh^r(y) = h^r(d)\cdot 1 = h^{r-1}(d)h(d)\cdot 1$$

$$= h^{r-1}(d)Eh(y), \tag{2.14}$$

where $r \geq 1$. When $r = 2$, $Eh^2(y) = h^2(d)\cdot 1 = h(d)Eh(y)$. For the vector function $h(y), Eh(y)h'(y) = h(d)Eh'(y) = h(d)h'(d)\cdot 1$.

**Exercise 2**   Let $y \sim N(\mu, \Sigma)$. Then show that $Ey = \mu$ and $V(y) = \Sigma$.

*Solution*   Let $h(y) = y$. Then from Lemma 1 $Ey = d \cdot 1 = (\mu + \Sigma(\partial/\partial\mu)) \cdot 1 = \mu$. Now $V(y) = Eyy' - \mu\mu'$. But from (2.12) in Lemma 1, $Eyy' = dd' \cdot 1 = d\mu' = (\mu + \Sigma(\partial/\partial\mu))\mu' = \mu\mu' + \Sigma$ so that $V(y) = \Sigma$.

Two points are important to remember. First, higher order derivatives should be obtained recursively, for example $d^2 \cdot 1 = d(d \cdot 1)$ rather than doing the square of $(\mu + \sigma^2(\partial/\partial\mu))$ and then operating it on 1. Second, when $Ey = \mu = 0$ then $Eh(y)$ follows by first considering $\mu \neq 0$ in deriving $h(d) \cdot 1$ and then substituting $\mu = 0$ in the final result. For example, $E(y - \mu)^2 = (d - \mu)^2 \cdot 1 = 0$ is not correct, but $E(y - \mu)^2 = \sigma^2$ from Exercise 2 or alternatively $E(y - \mu)^2 = d_0^2 \cdot 1 = \mu_0^2 + \sigma^2 = \sigma^2$ for $\mu_0 = 0$, where $d_0 = \mu_0 + \sigma^2(\partial/\partial\mu_0)$ and we first consider $E(y - \mu) = \mu_0 \neq 0$.

**Exercise 3**   Let $y \sim N(\mu, \Sigma)$. Then

$$E(y'Ny)^r = (d'Nd)^r \cdot 1 = (d'Nd)^{r-1} E(y'Ny), \qquad (2.15)$$

where $N$ is a symmetric matrix and $r \geq 1$.

*Solution*   Taking $h(y) = y'Ny$, the result in (2.15) follows from (2.14). Alternatively, substitute $h(y) = (y'Ny)^r$ in (2.11).

From (2.15) we note that

$$E(y'Ny) = (d'Nd) \cdot 1 = \operatorname{tr} N(dd' \cdot 1) = \mu'N\mu + \operatorname{tr}(N\Sigma), \qquad (2.16)$$

where $dd' \cdot 1 = \mu\mu' + \Sigma$ from Exercise 1. Further

$$E(y'Ny)^2 = (d'Nd)E(y'Ny) = \operatorname{tr} N[dd'\{\mu'N\mu + \operatorname{tr}(N\Sigma)\}]$$

$$= (\mu'N\mu)(\mu'N\mu + \operatorname{tr} N\Sigma) + 4\mu'N\Sigma N\mu$$

$$+ \operatorname{tr}[(N\Sigma)\{(\mu'N\mu) + \operatorname{tr}(N\Sigma) + 2N\Sigma\}]. \qquad (2.17)$$

When $\mu = 0$ and $\Sigma = I$, $E(y'Ny) = \operatorname{tr} N$ and $E(y'Ny)^2 = (\operatorname{tr} N)^2 + 2\operatorname{tr} N^2$. Further when $N$ is an idempotent matrix of rank $m \leq n$ then $E(y'Ny) = m$ and $E(y'Ny)^2 = m(m + 2)$, which is the well-known result for the moments of a $\chi^2 = y'Ny$ variable with $m$ degrees of freedom (d.f.).

The results in (2.16) and (2.17) also hold for $y'Ny$ when $N$ is not a symmetric matrix. In this case we need to replace $N$ by the symmetric matrix $(N + N')/2$ since $y'Ny = y'(N + N')y/2$.

**Exercise 4** Let $y \sim N(\mu, I)$ and $N_1$ and $N_2$ be two symmetric matrices. Then

$$E(y'N_1y)(y'N_2y) = \prod_{i=1}^{2} \mu'N_i\mu + 2\sum_{i=1}^{2}(\mu'N_iN_{3-i}\mu)$$

$$+ \sum_{i=1}^{2}(\mu'N_i\mu)\text{tr}\, N_{3-i}$$

$$+ \prod_{i=1}^{2}\text{tr}\, N_i + \sum_{i=1}^{2}\text{tr}\, N_iN_{3-i}. \qquad (2.18)$$

*Solution* From (2.11) or (2.12)

$$E(y'N_1y)(y'N_2y) = (d'N_1d)(d'N_2d)\cdot 1$$
$$= (d'N_1d)\text{tr}\, N_2(dd'\cdot 1)$$
$$= \text{tr}\, N_1dd'\{Ey'N_2y\}.$$

Using $E(y'N_2y)$ from (2.16) we then get the result in (2.18).

When $N_1 = N_2$, (2.18) reduces to (2.17) with $\Sigma = I$.

Let $y \sim N(\mu, \Sigma)$. Then

$$EH(y) = H(d)\cdot 1, \qquad (2.19)$$

where $H(y)$ is an $m \times m$ matrix of elements $h_{ij}(y), i = 1, \ldots, m, j = 1, \ldots, m$.

This follows by noting that $Eh_{ij}(y) = h_{ij}(d)$ from Lemma 1.

In deriving the moments of econometric estimators we often encounter a scalar function $g(y)$, which is an inverse function of $y$. More specifically we often find $g(y) = w^{-r}$, where $w = y'Ny$ and $N$ is any symmetric (often nonnegative definite) matrix, and $r$ is a nonnegative real number. For such a $g(y)$ we can present $Eg(y)$ in the following Lemma.

**Lemma 2** *If $w = y'Ny$ is a real valued quadratic form in the vector $y \sim N(\mu, \Sigma)$, and the rank of $N > 2r$ then*

$$Ew^{-r} = (\Gamma(r))^{-1}\int_0^{\infty} t^{r-1}|N_0|^{-1/2}\exp\left\{-\frac{1}{2}\mu'N_0^*\mu\right\}dt, \qquad (2.20)$$

*where $N_0 = I + 2t\Sigma N = \Sigma(\Sigma^{-1} + 2tN)$ and $N_0^* = 2tNN_0^{-1} = \Sigma^{-1} - \Sigma^{-1}(\Sigma^{-1} + 2tN)^{-1}\Sigma^{-1}$.*

**Proof** First we note from the gamma integral that

$$w^{-r} = (\Gamma(r))^{-1}\int_0^{\infty} t^{r-1}\exp\{-tw\}dt. \qquad (2.21)$$

Thus

$$Ew^{-r} = (\Gamma(r))^{-1} \int_0^\infty t^{r-1} E \exp\{-tw\} \, dt. \qquad (2.22)$$

But $E \exp\{-tw\} = \int \exp\{-ty'Ny\} f(y) \, dy = |N_0|^{-1/2} \exp\{-\frac{1}{2}\mu' N_0^* \mu\}$, where we use $y'Ay - 2b'y = (y - A^{-1}b)'A(y - A^{-1}b) - b'A^{-1}b$ for some matrix $A$ and vector b. The result in (2.20) then follows. (Q.E.D.)

The matrix $N_0$ is such that $|N_0| = |\Sigma| \, |\Sigma^{-1} + 2tN| = |I + 2t\Sigma^{1/2}N\Sigma^{1/2}|$ and

$$|N_0| = \prod_{j=1}^n (1 + 2t\lambda_j), \qquad (2.23)$$

where $\Sigma = \Sigma^{1/2}\Sigma^{1/2}$ and we use $P$ to be an orthogonal matrix such that $P'\Sigma^{1/2}N\Sigma^{1/2}P = \wedge$ and $\wedge$ is a diagonal matrix of eigenvalues $\lambda_1, \ldots, \lambda_n$ of $\Sigma^{1/2}N\Sigma^{1/2}$. In econometric applications the structures of $\mu, \Sigma$, and $N$ are usually known. Further, $N_0^* = \Sigma^{-1} - \Sigma^{-1}(\Sigma^{-1} + 2tN)^{-1}\Sigma^{-1} = \Sigma^{-1/2}(I - (I + 2t\Sigma^{1/2}N\Sigma^{1/2})^{-1})\Sigma^{-1/2}$. A series representation of $Ew^{-r}$ is given in Srivastava and Khatri (1979, ch. 2), Phillips (1986), and Smith (1988).

In a special case where $\Sigma^{1/2}N\Sigma^{1/2}$ or $N\Sigma$ is an idempotent matrix ($N\Sigma N = N$) of rank $p$ = rank of $N\Sigma = \text{tr}(N\Sigma)$, then $y'Ny$ is a noncentral $\chi^2$ with $p$ degreees of freedom. In the case, $\lambda_1 = \lambda_2 = \cdots = \lambda_p = 1$ and $\lambda_{p-1} = \cdots = \lambda_n = 0$ so the result in (2.20) along with (2.23) can be written as an infinite series. This gives the $r$th inverse moment of the noncentral $\chi^2$ distribution as

$$Ew^{-r} = 2^{-r} \frac{\Gamma((p/2) - r)}{\Gamma(p/2)} e^{-\theta} \,_1F_1\left(\frac{p}{2} - r; \frac{p}{2}; \theta\right), \qquad (2.24)$$

where $\theta = (\mu'\Sigma^{-1/2}N\Sigma^{-1/2}\mu)/2$ is a noncentrality parameter and

$$_1F_1(a; c; \theta) = \frac{\Gamma c}{\Gamma a} \sum_{i=0}^\infty \frac{\Gamma(a + i)}{\Gamma(c + i)} \frac{\theta^i}{i!} \qquad (2.25)$$

is a confluent hypergeometric function, see Appendix A.8.1 and A.9. Further if $\mu = 0$, (2.24) reduces to

$$Ew^{-r} = 2^{-r} \frac{\Gamma((p/2) - r)}{\Gamma(p/2)}, \qquad (2.26)$$

which is the $r$th inverse moment of the central $\chi^2$ distribution. If $r$ is negative, (2.26) gives the moments of a central $\chi^2$ distribution.

If $N$ is a stochastic matrix but independent of $y$, then

$$Ew^{-r} = E(y'Ny)^{-r} = E_N(Ew^{-r}|N), \qquad (2.27)$$

which can be evaluated by taking the expectation of $Ew^{-r}$ with respect to the elements of $N$.

An important application of Lemma 2 is in obtaining the $r$th moment of the ratio of quadratic forms, $q = y'N_1y/y'Ny$. This is given in the following Lemma.

**Lemma 3** *Let $y \sim N(\mu, \Sigma)$, and $N_1$ and $N$ be two symmetric matrices. Then, for $r \geq 1$,*

$$Eq^r = E\left(\frac{y'N_1y}{y'Ny}\right)^r = (d'N_1d)^r E(y'Ny)^{-r} \tag{2.28}$$

*where $d$ is the operator in (2.9). For $r = 1, 2$ we get*

$$Eq = \int_0^\infty |N_0|^{-1/2}\left(\text{tr}(N_1N_2) + \mu^{*'}N_2N_1N_2\mu^*\right)\exp\{-\tfrac{1}{2}\mu'N_0^*\mu\}\,dt,$$

$$Eq^2 = \int_0^\infty t|N_0|^{-1/2}\Big[\left(\text{tr}(N_1N_2) + \mu^{*'}N_2N_1N_2\mu^*\right)^2 \tag{2.29}$$

$$+ 2\text{tr}(N_1N_2)^2 + 4\mu^{*'}N_2N_1N_2N_1N_2\mu^*\Big]\exp\left(-\tfrac{1}{2}\mu'N_0^*\mu\right)dt,$$

*where $\mu^* = \Sigma^{-1}\mu, N_2 = N_0^{-1}\Sigma = \Sigma(I - N_0^*\Sigma)$.*

**Proof** From Lemma 1 (substituting $h(y) = (y'N_1y)^r$ and $g(y) = (y'Ny)^{-r}$) we can write

$$Eq^r = (d'N_1d)^r Ew^{-r},$$

where $Ew^{-r}$ is as given in Lemma 2. For $r = 1$, $Eq = (d'N_1d)\,Ew^{-1} = \text{tr}(N_1dd'Ew^{-1})$, which gives $Eq$ in (2.29). Further for $r = 2$, $Eq^2 = (d'N_1d)^2Ew^{-2} = (d'N_1d)\text{tr}(N_1dd'Ew^{-2})$, which gives $Eq^2$ in (2.29). (Q.E.D.)

Sawa (1972) used a result for the joint moment generating functions (mgf) of $w_1 = y'N_1y$ and $w_2 = y'Ny$, $M(\theta_1, \theta_2)$, and obtained the $r$th moment of $q$ as

$$Eq^r = E\left(\frac{w_1}{w_2}\right)^r = \frac{1}{\Gamma r}\int_0^\infty \theta_2^{r-1}\left[\frac{\partial^r}{\partial\theta_1^r}M(\theta_1, -\theta_2)\right]_{\theta_1=0}d\theta_2 \tag{2.30}$$

provided the expectation exists. The mgf is

$$M(\theta_1, \theta_2) = E\exp\{\theta_1y'N_1y + \theta_2y'Ny\},$$

$$= |I - 2C|^{1/2}\exp(-\tfrac{1}{2}\eta'\eta)\exp\left(\tfrac{1}{2}\eta'(I - 2C)^{-1}\eta\right), \tag{2.31}$$

where $\eta = L^{-1}\mu$, $C = L'(\theta_1N_1 + \theta_2N)$ and $L$ is the matrix such that $\Sigma = LL'$. A choice of $L$ is $\Sigma^{1/2}$ as described above. For $r = 1, 2$ one can verify that (2.30) gives the results in (2.29). Magnus (1986) provides an explicit expression for $Eq^r$. His result is given below.

**Lemma (Magnus)** *Let $y \sim N(\mu, \Sigma = LL')$. Let $N_1$ be a symmetric matrix and $N$ be a positive semi definite matrix, $N \neq 0$. Let $P$ be an orthogonal* *matrix and $D$ be a diagonal matrix such that $P'L'NLP = D$ and define $N_1^* = P'L'N_1LP$, $\mu^* = P'L^{-1}\mu$. Then, if the expectation exists, for $r = 1, 2, \ldots$*

$$Eq^r = \frac{\exp\left(-(\frac{1}{2})\mu'\Sigma^{-1}\mu\right)}{\Gamma(r)} \sum_v \gamma_r(v) \int_0^\infty t^{r-1}|\Delta|\exp\left(\frac{\xi'\xi}{2}\right)$$

$$\times \prod_{j=1}^r (\operatorname{tr} R^j + j\xi'R^j\xi)^{n_j} \, dt, \tag{2.32}$$

*where the summation is over all $1\times r$ vectors $v = (n_1, n_2, \ldots, n_r)$ where elements $n_j$ are non-negative integers satisfying $\sum_{j=1}^r jn_j = r$,*

$$\gamma_r(v) = r!2^r \prod_{j=1}^r [n_j(2j)n_j]^{-1} \tag{2.33}$$

*and $\Delta$ is a diagonal positive definite matrix, $R$ is a symmetric matrix and $\xi$ is a vector given by*

$$\Delta = (I + 2tD)^{-1/2}, \quad R = \Delta N_1^*\Delta, \quad \xi = \Delta\mu^*. \tag{2.34}$$

*For the proof see Magnus who also gives the condition of existence of the moments in (2.30). This is given below.*

**Lemma (Magnus)**   *Let $N_1$ be the symmetric $n \times n$ matrix and $N$ be a $n \times n$ positive semi definite of rank $m \geq 1$. If $m \leq n - 1$, let $Q$ be an $n \times (n - m)$ matrix of full column rank $n - m$ such that $L'NLQ = 0$*

1. *If $m \leq n-1$ and $L'N_1LQ = 0$, or if $m = n$ then $Eq^r$ exists for all $r \geq 0$*
2. *If $m \leq n - 1$, $Q'L'N_1LQ = 0$ and $L'N_1LQ \neq 0$ then $Eq^r$ exists for $0 \leq r < m$ and does not exist for $r \geq m$, and*
3. *If $m \leq n - 1$ and $Q'L'N_1LQ \neq 0$ then $Eq^r$ exists for $0 \leq r < m/2$ and does not exist for $r \geq m/2$.*

A large number of econometric estimators are in terms of the ratio of bilinear to quadratic forms, that is,

$$q = \frac{y_2'M_1y_1}{y_2'My_2}, \tag{2.35}$$

where $y_1$ and $y_2$ are $n \times 1$ vectors and $M_1$ and $M$ are $n \times n$ symmetric matrices. Our problem is to obtain $Eq^r$. Here we show that this result can be obtained from the moments of the ratio of quadratic forms given above. For this we first note that

$$y_2'M_1y_1 = y'N_1y \quad \text{and} \quad y_2'My_2 = y'Ny, \tag{2.36}$$

where

$$y = \begin{bmatrix} y_1 \\ y_2 \end{bmatrix}, \quad N_1 = \frac{1}{2}\begin{bmatrix} 0 & M_1 \\ M_1 & 0 \end{bmatrix}, \quad N = \begin{bmatrix} 0 & 0 \\ 0 & M \end{bmatrix}. \tag{2.37}$$

The important point is that the bilinear form $y_2' M_1 y_1$ can be written as a quadratic form. Thus

$$Eq^r = E\left(\frac{y_2' M_1 y_1}{y_2' M y_2}\right)^r = E\left(\frac{y' N_1 y}{y' N y}\right)^r \qquad (2.38)$$

is as given above with $y \sim N(\mu, \Sigma)$ being a $2n \times 1$ vector and

$$\mu = \begin{bmatrix} \mu_1 \\ \mu_2 \end{bmatrix}, \qquad \Sigma = \begin{bmatrix} \Sigma_{11} & \Sigma_{12} \\ \Sigma_{21} & \Sigma_{22} \end{bmatrix}; \qquad (2.39)$$

$\mu_i = E y_i$ and $\Sigma_{ij} = E y_i y_j'$ for $i, j = 1, 2$.

The number of econometric estimators and test statistics that can be written as the ratio of quadratic forms or the ratio of bilinear to quadratic forms are quite large. We present some of them below. The details on them and others are discussed in the relevant chapters.

**Exercise 5**  Consider the regression model $y = X\beta + u$ where $y$ is an $n \times 1$ vector, $X$ is an $n \times k$ nonstochastic matrix and $u$ is an $n \times 1$ disturbance vector. Show that the goodness of fit statistic $R^2$ and Durbin–Watson statistic (D–W) are

$$R^2 = \frac{y' N_1 y}{y' N y}, \quad \text{D–W} = \frac{y' M_1 y}{y' M y}$$

where $N = I - \iota \iota'/n, N_1 = N - M, M = I - X(X'X)^{-1}X', M_1 = MAM; \iota$ is an $n \times 1$ vector of unit elements and $A$ is an $n \times n$ matrix of known constants.

*Solution*  If the regression contains an intercept, that is, the first column of $X$ contains unit elements, it is well known that (e.g. see Greene 2000)

$$R^2 = 1 - \frac{\hat{u}'\hat{u}}{(y - \bar{y})'(y - \bar{y})}, \quad \text{D–W} = \frac{\hat{u}'A\hat{u}}{\hat{u}'\hat{u}}$$

where $\hat{u} = y - X\hat{\beta} = My, \bar{y} = \iota' y/n$ and $M^2 = M$. Using these in $R^2$ and D–W the results in Exercise 5 follow.

**Exercise 6**  Consider a single equation of the system of simultaneous equations as

$$y_1 = \gamma y_2 + u,$$

where $y_1$ and $y_2$ are $n \times 1$ vectors of observations on the endogenous variables, $\gamma$ is a scalar and $u$ is $n \times 1$. Show that the 2SLS estimator of $\gamma$ is

$$\hat{\gamma} = \frac{y' N_1 y}{y' N y},$$

where $y, N_1$, and $N$ are as in (2.37) with $M_1 = M = \bar{M} = X(X'X)^{-1}X'; X$ is an $n \times k$ matrix of exogenous variables appearing in the remaining equations of the system.

*Solution*    The well known form of the 2SLS $\hat{\gamma}$ is

$$\hat{\gamma} = \frac{y_2' \bar{M} y_1}{y_2' \bar{M} y_2},$$

see, for example, Theil (1971), Greene (2000). In its current setup $\hat{\gamma}$ is the ratio of a bilinear to quadratic forms. However, using (2.37) and $M_1 = M = \bar{M}$ the result follows immediately.

## 2.3    Exact Moments: Nonnormal Case

Here we first consider the case of discrete distributions and then take up the case of the continuous distributions. In each case we explore an operator corresponding to the operator $d$ in the normal case, which can help to provide the moments of a function of $y$.

### 2.3.1    Binomial Distribution

Let $y$ be a scalar random variable, which is distributed as binomial with $Ey = m\pi = \mu$ and $\sigma^2 = V(y) = m\pi(1 - \pi)$; $\pi$ is the probability of success in a given trial. The density function of $y$ can be written as

$$f(y) = \binom{m}{y} \pi^y (1 - \pi)^{m-y}, \quad y = 0, 1, \dots, m. \tag{2.40}$$

Then it can be verified that

$$\frac{\partial}{\partial \pi} f(y) = \frac{(y - m\pi)}{\pi(1 - \pi)} f(y) \tag{2.41}$$

or

$$(y - d)f(y) = 0, \tag{2.42}$$

where

$$d = m\pi + \pi(1 - \pi)\frac{\partial}{\partial \pi} \tag{2.43}$$

Thus the operator (2.4) and hence Lemma 1 for the normal case goes through for the binomial distribution. This is, for the scalar $y$,

$$Eh(y) = h(d) \cdot 1. \tag{2.44}$$

**Exercise 7**    Suppose $y$ is distributed as a binomial with parameter $\pi$ and density in (2.40). Show that

$$Ey = m\pi \quad \text{and} \quad V(y) = m\pi(1 - \pi).$$

*Solution*    $Ey = d \cdot 1 = (m\pi + \pi(1 - \pi)\partial/\partial\pi) \cdot 1 = m\pi$. Further $Ey^2 = (m\pi + \pi(1 - \pi)\partial/\partial\pi)^2 \cdot 1 = (m\pi + \pi(1 - \pi)\partial/\partial\pi) m\pi = (m\pi)^2 + m\pi(1 - \pi)$. Thus $V(y) = Ey^2 - (Ey)^2 = m\pi(1 - \pi)$.

## 2.3.2  Poisson Distribution

Let $y$ be a scalar random variable, which is distributed as a Poisson with $Ey = \lambda = \mu$ and $V(y) = \lambda = \sigma^2$. The density function of $y$ is

$$f(y) = \frac{e^{-\lambda}\lambda^y}{y!}, \quad y = 0, 1, 2, \dots . \tag{2.45}$$

Then it can be verified that

$$\frac{\partial}{\partial\lambda}f(y) = \frac{(y - \lambda)}{\lambda}f(y) \tag{2.46}$$

or

$$(y - d)f(y) = 0, \tag{2.47}$$

where

$$d = \left(\lambda + \lambda\frac{\partial}{\partial\lambda}\right) = \mu + \sigma^2\frac{\partial}{\partial\mu}. \tag{2.48}$$

Thus the operator (2.4) and Lemma 1 for the normal case hold for the case of Poisson distribution also. That is $Eh(y) = h(d) \cdot 1$.

**Exercise 8**  If $y$ is distributed as a Poisson with the density in (2.45), show that $Ey = \lambda$ and $V(y) = \lambda$.

*Solution*  $Ey = d \cdot 1 = (\lambda + \lambda(\partial/\partial\lambda)) \cdot 1 = \lambda$ and $Ey^2 = d^2 \cdot 1 = (\lambda + \lambda(\partial/\partial\lambda))\lambda = \lambda^2 + \lambda$. Thus $V(y) = \lambda^2 + \lambda - \lambda^2 = \lambda$.

**Exercise 9**  If $y_i, i = 1, \dots, n$, is independent identically distributed (i.i.d) random variables with the Poisson density in (2.45), and $y$ is an $n \times 1$ random vector. Then show that, for a symmetric matrix $N$ of constants,

$$E(y'Ny) = \lambda^2(\iota'N\iota) + \lambda\operatorname{tr} N.$$

*Solution*  $E(y'Ny) = \operatorname{tr} N(Eyy')$. Now $Ey_i^2 = \lambda^2 + \lambda$ and $E(y_iy_j) = (Ey_i)(Ey_j) = \lambda^2$ from the exercise above. Using these the result follows.

We now turn to the continuous distributions.

## 2.3.3  Gamma Distribution

Let $y$ be a scalar random variable with two parameters gamma density

$$f(y) = \frac{\lambda^r}{\Gamma r}y^{r-1}e^{-\lambda y}, \quad y > 0. \tag{2.49}$$

For this density $\mu = Ey = r/\lambda$ and $\sigma^2 = V(y) = r/\lambda^2$. Further

$$\frac{\partial}{\partial\lambda}f(y) = \left(\frac{r}{\lambda} - y\right)f(y) \tag{2.50}$$

or

$$(y - d)f(y) = 0, \tag{2.51}$$

where

$$d = \frac{r}{\lambda} - \frac{\partial}{\partial\lambda} = \mu + \sigma^2 \frac{\partial}{\partial\mu}. \tag{2.52}$$

Thus the operator $d$ and Lemma 1 hold for gamma density as well. That is $Eh(y) = h(d) \cdot 1$.

**Exercise 10**  Suppose $y_i, i = 1, \ldots, n$, is the i.i.d. random variables with the gamma density in (2.49). Show that

$$E(y'Ny) = \frac{r^2}{\lambda^2} \iota' N\iota + \frac{r}{\lambda^2} \mathrm{tr}(N).$$

*Solution*  First $Ey_i = d \cdot 1 = ((r/\lambda) - (\partial/\partial\lambda)) \cdot 1 = r/\lambda$ and $Ey_i^2 = d.d \cdot 1 = (r/\lambda)^2 + r/\lambda^2$. Using this in $E(y'Ny) = \mathrm{tr}\, N(Eyy')$ we get the result.

We note that gamma distribution includes exponential density $(r = 1)$.

$$f(y) = \lambda e^{-\lambda y}, \quad y > 0 \tag{2.53}$$

and $\chi^2(\lambda = 1/2), f(y) = y^{r-1}e^{-(1/2)y}/2^r\Gamma r$, as the special cases. For these cases also $Eh(y) = h(d) \cdot 1$.

## 2.3.4  Exponential Family

Consider a scalar random variable with an exponential family of densities as

$$f(y) = a(\theta)b(y)\exp[c(\theta)g(y)], \tag{2.54}$$

where $\theta$ is a scalar parameter. For this density

$$\frac{\partial f(y)}{\partial\theta} = \left[\frac{a^{(1)}(\theta)}{a(\theta)} + c^{(1)}(\theta)g(y)\right]f(y), \tag{2.55}$$

which gives

$$\left[-\frac{a^{(1)}(\theta)}{a(\theta)c^{(1)}(\theta)} + \frac{1}{c^{(1)}(\theta)}\frac{\partial}{\partial\theta}\right]f(y) = g(y)f(y) \tag{2.56}$$

or

$$(g(y) - d)f(y) = 0, \tag{2.57}$$

where the operator $d$ is

$$d = -\frac{a^{(1)}(\theta)}{a(\theta)c^{(1)}(\theta)} + \frac{1}{c^{(1)}(\theta)}\frac{\partial}{\partial\theta}. \tag{2.58}$$

If $g(y)$ is linear in $y$, for example, $g(y) = y$ then $(y - d)f(y) = 0$ from (2.57) and we get $Eh(y) = h(d) \cdot 1$. However, if $g(y)$ is not linear in $y$ then

$$Eg(y) = \int_y g(y)f(y)\,dy$$

$$= \int (g(y) - d + d)f(y)\,dy$$

$$= d \cdot 1 \qquad (2.59)$$

and $E[h(g(y))] = h(d) \cdot 1$. Thus we can obtain the moments of the form $h(g(y))$ for every analytical function of $h$.

In the special case of a standard exponential family

$$f(y) = a(\theta)\exp[\theta y]. \qquad (2.60)$$

$g(y) = y$ is linear, $c(\theta) = \theta$ and $b(y) = 1$. For this case the operator $d$ in (2.58) reduces to

$$d = -\frac{a^{(1)}(\theta)}{a(\theta)} + \frac{\partial}{\partial\theta} = Ey + \frac{\partial}{\partial\theta}. \qquad (2.61)$$

Further, for the exponential density in (2.53) $d = ((1/\lambda) - (\partial/\partial\lambda))$.

## 2.3.5   $K$-Parameter Exponential Density

Let us consider a $K$-parameter exponential family as

$$f(y) = f(y;\theta_1,\ldots,\theta_K) = a(\theta_1,\ldots,\theta_K)b(y)\exp\left[\sum_{j=1}^K c_j(\theta_1,\ldots,\theta_K)g_j(y)\right].$$
$$(2.62)$$

Then, for $i, j = 1,\ldots,K$,

$$\frac{\partial f(y)}{\partial\theta_i} = \frac{a_i^{(1)}}{a}f(y) + \left(\sum_{j=1}^K c_{ji}g_j(y)\right)f(y), \qquad (2.63)$$

where $c_{ji} = \partial c_j/\partial\theta_i$. This gives

$$(g_i(y) - d_i)f(y) = 0, \qquad (2.64)$$

where $g_i(y) = \sum_{j=1}^K c_{ji}g_j(y)$ and $d_i = ((-a_i^{(1)}/a) + (\partial/\partial\theta))$; $a = a(\theta_1,\ldots,\theta_K)$ and $a_i^{(1)} = \partial a/\partial\theta_i$.

We note that the normal density with $\mu = \theta_1$ and $\sigma^2 = \theta_2$ is a special case of the $K = 2$ parameter exponential family. Other densities described above can also be seen as special cases.

## 2.3.6    Mixtures of Distributions

A family of mixtures of distributions can be written by considering the conditional distribution of $y$ containing a parameter $\theta$, say, $f(y|_\theta)$, weighting it by a distribution of $\theta$, say, $f(\theta)$, and then integrating with respect to $\theta$. This gives

$$f(y) = \int_{-\infty}^{\infty} f(y|_\theta)f(\theta)\,d\theta$$

$$= E_\theta[f(y|_\theta)], \qquad (2.65)$$

where $E_\theta$ represents the expectation with respect to random variable $\theta$ with density $f(\theta)$. For example, if $f(y|_\theta)$ is a normal density with mean $\beta$ and variance $\theta$, and $f(\theta)$ is an inverted gamma density then $f(y)$ is a $t$ density. In general $f(y)$ is a mixture of normal density if $f(y|_\theta)$ is normal.

Using (2.65)

$$Eh(y) = \int_y h(y)f(y)\,dy = \int_y h(y)E_\theta[f(y|_\theta)]\,dy$$

$$= E_\theta \int h(y)f(y|_\theta)\,dy$$

$$= E_\theta[E(h(y)|_\theta)]. \qquad (2.66)$$

This implies that the moments of $h(y)$, under (2.65), can be obtained in two steps: (*a*) obtain the expectations under a conditional density $f(y|_\theta)$ (*b*) take expectation of these results with respect to $\theta$.

**Exercise 11**    Suppose $f(y|_\sigma)$ is a normal density with the mean zero and variance $\sigma^2$, and $f(\sigma)$ is an inverted gamma density

$$f(\sigma) = \frac{2}{\Gamma(m/2)} \left(\frac{m}{2}\right)^{m/2} \frac{1}{\sigma^{m+1}} e^{-(m/2)(1/\sigma^2)}$$

Show that $f(y)$ is a $t$-density with $m$ d.f. as

$$f(y) = \frac{\Gamma\left[(m+1)/2\right]}{\Gamma(m/2)\Gamma(\frac{1}{2})} \frac{1}{m^{1/2}} \left(1 + \frac{y^2}{m}\right)^{-(m+1)/2}$$

*Solution*    From (2.65),

$$f(y) = \int_0^{\infty} f(y|_\sigma)f(\sigma)\,d\sigma$$

$$= \frac{1}{\Gamma(m/2)} \left(\frac{2}{\pi}\right)^{1/2} \left(\frac{m}{2}\right)^{m/2} \int_0^{\infty} e^{-(1/2\sigma^2)(y^2+m)}\sigma^{-(m+2)}\,d\sigma.$$

Now using the variable transformation $(y^2 + m)/2\sigma^2 = z$ and the gamma integral we can easily verify the required result in the exercise.

**Exercise 12** Suppose $y$ is a $t$-density with zero mean and $m$ d.f. Show that, for $m > 2$,

$$Ey = 0, \quad V(y) = Ey^2 = \frac{m}{m-2}$$

*Solution* Using (2.66) and the above exercise

$$Ey = E_\sigma[E(y|_\sigma)] = 0$$

$$Ey^2 = E_\sigma[E(y^2|_\sigma)] = E_\sigma[\sigma^2]$$

$$= \int_\sigma \sigma^2 f(\sigma) \, d\sigma,$$

where $f(\sigma)$ is the inverted gamma density. The integral in the last equality is a second moment of the inverted gamma density, which is $(\Gamma(m-2)/2)/(\Gamma(m/2))(m/2) = m/(m-2), m > 2$, see Zellner (1971: 372). Hence the result in the exercise follows.

### 2.3.7 Edgeworth Density or Gram–Charlier Density

Suppose $y_i$ is distributed with mean $\mu_i$ and variance $\sigma_i^2$. Then the Edgeworth density of or Gram–Charlier series expansion of $f(y_i)$ is

$$f(y_i) = \sum_{j=0}^\infty c_j \left(\frac{d}{dy_i}\right)^j f(y_i \mid \mu_i, \sigma_i^2), \tag{2.67}$$

where $f(y_i \mid \mu_i, \sigma_i^2)$ represents the normal density, that is, $N(\mu_i, \sigma_i^2)$, and $c_j$ is as given in (A.10) (see Appendix A.2 and A.8.2). Davis (1976) gave an alternative convenient representation of (2.67), which is

$$f(y_i) = E_{w_i}[f(y_i \mid \mu_i + w_i, \sigma_i^2)], \tag{2.68}$$

where $f(y_i \mid \mu_i + w_i, \sigma_i^2)$ is $N(\mu_i + w_i, \sigma_i^2)$ and $w_i$ is a pseudo variate with mean and variance 0, and higher order cumulants the same as those of $y_i(E(w_i^j) = (-1)^j j! c_j)$.

As in the case of mixtures density, the moments of $h(y)$ under the Edgeworth density can be obtained in two steps: (*a*) obtain the results under $y \mid \mu + w \sim N(\mu + w, I)$ (*b*) take expectation of these results with respect to $w$. That is

$$Eh(y) = E_w[E(h(y) \mid w)], \tag{2.69}$$

where $E(h(y) \mid w)$ is the expectation of $h(y)$ when $y \mid \mu + w \sim N(\mu + w, I)$.

**Exercise 13** Suppose an $n \times 1$ random vector $y$, with i.i.d. elements, follows an Edgeworth density with mean 0 and variance $I$. Let $\bar{y} = \sum_1^n y_i/n$ be the sample average. Show that

$$E\bar{y} = 0, \quad V(\bar{y}) = 1/n.$$

*Solution* Using (2.68) $E\bar{y} = Ey_i = E_{w_i}[E(y_i \mid w_i)] = E_{w_i}[w_i] = 0$. Further $V(\bar{y}) = V(y_i)/n = (1/n)Ey_i^2 = (1/n)E_{w_i}[Ey_i^2 \mid w_i] = (1/n)E_{w_i}[1] = 1/n$.

## 2.4   Exact Moments: General Case

Let $Y$ be an $n \times p$ matrix whose $n$ independent row vectors are distributed according to a $p$-dimensional normal law with means given by $\bar{Y} = EY$ and variance covariance matrix $\Omega = I_p$. Then the density function of $Y$ can be written as

$$f(Y) = (2\pi)^{-np/2} \exp\left\{-\tfrac{1}{2}\operatorname{tr}\left(Y - \bar{Y}\right)\left(Y - \bar{Y}\right)'\right\}.$$

Further, the distribution of $A = Y'Y$ is noncentral Wishart (see Rao 1973) with $n$ d.f. and

$$\ominus = \bar{Y}'\bar{Y}/2$$

as the mean sigma matrix.

The density function of $A$ is

$$f(A) = c \exp\left\{-\frac{1}{2}\operatorname{tr} A\right\} \exp(-\operatorname{tr}\ominus)\,|A|^{(n-p-1)/2}\,{}_0F_1\left(\frac{n}{2};\frac{1}{2}\ominus A\right)$$

$$c = 2^{-np/2}\Gamma_p(n/2); \Gamma_p(a) = \pi^{p(p-1)/4}\prod_1^p \Gamma\left(a - \left(\frac{i-1}{2}\right)\right)$$

is the multivariate gamma function,

$$pFq\left(a_1, \ldots, a_p, b_1, \ldots, b_q; M\right) = \sum_{j=0}^{\infty}\sum_{\lambda}\frac{(a_1)_\lambda \cdots (a_p)_\lambda}{(b_1)_\lambda \cdots (b_q)_\lambda}\frac{C_\lambda(M)}{j!}$$

represents the hypergeometric function of matrix argument (Constantine 1963), James (1964), $\Sigma_\lambda$ denotes the summation over the partitions $\lambda = (j_1, j_2, \ldots, j_s)$ of $\lambda$ such that $j_1 \geq j_2 \cdots \geq j_s \geq 0$ and $\Sigma_1^s j_i = j$, $(a)_\lambda = \Pi_{i=1}^s \Gamma(a + j_i)/\Gamma(a)$, and $C_\lambda(M)$ denotes the zonal polynomial of degree $j$ and they are symmetric functions of the eigenvalues of $M$ (e.g. see James 1964).

The $r$th inverse moment of the determinant of $A$ can be written from Constantine (1963: 1279) as

$$E|A|^{-r} = 2^{-pr}\frac{\Gamma_p\left((n/2) - r\right)}{\Gamma_p\left(n/2\right)}\exp\{-\operatorname{tr}\ominus\}{}_1F_1\left(\frac{n}{2} - r; \frac{n}{2};\ominus\right),$$

where $n > 2r + p - 1$, and ${}_1F_1$ is the confluent hypergeometric function given above for p = q = 1.

Before stating the main result, we introduce a differential operator

$$D = \bar{Y} + \frac{\partial}{\partial\bar{Y}},$$

which is such that $Df(Y) = Yf(Y)$ or $(D - Y)f(Y) = 0$. This follows immediately by using the procedure (2.2) on $f(Y)$. Furthermore, if $H(Y)$ is any integer matrix valued analytic function of $Y$, then by using its Taylor series expansion around $D$ and noting that $(D - Y)f(Y) = 0$ we get

$$H(Y)f(Y) = H(D)f(Y).$$

We can now state our result.

**Lemma 4**  *Let $r$ be a positive integer such that $n > 2r + p - 1$, then the $r$th inverse moment of the noncentral wishart matrix $A = Y'Y$ is given by*

$$EA^{-r} = (\text{adj.}\, D'D)^r \, E|A|^{-r},$$

*where adj. $D'D$ is the adjoint of the matrix $D'D$, and the matrix operator $D$ and the expectation $E|A|^{-r}$ are given above.*

**Proof**  The result follows by noting that

$$
\begin{aligned}
E(Y'Y)^{-r} = EA^{-r} &= E(A^{-1}|A|)^r|A|^{-r}, \\
&= E(\text{adj.}\, A)^r|A|^{-r}, \\
&= EH(Y)|A|^{-r}, \\
&= EH(Y)f(Y)f^{-1}(Y)|A|^{-r}, \\
&= EH(D)f(Y)f^{-1}(Y)|A|^{-r}, \\
&= H(D)E|A|^{-r},
\end{aligned}
$$

where $H(Y) = (\text{adj.}\, A)^r = (\text{adj.}\, Y'Y)^r$, $H(D) = (\text{adj.}\, D'D)^r$ and use has been made of $H(Y)f(Y) = H(D)f(Y)$. (Q.E.D.)

**Remark 1**  Let $A = Y'NY$ be the matrix quadratic form in $Y$ with $N$ as an idempotent matrix of rank $m \leq n$. Then $A$ is noncentral wishart with $m$ d.f., and $EA^{-r}$ is as given above with $\ominus = \bar{Y}'N\bar{Y}/2$.

**Remark 2**  When $p = 1$, then $A = Y'Y = |A|$ is the noncentral chi-square and adj. $D'D = 1$. Thus, $EA^{-r} = E|A|^{-r}$ where $E|A|^{-r}$ is as given for $p = 1$. This compares with the $r$th inverse moment of the noncentral chi- square given in 2.2.

For an application consider the regression model

$$y = X\beta + u,$$

where $y$ is an $n \times 1$ vector, $X$ is an $n \times p$ matrix of $p$ stochastic regressors such that $X'X = A$ is noncentral wishart matrix with $n$ d.f. and the mean-sigma matrix $\ominus$, and $u$ is an $n \times 1$ disturbance vector with the mean 0 and the covariance matrix $\sigma^2 I_n$. For the sake of simplicity we assume that $X$ and $u$ are independent.

The least-squares (LS) estimator of $\beta$ is

$$b = (X'X)^{-1}X'y \quad \text{or} \quad b - \beta = (X'X)^{-1}X'u.$$

Since $X$ and $u$ are independent, $E(b - \beta) = 0$. Further

$$V(b) = E(b - \beta)(b - \beta)' = \sigma^2 E(X'X)^{-1} = \sigma^2 EA^{-1},$$

where $EA^{-1} = (\text{adj. } D'D)E|A|^{-1}$ provided $n > p + 1$. When $p = 1$, we get

$$V(b) = \frac{\sigma^2 2^{-1}}{\sigma_x^2} \frac{\Gamma((n/2) - 1)}{\Gamma(n/2)} \exp\{-\theta\} {}_1F_1\left(\frac{n}{2} - 1; \frac{n}{2}; \theta\right),$$

where $\theta = \bar{X}'\bar{X}/2\sigma_x^2$, $\bar{X} = EX$ and $\sigma_x^2 = V(X)$.

Further for large $n$ or small $\sigma_x$ we get the approximate variance, up to $O(1/\theta^2)$

$$V(b) = \frac{\sigma^2 2^{-1}}{\sigma_x^2 \theta}\left[1 + \frac{4 - n}{2\theta}\right],$$

by using the expansion of ${}_1F_1$ in Appendix A.9.1. This can also be obtained by the small-$\sigma$ expansion method of approximation to $E(x'x)^{-1}$ in 2.5.2 where $X = x = \mu + \sigma_x V$ and $V \sim N(0, I)$. This gives, up to $O(\sigma_x^2)$,

$$E(x'x)^{-1} = (\mu'\mu)^{-1}E\left[1 + \frac{2\sigma_x V'\mu + \sigma_x^2 V'V}{\mu'\mu}\right]^{-1}$$

$$= \frac{1}{\mu'\mu}E\left[1 - \frac{2\sigma_x V'\mu + \sigma_x^2 V'V}{\mu'\mu} + \frac{4\sigma_x^2(\mu'V)^2}{(\mu'\mu)^2}\right]$$

$$= \frac{1}{\mu'\mu}\left[1 - \frac{n\sigma_x^2}{\mu'\mu} + \frac{4\sigma_x^2}{\mu'\mu}\right],$$

which gives $V(b)$, up to $O(1/\theta^2)$, as given above with $\mu'\mu = 2\theta\sigma_x^2$.

## 2.5   Approximations of Moments

In the above sections we looked into the techniques of obtaining the exact moments of econometric estimators and test statistics. These techniques require the specification of the density of the data vector $y$, for example, normal, and they provide the results, which hold for any size of the data. The exact results are, however, difficult to derive under a general nonnormal framework. Even under a specified density the exact expressions for the moments in many situations are sufficiently intricate and do not lend themselves to further algebraic manipulations for deducing any clear inference. This is despite the fact that Lemma 3 provides a much simpler way of obtaining exact moments compared with previous studies described there. In some situations, especially in the commonly used empirical econometric models such as dynamic models, sample selection models, probit models, the numerical evaluations of exact expressions may be extremely difficult or cannot be derived by the presently known mathematical and statistical tools. In view of the above problems with the exact results, obtaining the approximate moments have been popular in econometrics since they are simpler to derive, provide simpler expressions, easier to calculate, and often provide useful inferences. Further, the approximations presented here are useful for the moderately large samples and they lie between the often unknown exact sample results, and infinite sample limiting results, which are routinely discussed in text books and used in applied work even though they give poor results for small and moderately large samples. Here we look into the following approaches of deriving approximate moments (*a*) large sample approximations, (*b*) small-$\sigma$ approximation, (*c*) Laplace approximations.

## 2.5.1 Large Sample Approximations: Normal and Nonnormal

The large sample method, also known as Nagar's (1959) approximation, of obtaining the approximate moments essentially involves the asymptotic expansion of the sampling error (the difference between the statistic and the parameter) such that the successive terms are in descending order of sample size $n$ in probability. Suppose $\theta$ is a $k \times 1$ parameter vector and $\hat{\theta} = h(y)$ is its estimator so that the sampling error is $\hat{\theta} - \theta$. Then the asymptotic expansion, obtained by using the Taylor Series expansion, is of the form

$$\hat{\theta} - \theta = \xi_0 + \xi_{-1/2} + \xi^*, \tag{2.70}$$

where $\xi_0$ is a fixed quantity in the sense that it does not vary stochastically with $n$. In other words, $\xi_0$ contains forms of order $O_p(n^0) = O_p(1)$ (see Appendix for definitions of small $o$ and capital $O$). Similarly $\xi_{-1/2}$ denotes the expression in which terms are of order $O_p(n^{-1/2})$. Lastly, $\xi^*$ is the remainder term containing terms of higher order of smallness than $O_p(n^{-1/2})$ to mean that the terms in $\xi^*$ are of order $O_p(n^{-(1/2)-s})$ with $s > 0$.

When $\xi_0 = 0, \hat{\theta}$ will be a consistent estimator so that $\xi_0$ provides a measure for inconsistency of the estimator $\hat{\theta}$. Thus assuming $\hat{\theta}$ to be a consistent estimator, we have the asymptotic expansion

$$\hat{\theta} - \theta = h(y) = \xi_{-1/2} + \xi^* \tag{2.71}$$

whence it follows that we can approximate the estimation error by $\xi_{-1/2}$. Now the properties of $\xi_{-1/2}$ shed light on the properties of $\hat{\theta}$ subject to the usual qualification that $n$ is large enough for the approximation to be satisfactory and reasonably good. We point out here that the Taylor series in (2.70) and (2.71) are the large-$n$ asymptotic expansions in the sense that they are absolutely convergent for large $n$, though they may be divergent for a fixed $n$. Thus the truncations may provide good approximations or make sense for moderately large samples. For details on the validity of asymptotic expansions of non-stochastic series see Whittaker and Watson (1965), and Appendix A.3, and for stochastic series see Sargan (1975, 1976), Phillips (1977$b$), and Appendix A.3.1.

Once the asymptotic expansion is written the large sample asymptotic approximation of the bias $\hat{\theta}$ to $O(n^{-1/2})$ is given by $E(\xi_{-1/2})$ while the large sample asymptotic approximation to $O(n^{-1})$ for the mean squared error (MSE) is $E\xi_{-1/2}^2$. It may be pointed out that the distribution of $n^{1/2}\xi_{-1/2}$ is nothing but the conventional limiting (asymptotic) distribution of $n^{1/2}(\hat{\theta} - \theta)$.

As an extension of the above approach, if we retain higher order terms in the expansion of $\hat{\theta} - \theta$ we get large sample asymptotic approximations of higher orders. Suppose that we use an infinite Taylor series expansion for the estimation error $\hat{\theta} - \theta$ and group the terms according to the order of magnitude in probability. This yields

$$\hat{\theta} - \theta = \sum_{j=1}^{\infty} \xi_{-j/2}$$

$$= \xi_{-1/2} + \xi_{-1} + \cdots + \xi_{-q/2} + \xi^*, \tag{2.72}$$

where $\xi^* = O_p(n^{-(q/2)-s})$, $s > 0$ , and the expression for $\xi_{-j/2}$ is of $O_p(n^{-j/2})$ consisting of sums and products of sample averages. Now if we approximate the estimation error $\hat{\theta} - \theta$ by the truncated sum $\xi = \xi_{-1/2} + \cdots + \xi_{-q/2}$ of first $q$ terms in the expansion and neglect the remaining terms, the difference between the estimation error and the truncated sum is of $O_p(n^{-q/2})$. The properties of the truncated sum $\xi$ provide useful information about the properties of $\hat{\theta}$ provided $n$ is sufficiently large for the accuracy of the approximation. Of course, while the accuracy of these approximations will chiefly depend upon the magnitude of $n$ it may also be affected by the other parameters of the econometric model and the nature of data under consideration.

Regarding the properties of $\hat{\theta} - \theta = h(y)$ we note that the first-order bias and MSE (asymptotic bias to $O(n^{-1/2})$ and MSE to $O(n^{-1})$) are obtained by taking expectation of first term on the right-hand side in (2.72) and its product, respectively. The second-order bias to $O(n^{-1})$ is defined as the expectation of the first two terms on the right-hand side in (2.72). Further the second-order MSE, up to $O(n^{-2})$, is

$$E(\hat{\theta} - \theta)(\hat{\theta} - \theta)' = E[h(y)h(y)']$$

$$= E\Big[\xi_{-1/2}\xi'_{-1/2} + \xi_{-1/2}\xi'_{-3/2} + \xi_{-3/2}\xi'_{-1/2} + \xi_{-1}\xi'_{-1}\Big]$$

$$= A_{-1} + A_{-2} \qquad\qquad\qquad (2.73)$$

where

$$A_{-1} = O(n^{-1}) = E(\xi_{-1/2}\xi'_{-1/2})$$

and

$$A_{-2} = O(n^{-2}) = E\Big(\xi_{-1/2}\xi'_{-3/2} + \xi_{-3/2}\xi'_{-1/2} + \xi_{-1}\xi'_{-1}\Big).$$

In Chapter 3 it is indicated that these approximate moments are the moments of the Edgeworth expansion of the distribution of $\hat{\theta}$. We note that $A_{-1}$ is the asymptotic variance (MSE) and $A_{-2}$ can be interpreted as a correction term for the moderately large samples. Similarly one can consider third-order approximations of bias and MSE by considering first four terms, see Akahira and Takeuchi (1981) for details.

To see the nature of the elements $\xi_{-j/2}$ for an econometric estimator or test statistic, consider $\hat{\theta} = h(y)$ for the econometric models $y = \mu + u$ where $\mu = Ey$ is an $n \times 1$ vector. We can write the Taylor series expansion of $h(y)$ around $\mu$ as

$$\hat{\theta} - \theta = u'\Delta + \tfrac{1}{2}u'\Delta^2 u + \tfrac{1}{6}(u'\Delta^2 u)u'\Delta + \tfrac{1}{24}(u'\Delta^2 u)^2 + \cdots$$

$$= \xi_{-1/2} + \xi_{-1} + \xi_{-3/2} + \xi_{-2} + \cdots,$$

where $\theta = h(\mu)$,

$$\Delta = \frac{\partial h(y)}{\partial y}\Big|_{y=\mu}, \qquad \Delta^2 = \frac{\partial^2 h(y)}{\partial y \partial y'}\Big|_{y=\mu}.$$

The $\xi_{-j/2}$ is the collection of terms of $O_p(n^{-j/2})$, which depend on the orders of $u'\Delta, u'\Delta^2 u$, and $(u'\Delta^2 u)^2$ for the estimator under consideration. An alternative equivalent expression of the Taylor expansion can also be written as

$$\hat{\theta} - \theta = \nabla u + \nabla^2[u \otimes u] + \tfrac{1}{6}\nabla^3[u \otimes u \otimes u] + \tfrac{1}{24}\nabla^4[u \otimes u \otimes u \otimes u],$$

where $\otimes$ is the kronecker product and

$$\nabla = \frac{\partial}{\partial y'}h(y)\Big|_{y=\mu}, \qquad \nabla^2 = \frac{\partial}{\partial y'}\nabla\Big|_{y=\mu}$$

are $1 \times n$ and $1 \times n^2$ vectors. Similarly $\nabla^3 = (\partial/\partial y')\nabla^2|_{y=\mu}$ and $\nabla^4 = (\partial/\partial y')\nabla^3|_{y=\mu}$ are $1 \times n^3$ and $1 \times n^4$ vectors of recursive derivatives. This form of Taylor series expansion will be useful for the nonlinear estimators given below. Also it provides results for nonnormal $u$ more easily.

To see the examples of the expressions of $\xi_{-j/2}$ we consider the asymptotic expansion of the LS estimator in the linear model $y = X\beta + u = \mu + u$, where $\mu = Ey = X\beta$ and $X$ is nonstochastic with $X'X = O(n)$. Then $\hat{\beta} = h(y) = (X'X)^{-1}X'y$ gives

$$\hat{\beta} - \beta = (X'X)^{-1}X'u = \xi_{-1/2},$$

where $\xi_{-1/2} = (X'X)^{-1}X'u$ is $O_p(n^{-1/2})$ because $X'u = O_p(n^{1/2})$. Note that this result also follows using the Taylor expansion above since $\beta = h(\mu), \nabla = (X'X)^{-1}X'$ and $\nabla^2 = 0 = \nabla^3 = \nabla^4$.

When $X$ is stochastic we can write $X'X/n = X'X/n + D - D$ where $D = 1/nEX'X$ is $O(1)$. Then, assuming $C = (X'X/n) - D = O_p(n^{-1/2})$,

$$\hat{\beta} - \beta = \left(\frac{X'X}{n}\right)^{-1}\frac{X'y}{n} = (C + D)^{-1}\frac{X'u}{n}$$

$$= D^{-1}(I + CD^{-1})^{-1}\frac{X'u}{n}$$

$$= D^{-1}(I - CD^{-1} + (CD^{-1})^2 - \cdots)X'u/n$$

$$= D^{-1}\frac{X'u}{n} - D^{-1}CD^{-1}\frac{X'u}{n} + D^{-1}(CD^{-1})^2\frac{X'u}{n}$$

$$= \xi_{-1/2} + \xi_{-1} + \xi_{-3/2}.$$

Again $\xi_{-1/2} = D^{-1}(X'u/n)$, $\xi_{-1} = -D^{-1}CD^{-1}(X'u/n)$ and $\xi_{-3/2} = D^{-1}(CD^{-1})^2(X'u/n)$. The bias and MSE of $\hat{\beta}$ then follow from (2.73).

**Nonlinear Estimators**  The asymptotic expansion given above can be used for the econometric statistic $\hat{\theta} = h(y)$ where the explicit form of $h(y)$ is known. However, for many statistics, for example, nonlinear maximum likelihood (ML) and method of moments, the form of $h(y)$ is not known. For these cases we develop the asymptotic expansion below. As a special case this also provides the results for $\hat{\theta}$, with explicit forms of $h(y)$. Let us consider the class of estimators $\hat{\theta}$, which may be written as the solution of a set of moment equations of the form $\psi_n = \psi_n(\theta) = 1/n\sum_1^n g_i(\theta) = 0$, that is

$$\psi_n(\hat{\theta}) = \frac{1}{n}\sum_1^n g_i(\hat{\theta}) = 0, \qquad (2.74)$$

where $g_i(\theta) = g(z_i, \theta)$ is a known $k \times 1$ vector valued function of the $m$-dimensional i.i.d. data $z_i$ and a $k$ dimensional parameter vector $\theta$ such that $E[g_i(\theta)] = 0$ only for true value of $\theta$ and for all $i$. The special cases of this are ML estimators, LS and other extremum estimators, many generalized method of moments estimators, and certain two step estimators, which involve a nuisance parameter. The obvious difficulty with nonlinear estimators is that they cannot be expressed as explicit functions of the data. Because of this, obtaining their exact moments are extremely difficult. Obtaining the asymptotic expansion of the form (2.72) is also not straightforward for the nonlinear estimators. Rilstone, Srivastava, and Ullah (RSU) (1996), assuming that $\hat{\theta}$ is arbitrarily closed to $\theta$, used iterative techniques to derive approximate solutions to the first-order conditions $\psi_n(\hat{\theta}) = 0$, also see De Bruijn (1961) and Barndorff-Nielsen and Cox (1979). For this solution RSU (1996) made the following assumptions:

**Assumptions 1**  The $s$th order derivatives of $g_i(\theta)$ exist in a neighborhood of $\theta$ and $E||\nabla^s g_i(\theta)||^2 < \infty$, where $||A||$, for a matrix $A$, denotes the usual norm, trace $[AA']^{1/2}$, and $\nabla^s A(\theta)$ is the matrix of $s$th order partial derivations of a matrix $A(\theta)$ with respect to $\theta$ and obtained recursively.

**Assumptions 2**  For some neighborhood of $\theta$, $(\nabla \psi_n(\theta))^{-1} = O_p(1)$.

**Assumptions 3**  $||\nabla^s g_i(\theta) - \nabla^s g_i(\theta_0)|| \le ||\theta - \theta_0|| M_i$ for some neighborhood of $\theta_0$, where $E|M_i| \le C < \infty$, $i = 1, 2, \dots$

Note that the above assumptions, with $s \ge 1$, are sufficient for $\sqrt{n}(\hat{\theta} - \theta) \to N(0, \Pi_1)$ as $n \to \infty$, $\Pi_1 = (E\nabla g_1)^{-1} E g_1 g_1' (E\nabla g_1)'^{-1}$. This provides an important result that $\hat{\theta} - \theta = O_p(n^{-1/2})$, which is useful in developing the following Lemma.

**Lemma (RSU 1996)** *Let Assumptions 1–3 hold for some $s \ge 3$. Then*

$$\hat{\theta} - \theta = \xi_{-1/2} + \xi_{-1} + \xi_{-3/2} + O_p(n^{-2}), \tag{2.75}$$

*where*

$$\xi_{-1/2} = -Q\psi_n, \quad \xi_{-1} = -QV\xi_{-1/2} - \tfrac{1}{2}Q\bar{H}_2\{\xi_{-1/2} \otimes \xi_{-1/2}\}$$

$$\xi_{-3/2} = -QV\xi_{-1} - \tfrac{1}{2}QW\{\xi_{-1/2} \otimes \xi_{-1/2}\} - \tfrac{1}{2}Q\bar{H}_2\{(\xi_{-1/2} \otimes \xi_{-1})$$

$$+ (\xi_{-1} \otimes \xi_{-1/2})\} - \tfrac{1}{6}Q\bar{H}_3(\xi_{-1/2} \otimes \xi_{-1/2} \otimes \xi_{-1/2}); \tag{2.76}$$

*a bar over a function indicates its expectation so that $\bar{A}(\theta) = EA(\theta)$, $H_j = \nabla^j \psi_n$, $j = 1, 2, 3$, $Q = (\bar{H}_1)^{-1}$, $V = H_1 - \bar{H}_1 = 1/n\Sigma_1^n V_i, V_i = \nabla g_i - \bar{\nabla} g_i$ and $W = H_2 - \bar{H}_2 = n^{-1}\Sigma W_i$; $W_i = \nabla^2 g_i - \bar{\nabla}^2 g_i$.*

The proof of the above lemma follows by first writing the first-order Taylor series expansion of $\psi_n(\hat{\theta})$ as

$$0 = \psi_n(\hat{\theta}) = \psi_n(\theta) + \nabla\psi_n(\bar{\theta})(\hat{\theta} - \theta),$$

where $\bar{\theta}$ is between $\hat{\theta}$ and $\theta$. This gives

$$
\begin{aligned}
\hat{\theta} - \theta &= -[\nabla \psi_n(\bar{\theta})]^{-1} \psi_n(\theta), \\
&= -[\nabla \psi_n(\theta)]^{-1} \psi_n(\theta) - [\nabla \psi_n^{-1}(\bar{\theta}) - \nabla \psi_n^{-1}(\theta)] \psi_n(\theta), \\
&= \epsilon_{-1/2} + \varepsilon_{-1},
\end{aligned}
\tag{2.77}
$$

where $\epsilon_{-1} = -[\nabla \psi_n^{-1}(\bar{\theta}) - \nabla \psi_n^{-1}(\theta)] \psi_n(\theta) = O_p(n^{-1})$. We note here that $\epsilon_{-1/2} = O_p(n^{-1/2})$ and this is the term upon which the usual asymptotic distribution of $\hat{\theta}$ is based.

Now write the second-order Taylor series expansion of $\psi_n(\hat{\theta})$ as

$$
0 = \psi_n(\hat{\theta}) = \psi_n(\theta) + \nabla \psi_n(\hat{\theta} - \theta) + \tfrac{1}{2} \nabla^2 \psi_n(\bar{\theta})[(\hat{\theta} - \theta) \otimes (\hat{\theta} - \theta)].
\tag{2.78}
$$

We then get

$$
\hat{\theta} - \theta = -[\nabla \psi_n]^{-1} \psi_n - \tfrac{1}{2} [\nabla \psi_n]^{-1} \nabla^2 \psi_n(\bar{\theta})(\hat{\theta} - \theta) \otimes (\hat{\theta} - \theta).
\tag{2.79}
$$

Finally the result in Lemma follows by taking the third-order Taylor series expansion as

$$
\begin{aligned}
0 = \psi_n(\hat{\theta}) &= \psi_n + \nabla \psi_n(\hat{\theta} - \theta) + \tfrac{1}{2} \nabla^2 \psi_n[(\hat{\theta} - \theta) \otimes (\hat{\theta} - \theta)] \\
&\quad + \tfrac{1}{6} \nabla^3 \psi_n[(\hat{\theta} - \theta) \otimes (\hat{\theta} - \theta) \otimes (\hat{\theta} - \theta)]
\end{aligned}
\tag{2.80}
$$

and substituting (2.77) and (2.79) in this equation, see RSU (1996).

Combining the result in the above lemma with (2.72) and (2.73) and evaluating the expectations using the techniques in the Appendix we get the following Proposition.

**Proposition (RSU 1996)**   Let Assumptions 1–3 hold for some $s \geq 2$. Then the bias of $\hat{\theta}$ to order $O(n^{-1})$ is

$$
B(\hat{\theta}) = \frac{1}{n} Q \left\{ \overline{V_1 d_1} - \frac{1}{2} \bar{H}_2 \overline{[d_1 \otimes d_1]} \right\},
\tag{2.81}
$$

where $Q = [\bar{\nabla} g_i]^{-1}, V_i = [\nabla g_i - \bar{\nabla} g_i]$, and $d_i = Q g_i$. Further if Assumptions 1–3 hold for some $s \geq 3$, then the MSE of $\hat{\theta}$ to order $O(n^{-2})$ is

$$
\text{MSE}(\hat{\theta}) = \frac{1}{n} \Pi_1 + \frac{1}{n^2} (\Pi_2 + \Pi_2') + \frac{1}{n^3} (\Pi_3 + \Pi_4 + \Pi_4'),
\tag{2.82}
$$

where

$$\Pi_2 = Q\left\{-\overline{V_1 d_1 d_1'} + \tfrac{1}{2}\bar{H}_2\overline{\{d_1 \otimes d_1\}d_1'}\right\},$$

$$\Pi_3 = Q\left\{\overline{V_1 d_1 d_2' V_2'} + \overline{[V_1 d_2 d_1' V_2']} + \overline{[V_1 d_2 d_2' V_1']}\right\}Q$$
$$+ \tfrac{1}{4}Q\bar{H}_2\overline{[d_1 \otimes d_1]}\,[d_2' \otimes d_2'] + \overline{[d_1 \otimes d_2][d_1' \otimes d_2']}$$
$$+ \overline{[d_1 \otimes d_2][d_2' \otimes d_1']}\bar{H}_2'\,Q$$
$$- \tfrac{1}{2}Q\left\{\overline{V_1 d_1 d_2' \otimes d_2'} + \overline{V_1 d_2[d_1' \otimes d_2']} + \overline{V_1 d_2[d_2' \otimes d_1']}\right\}\bar{H}_2'\,Q$$
$$- \tfrac{1}{2}Q\bar{H}_2\left\{\overline{d_1 \otimes d_1 d_2' V_2'} + \overline{[d_1 \otimes d_2]\,d_1' V_2'} + \overline{[d_1 \otimes d_2]\,d_2' V_1'}\right\}Q, \qquad (2.83)$$

$$\Pi_4 = Q\left\{\overline{V_1 Q V_1 d_2 d_2'} + \overline{V_1 Q V_2 d_1 d_2'} + \overline{V_1 Q V_2 d_2 d_1'}\right\}$$
$$- \tfrac{1}{2}Q\left\{\overline{V_1 Q\bar{H}_2\,[d_1 \otimes d_2']\,d_2'} + \overline{V_1 Q\bar{H}_2\,[d_2 \otimes d_1]\,d_2'} + \overline{V_1 Q\bar{H}_2\,[d_2 \otimes d_2]\,d_1'}\right\}$$
$$+ \tfrac{1}{2}Q\left\{\overline{W_1[d_1 \otimes d_2]\,d_2'} + \overline{W_1[d_2 \otimes d_1]\,d_2'} + \overline{W_1[d_2 \otimes d_2]\,d_1'}\right\}$$
$$- \tfrac{1}{2}Q\bar{H}_2\left\{\overline{[d_1 \otimes Q V_1 d_2]\,d_2'} + \overline{[d_1 \otimes Q V_2 d_1]\,d_2'} + \overline{[d_1 \otimes Q V_2 d_2]\,d_1'}\right\}$$
$$+ \tfrac{1}{4}Q\bar{H}_2\left\{\overline{d_1 \otimes Q\bar{H}_2\,[d_1 \otimes d_2]\,d_2'} + \overline{d_1 \otimes Q\bar{H}_2\,[d_2 \otimes d_1]\,d_2'}\right.$$
$$\left.+ \overline{d_1 \otimes Q\bar{H}_2[d_2 \otimes d_2]d_1'}\right\}$$
$$- \tfrac{1}{2}Q\bar{H}_2\left\{\overline{[Q V_1 d_1 \otimes d_2]\,d_2'} + \overline{[Q V_1 d_2 \otimes d_1]\,d_2'} + \overline{[Q V_1 d_2 \otimes d_2]\,d_1'}\right\}$$
$$+ \tfrac{1}{4}Q\bar{H}_2\left\{\overline{[Q\bar{H}_2\,[d_1 \otimes d_1] \otimes d_2]\,d_2'} + \overline{[Q\bar{H}_2\,[d_1 \otimes d_2] \otimes d_1]\,d_2'}\right\}$$
$$+ \tfrac{1}{4}Q\bar{H}_2\left\{\overline{[Q\bar{H}_2\,[d_1 \otimes d_2] \otimes d_2]\,d_1'}\right\} - \tfrac{1}{6}Q\bar{H}_3\left\{\overline{[d_1 \otimes d_1 \otimes d_2]\,d_2'}\right.$$
$$+ \overline{[d_1 \otimes d_2 \otimes d_1]\,d_2'} + \overline{[d_1 \otimes d_2 \otimes d_2]\,d_1'}\right\}.$$

We note that the MSE is a corrected version of RSU (1996) where $1/4, -1/2, -1/2$ in $\Pi_3$ are $1,1,1$ respectively and $Q\bar{H}_2$ before the curly bracket in the last but one term in $\Pi_4$ is missing, see Bao and Ullah (2002). A number of remarks are worth making with respect to the above expression. First, the second-order bias depends explicitly on the curvature of the model, $\nabla_g^2$ and $\nabla g$. This expression allows one to evaluate the influence of second-order terms on the location of the estimator. For highly nonlinear models, this term may be relatively large and one may be interested in estimating it either directly or by some resampling technique or at least taking it into account informally when making inferences.

For models that are linear in the parameters, the second term is zero. For linear regression models estimated with LS or generalized least squares, the first term is also zero from the orthogonality property of the disturbances and the regressors.

A third point is that the simple structure of the second-order bias suggests a natural estimate from the sample analogue evaluated at the estimated value of $\theta$, for example, $E(\nabla g_i) = \sum_1^n \nabla g_i(\hat{\theta})/n$. However, this should be interpreted with some care; see, for example, Phillips and Park (1987).

A final point to be emphasized is that, apart from the existence of moments, this result does not require any distributional assumptions regarding the random variables in the model. In particular, there is no need to assume, say, normality of the $z_i$'s. This remark also holds with respect to the derivation of the second-order MSE of $\hat{\beta}$.

As with the second-order bias, the second-order MSE is shown to be the expectation of sums and products of sums of zero mean random matrices. The second-order MSE is thus a combination of the usual $O(n^{-1})$ first-order asymptotic covariance matrix, $\Pi_1$, and a number of second-order terms. As will be seen in the examples, many of the higher-order terms are equal to zero under various symmetry, linearity, and exogeneity assumptions.

A few additional remarks are worth making with respect to the form of the second-order MSE. In this form the MSE is not necessarily positive definite, although one might expect it to be for most samples. This should not be surprising since, for example, high-order Edgeworth expansions are generally not valid distribution functions. The fact that the MSE may not be positive definite could actually be reassuring in some practical contexts. Most applied researchers have probably been in a situation where the usual standard errors seem to overestimate the sample variability of their estimator. For example, they may have observed that a given coefficient seems quite robust for various data sets or slightly different model specifications. One possible explanation could be that the asymptotic variance overstates the true dispersion of their estimate. The result in Proposition could thus provide a motivation for constructing alternative variance estimates.

Also important to note is under what conditions the high-order terms may have a substantial impact on the finite-sample precision of an estimator. Referring back to the definitions of the random variables it can be seen that the higher-order terms are comprised of expressions that depend on the second- and third-order derivatives of the model. Thus, a general rule of thumb would seem that variance estimates based on $\Pi_1$ will tend to lack precision for most nonlinear models. The terms to $O(1/n^2)$ can also be used to evaluate the effect of nonnormality on the MSE of $\hat{\theta}$. This can be done by comparing the expression of the MSE under nonnormality with that under normality.

Some additional points should be made with respect to application of the above results. First is that one can consider a bias-corrected estimator: $\hat{\theta}_{BC} = \hat{\theta} - \delta$ where $\delta = B(\theta) = n^{-1}Q\left\{\overline{V_1 d_1} - \frac{1}{2}\bar{H}_2\left[\overline{d_1 \otimes d_1}\right]\right\}$. It is straightforward that this estimator is unbiased to order $O(n^{-1})$.

Notice that $\hat{\theta}_{BC}$ is an estimator in the true sense only when $\delta$ is known. Generally, $\delta$ will involve several unknown quantities (parameter values and population moments) and consequently $\hat{\theta}_{BC}$ as such may not be feasible. A simple solution is then to replace these unknown quantities by their estimators or sample analogues. This will provide an estimator of $\delta$. Using such an estimator, $\hat{\delta}$ (say), one can propose the estimator $\tilde{\theta}_{BC} = \hat{\theta} - \hat{\delta}$, which will be unbiased to order $O(n^{-1})$ provided that $\hat{\delta}$ is a consistent estimator of $\delta$; see more on bias correction by MacKinnon and Smith (1998).

With respect to efficiency issues it is well established that the bias-corrected MLE is second-order efficient with respect to the mean squared error criterion, see Rothenberg (1984$a$). Further discussion of the efficiency properties of feasible versions of $\hat{\theta}_{BC}$ will demand inclusion of higher-order terms. This would be a difficult exercise, although for some particular examples it may not be that difficult. In RSU (1996) they report on how estimates of $\hat{\theta}_{BC}$ and $\tilde{\theta}_{BC}$ perform in a Monte Carlo setting for the exponential regression model. Results there indicate that bias corrections can lead to substantial improvements in inferences.

**Exercise 14**   Consider a population with mean $\mu$ and variance $\sigma^2$. Let $\bar{y} = \sum_1^n y_i/n$ and $s^2 = \sum_1^n(y_i - \bar{y})^2/(n-1)$ be the sample estimates based on the i.i.d. sample $y_i$, $i = 1, \ldots, n$. Obtain the exact and large-$n$ approximate bias and MSE of

$$(a)\ \bar{y} \quad (b)\ \frac{1}{\bar{y}}.$$

*Solution*   First we write

$$\bar{y} - \mu = \frac{1}{n}\sum_{i=1}^n (y_i - \mu) = \frac{1}{n}\sum_{i=1}^n g_i(\mu) = \psi_n(\mu) = \psi_n,$$

where $g_i(\mu) = y_i - \mu$ is such that $E\,g_i(\mu) = 0$. Then $E(\bar{y} - \mu) = 0$, that is the exact bias is zero. Further the exact $\mathrm{MSE}(\bar{y}) = V(\bar{y}) = \sigma^2/n$.

Now to obtain the approximate bias and MSE we first note from the Lemma that

$$\hat{\theta} - \theta = \bar{y} - \mu = \zeta_{-1/2}.$$

Thus in this case the exact approximate and asymptotic results are the same.

Regarding $1/\bar{y}$ we note that the exact mean

$$E\frac{1}{\bar{y}} = \int_{y_1}, \ldots, \int_{y_n} \frac{1}{\bar{y}} f\,(y_1, \ldots, y_n)\,dy_1, \ldots, dy_n$$

cannot be obtained without specifying the form of a density $f(\ )$. For example, if $y_i$'s are normal $\bar{y}$ is $N(\mu, \sigma^2/n)$ and $E(1/\bar{y})$ is infinite. Further the MSE of $1/\bar{y}$ is also infinite. However, for some nonnormal distribution $E(1/\bar{y})$ may exist, but it may be difficult to obtain explicit expressions.

To obtain the approximate moments we write

$$\frac{1}{n}\sum_1^n (1 - y_i\theta) = \frac{1}{n}\sum_1^n g_i(\theta) = \psi_n(\theta)$$

so that $\psi_n(\hat{\theta}) = 0$ gives $\hat{\theta} = 1/\bar{y}$ and $E\, g_i(\theta) = 0$ for $\theta = 1/\mu$. Then, the bias of $1/\bar{y}$ follows from the Proposition, where

$$\theta = \frac{1}{\mu}, \quad V_1 = (\mu - y_1), \quad d_1 = \frac{-(1 - y_1\theta)}{\mu}$$

$$H_2 = \nabla^2 g_1 = 0$$

so that

$$\overline{V_1 d_1} = E(V_1 d_1) = -(1/\mu)\, E\big[\mu - \mu y_1 \theta - y_1 + y_1^2\theta\big] = -\sigma^2\theta/\mu,$$

$$\bar{H}_2 = 0, \overline{d_1 \otimes d_1} = (\mu^2 + \sigma^2)/\mu^2 = 1 + \sigma^2/\mu^2.$$

This gives

$$B(\hat{\theta}) = -\frac{1}{n\mu}\left[-\frac{\sigma^2\theta}{\mu}\right] = \frac{\sigma^2\theta}{n\mu^2} = \frac{\sigma^2}{n\mu^3},$$

where the last equality is for $\theta = 1/\mu$. The MSE can be similarly obtained for $\theta = 1/\mu$ as

$$\text{MSE}(\hat{\theta}) = \frac{\sigma^2}{n\mu^4} + \frac{\sigma^3}{n^2\mu^6}\left[9\sigma - 2\gamma_1\mu\right],$$

where $\gamma_1$ is the skewness coefficient.

From the above exercise we note that the bias goes to zero as $n \to \infty$, and it is monotonically decreasing function of $\mu$. Further the bias-corrected estimator can be written as $\tilde{\theta}_{\text{BC}} = \hat{\theta} - s^2/n\bar{y}^3$. Also, the MSE for the positively skewed distributions with $\mu > 0$ is smaller compared with the symmetric distributions.

## 2.5.2    Small-$\sigma$ Approximations: Normal and Nonnormal

The small-$\sigma$ (disturbance) method of obtaining the approximate moments, first proposed by Kadane (1971) for the normal case and later explored by Ullah, Srivastava, and Roy (1995) for the nonnormal case, involves the asymptotic expansion of the sampling error such that the successive terms are in descending order of $\sigma$, the standard deviation, in probability. That is the sampling error $\hat{\theta} - \theta$, using the Taylor series expansion, is of the form

$$\hat{\theta} - \theta = \sum_{j=1}^{\infty} \sigma^j \zeta_j$$

$$= \sigma\zeta_1 + \sigma^2\zeta_2 + \cdots + \sigma^q\zeta_q + \zeta^*, \qquad (2.84)$$

where $\zeta_j$ is the $j$th term of the series, and $\zeta^* = O(\sigma^{q+s})$, $s > 0$.

The technique for obtaining the small-$\sigma$ asymptotic approximations can be explained by first noting that a class of econometric models can be written as

$$y = \mu + \sigma u, \tag{2.85}$$

where $y$ is an $n \times 1$ vector, $\mu = E\, y$ is an $n \times 1$ vector, and $u$ is an $n \times 1$ vector of disturbances with finite first four moments. For example, a univariate population with the scalar mean $\mu$ and a multivariate regression model with $\mu = X\,\beta$ are special cases of the above model. For these models $\hat{\theta} = h\,(y) = h(\mu + \sigma\, u)$, by expanding around $\mu$, gives

$$\hat{\theta} - \theta = \sigma\,\zeta_1 + \sigma^2\zeta_2 + \sigma^3\zeta_3 + \sigma^4\zeta_4 + \cdots, \tag{2.86}$$

where

$$\theta = h(\mu), \quad \zeta_1 = \sum_i u_i \left[ \frac{\partial h\,(y)}{\partial\, y_i} \right]_{y=\mu} = [\nabla h\,(y)]_{y=\mu}\, u,$$

$$\zeta_2 = \frac{1}{2} \sum_i \sum_j u_i\, u_j \left[ \frac{\partial^2\, h(y)}{\partial\, y_i\, \partial\, y_j} \right]_{y=\mu} = \frac{1}{2} [\nabla^2\, h(y)]_{y=\mu}\, [u \otimes u],$$

$$\zeta_3 = \frac{1}{6} \sum_i \sum_j \sum_k u_i\, u_j\, u_k \left[ \frac{\partial^3\, h(y)}{\partial\, y_i\, \partial\, y_j\, \partial\, y_k} \right]_{y=\mu} = \frac{1}{6} [\nabla^3\, h(y)]_{y=\mu}\, [u \otimes u \otimes u],$$

$$\zeta_4 = \frac{1}{24} \sum_i \sum_j \sum_k \sum_\ell u_i\, u_j\, u_k\, u_\ell \left[ \frac{\partial^4\, h(y)}{\partial\, y_i\, \partial\, y_j\, \partial\, y_k\, \partial\, y_\ell} \right]_{y=\mu}$$

$$= \frac{1}{24} [\nabla^4\, h(y)]_{y=\mu} [u \otimes u \otimes u \otimes u], \tag{2.87}$$

where $\nabla h(y) = (\partial/\partial y')\, h(y)$ is a $1 \times n$ vector, $\nabla^2\, h(y) = \partial/\partial y' \nabla h(y)$ is a $1 \times n^2$ vector and so on as defined in 2.5.1. If $\hat{\theta} = h(y)$ is a $k \times 1$ vector then $\nabla h(y)$ is a $k \times n$ matrix.

The Taylor series expansion may be convergent or divergent. However, if we consider $\sigma$ to be small and close to zero it can be regarded as an asymptotic expansion where the terms are in decreasing order of magnitude in $\sigma$. In that case one can retain the first few terms and study the properties of this truncated sum. These properties are referred to as small-$\sigma$ (disturbance) asymptotic properties of $\hat{\theta}$.

For example, the bias to order $O(\sigma^2)$ and MSE to $O(\sigma^4)$, respectively, are given by

$$\text{Bias}(\hat{\theta}) = \sigma E\zeta_1 + \sigma^2 E\zeta_2 \tag{2.88}$$

and

$$\text{MSE}(\hat{\theta}) = \sigma^2 E\zeta_1\zeta_1' + \sigma^3[E\zeta_1\zeta_2' + E\zeta_2\zeta_1'] + \sigma^4[E\zeta_2\zeta_2' + E\zeta_3\zeta_1' + E\zeta_1\zeta_3']. \tag{2.89}$$

Obviously, how successful and satisfactory these approximations are in any given practical application depends upon the smallness of $\sigma$ among other things. Since $\sigma$ measures the variability in the disturbance term of an econometric model, the assumption that $\sigma$ is small, or tends to zero, implies that the postulated econometric model is assumed to explain $y$ well. Thus the smallness of $\sigma$ is an appealing assumption and it is consistent with the philosophy of large-$n$ (small $1/n$) asymptotics in 2.5.1.

We thus observe that the methodology for deriving the small-$\sigma$ asymptotic approximations is similar to that of large sample asymptotic approximations. However, the latter requires the number of observations to be large while the former needs no such condition. Even the assumptions like the finiteness of the limiting value of sample moments such as $X'X/n$, required in regression contexts, are not needed. This also makes small-$\sigma$ expansions easier to derive since one does not have to determine the order of magnitude of the terms $\zeta_j$ in (2.87) in contrast to the large-$n$ expansions, which need to evaluate the order of magnitudes of $\xi_j$ in (2.72) or (2.75) as $n$ goes to infinity.

We can now present a more explicit expression for the bias to $O(\sigma^2)$ and MSE to $O(\sigma^4)$ of a general class of linear and nonlinear estimators $\hat{\theta}$ of the parameter vector $\theta$ in the model $y = \mu + \sigma u$. We make the following assumptions about the elements $u_i$, $i = 1, \ldots, n$, of the vector $u$.

**Assumptions 4**   The elements of the vector $u$ are independently and identically distributed such that

$$Eu_i = 0, \quad Eu_i^2 = 1, \quad Eu_i^3 = \gamma_1, \quad Eu_i^4 = \gamma_2 + 3,$$

where $\gamma_1$ and $\gamma_2$ are measures of skewness and kurtosis of the distribution.

**Assumptions 5**   The $h(y)$ and the $s$th order derivatives of $h(y)$ exist in the neighborhood of $Ey = \mu$.

Now we can state the result due to Ullah, Srivastava, and Roy (USR) (1995).

**Theorem (USR)**   *Under the assumptions 4 and 5 the expectation of $\hat{\theta} = h(y)$ is*

$$E\big(\hat{\theta} - \theta\big) = \sigma^2 \Delta_2 + \sigma^3 \gamma_1 \Delta_3 + \sigma^4 [\gamma_2 \Delta_4 + 3\Delta_{22}], \tag{2.90}$$

*where for $i$, $j = 1, \ldots, n$ and $s = 2, 3, 4$.*

$$\Delta_s = \frac{1}{s!} \sum_i \left[ \frac{\partial^s h(y)}{\partial y_i^s} \right]_{y=\mu}, \quad \Delta_{22} = \frac{1}{4!} \sum_i \sum_j \left[ \frac{\partial^4 h(y)}{\partial y_i^2 \, \partial y_j^2} \right]_{y=\mu}. \tag{2.91}$$

**Proof**   The proof follows by taking expectations in (2.86) from the Appendix, and simplifying the resulting terms.                                        (Q.E.D.)

The following observations may be deduced from our results given above.

First, the result in Theorem provides the mean of a general function $h(y)$ of the nonnormal vector $y$. The results for various econometric estimators and test statistics follow from this general result. The higher order moments also follow from the direct use of the Theorem. For example, for the $r$th moment of $h(y)$ we need to evaluate $Eg(y)$ where $g(y) = h^r(y)$ and this expectation can be obtained by replacing $g(y)$ with $h(y)$ in the Theorem.

Second, the result in the Theorem shows that the moments of econometric estimators and test statistics can be easily obtained by simply evaluating their first four derivatives at the mean value, $Ey = \mu$. Since a large class of econometric estimators and test statistics are the ratios of quadratic forms in $y$ or products of quadratic forms in $y$ and polynomials in $y$ their derivatives can be obtained by simple and well-known calculus methods.

Alternatively, the derivatives of any given function $h(y)$ can be obtained either numerically or analytically by using recently developed computer software, for example, Mathematica.

Third, from the Theorem we observe that, up to $O(\sigma^2)$, the moments for both normal and nonnormal cases are the same. However, up to $O(\sigma^4)$, the behavior of the moments in the nonnormal case can be quite different from those in the normal case where $\gamma_1 = 0 = \gamma_2$. In fact, if the true distribution of $y$ is not normal and we falsely assume it to be normal then the moments can be under or overestimated by the magnitude

$$\sigma^3 \gamma_1 \Delta_3 + \sigma^4 \gamma_2 \Delta_4, \tag{2.92}$$

where $\Delta_3$ and $\Delta_4$ are as given in (2.91). It is clear from this result that the third- and fourth-order derivatives of $h(y)$ at $y = \mu$ and the magnitudes of skewness and kurtosis of the distributions are the main determinants of the magnitude of misspecification error on the moments of $h(y)$.

Fourth, we observe from the Theorem that the bias of $h(y)$, up to $O(\sigma^2)$, depends crucially on the curvature properties (second derivatives) of $h(y)$. For example, for the econometric estimators and test statistics, which are the concave/convex functions of $y$, the directions of bias are negative/positive. Of course for estimators, which are linear functions of $y$, for example, the LS estimator in the linear regression case with fixed regressors, the $\Delta_{22}$ as well as $\Delta_s$ are equal to zero for $s = 2, 3, 4$ and therefore they become unbiased.

Finally, we observe from the Theorem that the estimator $\tilde{\theta} = h^*(y)$, where

$$h^*(y) = [h(y) - h(\mu)] - \sigma^2 \Delta_2, \tag{2.93}$$

has the zero mean up to $O(\sigma^2)$. This result is useful in providing bias-adjusted econometric estimators. The analysis of efficiency properties of these bias-adjusted estimators will be a useful subject of future research.

Further, we note that the above results are useful for the estimators, which have explicit solutions so that $h(y)$ is known. This may not be the case for some nonlinear estimators $\hat{\theta}$ which are the solution of $\psi_n(\hat{\theta}) = 0$, see (2.74). For these estimators the bias to $O(\sigma^2)$ and MSE to $O(\sigma^4)$ may be the same as the bias to $O(1/n)$ and MSE to $O(1/n^2)$ given in (2.81) and (2.82), respectively.

In general the results from the two approaches are not the same and the question arises, which of these two approaches give more accurate results. This issue is explored in the book. Often it is the case that for small samples and small-$\sigma$ the accuracy of results based on small-$\sigma$ asymptotics is better compared with large-$n$ asymptotics. In some cases the results of large-$n$ asymptotics can be derived from the small-$\sigma$ results, and in some special cases these two approaches give the same results. A trivial example is the properties of the sample mean as an estimator of the population mean $\mu$ in the model $y_i = \mu + \sigma u_i$, $i = 1, \ldots, n$ where $E u_i = 0$ and $V(u_i) = 1$. In this case as indicated in Exercise 14, the exact sampling error is

$$\bar{y} - \mu = \sigma \frac{1}{n} \sum_1^n u_i = \sigma \bar{u} \tag{2.94}$$

so that the infinite series expansion contains only the first term which is of $O(\sigma)$, or $O_p(1/\sqrt{n})$ due to limiting behavior of $\bar{u}$. Thus the large-$n$ expansion is the same as small-$\sigma$ and it is also reflected in the MSE $(\bar{y}) = V(\bar{y}) = \sigma^2/n$. Similarly in the regression model $y = \mu + \sigma u$, $\mu = X\beta$, the sampling error of the LS estimator is $\hat{\beta} - \beta = \sigma(X'X)^{-1} X'u = \sigma\zeta_1 = O(\sigma)$, which is the same as the $O_p(n^{-1/2})$ expansion in 2.5.1. Thus the large-$n$ and small-$\sigma$ expansions are the same and so is the $V(\hat{\beta}) = \sigma^2(X'X)^{-1}$. In Exercise 15 we consider a case where the two approximations are different. We also show in Chapters 4 and 6 that the moment approximations by these two approximations are different for the goodness of fit measure $R^2$ and dynamic models, but they are the same for the instrumental variables estimators in Chapter 7. Ullah (2002) proposes using Kullback–Leibler divergence measure for evaluating the quality of two and more approximations methods.

**Exercise 15**   Obtain the small-$\sigma$ asymptotic expansion of $\hat{\theta} = 1/\bar{y}$ where $\bar{y}$ is the sample mean estimator of $\mu$ in the model $y_i = \mu + u_i$, $i = 1, \ldots, n$.

*Solution*   Since $1/\bar{y} = \hat{\theta} = h(y)$, we get $h(\mu) = 1/\mu = \theta$.
Further

$$\frac{\partial^s h(y)}{\partial y_i} = (-1)^s \frac{s!\, \bar{y}^{-(s+1)}}{n^s}, \qquad \frac{\partial^4 h(y)}{\partial y_j^2\, \partial y_i^2} = \frac{4!}{n^4} \bar{y} - 4.$$

This gives

$$E\frac{1}{\bar{y}} = \frac{1}{\mu} + \frac{\sigma^2\, \mu^{-3}}{n} - \frac{\sigma^3\, \gamma_1}{n^2} \mu^{-4} + \sigma^4 \left[ \frac{(\gamma_2 + 3n)\mu^{-5}}{n^3} \right],$$

which is, upto $O(\sigma^2)$, the same as the bias to $O(1/n)$ in Exercise 14. To obtain MSE we need to obtain

$$\text{MSE}(\hat{\theta}) = E\frac{1}{\bar{y}^2} + \frac{1}{\mu^2} - \frac{2}{\mu}E\frac{1}{\bar{y}}.$$

Now consider $1/\bar{y}^2 = g(y)$. Then $g(\mu) = 1/\mu^2$,

$$\frac{\partial^s g(y)}{\partial y_i^s} = \frac{(-1)^s(s+1)!}{n^s}\mu^{-(s+2)}, \quad \frac{\partial^4 g(y)}{\partial y_j^2 \partial y_i^2} = \frac{5!}{n^4}\mu^{-6}.$$

Using this

$$E\frac{1}{\bar{y}^2} = \frac{1}{\mu^2} + \frac{2\,\sigma^2}{n}\mu^{-4} - \frac{3\sigma^3\gamma_1}{n^2}\mu^{-5} + \frac{4\sigma^4}{n^3}\left[(\gamma_2+3n)\mu^{-6}\right].$$

Thus

$$\begin{aligned}
\text{MSE}(\hat{\theta}) &= \frac{3\sigma^2}{n}\mu^{-4} - \frac{4\sigma^3\gamma_1}{n^2}\mu^{-5} + \frac{5\sigma^4}{n^3}(\gamma_2+3n)\,\mu^{-6} \\
&\quad - \frac{2}{\mu}\left[\frac{\sigma^2}{n}\mu^{-3} - \frac{\sigma^3\gamma_1}{n^2}\mu^{-4} + \frac{\sigma^4}{n^3}(\gamma_2+3n)\,\mu^{-5}\right] \\
&= \frac{\sigma^2}{n}\mu^{-4} - \frac{2\,\sigma^3\gamma_1}{n^2}\mu^{-5} + \frac{3\sigma^4}{n^3}(\gamma_2+3n)\,\mu^{-6}.
\end{aligned}$$

The above exercise provides an example where the bias to $O(n^{-1})$ and $O(\sigma^2)$ are the same but the MSE expressions to $O(\sigma^4)$ differs with the MSE to $O(n^{-2})$ by the term $(3\sigma^4/n^3)\,\gamma_2\mu^{-6}$. However, knowing MSE to $O(\sigma^4)$ one can derive the expression of the MSE up to $O(n^{-2})$ by dropping $\left(3\sigma^4/n^3\right)\gamma_2\,\mu^{-6}$.

**Exercise 16** Show that the $r$th order moment of the ratio of quadratic forms $y'N_1y/y'N_2y$, up to $O(\sigma^4)$, where $N_1$ and $N_2$ are symmetric matrices and the $n \times 1$ vector $y$ follows $y = \mu + \sigma\,u$, is given by

$$E\left[\left(\frac{y'N_1y}{y'N_2y}\right)^r\right] = (\theta_1)^r(\theta_2)^{-r}\left[1 + \sigma^2\lambda_2 + \sigma^3\gamma_1\lambda_3 + \sigma^4(\gamma_2\lambda_4 + \lambda_4^*)\right],$$

where

$$\lambda_2 = \text{tr}(A_2 + \underline{A}_2), \quad \lambda_3 = \mu'\left[N_1(I * A_3) + N_2(I * \underline{A}_3)\right]\iota,$$

$$\lambda_4 = \text{tr}[A_4(I * N_1) + \underline{A}_4(I * N_2)] + \text{tr}[A_4^*(I * N_1\mu\mu'N_1) + \underline{A}_4^*(I * N_2\mu\mu'N_2)],$$

$$\lambda_4^* = (\text{tr}\,N_1)(\text{tr}\,A_4) + (\text{tr}\,N_2)(\text{tr}\,\underline{A}_4) + +2\,\text{tr}(N_1A_4 + N_2\underline{A}_4)$$

$$\quad + \left(\mu'N_1^2\mu\right)(\text{tr}\,A_4^*) + \left(\mu'N_2^2\mu\right)(\text{tr}\,A_4^*) + 2\,\mu'(N_1A_4^*N_1 + N_2\underline{A}_4^*N_2)\mu.$$

Further,

$$\theta_1 = \mu' N_1 \mu, \theta_2 = \mu' N_2 \mu \neq 0, A_1 = 2 c_1 N_1,$$

$$A_2 = c_1 N_1 + 2 N_1 \mu \mu' (c_2 N_1 + c_1 \underline{c}_1 N_2),$$

$$A_3 = 2 c_2 N_1 + 2 c_1 \underline{c}_1 N_2 + \tfrac{4}{3} c_3 N_1 \mu \mu' N_1 + 4 c_1 \underline{c}_2 N_2 \mu \mu' N_2,$$

$$A_4 = \tfrac{1}{2} c_2 N_1 + \tfrac{1}{2} c_1 \underline{c}_1 N_2 + 2 c_3 N_1 \mu \mu' N_1 + 2 c_1 \underline{c}_2 N_2 \mu \mu' N_2 + 4 \underline{c}_1 c_2 N_1 \mu \mu' N_2,$$

$$A_4^* = \tfrac{2}{3} c_4 N_1 \mu \mu' N_1 + 2 c_2 \underline{c}_2 N_2 \mu \mu' N_2 + \tfrac{8}{3} \underline{c}_1 c_3 N_1 \mu \mu' N_2;$$

$$c_j = r(r-1) \cdots (r - j + 1)/\theta_1^j \text{ for } 1 \leq j < r \text{ and } 0 \text{ for } j > r,$$

and $\underline{c}_j$ is the same as $c_j$ with $r$ replaced by $-r$ and $\theta_1$ by $\theta_2$. Further $\underline{A}_j$ is $A_j$ with $\overline{c_j}$ interchanged with $\underline{c}_j$ and $N_1$ with $N_2$.

*Solution*　The result follows by substituting the first four derivatives of $h(y) = (y' N_1 y/y' N_2 y)^r$ in (2.90) and simplifying the results. An alternative proof follows by directly substituting $y = \mu + \sigma u$ in $(y' N_1 y)/(y' N_2 y)$, then expanding

$$(y' N_2 y)^{-1} = (\mu' N_2 \mu)^{-1} \left[ \frac{1 + 2\sigma \mu' N_2 \mu + \sigma^2 \mu' N_2 \mu}{\mu' N_2 \mu} \right]^{-1},$$

and taking expectations using Appendix A.5. This is the approach taken in Ullah and Srivastava (1994).

An alternative expression, which will be easier in special cases, can be written as

$$E \left( \frac{y' N_1 y}{y' N_2 y} \right)^r = \theta_1^r \theta_2^{-r} \left[ 1 + \sigma^2 \lambda_2 + \sigma^3 \lambda_3 + \sigma^4 \lambda_4 \right], \tag{2.95}$$

where

$$\lambda_2 = E[u' (A_2 + \underline{A}_2) u],$$

$$\lambda_3 = E[(u' M_1 \mu) (u' A_3 u) + (u' M_2 u) (u' \underline{A}_3 u)],$$

$$\lambda_4 = E\big[ (u' M_1 u) (u' A_4 u) + (u' M_1 u)^2 u' A_4^* u$$

$$+ (u' M_2 u) (u' \underline{A}_4 u) + (u' M_2 u)^2 u' \underline{A}_4^* u\big].$$

These expectations can be evaluated from the results in Appendix A.5.

The result for the normal case follows by substituting $\gamma_2 = \gamma_1 = 0$. Thus the moments can be under- or overestimated by falsely assuming normality by the magnitude

$$\theta_1^r \theta_2^{-r} \sigma^3 \left[ \gamma_1 \lambda_3 + \sigma \gamma_2 \lambda_4 \right]. \tag{2.96}$$

These results can also be extended for obtaining expectations of $E(y' N_1 y)^{r_1}(y' N_2 y)^{-r_2}$. In this case the result is the same as in Exercise 16 except that $c_j = r_1(r_1 - 1) \cdots (r_1 - j + 1)/\theta_1^j$ and $\underline{c}_j$ is $c_j$ with $r_1$ replaced by $-r_2$ and $\theta_1$ by $\theta_2$.

The results for the special cases of the ratio of quadratic forms will be considered in detail in the following chapters.

Finally the results can be generalized for the case where

$$H(Y) = (Y' N_2 Y)^{-r}(Y' N_1 Y)^r \tag{2.97}$$

and

$$Y = M + \sigma U, \tag{2.98}$$

where $Y$ is $n \times k$, $M = EY$ is $n \times k$ and $U = ((u_{it})) = (u_1, \ldots, u_k)$ is an $n \times k$ matrix of random errors. Again taking the expectations of the expansion of $H(Y)$ after substituting $Y = M + \sigma U$ we can write

$$E[H(Y)] = \Theta_2^{-r} \Theta_1^r + \sigma^2 \Delta_2 + \sigma^3 \Delta_3 + \sigma^4 \Delta_4, \tag{2.99}$$

where $\Theta_j = M' N_j M$ with $|\Theta_j| \neq 0$, for $j = 2, 3, 4$ and $\Delta_j = E[\Theta_2^{-r} V_j \Theta_1^r + \underline{V}_j \Theta_2^{-r} \Theta_1^{-r} + \underline{V}_{j-1} \Theta_2^{-r} V_1 \Theta_1^r + b_j \underline{V}_1 \Theta_2^{-r} V_{j-1} \Theta_1^r + a_j(\underline{V}_{j-2} \Theta^{-r} V_{j-2} \Theta^r)]$; $a_j = 0$ for $j = 2, 3$, $b_j = 0$ for $j = 2$ and 1 for $j = 3, 4$; $V_1 = c_1 A_1$ and

$$V_2 = c_1 B_1 + c_2 A_1^2, \ V_3 = c_2(A_1 B_1 + B_1 A_1) + c_3 A_1^3$$

$$V_4 = c_2 B_1^2 + c_3(A_1^2 B_1 + B_1 A_1^2 + A_1 B_1 A_1) + c_4 A_1^4;$$

$$A_\ell = (M' N_\ell U + U' N_\ell M)\Theta_\ell^{-1},$$

$$B_\ell = U' N_\ell U \Theta_\ell^{-1}, \quad \ell = 1, 2; \tag{2.100}$$

$c_j$ and $\underline{c}_j$ are the same as in Exercise 16 without $\theta_1$ and $\theta_2$. Finally the expression for $\underline{V}_j$ is the same as that of $V_j$ except that $r, N_1, \Theta_1$ are replaced by $-r$, $N_2, \Theta_2$ respectively.

An explicit expression of $\Delta_j$ can be written by substituting the expectations from Appendix A.7. This will be quite lengthy. But an easier expression may appear when applied to some econometric estimators in the special cases.

It is to be pointed out here that the sampling error of the econometric estimators are generally the functions of sample size and the parameter $\sigma$. Thus fixing $\sigma$ one can obtain the asymptotic expansion for large $n$ or fixing $n$ one can obtain the asymptotic expansion for small-$\sigma$. For many other econometric estimators the sampling error may be a function of $n$, $\sigma$, and other parameters. For example, in a regression model with first-order serial correlation the sampling error will be a function of $n$, $\sigma$, and the correlation coefficient parameter $\rho$. In this case, while not studied in this book, one could consider the asymptotic expansion with respect to small or large $\rho$ fixing $n$ and $\sigma$.

## 2.5.3    Results for Non-i.i.d Cases

All the above results are given for the case where the error in the models is i.i.d. satisfying assumption 4. These results can be generalized for the case where $u_i$ is non i.i.d and nonnormal such that, for $i, j, k, l = 1, \ldots, n$,

$$Eu_i = 0, \quad Eu_iu_j = \sigma_{ij}, Eu_iu_ju_k = \sigma_{ijk}, Eu_iu_ju_l = \sigma_{ijkl}.$$

For large classes of econometric models the errors will be non-i.i.d, for example, the models with heteroskedasticity and/or dependent time series models. In such cases the expectation of $\hat{\theta} = h(y)$ is

$$E(\hat{\theta} - \theta) = \sigma^2\lambda_2 + \sigma^3\lambda_3 + \sigma^4\lambda_4,$$

where

$$\lambda_2 = \frac{1}{2}\sum_i\sum_j\sigma_{ij}\Delta_{ij}, \quad \lambda_3 = \frac{1}{6}\sum_i\sum_j\sum_k\sigma_{ijk}\Delta_{ijk},$$

$$\lambda_4 = \frac{1}{24}\sum_i\sum_j\sum_k\sum_l\sigma_{ijkl}\Delta_{ijkl}$$

$$\Delta_{ij} = \frac{\partial^2 h(y)}{\partial y_i\partial y_j}, \quad \Delta_{ijk} = \frac{\partial^3 h(y)}{\partial y_i\partial y_j\partial y_k}, \quad \Delta_{ijkl} = \frac{\partial^4 h(y)}{\partial y_i\partial y_j\partial y_k\partial y_l}$$

are all evaluated at $y = \mu$. Under the i.i.d. assumption this result reduces to the result in Theorem (URS). The proof of the above result follows by taking the expectations of the asymptotic expansion in (2.87), also see Ullah (2002).

Lastly the expectation of $\hat{\theta} = h(y) = y'N_1y/y'N_2y$, when $y = \mu + u$ distributed with $Ey = \mu$ and $u$ is a non i.i.d vector, can be obtained as a special case of the above result. When $u \sim N(0, \Sigma)$ or $y \sim N(\mu, \Sigma)$ then we can also obtain

$$E\hat{\theta} = E\left(\frac{y'N_1y}{y'N_2y}\right)^r = E\left(\frac{y^{*'}N_1^*y^*}{y^{*'}N_2^*y^*}\right)^r,$$

where $y^* = \Sigma^{-1/2}y \sim N\left(\mu^* = \Sigma^{-1/2}\mu, \sigma^2 I\right)$, $N_1^* = \Sigma^{1/2}N\Sigma^{1/2}$, and $N_2^* = \Sigma^{1/2}N_2\Sigma^{1/2}$. The matrix $\Sigma^{1/2} = Q\wedge^{1/2}Q'$, $\wedge$ is the matrix of eigenvalues of $\Sigma$ and $Q$ is the orthogonal matrix of corresponding eigenvectors. The result now follows from Exercise 16.

The result for the large-$n$ expansion of $E(\hat{\theta} - \theta)$ can also be written from the large-$n$ asymptotic expansions of $\hat{\theta} - \theta$ in 2.5.1. For example, for the large class of econometric estimators given by (2.74) the bias, up to $O(n^{-1})$, and MSE, up to $O(n^{-2})$ can be obtained when the observations are non i.i.d. and nonnormal by using (2.73) and (2.75). This is given by

$$B(\hat{\theta}) = Q\left[\overline{Vd} - \tfrac{1}{2}\bar{H}_2\left(\overline{d \otimes d}\right)\right], \tag{2.101}$$

where $d = Q\psi_n$ and $Q$, $V$, and $\bar{H}_2$ are given in 2.5.1. Further the MSE, up to $O(n^{-2})$, is

$$\text{MSE}(\hat{\theta}) = \Pi_1^* + \left(\Pi_2^* + \Pi_2^{*'}\right) + \left(\Pi_3^* + \Pi_4^* + \Pi_4^{*'}\right), \tag{2.102}$$

where

$$\Pi_1^* = \overline{dd'}, \Pi_2^* = Q\left[-\overline{Vdd'} + \tfrac{1}{2}\bar{H}_2\overline{(d\otimes d)\,d'}\right],$$

$$\Pi_3^* = Q\left[\overline{Vdd'V'} + \tfrac{1}{4}\bar{H}_2\overline{(d\otimes d)\,(d'\otimes d')}\bar{H}_2{}' - \tfrac{1}{2}\overline{Vd\,(d'\otimes d')}\bar{H}_2{}'\right.$$

$$\left. -\tfrac{1}{2}\bar{H}_2\overline{(d\otimes d)\,d'V'}\right]Q,$$

$$\Pi_4^* = Q\left[\overline{VQVdd'} - \tfrac{1}{2}\overline{VQ}\bar{H}_2\,\overline{(d\otimes d)\,d'} + \tfrac{1}{2}\overline{W\,(d\otimes d)\,d'} - \tfrac{1}{2}\bar{H}_2\overline{(d\otimes(QVd))\,d'}\right.$$

$$+\tfrac{1}{4}\bar{H}_2\overline{(d\otimes(Q\bar{H}_2\,(d\otimes d)))\,d'} - \tfrac{1}{2}\bar{H}_2\overline{((QVd)\otimes d)\,d'}$$

$$\left. +\tfrac{1}{4}\bar{H}_2\overline{((Q\bar{H}_2\,(d\otimes d))\otimes d)\,d'} - \tfrac{1}{6}\bar{H}_3\overline{(d\otimes d\otimes d)\,d'}\right],$$

where $W$ and $\bar{H}_3$ are given in 2.5.1. In many applications it may be easier to obtain the bias and MSE of an estimator directly by using (2.75) and (2.76) with (2.73), see Bao and Ullah (2002). For the i.i.d case the above results reduce to the results in (2.81) and (2.82).

### 2.5.4 The Laplace Approximation: Normal and Nonnormal

The Laplace method is a method of approximating a definite integral by evaluating it in a small neighborhood around the point where it attains it's maximum value. For this to work well the neighborhood of this point must dominate compared with all other regions in the range of integration. Specifically, consider the integral of the form $\int_a^b e^{tg(x)}p(x)dx$ where $t$ is a "large" positive constant, the first two derivatives of $g(x)$ and $p(x)$ exist, $a < b$ and both may be either finite or infinite, $p(x)$ has only one maximum at $x = x_0$ where $a \le x_0 \le b$, and $x_0$ are finite. If $g(x)$ attains its maximum at $x = x_0$ then the integral around $x = x_0$ will dominate compared to all other regions. Therefore replace $g(x)$ by the first two non-zero terms and $p(x)$ by the first non-zero term of their respective Taylor series expansions around $x = x_0$. The Taylor expansions are:

$$p(x) = p(x_0) + p^{(1)}(x_0)(x-x_0) + p^{(2)}(x_0)\tfrac{1}{2}(x-x_0)^2 + \cdots$$

$$g(x) = g(x_0) + g^{(1)}(x_0)(x-x_0) + g^{(2)}(x_0)\tfrac{1}{2}(x-x_0)^2 + \cdots$$

so that for $p(x_0) \ne 0$, and the case where $x_0 = b$, $b \ge 0$, and $g^{(1)}(x) > 0$ in the range of integration we get:

$$\int_a^b e^{tg(x)}p(x)\,dx \approx \int_a^b e^{t\left[g(x_0)+g^{(1)}(x_0)(x-x_0)\right]}p(x_0)\,dx \qquad (2.103)$$

$$= p(x_0)e^{t\left[g(x_0)-g^{(1)}(x_0)x_0\right]}\int_a^b e^{tg^{(1)}(x_0)x}\,dx.$$

Since the region around $b$ dominates anyway we may extend the range of integration to $(-\infty, b)$ to get:

$$\approx p(x_0)e^{t\left[g(x_0)-g^{(1)}(x_0)x_0+b\right]}\left[tg^{(1)}(x_0)\right]^{-1} \qquad (2.104)$$

so that for large $t$:

$$\int_a^b e^{tg(x)}p(x)dx \approx p(x_0)e^{g(x_0)t}\left[tg^{(1)}(x_0)\right]^{-1}. \qquad (2.105)$$

For a rigorous treatment of this method see Olver (1974) Chapter 7 or De Bruijn (1958) Chapter 4. An example of a use of this method is in Lieberman (1994a) where he uses it to approximate the moments of a ratio of quadratic forms. His basic technique is to use the moment generating function to get the estimator (represented as a ratio of quadratic forms) into the same structure as the left-hand side of (2.104) and then apply the Laplace method. This technique will be used below to approximate the moments of estimators that can be written as a ratio of quadratic forms. As indicated above, many econometric estimators can be written in terms of a ratio of quadratic forms.

Let us consider the ratio of quadratic forms $(y' N_1 y)/(y' N_2 y)$, where $N_1$ is symmetric and $N_2$ is positive definite. Let $M(w_1, w_2)$ be the *m. g. f.* of $y' N_1 y$ and $y' N_2 y$ given by

$$M(w_1, w_2) = E[\exp(w_1 y' N_1 y + w_2 y' N_2 y)]$$

$$= \int_y \exp(w_1 y' N_1 y + w_2 y' N_2 y)f(y)\,dy, \qquad (2.106)$$

where $f(y)$ is the density of $y$. Then it can easily be verified that the exact $r$th moment

$$E\left(\frac{y' N_1 y}{y' N_2 y}\right)^r = \int_{-\infty}^0 \cdots \int_{-\infty}^0 \frac{\partial^r M(w_1, w_2)}{\partial w_1^r}\Big|_{w_1=o}\,dw_{21},\ldots,dw_{2r}, \qquad (2.107)$$

where $w_2 = \sum_{j=1}^r w_{2j}$. An alternative representation for $E(y' N_1 y/y' N_2 y)^r$ is given in (2.30). When $y$ follows an Edgeworth density the $M(w_1, w_2)$ and exact moments are analyzed by Peters (1989), also see Knight (1985). In general, under nonnormality, any tractable exact formula for these moments do not exist. That is the solution of multiple integrals in (2.107), under a general class of nonnormality, is not available. In view of this Lieberman (1994a) provided an approximation of this multiple integral or the $r$th moment by using the Laplace approximation method. This is an alternative to the small-$\sigma$ and large-$n$ approximation methods discussed above. Assuming that $E(y' N_2 y)$ and $E(y' N_1 y)^r$ exist, $r \geq 1$, the following theorem holds.

**Theorem (Lieberman 1994a)** *The Laplace approximation for the $r$th moment of $(y' N_1 y)/(y' N_2 y)$ about the origin is*

$$E\left(\frac{y' N_1 y}{y' N_2 y}\right)^r = \frac{E(y' N_1 y)^r}{(E(y' N_2 y))^r} \qquad (2.108)$$

**Proof** First we write the integrand in the multiple integral (2.107) in a form suitable for the application of the Laplace method as

$$\frac{\partial^r M(w_1, w_2)}{\partial w_1^r}\bigg|_{w_1=0} = M^{(r)}(0, w_2) \exp\{g(0, w_2)\}, \tag{2.109}$$

where $w_2 = \sum_{j=1}^r w_{2j}$ and

$$M^{(r)}(0, w_2) = \frac{\partial^r M(w_1, w_2)}{\partial w_1^r}\bigg|_{w_1=0} / M(0, w_2) \tag{2.110}$$

$$g(0, w_2) = \log M(0, w_2).$$

Now since $y' N_2 y$ is assumed to be positive definite

$$g^{(1)}(0, w_2) = \frac{\partial g(0, w_2)}{\partial w_2} = \frac{1}{M(0, w_2)}\frac{\partial}{\partial w_2} M(0, w_2)$$

$$= \frac{\int (y' N_2 y) \exp\{w_2 y' N_2 y\} f(y)\, dy}{\int \exp\{w_2 y' N_2 y\} f(y)\, dy} > 0. \tag{2.111}$$

On the range $-\infty$ to $0$, the monotonicity of $g(0, w_2)$ implies that its maximum is attained at the boundary points $w_{21} = \cdots w_{2r} = 0$ or $w_2 = 0$. Therefore, applying the method of Laplace around the point of maximum $0$, we have

$$E\left(\frac{y' N_1 y}{y' N_2 y}\right)^r = \int_{-\infty}^0 \cdots \int_{-\infty}^0 M^{(r)}(0, w_2) \exp\{g(0, w_2)\}\, dw_{21}, \ldots, dw_{2r}$$

$$\simeq M^{(r)}(0, 0) \exp\{g(0, 0)\} / \prod_{j=1}^r g^{(1)}(0, 0). \tag{2.112}$$

But $M^r(0, 0) = E(y' N_1 y)^r$ and $g^{(1)}(0, 0) = E(y' N_2 y)$. Therefore the result in the Theorem follows. (Q.E.D.)

Lieberman (1994a) provides sufficient conditions under which the Laplace approximation will have an error of $O(n^{-1})$. These conditions are (i) $p$th cumulant of $y' N_2 y$, $\kappa_p$, is $O(n)$, (ii) $E(y' N_1 y)^r = O(n^r)$, (iii) The $\gamma = 1 + m$ order and $\delta = r + m$ degree generalized cumulant of the product of $(y' N_1 y)^\kappa$ and $(y' N_2 y)^m$, $\kappa_{rm}$, is $O(n^\ell)$ with $\ell \leq r$. These conditions are satisfied for the ratio of independent chi-squares each with $O(n)$ d.f. In general, these conditions provide the Laplace expansion of the $r$th moment as

$$E\left(\frac{y' N_1 y}{y' N_2 y}\right)^r = \frac{E(y' N_1 y)^r}{(E y' N_2 y)^r} + \lambda_{n_1} + \lambda_{n_2} + O(n^{-3}), \tag{2.113}$$

where

$$\lambda_{n1} = \binom{r+1}{2} \left[ \frac{(E(y'\,N_1\,y)\kappa_2)}{(E\,y'\,N_2\,y)^{r+2}} \right] - r \left[ \frac{\kappa_{r1}}{(E\,y'\,N_2\,y)^{r+1}} \right] = O(n^{-1}) \qquad (2.114)$$

$$\lambda_{n2} = \binom{r+1}{2} \left[ \frac{\kappa_{r2}}{(E\,y'\,N_2\,y)^{r+2}} \right] - 3\binom{r+2}{3} \left[ \frac{3\,(E(y'\,N_1\,y)^r)\,\kappa_3 + \kappa_{r1}\,\kappa_2}{(E\,y'\,N_2\,y)^{r+3}} \right]$$

$$+ 3\binom{r+3}{4} \frac{(E(y'\,N_1\,y)^r)\,\kappa_2^2}{(E\,y'\,N_2\,y)^{r+4}} = O(n^{-2}), \qquad (2.115)$$

where the generalized cumulants

$$\kappa_{r1} = E((y'\,N_1\,y)^r y'\,N_2\,y) - E(y'\,N_1\,y)^r E(y\,N_2\,y) \qquad (2.116)$$

$$\kappa_{r2} = E\left\{ (y'\,N_1\,y)^r\,(y'\,N_2\,y)^2 \right\} - 2E(y'\,N_2\,y)\,E((y'\,N_1\,y)^r(y'\,N_2\,y))$$

$$- E\big((y'\,N_2\,y)^2\,E(y'\,N_1\,y)^r\big) + 2(Ey'\,N_2\,y)^2\,E(y'\,N_1\,y)^r \qquad (2.117)$$

can be evaluated by using the expectations in Appendix.

We note that unlike the large-$n$ and small-$\sigma$ expansions, which hold for a general class of estimators expressed as $h(y)$, the Laplace approximation is for the class of econometric estimators, which can be written as the ratio of quadratic forms. It will be useful to extend the above results for the Laplace approximations of the moments of $h(y)$. It is also conjectured here that the Laplace approximation would go through for the estimators, which are the ratio of quadratic forms in the $n \times k$ random matrix $Y$. That is

$$E\big[(Y'\,N_2\,Y)^{-r}(Y'\,N_1\,Y)^r\big] = (E\,Y'\,N_2\,Y)^{-r}\,E(Y'\,N_1\,Y)^r. \qquad (2.118)$$

## 2.6  Summary and Survey

In this chapter we have provided the techniques of obtaining exact and approximate moments of a function of random vector/matrix. The exact technique is based on the work of Ullah (1990), large-$n$ approximation is based on Nagar (1959) and Rilstone, Srivastava, and Ullah (1996) results; small-$\sigma$ approximation is based on the results due to Kadane (1971), Ullah, Srivastava, and Roy (1995), and Ullah (2002); and Laplace approximation is due to Lieberman (1994a). A special case of the function considered is the ratio of quadratic forms, which contains a large class of econometric estimators and test statistics. The exact and approximate moments of this are also presented using the above techniques. There is a vast statistics literature on deriving the moments of the ratio of quadratic forms, see for example, Mathai and Provost (1992). This dates back to the work of Von Neumann (1941) on obtaining the moments of the ratio of mean successive differences to the sample variance. Gurland (1956) derived the expectation of the ratio of quadratic forms in normal variables. White (1957), and Shenton and Johnson (1965) analyzed the moments of the LS estimator of the correlation coefficient $\rho$ in $y_i = \rho\, y_{i-1} + u_i$, which can be expressed as the ratio of quadratic forms in normal variables, see Chapter 6. Sawa (1972) obtained the moments of the ratio of quadratic forms using the joint moment generating function of two quadratic forms, also see Hoque (1985). Dwivedi and Chaubey (1981), Chaubey and Talukdev (1983), and Morin-Wahhab (1985) studied the moments of the ratio $(x_\ell^2 + \lambda\, x_m^2)/(x_p^2 + \eta\, x_m^2)$, where $x_\ell^2$, $x_m^2$, and $x_p^2$ are mutually independent chi-square variables. Note that this ratio can be expressed as $(y'\, N_1\, y)/(y'\, N_2\, y)$. Magnus (1986) provided the conditions of existence of moments and gave the expression in terms of an integral. Smith (1989) provided the expressions in terms of zonal polynomials. For a more general ratio where the numerator is $y'\, N_1\, y + \delta_1'\, y + \delta_2$ and the denominator is $y'\, N_2\, y + \delta_3'\, y + \delta_4$ the results, based on the extended version of Sawa's (1972) result, can be found in Mathai and Provost (1992).

All the above results are for the normal case. For the nonnormal case, an extension of Sawa's (1972) result is given in Peters (1989) for the Edgeworth density, also see Knight (1985) and Provost (1989a,b,c).

The approximation techniques given in this chapter provide the moments for the general class of functions that also includes the ratio of quadratic forms. Both the normal and nonnormal cases are considered. Also the results are analyzed for both the i.i.d and non-i.i.d observations and for linear and nonlinear models. These techniques for approximations along with the techniques for exact moments are applied for various econometric models in Chapters 4–7.

# 3

# Finite Sample Distributions

## 3.1 Introduction

In the earlier chapter, we discussed the techniques of evaluating the exact and approximate moments of the econometric estimators and test statistics. This was done by providing the moments of a general function $h(y)$ of the random vector $y$ and then specializing to the ratio of quadratic forms. It was indicated that the expressions of exact moments may often be very complicated and so the approximate moments are useful tools to study the behavior of various statistics. However, in many practical situations in econometrics just studying moments of econometric estimators or test statistics is not enough. For example, one needs to study the whole sampling distribution of various statistics in order to construct confidence intervals (regions) and test the hypotheses. Also, sometimes one or more estimators do not possess moments so that the comparison of estimators on the basis of moments become infeasible. In such cases one can consider coverage probability as the performance criterion, which prefers the estimator with high probabilities of being close to the true value of the parameter. This requires the knowledge of the sampling distribution of the estimators.

As in the case of the exact expressions for the moments of estimators, the exact probability distributions are generally difficult to derive. Also the expressions, if derived, are often difficult to be fruitfully used and they require extensive numerical calculations. This has stimulated the development of several approximation techniques, which provide easier asymptotic expansions for the density and distributions functions.

## 3.2 Exact Distribution

As in Chapter 2, consider $h(y)$ to be the real valued function of an $n \times 1$ random vector $y$. Then we can write the distribution function of

51

$q = h(y)$ as

$$F(q_0) = P(h(y) \le q_0) = \int_{q \le q_0} f(q) \, dq \qquad (3.1)$$

$$= E[I(q)]$$

where $f(q)$ is the density function of $h(y)$ and $I(\cdot)$ is an indicator function, which takes the value 1 if $q = h(y) \le q_0$ and 0 otherwise. Note that $I(q)$ is not a continuous function of $y$ so we cannot use the results of Chapter 2 to obtain $E[I(q)]$.

An alternative expression for the distribution function is to obtain the characteristic function (c.f.) and then use the inversion formula. The c.f. of $h(y)$ is

$$\psi(t) = E \exp\{it h(y)\} = \int_y \exp\{i\, t h(y)\}\, f(y)\, dy, \qquad (3.2)$$

and the density function of $q = h(y)$ is

$$f(q) = \frac{1}{2\pi} \int_{-\infty}^{\infty} \exp\{-i\, t\, q\}\, \psi(t)\, dt \qquad (3.3)$$

provided $\psi(t)$ is absolutely integrable, see Appendix Section A.8.3.

It is clear that, unlike the exact expectation of $h(y)$ in Chapter 2, a simple expression for the distribution of a general $h(y)$ may not be possible. However, as noted in Chapter 2, a large class of econometric estimators and test statistics $h(y)$ are in the form of the ratio of quadratic forms. Thus we turn to the distribution of such $h(y)$ in the following section.

### 3.2.1    Distribution of Ratio of Quadratic Forms

Let us write the ratio of quadratic forms as

$$q = \frac{y' N_1 y}{y' N_2 y} = h(y) \qquad (3.4)$$

where $y$ is an $n \times 1$ random vector with the mean vector $\mu$ and covariance matrix $\Sigma$, and both $N_1$ and $N_2$ are $n \times n$ nonstochastic matrices. Then

$$F(q_0) = P[q \le q_0] = P[y' N_1 y \le q_0 y' N_2 y] \qquad (3.5)$$

$$= P[y' N y \le 0],$$

where $N = N_1 - q_0 N_2$. Since the covariance matrix of $y$ is $\sum$ we can also write (3.5) as

$$F(q_0) = P[y' \Sigma^{-1/2} \Sigma^{1/2} N \Sigma^{1/2} \Sigma^{-1/2} y \le 0]$$

$$= P[y' \Sigma^{-1/2} P P' \Sigma^{1/2} N \Sigma^{1/2} P P' \Sigma^{-1/2} y \le 0]$$

$$= P[z' \Lambda z \le 0] = P\left[\sum_{i=1}^{n} \lambda_i z_i^2 \le 0\right], \qquad (3.6)$$

where $z = P' \Sigma^{-1/2} y$ and $P$ is an orthogonal matrix of eigenvectors of $\Sigma^{1/2} N \Sigma^{1/2}$ such that $P' \Sigma^{1/2} N \Sigma^{1/2} P = \Lambda$, a diagonal matrix of eigenvalues $\lambda_1, \ldots, \lambda_n$ of $\Sigma^{1/2} N \Sigma^{1/2}$; $\Sigma^{1/2} = Q D^{1/2} Q'$ where $D$ is the diagonal matrix of eigenvalues of $\sum$ and $Q$ is the matrix of corresponding eigenvectors.

The equations (3.5) and (3.6) show that the distribution of the ratio of quadratic forms reduce to the distribution of an indefinite quadratic form $y' N y$, where $N$ is an indefinite matrix. There is a vast statistics literature studying the distribution of indefinite quadratic forms in the normal case, that is, $y \sim N(\mu, \Sigma)$. In this case $z \sim N(\mu_z = P' \Sigma^{-1/2} \mu, I)$ and

$$F(q_0) = P\left[\sum_1^n \lambda_i z_i^2 \leq 0\right] = P\left[\sum_1^n \lambda_i \chi^2(\mu_{zi}^2) \leq 0\right] \qquad (3.7)$$

where $\chi^2(\mu_{zi}^2)$ is a noncentral $\chi^2$ with one (degrees of freedom) d.f.

The infinite series representation of $F(q)$ in the normal case was given by Gurland (1955, 1956); also see Shah (1963), Press (1966), and Taneja (1976). However, the numerical evaluation of this is difficult. Imhof (1961) provided a numerical integral representation of (3.7), which is based on the Gil-Pelaez (1951) inversion formula for the indefinite quadratic form, also see Davies (1973). This formula is

$$P(z' \Lambda z \leq q_0^*) = \frac{1}{2} - \frac{1}{\pi} \int_0^\infty t^{-1} \text{Img} \left\{ \exp\left(-i t q_0^*\right) \psi(t) \right\} dt \qquad (3.8)$$

where Img $\{\in\}$ represents the imaginary part of $\in$ and

$$\psi(t) = \left[ \prod_{j=1}^n (1 - 2 i t \lambda_j)^{\frac{-n}{2}} \right] \exp \left\{ i \prod_{j=1}^n \mu_{zj}^2 \lambda_j t (1 - 2 i t \lambda_j)^{-1} \right\} \qquad (3.9)$$

is the c.f. of $z' \Lambda z$. Imhof (1961) has shown that (3.8) can be written as

$$P(z' \Lambda z \leq q_0^*) = \frac{1}{2} - \frac{1}{\pi} \int_0^\infty \frac{\sin \theta(v)}{v \rho(v)} dv, \qquad (3.10)$$

where

$$\theta(v) = \frac{1}{2} \sum_{j=1}^n \left( r_j \tan^{-1}(\lambda_j v) + \mu_{zj}^2 \lambda_j v \left(1 + \lambda_j^2 v^2\right)^{-1} \right) - \frac{v q_0^*}{2} \qquad (3.11)$$

$$\rho(v) = \prod_{j=1}^n \left(1 + \lambda_j^2 v^2\right)^{r_j/4} \exp \left\{ \frac{1}{2} \sum_{j=1}^n (\mu_{zj} \lambda_j v)^2 / \left(1 + \lambda_j^2 v^2\right) \right\}$$

and $r_j$'s are the multiplicities of the nonzero distinct $\lambda_j$s. For $q_0^* = 0$ we get $P(z' \Lambda z \leq 0) = F(q_0)$ by substituting $q_0^* = 0$ in (3.10) and (3.11).

Since $v \rho(v)$ is monotically increasing towards $+\infty$, in numerical work the integration in (3.10) is carried out for $0 \leq v \leq v^*$ only. Imhof's technique provides excellent accuracy and it is almost exact. Computer programs for evaluating the numerical integration of (3.10) are described in Koerts and Abrahamse (1969), and Davies (1980). An advantage of the Davies program is that both the truncation and numerical integration errors are controlled with guaranteed accuracy. For the numerical implementation of these programs the eigenvalues and corresponding eigenvectors of the matrix $\Sigma^{1/2}(N_1 - q_0 N_2)\Sigma^{1/2}$ are needed. These can always be found numerically, and in some cases analytically. Palm and Sneek (1984) have suggested modifications, which eliminate the need to compute eigenvalues. Evans and Savin (1984) have developed an algorithm, which is efficient with regard to time taken in calculating the eigenvalues and eigenvectors.

The distribution of $q$ can also be obtained directly by the numerical inversion formula in Gurland (1948). This is

$$F(q_0) = P(q \le q_0) = \frac{1}{2} - \frac{1}{\pi}\int_0^\infty \mathrm{Img}\left[\frac{\psi(t, -t\,q_0)}{t}\right]dt \qquad (3.12)$$

where $\psi(.\,,.)$ is the joint c.f. of $y'N_1 y$ and $y'N_2 y$.

Another numerical inversion formula, proposed by Martynov (1977), is

$$P(z'\Lambda z \le q_0^*) = 1 - \frac{1}{\pi}\tan^{-1}\left(\frac{1}{\alpha}\right) - \frac{1}{\pi}\int_0^\infty \frac{\exp\{-\alpha\,v\,q_0^*/2\}\sin(\theta(v))}{\rho(v)}\,dv \qquad (3.13)$$

where $q_0^* \ge 0$, $\alpha \ge 0$ and

$$\theta(v) = \sum_{j=1}^n \left\{\frac{1}{2}w_j\,v + \frac{\epsilon_j\,\mu_{zj}^2\,v}{2\left((\epsilon_j - \alpha\,v)^2 + v^2\right)}\right\} - \frac{v\,q_0^*}{2} \qquad (3.14)$$

$$\rho(v) = v\prod_{j=1}^n \left\{\left(\left(1 - \frac{\alpha\,v}{\epsilon_j}\right)^2 + \frac{v^2}{\epsilon_j^2}\right)^{1/4}\exp\left\{\frac{-\mu_{zj}^2\,v\left(\alpha\,\epsilon_j - (\alpha^2 + 1)v\right)}{2\left((\epsilon_j - \alpha\,v)^2 + v^2\right)}\right\}\right\};$$

$w_j(v) = \cot^{-1}\left(\frac{(\epsilon_j - \alpha\,v)}{v}\right)$, $\epsilon_j = 1/\lambda_j$, $j = 1, \ldots, n$. For large $q_0^* > 0$, (3.13) may be more efficient computationally compared with (3.10). The density function of $q$ can be obtained by the numerical differentiation of the distribution function. For more on numerical evaluations, see Beran (1975), Rice (1980), Helstrom (1983), Luigannini and Rice (1984), and Farebrother (1984, 2002).

We note that for the central case, $\mu_z = 0$, the integrand in (3.10) simplifies considerably. For alternative expressions in the central case, see Provost (1989b, c), Provost and Rudink (1991), and Forchini (2002); also see Hillier (2001) for the exact density function of $q$. For the simplified finite expressions in the central case where $z'\Lambda z$ is positive definite, see Mathai and Provost (1992, ch. 4).

## 3.3 Approximations of the Distribution of Quadratic Forms

There is an extensive statistics literature on the approximation of the distribution of $q = \sum_1^n \lambda_j z_j^2$. This includes the work of Patnaik (1949), who approximates the distribution of central $q$ by $\lambda \chi_\ell^2$ where $\lambda$ and $\ell$ are chosen so that $q$ and $\lambda \chi_\ell^2$ have the same first two moments. This gives $\lambda = \sum_1^n \lambda_j^2 / \sum_1^n \lambda_j$ and $\ell = \left(\sum_1^n \lambda_j\right)^2 / \left(\sum_1^n \lambda_j^2\right)$. Pearson (1959) considered a noncentral $q = \sum_1^n \lambda_j (z_j + b_j)^2$, where $z_j$s are standard normal and $b_j$ are constants, and suggested a three moment approximation of the distribution of $q$ as $c \chi_\ell^2 + b$ where $c = \theta_3/\theta_2$, $b = \theta_1 - \theta_2^2/\theta_3$, and $\ell = \theta_2^3/\theta_3^2$; $\theta_s = \sum_1^n \lambda_j^s(1 + s b_j^2)$ for $s = 1, 2, 3$. Thus $P(q \le q_0) = P(\chi_\ell^2 \le q_0^*)$ where $q_0^* = (q_0 - \theta_1)\sqrt{\theta_2}/\theta_3 + \ell$. In both Patnaik's and Pearson's approximations, $\ell$ can be fractional so that one needs to calculate $\chi_\ell^2$ by using interpolations. Alternatively one can use Wilson and Hilferty (1931) approximation. Imhof (1961) result indicates that Pearson approximation is much better than Patnaik's approximation, particularly in the upper tail.

Siddiqui (1965) looks into the approximation by quadratic bounds. Okatomo (1960) has provided an upper bound for the distribution of a central $q = \sum_1^n \lambda_j z_j^2$ where $z_j$s are independent $\chi_s^2$ with $n_j$ d.f. and $\lambda_j > 0$ for all $j$. His result is

$$P\left(\sum \lambda_j z_j^2 < q_0\right) \le P\left(\lambda \chi_m^2 < q_0\right) \tag{3.15}$$

where $\lambda = (\prod_j^n \lambda_j^{n_j})^{1/m}$, $m = \sum_{j=1}^n n_j$. Siotani (1964) shows that this approximation works well if the variation in $\lambda_j$s is not too large.

Jensen and Solomon (1972) considered a normal approximation of $q^* = (q/\theta_1)^r$, where $\theta_1 = E q = \sum \lambda_j \left(1 + b_j^2\right)$ as above, $q = \sum \lambda_j (z_j + b_j)^2$ with $\lambda_j > 0$, $b_j$ as bounded constants and $z_j$s are mutually independent standard normal, and $r$ is determined by the first three moments so that the leading term in the expansion in powers of $\theta_1^{-1}$ of the third central moment of $q^*$ vanishes. The distribution of $q^*$ is approximated by a normal distribution with mean and variance given by

$$E q^* = 1 + \theta_2 r(r-1)/\theta_1^2, \quad V(q^*) = 2 \theta_2 r^2/\theta_1^2. \tag{3.16}$$

Jensen and Solomon indicate better performance of this compared with Patnaik's and Pearson's. Solomon and Stephens (1978) have proposed another approximation to the density of $q$ by fitting a Pearson curve with the same first four moments as $q$. In another work Solomon and Stephens (1977) provide the approximation of the distribution of $q$ by $A \chi_p^{2d}$ where the constants $A$, $p$, and $d$ are found by matching the first three moments of $q$ and $A \chi_p^{2d}$. The computer routines are also provided by the authors for doing all the calculations. This approximation, except in the lower tail, performs better than the Jensen and

Solomon approximation. For other approximation procedures, see Oman and Zacks (1981), Robbins and Pitman (1949), and Moschopoulos (1983).

We note that most of the above approximations developed were useful during the period when the computer technology did not exist or was not advanced. With the current and future advancements in computers it will be more useful to calculate almost exact results by Imhof and other methods described above. However, the large-$n$ and small-$\sigma$ approximations considered in the later sections will be quite useful in practice.

# 3.4   Limiting Distributions

Often the approximate distributions will not be as accurate as the exact distributions. However, they may improve the accuracy over the limiting (asymptotic) distribution. This may especially be the case when the sample is small or moderately large and we use large-$n$ and small-$\sigma$ approximations given in the following sections. In view of this it is useful to look into the asymptotic distribution of $q$. This is given in the following theorem.

**Theorem**      *Let $q = y'Ay = \sum_i^n \sum_j^n a_{ij} y_i y_j$ where $y_i$s are independently distributed with zero mean. Further, suppose the following conditions are satisfied:*

1. *$E|y_i|^{4+2\delta} < \infty$ and $E(|y_i|^{4+2\delta})/(V(y_i))^{2+\delta}$ is uniformly bounded for all $y_i$ and some $\delta$ in $(0, 1)$.*
2. *$E(y_i^4)/(E y_i^2)^2 \geq 1 + d$ for some $d > 0$ and all $i$*
3. *The integers $j = 1, \ldots, n$ can be grouped into a finite number of sets $g_1, g_2, \ldots, g_r$ such that*

$$\lim_{n\to\infty} \left[ \frac{\|Q\|^2 - \sum_{\ell=1}^r \|Q_\ell\|^2}{\|Q\|^2} \right] = 0$$

*and*

$$\lim_{n\to\infty} \sum_{\ell=1}^r \left[ \frac{\|Q_\ell\|}{\|Q\|} \right]^{2+\delta} = 0,$$

*where $\|Q\| = (\sum_i^n \sum_j^n a_{ij}^2 V(y_i) V(y_j))^{1/2}$ and $\|Q_\ell\| = (\sum_i \sum_{j\epsilon g_\ell} a_{ij}^2 V(y_i) V(y_j))^{1/2}$. Then, as $n \to \infty$, $q$ is distributed as normal.*

**Proof**   See Whittle (1964).                                              (Q.E.D.)

The above theorem is as given in Mathai and Provost (1992: 180). If we consider the case where $y_i$s are identically distributed and $a_{ij} = a_{i-j}$ then the above Theorem holds under the conditions (a) $E|y_i|^{4+\delta} < \infty$ and (b) $\sum_{-\infty}^\infty a_j^2$ is finite. Grenader and Szegö (1958) showed the asymptotic normality of $q$ for the case where $y_i$ is a normally distributed stationary process with discrete time parameter with a spectral density bounded by zero and $\infty$ and $a_{jk} = a_{j-k} = 1/2\pi \int_{-\pi}^{\pi} w(\lambda) \exp i(j-k) \, d\lambda$ for $j, k = 1, \ldots, n$; $w(\lambda) = w(-\lambda)$ and $a_{j-k}$ being the elements of the Toeplitz matrix $A$, also see Avram (1988). Whittle (1964) indicates that the approximation of $q$ by a chi-square variable is better than the approximation of $q$ by a normal variable. Further, the normal limiting distributions are poor approximations when $n$ is not too large, see Burman (1987), and Konishi, Niki, and Gupta (1988) among others. In view of this we look into higher order approximation theory in Section 3.6.

## 3.5 Nonnormal Case

We note form (3.1) that

$$P\left[h(y) \leq q_0\right] = E\left[I(h(y))\right] = E\left[g(y)\right],$$

where $g(y) = I(h(y))$. Thus using the results in Chapter 2 we can obtain the distribution of $h(y)$, under the Edgeworth density and the mixtures of normal, by following two steps, $(a)$ obtain the density under the conditional normality; $(b)$ take expectation of these results with respect to the conditioning variable. Since the results for the special case of quadratic form $h(y) = y' N y$ under normality are given above they can be extended for the above nonnormal cases, see for example, Knight (1985, 1986). However, the results for the nonnormal cases like binomial, Poisson, exponential do not follow from the expectation results in Chapter 2 since $g(y)$ here is a discrete indicator function. This is another reason why approximations results in Section 3.6 are useful since they hold for general nonnormal cases. For more references on the distribution of quadratic forms under nonnormality see Menzefricke (1981), Khatri (1987), Anderson and Fang (1987), and Kwapien and Woyczynski (1987).

## 3.6 Large-$n$ Edgeworth Expansion

Let us consider the econometric estimators, which are asymptotically normal and which are expressed as $\hat{\theta} = h(y)$ with $\theta = h(\mu)$ where $\mu = E y$ and $V(y) = I$. Further denote a class of statistics as

$$Z_n = \frac{(h(y) - h(\mu))}{\sqrt{\nabla'\nabla}} \tag{3.17}$$

where $\nabla^{(s)}$ is the $s$th order derivative of $h(y)$ at $y = \mu$; $\nabla^{(1)} = \nabla$. Then $Z_n$ is said to admit an Edgeworth expansion to $O(n^{-1})$ if we can write

$F_n(z) = P(Z_n \leq z)$ as

$$F_n(z) = \Phi(z) + \frac{A(z)}{\sqrt{n}} + \frac{B(z)}{n} + o(n^{-1})$$
$$= F(z) + o(n^{-1}), \tag{3.18}$$

where $\Phi(z)$ is the standard normal distribution function and $A$ and $B$ are integrable functions, typically polynomials times the standard normal density $\phi(z)$. $\Phi$, the limiting distribution, is called as a first-order approximation to $F_n$ and the right side of (3.18), $F(z)$, a second-order approximation. The first and second moments of $F$ will be considered as second-order approximations to the first two moments of $Z_n$ and they will be the same as the large-$n$ Nagar's expansion discussed in Chapter 2.

The Edgeworth approximation, as described above, is essentially a finite number of terms of an asymptotic series expansion of the distribution function of an estimator or test statistic under consideration. The idea behind the approximation is to improve upon the gap between the exact distribution and the limiting distribution ($n \longrightarrow \infty$) by means of correction terms, which capture the higher order nature of $h(y)$. Essentially this is achieved by looking at the distribution of the approximation of $Z_n$ by a polynomial of higher order than the linear representation. The Edgeworth approximation thus obtained provides an improvement over the limiting distribution of the statistics based on the linear representation. This Edgeworth asymptotic expansion is closely related to the series (expansion) known as the Gram (1879)–Charlier (1905) series, which represents the density of an appropriately standardized statistic as a linear combination of the standardized normal density and its successive derivatives, see Appendix Section A.2.

To see an Edgeworth expansion and its relationship with the Gram–Charlier expansion let us consider the standardized statistic

$$Z_n = \frac{1}{\sqrt{n}} \sum_1^n Z_i = \frac{\sqrt{n}\,(\bar{y} - \mu)}{\sigma} = h(y), \tag{3.19}$$

where $Z_i = (y_i - \mu)/\sigma$ and $y_i$ are independent and identically distributed random variables with mean $\mu$, variance $\sigma^2$ and possess moments (and, hence, cumulants) up to order 4. Thus each of $Z_i$ and $Z_n$ have mean zero and variance 1 and $Z_n$ is the $n^{-1/2}$ time the sum of i.i.d random variables $Z_i$.

Let $\psi(t)$ be the c.f. and $K(t) = \log \psi(t)$ be the cumulant generating function (c.g.f, see Appendix Section A.1) of $Z_i$. Then, using Taylor series, c.g.f. can be expanded around the origin as

$$K(t) = \log \psi(t) = \log\left(E e^{itZ_i}\right) = \frac{1}{2!}(it)^2 + \frac{1}{3!}\kappa_3(it)^3 + \frac{1}{4!}\kappa_4(it)^4 + \cdots \tag{3.20}$$

and $\kappa_r = (i)^{-r} K^{(r)}(0)$ is the $r$th cumulant of the density $f$ of $Z_i$, $i = \sqrt{-1}$ and $K^{(r)}(0)$ is the $r$th derivative of $K(t)$ at $t = 0$. We note that $\kappa_1 = 0$ and

$\kappa_2 = 1$. From the c.g.f. we can obtain the c.f. as

$$\psi(t) = \exp\left[\log\psi(t)\right]$$

$$= \exp\left[\frac{(it)^2}{2!} + \frac{(it)^3}{3!}\kappa_3 + \frac{(it)^4}{4!}\kappa_4 + \cdots\right]$$

$$= e^{-(1/2)t^2}\exp\left[\sum_{j=3}^{\infty}\kappa_j\frac{(it)^j}{j!}\right]$$

$$= e^{-(1/2)t^2}\sum_{j=0}^{\infty}(-it)^j\,c_j, \tag{3.21}$$

where $c_0 = 1, c_1 = c_2 = 0, c_3 = -\kappa_3/3!, c_4 = \kappa_4/4!, c_5 = \kappa_5/5!, c_6 = \left(k_6 + 10\kappa_3^2\right)/6!$, see Appendix Section A.2 for $c_j$ when $j > 6$.

Now define $\psi_n(t), K_n(t), f_n(t)$, and $F_n$ to be the c.f., c.g.f., density and cumulative distribution of $Z_n$, respectively. Further note that the $r$th cumulant of $Z_n$ is $\kappa_r n^{(2-r)/2}$, for $r > 2$, see Cramér (1946: 225). Then the c.f. of $Z_n$ can be written as

$$\psi_n(t) = \left[\psi\left(\frac{t}{\sqrt{n}}\right)\right]^n$$

$$= e^{-(1/2)t^2}\exp\left[n\sum_{j=3}^{\infty}\left(\frac{it}{\sqrt{n}}\right)^j\frac{\kappa_j}{j!}\right]$$

$$= e^{-(1/2)t^2}\sum_{j=0}^{\infty}(-it)^j\,c_j^*, \tag{3.22}$$

where $c_0^* = c_0 = 1, c_1^* = c_2^* = 0, c_3^* = n^{-1/2}c_3, c_4^* = n^{-1}c_4, c_5^* = n^{-3/2}c_5, c_6^* = [(\kappa_6/n^2) + (10\kappa_3^2/n)]/6!$, and so on. An alternative derivation of $\psi_n$ can be obtained by obtaining the c.g.f. $K_n(t) = \log\psi_n(t) = n\log\psi(t/\sqrt{n})$, where $\log\psi(t/\sqrt{n})$ is obtained by writing $t$ with $t/\sqrt{n}$ in $\log\psi(t)$ given above. Then $\psi_n(t) = \exp\left[\log\psi_n(t)\right]$ will give the expansion as above.

Using the expansion of $\psi_n$ and the inversion theorem (Appendix Section A.8.3) the Gram–Charlier expansion (see Appendix Section A.2) can be written as

$$f_n(z) = \phi(z) + c_3^*\phi^{(3)}(z) + c_4^*\phi^{(4)}(z) + c_5^*\phi^{(5)}(z) + c_6^*\phi^{(6)}(z) + \cdots \tag{3.23}$$

$$= \phi(z)\left[1 - c_3^*H_3(z) + c_4^*H_4(z) - c_5^*H_5(z) + c_6^*H_6(z) + \cdots\right],$$

where $\phi(z)$ is a standard normal density and it is the limiting distribution of $Z_n$, $\phi^{(j)}(z)$ represent the $j$th derivative of $\phi(z)$ and $H_j(z)$ is the Hermite polynomial of degree $j$ defined as

$$H_j(z) = (-1)^j\frac{\phi^{(j)}(z)}{\phi(z)}. \tag{3.24}$$

Thus $H_3(z) = z^2 - 3z, H_4(z) = z^4 - 6z^2 + 3, H_5(z) = z^5 - 10z^3 + 15z, H_6(z) = z^6 - 15z^4 + 45z^2 - 15$.

We observe that the coefficient $c_j^*$ depends on $n$ and it is of order $O(n^{[j/3]-j/2})$, where $[j/3]$ stands for the highest integer not exceeding $(j/3)$. For instance, $c_3^*$ is of order $O(n^{-1/2})$, $c_4^*$ and $c_6^*$ are of order $O(n^{-1})$, $c_5^*$, $c_7^*$, and $c_9^*$ are of order $O(n^{-2/3})$, $c_8^*$, $c_{10}^*$, and $c_{12}^*$ are of order $O(n^{-2})$ and so on. Thus it is noticed that the order of the terms in the series expansion of $\psi_n(t)$ and $f_n(z)$ do not steadily decrease. To examine the implication of it, let us consider the Gram–Charlier (see Appendix) expansion (3.23) for $f_n(z)$ and suppose that we retain terms up to order $O(n^{-1})$ in order to improve upon the approximate $\phi(z)$ of $f(z)$. This means that the correction, to order $O(n^{-1})$, to be applied to $\phi(z)$ requires the inclusion of all the following terms,

$$\phi(z)\left[-c_3^* H_3(z) + c_4^* H_4(z) - c_5^* H_5(z) + c_6^* H_6(z)\right] \qquad (3.25)$$

the evaluation of which needs sixth order moments or equivalently sixth order cumulants. However, if we look at the explicit expressions for $c_3^*$, $c_4^*$, $c_5^*$, and $c_6^*$, we observe that merely two cumulants $\kappa_3$ and $\kappa_4$ are essential to evaluate the contributions to order $O(n^{-1})$ in $c_3^*$, $c_4^*$, $c_5^*$, and $c_6^*$. Thus actually we need not go for the knowledge of cumulants beyond fourth order. This kind of inadequacy continues to be present if we proceed further to retain terms of higher order in an attempt to obtain still better approximates for $f(z)$. Besides it, when we approximate $f_n(z)$ by the sum of a few terms in the expansion, this approximation can sometimes take, for instance, negative values violating the basic requirement of a probability density function. These limitations reduce the utility of Gram–Charlier series expansion for developing approximates of the functions $f_n(z)$ and $F_n(z)$.

An additional approximation developed from the Gram–Charlier series expansion, which contains the terms in declining powers of $n$ and the computation of terms to a certain specific order of magnitude in $n$ does not call for the knowledge of those moments or cumulants that are not really necessary, is given by the Edgeworth series expansion. This is obtained by reassembling the terms from the Gram–Charlier series expansion in the powers of $n^{-1/2}$. Such a series has the property that when we retain a finite number of terms for serving as an approximation, the remainder part has the same order of magnitude as the first neglected term. In this sense, the Edgeworth series is a proper asymptotic expansion obtained in terms of the parameter $n^{-1/2}$ by regrouping terms of the Gram–Charlier series.

Alternatively, to obtain the Edgeworth expansion of the distribution of $Z_n$, up to $O(n^{-1})$, we can first arrange $\psi_n(t)$ as a power series in $n^{-1/2}$ and write

$$\psi_n(t) = e^{-(1/2)t^2}\left[1 + \frac{1}{6\sqrt{n}}\kappa_3(it)^3 + \frac{1}{72n}\left(3\kappa_4(it)^4 + \kappa_3^2(it)^6\right) + \cdots\right].$$

The Edgeworth approximation to the density function for $Z_n$ in (3.26), up to $O(n^{-1})$, can then be obtained by applying the inversion theorem and dropping higher order terms. This is given by

$$f_n(z) = \phi(z) \left[ 1 + \frac{\kappa_3}{6} \frac{H_3(z)}{\sqrt{n}} + \frac{3\kappa_4 H_4(z) + \kappa_3^2 H_6(z)}{72n} \right]. \qquad (3.26)$$

Integrating the density function gives an Edgeworth (1905) approximation for the distribution function as

$$F_n(z) = \Phi(z) - \phi(z) \left[ \frac{\kappa_3 H_2(z)}{6\sqrt{n}} + \frac{3\kappa_4 H_3(z) + \kappa_3^2 H_5(z)}{72n} \right]. \qquad (3.27)$$

This can also be written as

$$F_n(z) = \Phi \left[ z - \frac{\kappa_3 (z^2 - 1)}{6\sqrt{n}} + \frac{3\kappa_4 (3z - z^3) + 2\kappa_3^2 (4z^3 - 7z)}{72n} \right] \qquad (3.28)$$

by using Hermite polynomials and Taylor Series expansion. These two representations of $O(n^{-1})$ Edgeworth approximations are referred to as Edgeworth-A and Edgeworth-B approximations, respectively, in Phillips (1978).

In general the Edgeworth asymptotic expansion has the form

$$f_n(z) = \phi(z) \left[ 1 + \sum_{i=1}^{j} p_i(z) n^{-i/2} \right] + R, \qquad (3.29)$$

where $p_i(z)$ is a polynomial in $z$ and $R$ is the remainder in the series after $j+1$ terms and it is $o(n^{-j/2})$. Further the distribution function is

$$F_n(z) = \Phi(z) + \phi(z) \sum_{i=1}^{j} q_i(z) n^{-i/2} + R. \qquad (3.30)$$

Note that $p_i(z) = (\phi(z))^{-1} d(q_i(z) \phi(z))/dz$.

The term of order $n^{-1/2}$ in Edgeworth expansion corrects the basic normal approximation for the effect of skewness and the term of order $n^{-1}$ corrects for the effects of kurtosis and skewness. The Edgeworth expansion only rarely converges as an infinite series given above. Usually, it is only available as an asymptotic expansion, meaning that the series is truncated after taking a given number of terms with the remainder $R$ having smaller order than the last term that has been included. That is the Edgeworth distribution expansion is valid for fixed $j$, if $R$ in $F_n(z)$ is $= o(n^{-j/2})$ as $n \longrightarrow \infty$. This needs $z_i$ to have finite moments to order $j + 2$ and $|\psi(t)|$ to be bounded away from one for larger $t$. This latter condition, known as Cramér's (1928) condition, holds if $z$ has a smooth distribution. For the validity of Edgeworth density expansion the $R = o(n^{-j/2})$ needs the finiteness of $(j + 2)$ moments and $\int |\psi(t)|^c dt < \infty$ for some $c \geq 1$, see Hall (1992). For further details on the conditions and proofs, see Feller (1971), Bhattacharya and Ghosh (1978), Cramér (1925, 1928), and Hall (1992).

**A General Expansion**   Most econometric estimators and test statistics, written as $Z_n$, are not a simple sum of i.i.d random variables, hence the classical asymptotic Edgeworth expansions are not directly useful. To develop their Edgeworth expansions we first write their asymptotic stochastic expansion (see Appendix Section A.3.1) as a power series in $n^{-1/2}$ as

$$Z_n = T_n + \frac{A_n}{\sqrt{n}} + \frac{B_n}{n} + \frac{R_n}{n^{3/2}}$$

$$= \xi_0 + \xi_{-1/2} + \xi_{-1} + O_p\left(n^{-3/2}\right), \tag{3.31}$$

where $\xi_{-i} = O_p\left(n^{-i}\right)$, $T_n$, $A_n$, and $B_n$ are well behaved random variables with limiting distributions as $n \longrightarrow \infty$. Suppose the limiting distribution of $T_n$ is $N(0,1)$. Further $R_n$ is stochastically bounded. Based on this stochastic expansion one can obtain the Nagar-type large-$n$ approximations of first four moments of $Z_n$, see Chapter 2. Let these be $EZ_n = a_1/\sqrt{n}$ and $V(Z_n) = 1 + (a_2/n)$ where $a_1$ and $a_2$ are nonstochastic terms of $O(1)$. Using these results define

$$Z_n^* = \frac{Z_n - EZ_n}{\sqrt{V(Z_n)}}, \tag{3.32}$$

which has zero mean, unit variance, and approximate third and fourth moments as $E(Z_n^*)^3 = a_3/\sqrt{n}$ and $E(Z_n^*)^4 = 3 + (a_4/n)$ where $a_3$ and $a_4$ are of $O(1)$. Then using (3.28) and replacing $a_3$ and $a_4$ by $\kappa_3$ and $\kappa_4$, respectively, we get the Edgeworth expansion, up to $O(n^{-1})$, as

$$P(Z_n \leq z) = P\left(Z_n^* \leq \frac{z - a_1/\sqrt{n}}{\sqrt{1 + a_2/n}}\right),$$

$$= P\left[Z_n^* \leq z - \frac{a_1}{\sqrt{n}} - \frac{a_2 z}{2n}\right],$$

$$= \Phi\left[z + \frac{\lambda_1 + \lambda_2 z^2}{6\sqrt{n}} + \frac{\lambda_3 z + \lambda_4 z^3}{72n}\right], \tag{3.33}$$

where

$$\lambda_1 = a_3 - 6a_1; \quad \lambda_3 = 9a_4 - 14a_3^2 - 36a_2 + 24a_1 a_3;$$

$$\lambda_2 = -a_3; \quad \lambda_4 = 8a_3^2 - 3a_4,$$

see Rothenberg (1984a).

The above method needs to develop large-$n$ first four moments in order to develop the classical expansion. An alternative is to obtain the c.f. of the stochastic expansion of $Z_n$ and then obtain the distribution function using the inversion theorem. We provide this result for a general class of econometric estimators and test statistic in a later section.

Another method of developing the Edgeworth expansion of econometric statistics is due to Sargan (1975). His approach is based on the observation that the estimators and associated statistics commonly employed in econometric work are not straightforwardly defined. They are expressed as functions of multivariate variables and involve functions of first- and second-order moments of observations, for example, the mean and standard deviation. These moments are generally consistent, and quite often unbiased too, estimators of their population counterparts. Their standard errors are generally of order $O(n^{-1/2})$. The estimation error (the difference between the estimator $\hat{\beta}$ and parameter $\beta$) is of order $O_p(n^{-1/2})$ and consequently $Z_n$ is $O_p(1)$. Motivated by it, suppose the estimation error $e$ is expressible as a function of two random vectors $p$ and $w$ where $p$ is a vector of stochastic variables following a multivariate normal distribution and $w$ is a vector of stochastic variables. The vectors $p$ and $w$ are assumed to be independently distributed. The functional form of $e$ is supposed to be such that it is equal to 0 when $p$ and $w$ are set as null vectors. In addition to the normality requirement of $p$, $\sqrt{n}w$ are assumed to have bounded moments of all orders. Further the function $e$ is assumed to satisfy a smoothness and invariability condition.

Under this setup, Sargan (1975, theorem 1) proved that the distribution function $F$ of $n^{1/2}e$ or the distribution $F_n$ of $Z_n$ can be approximated by few leading terms in the Edgeworth series expansion as $n \to \infty$. Up to order $O(n^{-1})$, this is given by Sargan (1975) as

$$F_n(z) = \Phi(z) - \phi(z)\left[g_0 + zg_1 + z^2g_2 + z^3g_3 + z^5g_4\right]$$

and alternatively

$$F_n(z) = \Phi\left(z - g_0 - zg_1^* - z^2g_2 - z^3g_2^*\right),$$

where $g$'s and $g^*$s are the functions of the derivatives of $e$ and moments of $p$ and $w$. For the applications of Sargan's result see Phillips (1979, 1980) and Ullah (1982), among others.

To show that $Z_n$ has a valid Edgeworth expansion up to $O(n^{-1})$ we need conditions on the behavior of $T_n, A_n$, and $B_n$ such that the approximation error is $O(n^{-1})$, this follows from the results of Chibishov (1980). When the Edgeworth expansion is obtained for the stochastic expansion of the estimation error function $e(p, w) = e$ then its validity has been studied by Bhattacharya and Ghosh (1978), Sargan (1975, 1976) and Phillips (1977b).

**Exercise 1** For the application of Edgeworth expansion consider a simple example. Suppose $y_i$ is i.i.d as $N(\mu, \sigma^2)$. Consider the problem of obtaining the Edgeworth approximation to the distribution of

$$Z_n = \sqrt{n}\frac{(\bar{y} - \mu)}{s},$$

where $s^2$ is an unbiased sample variance. Note that both $\overline{y} - \mu$ and $s^2 - \sigma^2$ are of $O_p(n^{-1/2})$. Thus noting that

$$\frac{1}{s} = \frac{1}{\sigma}\left[1 + \frac{s^2 - \sigma^2}{\sigma^2}\right]^{-1/2}$$

$$= \frac{1}{\sigma}\left[1 - \frac{1}{2}\left(\frac{s^2 - \sigma^2}{\sigma^2}\right) + \frac{3}{8}\left(\frac{s^2 - \sigma^2}{\sigma^2}\right)^2 + \cdots\right]$$

the asymptotic expansion of $Z_n$, up to $O(n^{-1})$, is

$$Z_n = T_n + \frac{A_n}{\sqrt{n}} + \frac{B_n}{n} = \xi_0 + \xi_{-1/2} + \xi_{-1},$$

where $T_n = \sqrt{n}(\overline{y} - \mu)/\sigma$, $A_n = -\frac{1}{2}S_nT_n$ and $B_n = \frac{3}{8}S_n^2T_n$ with $S_n = \sqrt{n}(s^2 - \sigma^2)/\sigma^2$.

Since $S_n$ and $T_n$ are independent, $T_n \sim N(0,1)$ and $(n-1)s^2/\sigma^2$ is a $\chi^2$ distribution with $n-1$ degrees function so that $ES_n = 0$ and $V(S_n) = 2n/(n-1)$ we can obtain the following approximate moments of $Z_n$.

$$EZ_n = 0, \quad V(Z_n) = 1 + \frac{2}{n},$$

$$EZ_n^3 = 0, \quad EZ_n^4 = 3 + \frac{18}{n}.$$

Further the approximate moments of $Z_n^*$ are $EZ_n^* = 0, V(Z_n^*) = 1, E(Z_n^*)^3 = 0$, $E(Z_n^*)^4 = 3 + 6/n$. Thus, using $a_1 = a_3 = 0$, $a_2 = 2$, and $a_4 = 6$ the Edgeworth expansion is

$$F_n(z) = \Phi\left[z - \frac{z + z^3}{4n}\right].$$

This is an approximation of the exact distribution of $Z_n$, which is a student-$t$ distribution.

In the above example $Z_n$ is a function of $p = T_n$ and $w = S_n$. These $p$ and $w$ are independent and all of their moments are finite. Thus one can also use Sargan's (1975) result to obtain Edgeworth expansion. This is left as an exercise for the reader. For more applications on Sargan's approach see Phillips (1977a, 1980, 1979), Anderson and Sawa (1973), Ullah (1982), Ullah, Carter and Srivastava (1984), Carter, M.S. Srivastava, V. K. Srivastava and Ullah (1990), among others.

**Exercise 2**   Consider a consumption function

$$y_{1t} = \alpha_0 + \alpha y_{2t} + u_t,$$

where $y_{1t}$ is aggregate consumption at time $t$, $y_{2t}$ aggregate income at time $t$, $\alpha$ the marginal propensity to consume and $\alpha_0$ is the coefficient of a predetermined variable, which assumes the value 1 for all observations; further, it contains the identity

$$y_{2t} = x_t + y_{1t}$$

$x_t$ = net investment at time $t$. In this case, $y_1, y_2$ are interpreted as endogenous variables and $x$ is exogenous or predetermined.

We assume that $n$ observations are available on all variables, and the reduced form exists:

$$y_{1t} = \frac{\alpha_0}{1 - \alpha} + \frac{\alpha}{1 - \alpha} x_t + \frac{1}{1 - \alpha} u_t$$

$$y_{2t} = \frac{\alpha_0}{1 - \alpha} + \frac{1}{1 - \alpha} x_t + \frac{1}{1 - \alpha} u_t,$$

that is, $\alpha \neq 1$. In fact, we assume $0 \leq \alpha \leq 1$.

The two-stage least squares estimator of $\alpha$ is given by

$$a = \frac{\sum_{t=1}^n X_t \, y_{1t}}{\sum_{t=1}^n X_t \, y_{2t}},$$

where $X_t = x_t - \overline{x}$, $\overline{x} = (1/n) \sum_{t=1}^n x_t$.

A little algebraic manipulation will show that

$$Z_n = \sqrt{n} \frac{(a - \alpha)}{1 - \alpha} = \frac{\sqrt{n} z}{1 + z},$$

where

$$z = \frac{\sum_{t=1}^n X_t \, u_t}{\sum_{t=1}^n X_t^2}.$$

Then the stochastic asymptotic expansion of $Z_n$ can be written as

$$Z_n = \sqrt{n} z \, (1 + z)^{-1} = \sqrt{n} \left( z - z^2 + z^3 - z^4 + \cdots \right)$$

$$= \xi_0 + \xi_{-1/2} + \xi_{-1} + \xi_{-3/2} + \cdots$$

where $\xi_0 = \sqrt{n} z$, $\xi_{-1/2} = -\sqrt{n} z^2$, $\xi_{-1} = \sqrt{n} z^3$, and $\xi_{-3/2} = -\sqrt{n} z^4$. We note that $z = O_p\left(n^{-1/2}\right)$ because $1/n \sum_1^n X_t u_t$ is of $O_p(n^{-1/2})$ if $1/n \sum_1^n X_t^2$ is assumed to be bounded in probability as $n \to \infty$.

First we obtain the exact distribution of $Z_n$. For this we note that if we assume $X_t$ to be nonstochastic and $u_t$ are i.i.d normal random errors with mean 0 and variance $\sigma^2$, then $z \sim N(0, \delta^2)$ where

$$\delta^2 = \frac{\sigma^2}{\sum X_t^2}.$$

Therefore

$$P\left(Z_n < Z\right) = P\left[\sqrt{n}\left(\frac{z}{1+z}\right) < Z\right],$$

$$= P\left(z < \frac{Z}{\sqrt{n} - Z}\right) = P\left(z < z_0\right),$$

$$= \frac{1}{\delta\sqrt{2\pi}} \int_{-\infty}^{z_0} \exp\left(-\frac{1}{2}\frac{z^2}{\delta^2}\right) dz,$$

$$= \frac{1}{\sqrt{2\pi}} \int_{-\infty}^{z_0/\delta} \exp\left(-\frac{1}{2}z_*^2\right) dz_*,$$

where $z_* = z/\delta \sim N(0, 1)$. Thus we can obtain the exact distribution of $Z_n$ by using the standard normal distribution.

Now we obtain the Edgeworth approximation to the exact distribution of $Z_n$. For this, from the asymptotic distribution of $Z_n$ we first obtain the Nagar type approximate cumulants of $Z_n$ as

$$\kappa_1 = -\frac{\lambda}{\sqrt{n}} - 3\frac{\lambda^2}{n^{3/2}} - 15\frac{\lambda^3}{n^{5/2}} - \cdots,$$

$$\kappa_2 = \lambda + 8\frac{\lambda^2}{n} + 69\frac{\lambda^3}{n^2} + \cdots,$$

$$\kappa_3 = -6\frac{\lambda^2}{\sqrt{n}} - 116\frac{\lambda^3}{n^{3/2}} - \cdots,$$

$$\kappa_4 = 72\frac{\lambda^3}{n} + 2448\frac{\lambda^4}{n^2} + \cdots,$$

where $\lambda = n\delta^2$.

The characteristic function of the distribution that possesses these cumulants can be written from (3.21) as

$$\exp\left[(it)\kappa_1 + \frac{(it)^2}{2!}\left(\kappa_2 - \lambda\right) + \frac{(it)^3}{3!}\kappa_3 + \frac{(it)^4}{4!}\kappa_4 + \cdots\right]\exp\left(-\frac{1}{2}t^2\lambda\right)$$

$$= \exp\left[\left(-\lambda(it) - \lambda^2(it)^3\right)(1/\sqrt{n}) + \left(4\lambda^2(it)^2 + 3\lambda^3(it)^4\right)\right.$$

$$\left. \times (1/n) + o(1/n)\right]\exp\left(-\frac{1}{2}t^2\lambda\right),$$

where $o(1/n)$ represents terms of lower order than $1/n$.

If we expand the exponential in the usual manner, we can write the characteristic function as

$$\left(1 + \frac{1}{\sqrt{n}}a + \frac{1}{n}b + o(1/n)\right)\exp\left(-\frac{1}{2}t^2\lambda\right)$$

$$a = -\lambda\,(it) - \lambda^2\,(it)^3$$

$$b = \frac{9}{2}\lambda^2\,(it)^2 + 4\lambda^3\,(it)^4 + \frac{1}{2}\lambda^4\,(it)^6\,.$$

If we retain the leading term of the expansion, the characteristic function is $\exp((-1/2)t^2\lambda)$. This is the characteristic function of a normal distribution with mean zero and variance $\lambda$. Therefore, the limiting distribution of $Z_n$ is normal with mean zero and variance $\lambda$.

If we retain terms to order $1/\sqrt{n}$, we get an approximation to the characteristic function as

$$\left(1 + \frac{1}{\sqrt{n}}a\right)\exp\left(-\frac{1}{2}t^2\lambda\right).$$

Applying the Inversion Theorem we get the Edgeworth approximation, to order $1/\sqrt{n}$, of the probability density function of $Z_n$ as

$$\left[1 + \frac{1}{\sqrt{n}}\left(2Z_n - \frac{Z_n^3}{\lambda}\right)\right]\frac{1}{\sqrt{\lambda}}\phi\left(\frac{Z_n}{\sqrt{\lambda}}\right).$$

Since $Z_n$ is the ratio of normal variables the exact moments or cumulants (moments of the exact distribution) are infinite. The approximate cumulants can be obtained from the Edgeworth expansion of the density of $Z_n$. These results will be identical to the Nagar type approximate cumulants given above.

## 3.7   Small-σ Edgeworth Expansion of $h(y)$ (Normal and Nonnormal)

In order to obtain the asymptotic distribution of $\xi = h(y) - h(\mu)$ we consider $Z_n = \xi/\sigma\sqrt{\nabla'\nabla}$, and using the expansion of $h(y)$ around $\mu$ with $y - \mu = \sigma\,u$ we write

$$Z_n = \xi_0 + \sigma\,\xi_1 + \sigma^2\,\xi_2 + O_p(\sigma^3), \tag{3.34}$$

where $\xi_0 = (u'\,\nabla)/\sqrt{\nabla'\,\nabla}$, $\xi_1 = \frac{1}{2}((\nabla^{(2)'}\,(u \otimes u))/\sqrt{\nabla'\nabla})$; $\xi_2 = ((\nabla)^{(3)'}\,(u \otimes u \otimes u))/\,6\sqrt{\nabla'\,\nabla}$ are evaluated at $y = \mu$.

Consider the characteristic function $Z_n$ as

$$\psi(t) = E\, e^{itZ_n} = E\left[e^{it\xi_0} e^{it(\sigma\xi_1 + \sigma^2\xi_2)}\right],$$

$$= E e^{it\xi_0}\left[1 + \sigma it\xi_1 + \sigma^2 it\left(\xi_2 + \frac{it\xi_1^2}{2}\right) + O_p(\sigma^3)\right],$$

$$= E e^{it\xi_0} + \sigma it E\left[\xi_1 e^{it\xi_0}\right] + \sigma^2 it E\left[\left(\xi_2 + \frac{it\xi_1^2}{2}\right) e^{it\xi_0}\right],$$

$$= \psi_{\xi_0}(t) + \sigma it\gamma_1(t) + \sigma^2 it\gamma_2(t), \tag{3.35}$$

where $\gamma_1(t) = E\,\xi_1\, e^{it\xi_0}$, $\gamma_2(t) = E\left[\left(\xi_2 + (it\xi_1^2/2)\right) e^{it\xi_0}\right]$ and $\psi_{\xi_0}(t)$ is the c.f. of $\xi_0$. Then the density function is

$$f(Z_n) = \frac{1}{2\pi}\int_{-\infty}^{\infty} \exp(-i\,t\,Z_n)\psi(t)\,dt,$$

$$= f_0(Z_n) + \sigma\, f_1(Z_n) + \sigma^2\, f_2(Z_n), \tag{3.36}$$

where we use the results

$$\frac{1}{2\pi}\int_{-\infty}^{\infty} \exp(-i\,t\,Z_n)\,\psi_{\xi_0}(t)\,dt = f_0(Z_n) \tag{3.37}$$

$$\frac{1}{2\pi}\int_{-\infty}^{\infty} \exp(-i\,t\,Z_n)\,\gamma_1(t)\,dt = f_1(Z_n). \tag{3.38}$$

$$\frac{1}{2\pi}\int_{-\infty}^{\infty} \exp(-i\,t\,Z_n)\,\gamma_2(t)\,dt = f_2(Z_n). \tag{3.39}$$

In the case when $u \sim N(0,\,I)$, $\xi_0 \sim N(0,\,1)$, and we get

$$\psi_{\xi_0}(t) = E\, e^{i\,t\,\xi_0} = e^{-t^2/2} \tag{3.40}$$

$$\gamma_1(t) = \frac{1}{2\sqrt{\nabla'\nabla}}\, E\left[\left(\nabla^{(2)'} u \otimes u\right) e^{i\,t\,\xi_0}\right],$$

$$= \frac{1}{2\sqrt{\nabla'\nabla}}\, E\left[u'\, D\, u\, e^{i\,t\,\frac{u'\nabla}{\sqrt{\nabla'\nabla}}}\right],$$

$$= \frac{1}{2\sqrt{\nabla'\nabla}}\, e^{-t^2/2}\left[\text{tr}D + i^2 t^2\,\frac{\nabla' D\,\nabla}{\nabla'\nabla}\right], \tag{3.41}$$

where $D = (\partial^2\, h(y))/\partial y\, \partial y'$ at $y = \mu$ and the last equality follows from the Lemma 1 of Chapter 2 by taking $u \sim N(\delta,\, I)$, $h_1(u) = u'\, D\, u$, $h_2(u) = e^{i\,t\,\xi_0}$, and evaluating $E\, h_1(u)\, h_2(u) = h_1(\text{d})\, E(h_2(u)) = (d'\, D\, d)[e^{-(t^2/2)+it\delta_0}]$ with the mean of $\xi_0$ as $\delta_0$ and $d = \delta + (\partial/\partial\delta)$, and then letting $\delta \to 0$. This gives $f_{\xi_0}(Z_n) = \phi(Z_n)$ and

$f_1(Z_n) = Z_n/(2\sqrt{\nabla'\nabla}) \left\{ \operatorname{tr} D + (Z_n^2 - 3)\nabla' D \nabla/(\nabla'\nabla) \right\} \phi(Z_n)$. Hence, up to $O(\sigma)$,

$$f(Z_n) = \left[ 1 + \sigma \frac{Z_n}{2\sqrt{\nabla'\nabla}} \left\{ \operatorname{tr} D + \left( Z_n^2 - 3 \right) \frac{\nabla' D \nabla}{\nabla'\nabla} \right\} \right] \phi(Z_n). \qquad (3.42)$$

When $h(y)$ is a vector, the joint probability density function of a normalized form of $h(y) - h(\mu)$ can be evaluated in a similar manner, see Carter, M. S. Srivastava, V. K. Srivastava and Ullah (1990), Chaturvedi, Hoa, and Lal (1992) and Chaturvedi and Shukla (1990). The large-$n$ Edgeworth expansion of $Z_n$, up to $O(n^{-1})$, can be written similarly.

## 3.8 Remarks on the Edgeworth Expansion

1. The Edgeworth expansions are useful in comparing two asymptotically equivalent econometric statistics. But for the purposes of inference the quality of Edgeworth approximations in the tails is often not good in the sense that it can produce small or negative density in the tails, see Phillips (1977b, 1978). Under this scenario it is sensible to approximate ratios of tail probabilities $F_n(-z)/\Phi(-z)$ and $(1 - F_n(z))/(1 - \Phi(z))$ for $z = o(\sqrt{n})$ instead of $F_n$, see Phillips (1980). An additional point is to see the question of where to approximate the distribution. For this we look into the saddle point approximates, which provide improved performance in certain environments of the parameters, particularly in the tail parts of the distributions. Essentially the techniques involve using a cleverer inversion of the characteristic or moment generating function to obtain the approximations, see Daniels (1954, 1956). The resulting approximation has the features that the density function $f_n(z)$ is in powers of $n^{-1}$, not $n^{-1/2}$ and it is always positive. For applications of saddle point approximations, see Phillips (1978), Durbin (1979), Holly and Phillips (1979) and Lieberman (1994c) among others. It may be pointed out that the saddle point approximation is applied only in some specific situations, for instance, when the characteristic function is available or when a set of sufficient statistics for the estimation of parameters is available; see Daniels (1956) and Durbin (1979).

2. Let us write the statistic $Z_n = (\hat{\theta} - \theta)/\sqrt{V(\hat{\theta})}$, where $\hat{\theta} = h(y)$ and $V(\hat{\theta}) = \nabla' \nabla$ is the asymptotic Cramér-Rao bound for $\theta$ and $\hat{\theta}$ is asymptotically efficient with the Edgeworth expansion $F_n(z)$ up to $O(n^{-1})$, where first term is the limiting normal distribution and then there are terms of $O(n^{-1/2})$ and $O(n^{-1})$ terms. This is called in this book to be second-order approximation and the approximation up to first term is called the first-order approximation. This terminology is, however, different with those in Akahira and Takeuchi (1981), Pfangal and Wefelmeyer (1978), and others where the approximations up to $O(n^{-1/2})$ are considered second order and the approximations up to $O(n^{-1})$ as third-order.

3. For the estimation case, the maximum likelihood (ML) estimator $\hat{\theta}$ is known to be first-order efficient under general regularity conditions. If we correct the bias of the ML estimator to second order, then the variance of the bias-corrected ML, $\tilde{\theta} = \hat{\theta} - (b(\hat{\theta})/n)$, $b(\hat{\theta})/n$ is the bias term, is less than or equal to any other second-order bias corrected first-order efficient estimators, see Efron (1979, 1982). For example, it is well known that the bias-adjusted limited information ML estimator in a structural model is second-order efficient compared with the instrumental variables estimator. Rothenberg (1984a) provides a procedure of obtaining the second-order efficient estimator as

$$\hat{\theta}_k = \hat{\theta}_{k-1} - \frac{L^{(1)}\left(\hat{\theta}_{k-1}\right)}{L^{(2)}\left(\hat{\theta}_{k-1}\right)},$$

where $k = 1, 2$ and $L^{(1)}$ and $L^{(2)}$ represent the first and second derivatives of the log likelihood of a scalar $\theta$. Using an initial consistent estimator $\hat{\theta}_0$ will give $\hat{\theta}_1$, which is first-order equivalent to the ML estimator. Similarly $\hat{\theta}_2$ obtained is second-order efficient. In the case of testing $\theta = \theta_0$ against $\theta < \theta_0$, suppose $Z_n = \hat{\theta} - \theta_0 / \sqrt{V(\hat{\theta})}$ has a valid Edgeworth expansion $F_n(z)$ up to $O(n^{-1})$. Then the $\alpha$-percentage critical value $z^*$ is the value, which solves $F_n(z^*) = 1 - \alpha$. Test based on this $z^*$ is called a second-order size corrected test of size $\alpha$. Pfanzagl and Wefelmyer (1978) have shown that in the class of second-order size corrected tests the test based on the ML estimator $\hat{\theta}$ is locally uniformly more powerful compared with other first-order efficient $\hat{\theta}$.

4. Given the Edgeworth expansion of probability distribution of an econometric statistic, one can use it to obtain the approximate moments of the statistic. These moments will be the same as those obtained by using large-$n$ Nagar type moment expansions. Sargan (1974) showed that a large class of Nagar type large-$n$ moment expansions are valid as asymptotic approximations, provided only that the corresponding moments of the exact distribution exist and are of $O(1)$ as $n \to \infty$, also see Srinivasan (1970), and Basmann (1974) on this issue. This result of Sargan (1974) is important in view of the fact that for some econometric statistics, for example, the instrumental estimator for a just identified structural equation with normal errors, the exact moments do not exist but the Nagar type large-$n$ moments or the moments based on the Edgeworth distribution approximation or the bootstrap based moments are available. It should be pointed out that knowing the nonexistence moments may not be relevant in determining the underlying exact distribution function. For example, the instrumental variable estimator in the just identified structural equation case does not have any moment existing but it has a well defined distribution of the ratio of two normal random variables and also a well defined limiting distribution.

5. The analytical theory of Edgeworth expansions has made an important impact on the resampling techniques, such as the bootstrap and the jackknife,

of developing the sampling distributions and moments of econometric statistics. Hall (1992) discusses the link between Edgeworth expansion and the bootstrap and shows that the bootstrap may be used as a method for the estimating second-order Edgeworth expansion, also see Jeong and Maddala (1993), Vinod (1993), and Horowitz (2001) for the econometrics literature on the bootstrap. The role of analytical results on the Edgeworth expansion of the econometric estimators is now more important. For example, without knowing the analytical validity of the Edgeworth expansion or the forms of moments and distribution of the econometric statistics under consideration the bootstrap exercise has somewhat of a black box flavor. Also a problem with the resampling techniques is that they usually change with the particular resampling and they may be very time-intensive in the contexts of nonlinear and dependent time series models. The analytical results can also be useful to have qualitative or analytical knowledge about the finite sample distribution to place bounds on inferences about the parameters of interest. It can also provide a measure of the accuracy of resampling techniques.

6. The Edgeworth expansion is only a valid asymptotic expression in the sense that it works well for large or moderately large $n$. For a small fixed $n$ the second-order approximation error may not be smaller than that of the first order limiting normal approximation. This is because the second-order approximations for econometric statistics depend on the data structure of the economic variables and the cumulants. The approximate distributions usually depend on the unknown parameters, but they can be substituted with their consistent estimators and order of approximation adjusted accordingly. Finally the form of the Edgeworth expansion of the econometric statistics will depend upon the assumption of the distribution of observations.

7. We note here that while Edgeworth expansion provides the order of magnitude of the error from the limiting normal approximation as $n \to \infty$, it does not provide the absolute magnitude of the error when $n$ does not go to $\infty$. An important result, however, was given by Berry (1941) and Eseen (1945) as

$$\sup_z |F_n(z) - \Phi(z)| \leq \frac{c\,\beta_3}{n^{1/2}\,\sigma^3},$$

where $\beta_3 = E|z_i^3|$ and $c \geq 2.031$ is an absolute, universal constant, also see Petrov (1975) for nonidentically distributed variables and Bhattacharya (1975) for the multivariate distributions.

8. There is some work on the Edgeworth expansion of the ratio of polynomials in $y$. Let us consider $q = h(y) = h_1(y)/h_2(y)$ where $h_1(y) = a_0 + \sum a_i\, y^i + \sum_i \sum_j a_{ij}\, y^i\, y^j + \cdots$ and $h_2(y) = b_0 + \sum b_i\, y^i + \sum_i \sum_j b_{ij}\, y^i\, y^j + \cdots$ are arbitrary polynomial transformation of $y$, $a$'s and $b$'s are constants, and $y$ is a random vector with the elements, which could be dependent and nonidentically distributed. Note that the ratio of quadratic forms is a special case of $q$ above. The Edgeworth asymptotic expansion of $q$ can be obtained by the procedure described in this chapter, also see Phillips (1983). The Edgeworth

asymptotic expansion involves two types of errors, one due to the truncation of $h(y)$ by Taylor series and then due to the truncation of the Edgeworth expansion. Lieberman's (1997) result avoids the expansion of $q$ at the first stage, and hence the only error is due to the truncation of the Edgeworth expansion at some point, although it is possible to write it in infinite expansion. Using this one can obtain the Edgeworth asymptotic expansion by collecting terms of decreasing order of magnitude of $n^{-1/2}$.

9. Let $Z_n$ represent a statistic which has the Edgeworth asymptotic expansion given above. Denoting $Q_\alpha = Q_\alpha(n)$ for the $\alpha-$level quantile of $Z_n$, given by

$$Q_\alpha = \inf \{z : P(Z_n \leq z) \geq \alpha\}$$

and let $q_\alpha$ be the $\alpha-$level quantile of the standardized normal distribution, given by $\Phi(q_\alpha) = \alpha$. Then the expansion of $Q_\alpha$ in terms of $q_\alpha$ and $q_\alpha$ in terms of $Q_\alpha$ can be written from the Edgeworth expansion as

$$Q_\alpha = q_\alpha + \sum_{i=1}^{j} P_{i1}(q_\alpha) n^{-i/2} + \cdots,$$

$$q_\alpha = Q_\alpha + \sum_{i=1}^{j} P_{i2}(Q_\alpha) n^{-i/2} + \cdots,$$

where functions $P_{i1}$ and $P_{i2}$ are polynomials. The asymptotic expansions are called Cornish–Fisher expansions and they are available uniformly in $\varepsilon < \alpha < 1-\varepsilon$ for any $0 < \varepsilon < 0.5$. The polynomials $P_{i1}$ and $P_{i2}$ are completely expressed in term of the polynomials $q_i$ in (3.30). See Hall (1992).

10. Several econometrics statistics are nonpivotal/asymptotically nonpivotal in the sense that their exact/asymptotic distributions depend on the parameters of the models. The difference of the exact distribution from the estimated Edgeworth expansions or the bootstrap distribution of such asymptotically nonpivotal statistics is known to be of $O(n^{-1/2})$, which is the same as the difference of the exact distribution from the first order limiting approximation. In contrast for the asymptotically pivotal statistics having distributions free from the parameters, the exact distribution differs with the limiting Edgeworth approximation (bootstrap distribution) by $O(n^{-1})$. As an illustration, see Exercise 1 of Section 3.6 where the statistics $Z_n$ is pivotal with the Edgeworth expansion of $O(n^{-1})$ whereas the Edgeworth expansion of the distribution of the nonpivotal statistic in Exercise 2 is of $O(n^{-1/2})$. Thus the second-order Edgeworth expansions or bootstrap distributions for the pivitol statistics may have better approximation of their exact distributions, see Hall (1992) and Horowitz (2001).

11. We have discussed the techniques of obtaining the Edgeworth expansion of econometric statistics. One way to develop this is to obtain the first four moments (cumulants) of the statistics under consideration. This was done in

developing large-$n$ Edgeworth expansions of Exercises 1 and 2 in Section 3.6. Alternatively one can first obtain the characteristic function based on the asymptotic expansion of the statistic. This was followed for the econometric statistics $h(y)$ in Section 3.7 in developing its small-$\sigma$ Edgeworth expansion. It can similarly be followed for developing the large-$n$ Edgeworth expansions of a general class of econometric statistics with a large-$n$ asymptotic expansion as given in (2.75).

# 4

# Regression Model

## 4.1 Introduction

In this chapter, the regression model is considered and the application of results of Chapters 2 and 3 are demonstrated in the evaluation of moments and distribution of various statistics encountered in drawing inferences from the model. Most of the results for the normal distribution, it may be pointed out, have been obtained in the econometrics text books in a different way but here our objective is to illustrate the technique, which merely rests on the knowledge of multivariate normal distribution and its simple properties. The technique will appear to be more fruitful in subsequent chapters. The results for the nonnormal cases are also presented, which have rarely been discussed in the literature.

## 4.2 Model Specification and Least Squares Estimation

Let us postulate the following linear regression model:

$$y = X\beta + u, \tag{4.1}$$

where y is an $n \times 1$ vector of $n$ observations on the study variable, $X$ is an $n \times p$ matrix of $n$ observations on $p$ explanatory variables, $\beta$ is a $p \times 1$ vector of unknown regression coefficients and $u$ is an $n \times 1$ vector of disturbances.

For the estimation of coefficient vector $\beta$, the following assumptions are made:

1. The matrix $X$ has full column rank meaning thereby that there are no exact linear relationships among the explanatory variables and the number of observations do not fall short of the number of explanatory variables.

2. The matrix $X$ is nonstochastic.
3. The disturbance vector $u$ has mean vector null and variance covariance matrix $\sigma^2 I_n$ with $\sigma^2$ as the unknown disturbance variance and $I_n$ as the identity matrix of order $n \times n$.

The least squares (LS) estimator of $\beta$ is given by

$$\hat{\beta} = (X'X)^{-1}X'y, \tag{4.2}$$

which is the best linear unbiased estimator according to Gauss–Markov theorem. Writing $A = (X'X)^{-1}X'$ if $a_i$ denotes the $i$th row vector of A, the LS estimator of the $i$th element $\beta_i$ of $\beta$ can be expressed as

$$\hat{\beta}_i = a_i y. \tag{4.3}$$

Next, denoting $M = I_n - XA$, the residual vector is

$$\hat{u} = (y - X\hat{\beta}) = My \tag{4.4}$$

whence the residual sum of squares (RSS) is given by

$$\text{RSS} = \hat{u}'\hat{u} = y'My. \tag{4.5}$$

This provides an unbiased estimator of $\sigma^2$, the disturbance variance, as follows:

$$\hat{\sigma}^2 = \frac{\text{RSS}}{(n-p)} = \frac{y'My}{(n-p)}. \tag{4.6}$$

If the model contains an intercept term or equivalently if one of the explanatory variables in the model is constant, the coefficient of multiple determination is defined by

$$R^2 = 1 - \frac{\hat{u}'\hat{u}}{y'y - n\bar{y}^2} = 1 - \frac{y'My}{y'Ny} \tag{4.7}$$

$$= \frac{y'(N-M)y}{y'Ny}, \quad N = I_n - \frac{1}{n}\iota\iota',$$

which is the square of multiple correlation coefficient between the study variable and the explanatory variables. Here $\bar{y}$ denotes the mean of observations on the study variable and $\iota$ in the specification of matrix N is an $n \times 1$ vector with all elements unity.

If a correction for the degrees of freedom (d.f.) is applied to $R^2$, we obtain the adjusted $R^2$ given by

$$\bar{R}^2 = 1 - \left(\frac{n-1}{n-p}\right)\frac{y'My}{y'Ny}$$

$$= \left(\frac{n-1}{n-p}\right)R^2 - \left(\frac{p-1}{n-p}\right). \tag{4.8}$$

Next, consider the conventional $F$-ratio for testing $H_0{:}\beta = 0$, which is given by

$$F = \frac{1}{p\hat{\sigma}^2}\hat{\beta}'X'X\hat{\beta}$$

$$= \left(\frac{n-p}{p}\right)\frac{y'(I_n - M)y}{y'My}. \tag{4.9}$$

Note that this $F$ is related to $R^2$ given in (4.7), that is

$$F = \frac{(n-p)}{p}\frac{R^2}{1-R^2}. \tag{4.10}$$

Finally, let us consider the predictor

$$P = X\hat{\beta}, \tag{4.11}$$

which can be utilized either for predicting the actual values of study variable or for the mean values.

In case we wish to predict some future value (say, $y_f$) associated with pre-specified values of explanatory variables, the prediction or forecast is given by

$$\hat{y}_f = x_f\hat{\beta}, \tag{4.12}$$

where $x_f$ denotes a $1 \times p$ vector consisting of the pre-specified values of $p$ explanatory variables.

## 4.3 Properties of Estimators

### 4.3.1 Coefficients Estimators

Let us assume that the disturbances are normally distributed. Now if we write

$$z = \frac{1}{\sigma}y, \qquad \mu = \frac{1}{\sigma}X\beta \tag{4.13}$$

then $z$ has a normal distribution $N(\mu, I_p)$. Further, we observe from (2.4) and (2.9) that

$$d \cdot 1 = \left(\mu + \frac{\partial}{\partial\mu}\right) \cdot 1 = \mu$$

whence it follows that $d' \cdot 1 = \mu'$. Using it, we see that

$$dd' \cdot 1 = \left(\mu + \frac{\partial}{\partial\mu}\right)d' \cdot 1$$

$$= \left(\mu + \frac{\partial}{\partial\mu}\right)\mu' = \mu\mu' + I_n. \tag{4.14}$$

Thus using (2.11) we have

$$
\begin{aligned}
E(\hat{\beta}) &= \sigma E[(X'X)^{-1}X'z] \\
&= \sigma(X'X)^{-1}X'd \cdot 1 \\
&= \sigma(X'X)^{-1}X'\mu \\
&= \beta,
\end{aligned}
\tag{4.15}
$$

which establishes the unbiasedness of $\hat{\beta}$. Notice that the result (2.11) gives $Eh(z) = h(d) \cdot 1$, that is the expectation of a function of normal vector is simply that function with $z$ replaced by the nonstochastic operator $d$.

Similarly, the second-order moments of the elements of $\hat{\beta}$ are

$$
\begin{aligned}
E(\hat{\beta}\hat{\beta}') &= \sigma^2 E[(X'X)^{-1}X'zz'X(X'X)^{-1}] \\
&= \sigma^2(X'X)^{-1}X'[dd' \cdot 1]X(X'X)^{-1} \\
&= \sigma^2(X'X)^{-1}X'[\mu\mu' + I_n]X(X'X)^{-1} \\
&= \sigma^2(X'X)^{-1}X'\left[\frac{1}{\sigma^2}X\beta\beta'X' + I_n\right]X(X'X)^{-1} \\
&= \beta\beta' + \sigma^2(X'X)^{-1}.
\end{aligned}
\tag{4.16}
$$

Here $Ezz'$ is simply replaced by $dd' \cdot 1$ using (2.11). This result can be alternatively derived by using (2.14) recursively as follows:

$$
\begin{aligned}
E(\hat{\beta}\hat{\beta}') &= \sigma E\left[(X'X)^{-1}X'z\hat{\beta}'\right] \\
&= \sigma(X'X)^{-1}X'dE\hat{\beta}' \\
&= \sigma^2(X'X)^{-1}X'\left(\mu + \frac{\partial}{\partial\mu}\right)\mu'X(X'X)^{-1} \\
&= \sigma^2(X'X)^{-1}X'\mu\mu'X(X'X)^{-1} + \sigma^2(X'X)^{-1} \\
&= \beta\beta' + \sigma^2(X'X)^{-1}
\end{aligned}
\tag{4.17}
$$

whence it is deduced that the variance–covariance matrix of $\hat{\beta}$ is

$$
\begin{aligned}
E(\hat{\beta} - \beta)(\hat{\beta} - \beta)' &= E(\hat{\beta}\hat{\beta}') - \beta\beta' \\
&= \sigma^2(X'X)^{-1}.
\end{aligned}
\tag{4.18}
$$

It may be noticed that the above results can be obtained without assuming normality of disturbances, see Section 2.3.

Now let us evaluate the moments of $\hat{\beta}_i$ given by (4.3). First, from (4.13) we have

$$\begin{aligned}
E(\hat{\beta}_i) &= \sigma E(a_i z) \\
&= \sigma a_i d \cdot 1 \\
&= \sigma a_i \mu \\
&= a_i X \beta \quad [AX = I_p] \\
&= \iota_i \beta = \beta_i,
\end{aligned}$$
(4.19)

where $\iota_i$ denotes a $1 \times p$ vector with all elements 0 except the $i$th element, which is 1. In other words, $\iota_i$ is the $i$th row vector of an identity matrix $I_p$.

Next, consider the second-order moments. Following the manipulation indicated in (4.17), we have

$$\begin{aligned}
E(\hat{\beta}_j \hat{\beta}_i) &= \sigma E(a_j z \hat{\beta}_i) \\
&= \sigma a_j d E(\hat{\beta}_i) \\
&= \sigma^2 a_j \left( \mu + \frac{\partial}{\partial \mu} \right) a_i \mu \\
&= \sigma^2 \left[ a_j \mu a_i' \mu + a_j \frac{\partial}{\partial \mu} (a_i \mu) \right] \\
&= \sigma^2 \left[ a_j \mu a_i' \mu + a_j a_i' \right] \\
&= \beta_j \beta_i + \sigma^2 c_{ji},
\end{aligned}$$
(4.20)

where $c_{ji}$ denotes the $(j, i)$ the element of the matrix $C = (X'X)^{-1} = AA'$.

From (4.19) and (4.20) we can write

$$E(\hat{\beta}_j - \beta_j)(\hat{\beta}_i - \beta_i) = \sigma^2 c_{ji},$$
(4.21)

which leads to the expression (4.18).

Next, let us find the third-order moments:

$$\begin{aligned}
E(\hat{\beta}_h \hat{\beta}_j \hat{\beta}_i) &= \sigma E(a_h z \hat{\beta}_j \hat{\beta}_i) \\
&= \sigma a_h d \cdot E(\hat{\beta}_j \hat{\beta}_i) \\
&= \sigma^3 a_h \left( \mu + \frac{\partial}{\partial \mu} \right) (a_j \mu a_i \mu + a_j a_i') \\
&= \sigma^3 a_h \mu a_j \mu a_i \mu + \sigma^3 a_h \mu a_j a_i' \\
&\quad + \sigma^3 a_i \mu a_h a_j' + \sigma^3 a_j \mu a_h a_i' + \sigma^3 a_h \frac{\partial}{\partial \mu} (a_j a_i') \\
&= \beta_h \beta_j \beta_i + \sigma^2 \beta_h c_{ji} + \sigma^2 \beta_i c_{hj} + \sigma^2 \beta_j c_{hi}
\end{aligned}$$
(4.22)

from which, using (4.19) and (4.20), we find

$$E(\hat{\beta}_h - \beta_h)(\hat{\beta}_j - \beta_j)(\hat{\beta}_i - \beta_i) = 0. \qquad (4.23)$$

Similarly, we can obtain the fourth-order moments:

$$
\begin{aligned}
E(\hat{\beta}_g\hat{\beta}_h\hat{\beta}_j\hat{\beta}_i) &= \sigma E(a_g z \cdot \hat{\beta}_h\hat{\beta}_j\hat{\beta}_i) \\
&= \sigma a_g d \cdot E(\hat{\beta}_h\hat{\beta}_j\hat{\beta}_i) \\
&= \sigma^4 a_g \left(\mu + \frac{\partial}{\partial \mu}\right)(a_h \mu a_j \mu a_i \mu + a_h \mu c_{ji} + a_i \mu c_{hj} + a_j \mu c_{hi}) \\
&= \sigma^4 [a_g \mu (a_h \mu \cdot a_j \mu \cdot a_i \mu + a_h \mu c_{ji} + a_i \mu c_{hj} + a_j \mu c_{hi}) \\
&\quad + a_i \mu a_j \mu a_g a_h' + a_h \mu a_j \mu a_g a_i' + a_h \mu a_i \mu a_g a_j' \\
&\quad + a_g a_h' c_{ji} + a_g a_i' c_{hj} + a_g a_j' c_{hi}] \\
&= \beta_g \beta_h \beta_j \beta_i + \sigma^2 (\beta_g \beta_h c_{ji} + \beta_g \beta_i c_{hj} + \beta_g \beta_j c_{hi} \\
&\quad + \beta_h \beta_j c_{gi} + \beta_h \beta_i c_{gj} + \beta_i \beta_j c_{gh}) \\
&\quad + \sigma^4 (c_{gh} c_{ji} + c_{gi} c_{hj} + c_{gj} c_{hi}). \qquad (4.24)
\end{aligned}
$$

From above, we obtain

$$E(\hat{\beta}_g - \beta_g)(\hat{\beta}_h - \beta_h)(\hat{\beta}_j - \beta_j)(\hat{\beta}_i - \beta_i) = \sigma^4 (c_{gh} c_{ji} + c_{gi} c_{hj} + c_{gj} c_{hi}). \qquad (4.25)$$

Further higher-order moments can be straightforwardly found in a similar manner. It may be pointed out that the above results can also be derived from the moment generating function or characteristic function of $(\hat{\beta} - \beta)$ in the conventional manner but the process may be algebraically difficult for higher-order moments than the recursive kind of aforesaid procedure. When X is a stochastic matrix the results have been discussed in Chapter 2.

## 4.3.2   Residuals and Residual Sum of Squares

Consider the $i$th element of the residual vector $\hat{u}$ in (4.4):

$$\hat{u}_i = m_i y, \qquad (4.26)$$

where $m_i$ is the $i$th row vector of $M = [I_n - X(X'X)^{-1}X']$. The moments of $\hat{u}_i$ can be evaluated precisely in the same manner as indicated for $\hat{\beta}_i$. The resulting expressions can be further simplified by noting the following results

$$m_i X = 0, \qquad m_i m_j' = m_{ij} \qquad (4.27)$$

arising from the identity $MX = 0$ and the idempotency of $M$. Here $m_{ij}$ denotes the $(i,j)$th element of $M$. Thus we find

$$E\hat{u}_i = m_i Ey = \sigma m_i d \cdot 1 = m_i \mu = m_i \left(X\frac{\beta}{\sigma}\right) = 0.$$

Similarly,

$$E(\hat{u}_i \hat{u}_j) = \sigma^2 m_{ij}, \qquad E(\hat{u}_h \hat{u}_i \hat{u}_j) = 0, \tag{4.28}$$
$$E(\hat{u}_g \hat{u}_h \hat{u}_i \hat{u}_j) = \sigma^4 (m_{gh} m_{ij} + m_{gi} m_{hj} + m_{gj} m_{hi}).$$

In particular, we have

$$E(\hat{u}_i) = 0, \quad E(\hat{u}_i^2) = \sigma^2 m_{ii}, \tag{4.29}$$
$$E(\hat{u}_i^3) = 0, \quad E(\hat{u}_i^4) = 3\sigma^4 (m_{ii}^2).$$

Next, let us consider the moments of the RSS. Using (2.11), we have

$$\begin{aligned}
E(\text{RSS}) &= \sigma^2 E[(z'Mz)] \\
&= \sigma^2 \text{tr} M E(zz') \\
&= \sigma^2 \text{tr} M dd' \cdot 1 \\
&= \sigma^2 \text{tr} M(\mu\mu' + I_n) \\
&= \sigma^2 \mu' M \mu + \sigma^2 \text{tr} M \\
&= \sigma^2 (n - p) \tag{4.30}
\end{aligned}$$

because $M\mu = (1/\sigma) MX\beta = 0$. Similarly, we observe that

$$\begin{aligned}
E(\text{RSS})^2 &= \sigma^4 E(z'Mz)^2 \\
&= \sigma^4 (d'Md) E(z'Mz) \\
&= \sigma^4 \text{tr} M dd' [\mu' M \mu + (n - p)] \\
&= \sigma^4 [\text{tr} M dd' \cdot \mu' M \mu + (n - p) \text{tr} M dd' \cdot 1] \\
&= \sigma^4 \left[ \text{tr} M \left( \mu + \frac{\partial}{\partial \mu} \right) \left( \mu' + \frac{\partial}{\partial \mu'} \right) \mu' M \mu + (n - p) \text{tr} M(\mu\mu' + I_n) \right] \\
&= \sigma^4 [\text{tr} M(\mu' M \mu \cdot \mu\mu' + 2M\mu\mu' + 2\mu\mu' M + 2M) + (n - p) \text{tr} M] \\
&= \sigma^4 [2\text{tr} M^2 + (n - p) \text{tr} M] \\
&= \sigma^4 (n - p)(n - p + 2), \tag{4.31}
\end{aligned}$$

since $M^2 = M$. It can be shown in a similar manner that

$$\begin{aligned}
E(\text{RSS})^3 &= \sigma^6 (d'Md) E(z'Mz)^2 \\
&= \sigma^6 (n - p)(n - p + 2)(n - p + 4) \tag{4.32}
\end{aligned}$$

$$\begin{aligned}
E(\text{RSS})^4 &= \sigma^8 (d'Md) E(z'Mz)^3 \\
&= \sigma^8 (n - p)(n - p + 2)(n - p + 4)(n - p + 6). \tag{4.33}
\end{aligned}$$

Higher-order moments can be derived in the same way. From these results, one can find the expressions for moments of residual variance estimator $\hat{\sigma}^2$. For instance, the first four central moments of $\hat{\sigma}^2$ are

$$E(\hat{\sigma}^2 - \sigma^2) = 0, \qquad E(\hat{\sigma}^2 - \sigma^2)^2 = \frac{2\sigma^4}{(n-p)},$$

$$E(\hat{\sigma}^2 - \sigma^2)^3 = \frac{8\sigma^6}{(n-p)^2}, \qquad E(\hat{\sigma}^2 - \sigma^2)^4 = 12\frac{(n-p+4)\sigma^8}{(n-p)^3} \tag{4.34}$$

whence the Pearson's measures for the excess of skewness and kurtosis of the distribution of $\hat{\sigma}^2$ can be straightforwardly obtained:

$$\frac{E(\hat{\sigma}^2 - \sigma^2)^3}{[E(\hat{\sigma}^2 - \sigma^2)^2]^{3/2}} = \left(\frac{8}{n-p}\right)^{1/2} \tag{4.35}$$

$$\frac{E(\hat{\sigma}^2 - \sigma^2)^4}{[E(\hat{\sigma}^2 - \sigma^2)^2]^2} - 3 = \left(\frac{12}{n-p}\right) \tag{4.36}$$

implying that the distribution of $\hat{\sigma}^2$ is positively skewed and leptokurtic.

Sometimes we may be interested in finding out the inverse moments. These can be obtained from result (2.20). For instance, the $r$th inverse moment of the RSS is

$$E(\text{RSS})^{-r} = \frac{1}{\sigma^{2r}\Gamma(r)} \int_0^\infty t^{r-1} |I_n + 2tM|^{-1/2}$$
$$\times \exp\{-t\mu'M(I_n + 2tM)^{-1}\mu\}\, dt \tag{4.37}$$

provided that $r$ is less than $(1/2)(n-p)$.

Since $M$ is an idempotent matrix of rank $(n-p)$, it has only $(n-p)$ nonzero characteristic roots and these roots are all equal to one. Thus it is easy to see that $|I_n + 2tM| = (1 + 2t)^{(n-p)}$ and $\mu'M(I_n + 2tM)^{-1}\mu = 0$.

$$E(\text{RSS})^{-r} = \frac{1}{\sigma^{2r}\Gamma(r)} \int_0^\infty t^{r-1}(1 + 2t)^{-(1/2)(n-p)}\, dt. \tag{4.38}$$

Now applying the transformation $t_* = (1 + 2t)^{-1}$ we obtain the following expression

$$E(\text{RSS})^{-r} = \frac{1}{(2\sigma^2)^r\Gamma(r)} \int_0^1 (1 - t_*)^{r-1} t_*^{(1/2)(n-p)-r-1}\, dt_*$$
$$= \left(\frac{1}{2\sigma^2}\right)^r \frac{\Gamma\left(\frac{n-p}{2} - r\right)}{\Gamma\left(\frac{n-p}{2}\right)} \tag{4.39}$$

whence the $r$th inverse moment of $\hat{\sigma}^2$ is

$$E(\hat{\sigma}^2)^{-r} = \left(\frac{n-p}{2\sigma^2}\right)^r \frac{\Gamma\left(\frac{n-p}{2} - r\right)}{\Gamma\left(\frac{n-p}{2}\right)} \tag{4.40}$$

provided that $r < (1/2)(n-p)$.

If we are interested in the distribution of $(1/\hat{\sigma}^2)$, for example, in Bayesian inference, the mean and variance are

$$E\left(\frac{1}{\hat{\sigma}^2}\right) = \frac{(n-p)}{\sigma^2(n-p-2)} = \alpha \ (say); \quad (n-p) > 2$$

$$E\left(\frac{1}{\hat{\sigma}^2} - \alpha\right)^2 = \frac{2(n-p)^2}{\sigma^4(n-p-2)^2(n-p-4)}; \quad (n-p) > 4 \tag{4.41}$$

while the Pearson's measures of excess of skewness and kurtosis are

$$\frac{E\left(\frac{1}{\hat{\sigma}^2} - \alpha\right)^3}{\left[E\left(\frac{1}{\hat{\sigma}^2} - \alpha\right)^2\right]^{3/2}} = \frac{4[2(n-p-4)]^{1/2}}{(n-p-6)}; \quad (n-p) > 6$$

$$\frac{E\left(\frac{1}{\hat{\sigma}^2} - \alpha\right)^4}{\left[E\left(\frac{1}{\hat{\sigma}^2} - \alpha\right)^2\right]^2} - 3 = \frac{60(n-p-4)}{(n-p-6)(n-p-8)}; \quad (n-p) > 8. \tag{4.42}$$

It is thus seen that the distribution of inverted $\hat{\sigma}^2$ is positively skewed. Further, it is leptokurtic as $(n-p) > 8$.

### 4.3.3  $R^2$ and Adjusted $R^2$

Let us first consider the moment of $R^2$ defined by (4.7). The $r$th moment of $R^2$ is given by

$$E(R^2)^r = E\left[\frac{y'(N-M)y}{y'Ny}\right]^r, \tag{4.43}$$

where $N$ and $M$ are idempotent matrices. Here we restrict our attention to the first two moments only. The higher-order moments can be evaluated using the result (2.28) in a recursive manner. In particular the mean is

$$E(R^2) = \int_0^\infty |\Delta|^{1/2} \left[\text{tr}(N-M)\Delta + \mu'\Delta(N-M)\Delta\mu\right] \exp\{-t\mu'N\Delta\mu\} \, dt \tag{4.44}$$

with $\Delta = (I_n + 2tN)^{-1}$ provided that $n$ exceeds 3.

Since the regression model is assumed to contain an intercept term, the vector $\iota$ appears in X as one of the column vectors so that $M\iota = 0$. This implies that $MN = M$. Further, using the results

$$(D - gdd')^{-1} = D^{-1} + \frac{g}{1 - gd'D^{-1}d}D^{-1}dd'D^{-1}$$

$$|D + gdd'| = |D|\,(1 + gd'D^{-1}d)$$

(4.45)

for any nonsingular matrix $D$, vector $d$ and scalar $g$, it is easy to see that

$$\Delta = (I_n + 2tN)^{-1}$$

$$= \left[(1 + 2t)I_n - 2\left(\frac{t}{n}\right)\iota\iota'\right]^{-1}$$

$$= \left[\left(\frac{1}{1 + 2t}\right)I_n + \frac{2t}{n(1 + 2t)}\iota\iota'\right]$$

(4.46)

whence it follows that $|\Delta| = (1/(1 + 2t))^n[1 + 2(t/n)\iota'\iota] = (1/(1 + 2t))^{n-1}$ and $N\Delta = (1 + 2t)^{-1}N$. Further, we find $(N - M)\Delta = (1/(1 + 2t))(N - M)$, $\mu'\Delta(N - M)\Delta\mu = (1/(1 + 2t))^2\mu'\mu$, $\mu'N\Delta\mu = (1/(1 + 2t))\mu'\mu$, which when substituted in (4.44) yields

$$E(R^2) = \int_0^\infty \left[(p - 1) + \left(\frac{1}{1 + 2t}\right)\mu'\mu\right]\left(\frac{1}{1 + 2t}\right)^{(1/2)(n+1)}$$

$$\times \exp\left\{-\left(\frac{t}{1 + 2t}\right)\mu'\mu\right\}dt.$$

(4.47)

Applying the transformation $t_* = (1 + 2t)^{-1}$ we get

$$E(R^2) = \frac{1}{2}\int_0^1 \left[(p - 1) + t_*^2\mu'\mu\right]t_*^{(1/2)(n-3)}\exp\left\{-(1 - t_*)\frac{\mu'\mu}{2}\right\}dt_*$$

$$= \int_0^1 \left[\frac{1}{2}(p - 1) + t_*^2\theta\right]t_*^{(1/2)(n-3)}\exp\left\{-(1 - t_*)\theta\right\}dt_*,$$

(4.48)

where $\theta = (1/2)\mu'\mu = (1/2\sigma^2)\beta'X'X\beta$ is the noncentrality parameter.
An alternative expression for the mean is

$$E(R^2) = e^{-\theta}\sum_{j=0}^\infty \left(\frac{p - 1 + 2j}{n - 1 + 2j}\right)\frac{\theta^j}{j!},$$

(4.49)

which is the form obtained by Cramer (1987).

Similarly, using the result (2.29) it is easy to see that the second moment of $R^2$ is

$$E(R^4) = \int_0^1 \left[ \frac{1}{4}(p^2 - 1) + (p+1)\theta t_* + \theta^2 t_*^2 \right] (1 - t_*) t_*^{(1/2)(n-3)}$$
$$\times \exp\{-(1 - t_*)\theta\} \, dt_*$$
$$= e^{-\theta} \sum_{j=0}^{\infty} \left( \frac{p - 1 + 2j}{n - 1 + 2j} \right) \left( \frac{p + 1 + 2j}{n + 1 + 2j} \right) \frac{\theta^j}{j!} \tag{4.50}$$

provided that $n$ exceeds 5.

If we define the population counterpart of $R^2$ as

$$\phi = \frac{\beta' X' X \beta}{\beta' X' X \beta + n\sigma^2} = \frac{\theta}{\theta + (n/2)} \tag{4.51}$$

it is easy to see that $R^2$ serves as a consistent estimator of $\phi$; see Cramer (1987: 256–7). Further, it is obvious from (4.48) that $R^2$ is a biased estimator. For assessing the magnitude of bias, Cramer (1987) carried out a numerical evaluation of bias and standard deviation of $R^2$ for few selected values of $p$, $n$, and $\phi$, viz., $p = 2, 3, n = 5$, 10, 50, 200, and $\phi = 0.9$, 0.667, 0.5, 0.333. The numerical results revealed that $R^2$ as an estimator of $\phi$ has an upward bias, which can be substantial when the number of observations is small. However, the bias declines rapidly as $n$ grows large. When the bias is noticeable, $R^2$ has very large standard errors. The standard error appears to have a stronger dependence upon $\phi$ in comparison to $p$ and $n$, and it is this dependence, Cramer stated, that often leads to erroneous inferences from the value of $R^2$ taken as a measure of goodness of fit.

Next, let us consider the moments of adjusted $R^2$. These moments can be straightforwardly found from the moments of $R^2$. For instance, the mean is

$$E(\bar{R}^2) = \left( \frac{n-1}{n-p} \right) E(R^2) - \left( \frac{p-1}{n-p} \right)$$
$$= \left( \frac{n-1}{n-p} \right) e^{-\theta} \sum_{j=0}^{\infty} \left( \frac{p-1+2j}{n-1+2j} \right) \frac{\theta^j}{j!} - \left( \frac{p-1}{n-p} \right)$$
$$= \left( \frac{n-1}{n-p} \right) e^{-\theta} \sum_{j=0}^{\infty} \left( 1 - \frac{n-p}{n-1+2j} \right) \frac{\theta^j}{j!} - \left( \frac{p-1}{n-p} \right)$$
$$= \left( \frac{n-1}{n-p} \right) \left[ 1 - (n-p)e^{-\theta} \sum_{j=0}^{\infty} \left( \frac{1}{n-1+2j} \right) \frac{\theta^j}{j!} \right] - \left( \frac{p-1}{n-p} \right)$$
$$= 1 - (n-1)e^{-\theta} \sum_{j=0}^{\infty} \left( \frac{1}{n-1+2j} \right) \frac{\theta^j}{j!}. \tag{4.52}$$

Similarly, the second moment of $\bar{R}^2$ can be found:

$$E(\bar{R}^4) = \left(\frac{n-1}{n-p}\right)^2 E(R^4) - 2\frac{(n-1)(p-1)}{(n-p)^2} E(R^2) + \left(\frac{p-1}{n-p}\right)^2 \qquad (4.53)$$

whence an explicit expression for the variance of $\bar{R}^2$ can be obtained.

It is interesting to note from the above expression that $E(\bar{R}^2)$ does not explicitly depend upon $p$, the number of explanatory variables in the model, while $E(\bar{R}^2)$ does. As a consequence, Cramer (1987) observed from his numerical results that bias of $\bar{R}^2$ virtually vanishes and in fact it may be downward. Next, we observe that

$$\frac{E[\bar{R}^2 - E(\bar{R}^2)]^2}{E[R^2 - E(R^2)]^2} = \left(\frac{n-1}{n-p}\right)^2 \qquad (4.54)$$

from which it follows that $\bar{R}^2$ has larger variance than $R^2$. Thus, for a smaller number of observations, $\bar{R}^2$ may have smaller bias than $R^2$ but owing to larger variability it can be more unreliable than $R^2$.

### 4.3.4   The *F*-Ratio

The *F*-ratio given by (4.9) can be written as

$$F = \left(\frac{n-p}{p}\right) \cdot \frac{z'Hz}{z'Mz}; \quad H = X(X'X)^{-1}X' = XA \qquad (4.55)$$

so that its $r$th moment is given by

$$\begin{aligned}
E(F^r) &= \left(\frac{n-p}{p}\right)^r E\left(\frac{z'Hz}{z'Mz}\right)^r; \quad r < \frac{1}{2}(n-p) \\
&= \left(\frac{n-p}{p}\right)^r (d'Hd)^r E(z'Mz)^{-r} \\
&= \left(\frac{n-p}{p}\right)^r (d'Hd)^r E(\sigma^2 RSS)^{-r} \\
&= \left(\frac{n-p}{p}\right)^r (d'Hd)^r \left[\frac{\Gamma\left(\frac{n-p}{2} - r\right)}{2^r \Gamma\left(\frac{n-p}{2}\right)}\right] \\
&= \left(\frac{n-p}{2p}\right)^r \frac{\Gamma\left(\frac{n-p}{2} - r\right)}{\Gamma\left(\frac{n-p}{2}\right)} (d'Hd)^r \cdot 1,
\end{aligned} \qquad (4.56)$$

where use has been made of (2.28). Thus the mean is

$$\begin{aligned}
E(F) &= \frac{(n-p)}{p(n-p-2)} (d'Hd) \cdot 1 \\
&= \frac{(n-p)}{p(n-p-2)} (\mu'H\mu + \mathrm{tr}H) \\
&= \frac{(n-p)}{p(n-p-2)} (\mu'\mu + p). \qquad (4.57)
\end{aligned}$$

Similarly, setting $r = 2$ in (4.56), the second moment of $F$ is

$$E(F^2) = \frac{(n-p)^2}{p^2(n-p-2)(n-p-4)}(d'Hd)^2 \cdot 1$$

$$= \frac{(n-p)^2[(\mu'\mu + p)(\mu'\mu + p + 2) + 2\mu'\mu]}{p^2(n-p-2)(n-p-4)}, \qquad (4.58)$$

where we have used the result

$$\begin{aligned}
(d'Hd)^2 \cdot 1 &= (d'Hd)(d'Hd) \cdot 1 \\
&= (d'Hd)(\mu'\mu + p) \\
&= \mathrm{tr} H\left(\mu + \frac{\partial}{\partial\mu}\right)\left(\mu' + \frac{\partial}{\partial\mu'}\right) \cdot (\mu'\mu + p) \\
&= \mathrm{tr} H[(\mu'\mu + p)(\mu\mu' + I_p) + 2(2\mu\mu' + I_p)] \\
&= (\mu'\mu + p)(\mu'\mu + p + 2) + 2\mu'\mu. \qquad (4.59)
\end{aligned}$$

Similarly, the higher-order moments of $F$ can be found from (4.56) in a recursive way.

It may be mentioned that the expression for the $r$th moment of $F$ is essentially the $r$th moment of a singly noncentral $F$-distribution with $p$ and $(n - p)$ d.f. and $(\mu'\mu/2)$ the noncentrality parameter.

## 4.3.5 Prediction

Let us consider the predictor defined by (4.11):

$$P = X\hat{\beta} = X(X'X)^{-1}X'y. \qquad (4.60)$$

If it is employed for predicting the actual values of the study variable, the prediction error is

$$(P - y) = -My = -\hat{u} \qquad (4.61)$$

from which the predictive bias and the predictive mean squared error (MSE) or variance are

$$E(P - y) = -E(\hat{u}) = 0$$
$$E(P - y)'(P - y) = E(\hat{u}'\hat{u}) = \sigma^2(n - p). \qquad (4.62)$$

Higher-order moments of the prediction error can be determined from the moments of residuals (see Section 4.3.2). If the predictor is used for the mean values of study variable, the prediction error is given by

$$(P - E(y)) = P - X\beta. \qquad (4.63)$$

Now, utilizing results in Section 4.3.1, we have

$$E(P) = \sigma X(X'X)^{-1}X'E(z) = \sigma X(X'X)^{-1}X'\mu = X\beta$$
$$E(P'P) = \sigma^2 E[z'X(X'X)^{-1}X'z]$$
$$= \sigma^2 \text{tr}[X(X'X)^{-1}X'E(zz')]$$
$$= \sigma^2 \text{tr}[X(X'X)^{-1}X'(\mu\mu' + I_n)]$$
$$= \beta'X'X\beta + \sigma^2 p$$

from which the predictive bias and the predictive MSE or variance of the mean predictor are

$$E(P - X\beta) = 0$$
$$E(P - X\beta)'(P - X\beta) = E(P'P) - 2\beta'X'E(P) + \beta'X'X\beta = \sigma^2 p. \tag{4.64}$$

It is thus seen that the predictor $P$ is unbiased whether used for actual values or mean values of the study variable. However, it has smaller variability when used for mean values of study variable rather than for actual values if $n$ is larger than $2p$. Just the reverse happens when $n$ is smaller than $2p$.

Finally, suppose that a pre-specified value for each of the $p$ explanatory variables is assigned and thus a row vector $x_f$ is formed. Associated with this if $y_f$ is the true value of study variable, we have

$$y_f = x_f\beta + u_f$$

where $u_f$ is the disturbance term having the same distributional properties as the elements of $u$.

The prediction or forecast for $y_f$ is then defined by

$$\hat{y}_f = x_f\hat{\beta} = x_f(X'X)^{-1}X'y = \sigma x_f(X'X)^{-1}X'z. \tag{4.65}$$

Moments of $\hat{y}_f$ are easy to evaluate. For example, the mean is

$$E(\hat{y}_f) = \sigma x_f(X'X)^{-1}X'E(z) = \sigma x_f(X'X)^{-1}X'\mu = x_f\beta \tag{4.66}$$

whence it follows that $E(\hat{y}_f - y_f) = 0$. Similarly, we have

$$E(\hat{y}_f^2) = \sigma^2 x_f(X'X)^{-1}X'E(zz')X(X'X)^{-1}x_f'$$
$$= \sigma^2 x_f(X'X)^{-1}X'(\mu\mu' + I_n)X(X'X)^{-1}x_f'$$
$$= (x_f\beta)^2 + \sigma^2 x_f(X'X)^{-1}x_f'$$

so that the forecast variance is

$$E(\hat{y}_f - y_f)^2 = \sigma^2 x_f(X'X)^{-1}x_f'. \tag{4.67}$$

Higher-order moments can be evaluated in a similar manner.

## 4.3.6  Exact Moments Under Nonnormal

Since $R^2$ and $F$ are essentially ratio of quadratic forms, their exact moments under normality follow from the results in Chapter 2 and they have been discussed above. For a specific family of exponential density the results can be developed by the procedures described in Section 2.3. Further, since $R^2$ and $F$ are scale invariant, the exact results under normality will continue to hold for any spherically symmetric error density, a special case of which is multivariate $t$-density, see Ullah and Zinde-Walsh (1984), Ullah and Phillips (1986), Ohtani and Hasegawa (1993), Zellner (1976), King (1980), and Breusch, Robertson, and Welsh (1993). Furthermore the exact moments of $R^2$ and $F$ can also be written under the Edgeworth type density of disturbances from Peters (1989).

If, however, the interest is to compare the exact bias and MSE properties of $R^2$ and $\bar{R}^2$, without making distributional assumption and without deriving the explicit expressions of bias and MSE, it can be done by simply looking at the relationship between $R^2$ and $\bar{R}^2$. This is

$$\bar{R}^2 = (1+l)R^2 - l \quad l = \frac{p-1}{n-p} > 0. \tag{4.68}$$

Cramér (1987) has pointed out that $\bar{R}^2$ has the same probability limit as $R^2$ provided all the explanatory variables in the model are asymptotically cooperative in the sense that the limiting term of matrix $n^{-1}(X'MX)$ as $n \to \infty$ is finite and nonsingular. Consequently, both $R^2$ and $\bar{R}^2$ can be regarded as consistent estimators of their population counterpart $\phi$ $(0 \leq \phi \leq 1)$.

The efficiency properties of $R^2$ and $\bar{R}^2$ can now be studied by noting

$$\bar{R}^2 - R^2 = -l(1 - R^2) \leq 0. \tag{4.69}$$

Thus, $E(\bar{R}^2 - R^2) \leq 0$, which implies that $E\bar{R}^2 - \phi \leq ER^2 - \phi$, that is, $B(\bar{R}^2) \leq B(R^2)$ where $B(\bar{R}^2) = E\bar{R}^2 - \phi$. Similarly

$$V(\bar{R}^2) = (1+l)^2\, V(R^2), \tag{4.70}$$

so that

$$V(\bar{R}^2) \geq V(R^2), \tag{4.71}$$

that is, the exact variance of $\bar{R}^2$ will always be larger than that of $R^2$.

Turning to the MSE of $R^2$ and $\bar{R}^2$ we note from (4.68) that

$$(R^2 - \phi) - \left(\bar{R}^2 - \phi\right) = l(1 - R^2). \tag{4.72}$$

Therefore, squaring and taking expectations

$$\text{MSE}(R^2) - \text{MSE}(\bar{R}^2) = l[2(1 - \phi)E(1 - R^2) - (2 + l)E(1 - R^2)^2]$$

so that $\text{MSE}(\bar{R}^2) \leq \text{MSE}(R^2)$ provided

$$l + 2 \leq \frac{2(1 - \phi)E(1 - R^2)}{E(1 - R^2)^2}. \tag{4.73}$$

Because $1 - R^2 \geq (1 - R^2)^2$, $\quad E(1 - R^2) \geq E(1 - R^2)^2$. Thus it is clear that the comparison of MSE is not as straightforward as the bias and variance. Indeed it could be the case that in some situations MSE of $R^2$ is better behaved compared with $\bar{R}^2$ and vice versa. Some observations on this are given below on the basis of approximate results.

### 4.3.7  Approximate Moments

It is obvious that once $F$ and $R^2$ are written in a ratio of quadratic terms, their exact moments can be written in a straightforward way. However, these expression are complicated and one has to resort to numerical calculations to derive any meaningful conclusions. In such situations the approximations can be very useful. For this we first look at the large-sample approximations of $R^2$, which can be written as

$$R^2 - \phi = \xi_{-1/2} + \xi_{-1},$$

where $\xi_{-1/2} = (1 - \phi)(n\sigma^2)^{-1}[2(1 - \phi)u'MX\beta - \phi nw]$,

$$\xi_{-1} = (1 - \phi)(n\sigma^2)^{-1}u'[MX(X'MX)^{-1}X'M + \phi n^{-1}u'$$
$$- 4(1 - \phi)^2(n\sigma^2)^{-1}MX\beta\beta'XM]u$$
$$+ (1 - \phi)^2(n^2\sigma^4)^{-1}[\phi n^2 w^2 - 2(1 - 2\phi)nwu'MX\beta] \tag{4.74}$$

and $w = (n^{-1}u'u - \sigma^2)$. Using the expectation results in the Appendix Section A.5 it can be seen that, up to $O(n^{-1})$,

$$B(R^2) = \frac{(1 - \phi)}{n}[p - 1 + \phi(2\phi - 1) + \phi(1 - \phi)\gamma_2], \tag{4.75}$$

and hence

$$B(\bar{R}^2) = \frac{\phi(1 - \phi)}{n}[(2\phi - 1) + (1 - \phi)\gamma_2]. \tag{4.76}$$

Further the difference between $\text{MSE}(R^2)$ and $\text{MSE}(\bar{R}^2)$, up to $O(n^{-1})$, is

$$\text{MSE}(R^2) - \text{MSE}(\bar{R}^2) = \frac{2(p - 1)(1 - \phi)^2}{n^2}$$
$$\times \left[\frac{p - 1}{2} + \phi(4\phi - 5) + \phi(1 - 2\phi)\gamma_2\right]. \tag{4.77}$$

When $\gamma_2 = 0$ the above results are for the case of normal disturbances, see V. K. Srivastava, A. K. Srivastava, and Ullah (1995).

Several observations about bias and MSE can be made on the basis of above results. First while the bias of $R^2$ is monotonically increased with the number of regressors $p$ it is not the case with the bias of $\bar{R}^2$. This is consistent with the well known fact that $R^2$ is a monotonically increasing function of $p$. Second the bias of $R^2$ and $\bar{R}^2$ are not affected by the asymmetry of disturbances, though kurtosis does have its impact on the magnitude of bias. However,

$$B(R^2) - B(\bar{R}^2) = \frac{(p-1)(1-\phi)}{n} \geq 0. \tag{4.78}$$

Thus the magnitude of approximate bias of $R^2$ will be larger than that of $\bar{R}^2$ for the i.i.d. disturbances. This is consistent with the exact result above, which holds for all distributions, including non i.i.d.

As regards the variances of these estimators, we observe from (4.75) to (4.77) that the difference in variances of $R^2$ and $\bar{R}^2$ up to the order $O(n^{-2})$ is given by

$$D = V(R^2) - V(\bar{R}^2)$$

$$= \frac{2p\theta(1-\theta)^2}{n^2}[-2(2-\theta) - \theta\gamma_2]. \tag{4.79}$$

Now this $D$ is always negative because of positivity of $(\gamma_2 + 2)$ for all types of distributions. This result is also consistent with the exact result above which holds for all distributions, including those which are not i.i.d. Further, $D$ increases as $p$ grows large. This supports the result that the larger is the number of explanatory variables in the model, the more inefficient is $\bar{R}^2$ in comparison to $R^2$ according to the criterion of variance to order $O(n^{-2})$ irrespective of the nature of distribution of the disturbances.

However, variance is not an appropriate criterion for judging efficiency of biased estimators; the right choice is the MSE and, therefore, we should consider this for comparing the performance of $R^2$ and $\bar{R}^2$. Accordingly, from (4.77), $\bar{R}^2$ has a smaller MSE, to the order of our approximation, than $R^2$ when

$$p - 1 > 2\theta[(5 - 4\theta) - (1 - 2\theta)\gamma_2]. \tag{4.80}$$

Now if the disturbances are mesokurtic, that is, if they are normally distributed ($\gamma_2 = 0$), then the condition reduces to

$$p - 1 > 2\theta(5 - 4\theta), \tag{4.81}$$

which holds true for all values of $\theta$ so long as $p - 1$ exceeds 3; see Table 4.1.

Table 4.1
Evaluation of (4.81)

| $\theta$ | 0.0 | 0.1 | 0.2 | 0.3 | 0.4 | 0.5 | 0.6 | 0.7 | 0.8 | 0.9 | 1.0 |
|---|---|---|---|---|---|---|---|---|---|---|---|
| $2\theta(5-4\theta)$ | 0.00 | 0.92 | 1.68 | 2.28 | 2.72 | 3.00 | 3.12 | 3.05 | 2.88 | 2.52 | 2.00 |
| $2\theta(1-2\theta)$ | 0.00 | 0.16 | 0.24 | 0.24 | 0.16 | 0.00 | −0.24 | −0.56 | −0.96 | −1.44 | −2.00 |

Thus, when the distribution of disturbances is mesokurtic (normal), $\bar{R}^2$ is definitely superior to $R^2$ as long as the number of explanatory variables is four or more, in the sense that $\bar{R}^2$ has not only smaller bias but also smaller MSE too. This result may hold for three or less explanatory variables also provided $\theta$ is small enough, with $\theta \leq 0.2$ two explanatory variables are enough.

When the distribution of disturbances departs from normality, it follows from inequality (4.80) and the table given above that $\bar{R}^2$ is more efficient than $R^2$ for all platykurtic distributions ($-2 \leq \gamma_2 < 0$), at least as long as ($p - 1$) exceeds three. This result continues to remain true for all leptokurtic distributions ($\gamma_2 > 0$) also provided $\theta$ does not fall below 0.5, that is, the model does not fit the data very poorly. When $\theta$ is less than 0.5 so that the model fits poorly, the condition (4.80) for superiority of $\bar{R}^2$ over $R^2$ may require ($p - 1$) to be somewhat larger depending upon the value of $\gamma_2$ for leptokurtic distributions.

It is thus found that the adjusted $R^2(\bar{R}^2)$ is not that unreliable as it emerges out to be from variance viewpoint alone.

Now we turn to the question of the limitations of the approximate result. For this we make the following observations. It is interesting to note that both the results $B(R^2) \geq B(\bar{R}^2)$ and $V(R^2) \leq V(\bar{R}^2)$, based on large-$n$ approximations, are the same as the exact results. Also, under the normality assumption, a comparison of the exact bias of $R^2$ given in the table 1 of Cramer (1987) with the corresponding calculations of approximate bias above suggests that the two results are quite close. For example, when $p = 2$ ($k = 2$ in Cramer) and $\theta = 0.9$, we get the exact bias with approximate bias in parenthesis as 0.036 (0.034), 0.018 (0.017), 0.006 (0.006), 0.002 (0.002) for $n = 5$, 10, 30, 100, respectively. For $p = 3$, $\theta = 0.9$ and the same $n$ values, in order, we get 0.057 (0.054), 0.028 (0.027), 0.009 (0.009), 0.003 (0.003). Though not reported here, similar results were obtained for other values of $\theta$ considered in Cramer (1987). The same phenomenon occurred in the case of MSE comparisons of the exact versus the approximate results. Again, when $p = 2$ and $\theta = 0.9$, the exact and approximate values of $MSE(R^2) - MSE(\bar{R}^2)$ were $-0.001$ ($-0.0006$), $-0.00018$ ($-0.00015$), 0.0000 (0.0000) for $n = 5$, 10, and 30, respectively. Note that while the approximate difference in MSE is calculated by using (4.77), the exact value of difference is calculated by noting that we can rewrite this from (4.72) as $l[2(1 - \phi)(l + 1)B(R^2) - (2 + l)MSE(R^2) - l(1 - \phi)^2]$ and using the results in table 1 of Cramer. It is thus clear that the approximate numerical results in the normal case are very close to the corresponding exact results and they are identical when $n$ is thirty and above. Also, as indicated above, the analytical comparisons of the approximate bias and variance, in the general nonnormal case, provide the same results as those based on the exact results. Nevertheless, it remains the subject of a future study to see if the dominance condition in (4.80) and (4.81), based on the approximate MSE, will go through for the exact MSE case.

Now we consider the small-$\sigma$ approximation of the bias and MSE. These follow from the results in (2.91) or (2.95). For example, the bias up to $O(\sigma^2)$ is

$$B(R^2) = 1 - \phi + \frac{\sigma^2}{\beta'X'NX\beta}(p - n)$$

$$= \frac{\sigma^2 p}{\beta'X'NX\beta} \tag{4.82}$$

and hence

$$B(\bar{R}^2) = \frac{\sigma^2}{\beta'X'NX\beta}, \tag{4.83}$$

where we also use $1 - \phi = n\sigma^2 / (n\sigma^2 + \beta'X'NX\beta) \simeq n\sigma^2 / \beta'X'NX\beta$.

From the above results we note that the bias of $R^2$ depends on the number of regressors $p$ and it is a decreasing function of $\phi$ and $n$, since $\beta'X'NX\beta/\sigma^2$ can be written as $n\phi/(1 - \phi)$. The bias of $\bar{R}^2$ is also a decreasing function of $n$ and $\phi$, and it is considerably smaller than the bias of $R^2$ especially when $p$ is large.

Turning to Laplace approximations, we note from (2.108) that

$$ER^2 = \frac{E[y'(N - M)y]}{E(y'Ny)}, \qquad ER^4 = \frac{E[y'(N - M)y]^2}{[E(y'Ny)]^2}. \tag{4.84}$$

Further, using the expectations in the Appendix we get

$$B(R^2) = \frac{2\theta p + n(p - 1)}{(2\theta + n)(2\theta + n - 1)}, \qquad \theta = \frac{\beta'X'NX\beta}{2\sigma^2} = \frac{\mu'\mu}{2} \tag{4.85}$$

and

$$B(\bar{R}^2) = \frac{1}{(n - p)(2\theta + n)} \left[ \frac{n(2\theta p + n(p - 1))}{(2\theta + n - 1)} + (n - p)2\theta - np \right]. \tag{4.86}$$

Comparing the large-$n$, small-$\sigma$, and Laplace approximations we first observe that while both the small-$\sigma$ and Laplace results remain the same under the normal and nonnormal errors this is not the case with the large-$n$ approximation, which depends on $\gamma_2$. The MSEs, based on all the approximations, can be shown to be affected by $\gamma_2$ indicating that the distribution of $R^2$ is affected by the nonnormality. For the comparison of $ER^2$ based on these three approximations, see Smith (1996) where he indicates better accuracy of large-$n$ approximation. But as $\sigma$ decreases, with $n$ fixed, his calculations suggest that the accuracy of each approximation method improves.

The exact distributions of $R^2$ and $F$ can be evaluated by the Imhof procedure given in Chapter 3.

### 4.3.8   Hypothesis Testing

We consider the problem of testing that $\beta$ satisfies $q$ linear restrictions

$$H_0 : R\beta = s, \qquad H_1 : R\beta \neq s,$$

where $R$ is a $q \times q$ matrix of constants of rank $q$ and $s$ is a $q \times 1$ vector of constants.

Under the assumption of $u \sim N\left(0, \sigma^2 I_n\right)$ the log likelihood function is

$$\log L\left(\beta, \sigma^2\right) = -\frac{n}{2} \log\left(2\pi\right) - \frac{n}{2} \log \sigma^2 - \frac{1}{2\sigma^2}\left(y - X\beta\right)'\left(y - X\beta\right).$$

Let $\hat{\beta}_1$, $\hat{\sigma}_1^2$ be the unconstrained ML estimates under $H_1$ and consider $\tilde{\beta}_0, \tilde{\sigma}_0^2$ to be the constrained ML estimators under $H_0$, where $\hat{\sigma}_1^2$ and $\tilde{\sigma}_0^2$ are defined as in (4.6) with $n - p$ replaced by $n$ and RSS by $\text{RSS}_1$ and $\text{RSS}_0$, respectively, under $H_1$ and $H_0$. Further $\hat{\beta}_1 = \hat{\beta}$ is as given in (4.2) and

$$\tilde{\beta}_0 = \hat{\beta} - \left(X'X\right)^{-1} R' \left[R\left(X'X\right)^{-1} R'\right]^{-1}\left(R\hat{\beta} - s\right).$$

The usual $F$, Wald ($W$), Rao Score (RS) and the likelihood ratio (LR) test statistics are given as

$$F = \frac{\text{RSS}_0 - \text{RSS}_1}{\text{RSS}_1}\frac{\left(n - p\right)}{q},$$

$$W = \left(R\hat{\beta} - s\right)'\left[\hat{\sigma}_1^2 R\left(X'X\right)^{-1} R'\right]^{-1}\left(R\hat{\beta} - s\right),$$

$$\text{RS} = \left(R\hat{\beta} - s\right)'\left[\tilde{\sigma}_0^2 R\left(X'X\right)^{-1} R'\right]^{-1}\left(R\hat{\beta} - s\right),$$

$$\text{LR} = n\left[\log \tilde{\sigma}_0^2 - \log \hat{\sigma}_1^2\right],$$

where RS is also known as the Lagrange Multiplier test, see Bera and Ullah (1991) and Buse (1982).

The above statistics are such that $\text{RS} = W/\left(1 + W/n\right)$ and $\text{LR} = n \log\left(1 + W/n\right)$. Thus they follow the inequality $W \geq \text{LR} \geq \text{RS}$. Thus these test are not numerically equivalent. This inequality may not hold when the errors are not normal, see Ullah and Zinde-Walsh (1984, 1985). Further noting that $\text{RSS}_0 - \text{RSS}_1 = (R\hat{\beta} - s)'[R(X'X)^{-1}R']^{-1}(R\hat{\beta} - s)$ the three statistics $W$, LR, and RS are a function of the $F$-statistic since $W = nqF/\left(n - p\right)$. For a test of $H_0$ at $\alpha$ level of significance using exact distribution of $F$ let $z_F$ be its critical value. Then, based on the exact distributions, the critical values of three tests are $z_W = nqz_F/\left(n - p\right)$, $z_{\text{LR}} = n \log\left(1 + qz_F/n\right)$, and $z_{\text{RS}} = \left(qnz_F/n - p\right)/\left(1 + qz_F/n\right)$ so that when $H_0$ is true we have $P\left[W > z_W\right] = P\left[\text{LR} > z_{\text{LR}}\right] = P\left[\text{RS} > z_{\text{RS}}\right] = \alpha$. That is the exact tests have the correct significance level and hence they are equivalent in the sense of giving the same results regarding the acceptance or rejection of the null hypothesis. Also the exact tests have the same power function, which is the power function of the $F$-test. Thus though three tests are not numerically equivalent they do not provide conflicting results based on the respective critical values using exact distributions.

Under suitable regularity conditions it is well known that the three test statistics have the same asymptotic chi-square distribution with $q$ d.f., under the null hypothesis. Let $z$ be the critical value corresponding to the upper $\alpha$ percentage point of this chi-square distribution. Then the asymptotic tests, based on $z$, reject the null hypothesis if $W > z$, $RS > z$, and $LR > z$ provided $n$ goes to infinity. But the exact critical values of each of the tests may be substantially different from the asymptotic critical value $z$. Thus given the inequality among these three tests, for small or moderately large samples, the critical regions of them may not be the same $\alpha$-percentage. Thus these tests may give conflicting results by using the same asymptotic critical value, also the true powers of the asymptotic tests cannot be equal; see Berndt and Savin (1977), and also Evans and Savin (1982) for the calculations of probabilities of conflict and the true power of asymptotic tests.

The conflict between the asymptotic tests is essentially due to the fact that the significance levels are not correct for the actual sample of observations. For this we can develop Edgeworth expansions of each of the tests and determine the correction factors for the chi-square critical value $z$, which make the significance level of each test correct to order $n^{-1}$. For the Edgeworth expansion, up to $O(n^{-1})$, of the distribution of LR under $H_0$ and $H_1$, see Rothenberg (1984a). This Edgeworth expansion can be obtained by deriving the first four approximate cumulants of LR and then determining the characteristic function, see Chapter 3. This provides the Edgeworth corrected LR, as

$$\mathrm{LR}_e = \left(n - p + \frac{q}{2} - 1\right) \log\left(1 + \frac{W^*}{n}\right),$$

where

$$W^* = (n - p)\frac{(\mathrm{RSS}_0 - \mathrm{RSS}_1)}{\mathrm{RSS}_1} = \frac{(n - p)}{n}W.$$

This correction ensures that the LR has the correct significance level to order $n^{-1}$. $W^*$ is simply modified $W$ in which $n$ is replaced by $n - p$ in order to have an unbiased estimatior of the error variance. A similar modification in RS is

$$\mathrm{RS}^* = \frac{(n + q - p)}{n}\frac{W^*}{\left(1 + \frac{W^*}{n}\right)}.$$

To obtain the critical values of $W^*$ and $RS^*$ we note the following stochastic expansions of $W^*$ and $RS^*$, up to $O(n^{-1})$,

$$W^* = \mathrm{LR}_e\left(1 + (\mathrm{LR}_e - q + 2)/2n\right)$$
$$\mathrm{RS}^* = \mathrm{LR}_e\left(1 - (\mathrm{LR}_e - q - 2)/2n\right).$$

These give the critical values as

$$z_W = z\left(1 + (z - q + 2)/2n\right)$$
$$z_{RS} = z\left(1 - (z - q - 2)/2n\right).$$

The $W^*$ and $RS^*$ tests, based on these critical values, are referred size-corrected tests as in the $LR_e$ test. These size-corrected tests generally provide the right significance levels and hence negligible probability of conflict in practice. Further they have the same power to order $n^{-1}$, see Evans and Savin (1982) and Rothenberg (1984a).

The above results are valid under the normality of errors. It will be an interesting study to extend the above results for the nonnormal errors. The results in Ali and Sharma (1996), Ullah and Phillips (1986), Knight (1985), and Lieberman (1997) among others, will be useful in this context.

### 4.3.9   Nonlinear Regression Models

Consider a nonlinear model of the form

$$y_i = f\left(X_i, \beta\right) + u_i,$$

where $X_i$ is an i.i.d variable, $\beta$ is a scalar parameter and $u_i$ is i.i.d with $E\left(u_i \mid X_i\right) = 0$ and $V\left(u_i \mid X_i\right) = \sigma^2$. The estimator $\hat{\beta}$ of $\beta$ solves the moment condition

$$\Psi(\beta) = \frac{1}{n}\sum_1^n u_i X_i = \frac{1}{n}\sum_1^n q_i = 0,$$

where $q_i = u_i X_i$. The $j$th order derivative of $q_i$ with respect to $\beta$ is $\nabla^j q_i = -X_i f^{(j)}\left(X_i, \beta\right) = -X_i f_i^{(j)}$. Using the results (2.81) and (2.82) of Chapter 2 we get

$$B\left(\hat{\beta}\right) = -\frac{1}{2n} w^2 \bar{H}_2 Q$$

and

$$MSE\left(\hat{\beta}\right) = \frac{w^2}{n} + \frac{1}{n^2}\left\{3\sigma_x^2 w^2 Q^2 + \frac{15}{4}\bar{H}_2^2 Q^2 w^4 - \bar{H}_3 Q w^4\right\},$$

where $Q = \bar{H}_1^{-1}, \bar{H}_j = E(f_1^{(j)} X_1), \sigma_x^2 = E(f_1^{(1)} X_1 - \bar{H}_1)^2 = V(f_1^{(1)} X_1)$ and $w^2 = \sigma^2(EX_1^2)/\bar{H}_1^2$, which is also the asymptotic variance of $\hat{\beta}$.

When the model is linear the $\sigma_x^2 = V(X_1^2)$ and the last two terms in $M(\hat{\beta})$ are zero because $\bar{H}_2 = \bar{H}_3 = 0$. Also $B(\hat{\beta}) = 0$.

When $X$ is nonstochastic $\sigma_x^2 = 0$ and we replace $EX_1^2$ and $\bar{H}_j$ by $\Sigma X_i^2/n$ and $\Sigma f_i^{(j)} X_i/n$, respectively. Further the results for the case where $X_i$ and $u_i$ are non i.i.d, as in time series, follow from the results in (2.101) and (2.102).

# 5

# Models with Nonscalar Covariance Matrix of Errors

## 5.1 Introduction

In Chapter 4, we considered the regression model where the errors have a scalar covariance matrix. The regression coefficients were estimated by the method of least squares (LS). But a large class of econometric models are such where the covariance matrix of errors is nonscalar. Usually the error covariance matrix is unknown so an estimated matrix is obtained and the resulting estimators of $\beta$ are obtained by the feasible generalized least squares (FGLS) or by the maximum likelihood (ML) method. These contain the linear regression model where the errors are heteroskedastic or serially correlated, the seemingly unrelated regressions, random effect panel data model, and the limited dependent variables. The objective of this chapter is to analyze the exact and approximate distributions and moments of the feasible GLS and ML estimators of the parameters of these models. The results for several test statistics will also be explored.

## 5.2 General Model with Nonscalar Covariance Matrix

### 5.2.1 Exact Moments

Let us consider the linear model:

$$y = X\beta + u, \tag{5.1}$$

where $y$ is an $n \times 1$, $X$ is an $n \times k$ matrix of regressors having rank $k$, $\beta$ is a $k \times 1$ vector of parameters, and $u$ is an $n \times 1$ vector of unobserved random errors with

$$Eu = 0, \qquad V(u) = \Omega, \tag{5.2}$$

where $\Omega$ is an $n \times n$ nonsingular covariance matrix. Such a matrix appears in many econometrics models, such as those in heteroskedastic or serially correlated models. The LS estimator of $\beta$ is given by

$$b = (X'X)^{-1} X'y. \tag{5.3}$$

This estimator, conditional on X, has the following properties:

$$Eb = \beta, \qquad V(b) = (X'X)^{-1} X'\Omega X (X'X)^{-1}. \tag{5.4}$$

That is, the estimator is unbiased but it is not the best in the sense of having minimum variance in the class of linear unbiased estimators. This is because the covariance of error vector $u$ is $\Omega$ and not an identity matrix. In view of this, an alternative estimator, Aitken's GLS of $\beta$ is often used. This is, minimizing $u'\Omega^{-1}u$ subject to $\beta$,

$$\bar{\beta} = \left(X'\Omega^{-1}X\right)^{-1} X'\Omega^{-1}y. \tag{5.5}$$

When $\Omega$ is known, this GLS estimator, conditional on X, is the best linear unbiased estimator with

$$E\bar{\beta} = \beta \quad \text{and} \quad V\left(\bar{\beta}\right) = \left(X'\Omega^{-1}X\right)^{-1}. \tag{5.6}$$

Also $V\left(\bar{\beta}\right) \leq V(b)$ in the sense that $V(b) - V\left(\bar{\beta}\right)$ is a positive definite matrix. The GLS estimator $\bar{\beta}$ is not operational since in practice $\Omega$ is rarely, if ever, known. An operational or feasible estimator of the GLS estimator $\bar{\beta}$ can be obtained by developing consistent estimates of the $n^2$ elements of $\Omega$. Suppose, however, that $\Omega$ depends on an unknown $p$-dimensional parameter vector $\theta$ and is written as $\Omega = \Omega(\theta)$. The parameter vectors $\beta$ and $\theta$ are unrelated and can vary independently. If a reasonable consistent estimator $\hat{\theta}$ exists, it is natural to get an operational GLS estimator as

$$\hat{\beta} = \left(X'\hat{\Omega}^{-1}X\right)^{-1} X'\hat{\Omega}^{-1}y, \tag{5.7}$$

where $\hat{\Omega} = \Omega\left(\hat{\theta}\right)$. This estimator is well known to have the following limiting distribution

$$\sqrt{n}\left(\hat{\beta} - \beta\right) \sim N\left(0, \left(p\lim \frac{X'\Omega^{-1}X}{n}\right)^{-1}\right). \tag{5.8}$$

Further, the asymptotic variance of $\hat{\beta}$ is the same as the GLS $\bar{\beta}$ with known $\Omega$. Thus, the operational estimator is asymptotically efficient.

It will then be interesting to investigate how the asymptotic inference based on $\hat{\beta}$ differs from inference based on $b$ and $\bar{\beta}$ when $n$ is small or moderately large, but large relative to $p$ and $k$. For example, in the case where we have AR or moving average (MA) process, the number of parameters $p$ can be much smaller than $n$. We will take up these cases later after getting a general case of $\Omega(\hat{\theta})$.

First we note that the operational GLS estimator $\hat{\beta}$ is an unbiased estimator of $\beta$ when $\hat{\theta}$ is an even function of $u$ and $u$ follows a symmetric distribution. This is because, in this case

$$\hat{\beta} - \beta = \left( X'\hat{\Omega}^{-1} X \right)^{-1} X'\hat{\Omega}^{-1} u,$$

$$= \left( X'\Omega^{-1}\left(\hat{\theta}\right) X \right)^{-1} X'\Omega^{-1}\left(\hat{\theta}\right) u,$$

$$= H\left(\hat{u}\right) u, \tag{5.9}$$

where $H(\hat{u}) = (X'\Omega^{-1}(\hat{\theta})X)^{-1}X'\Omega^{-1}(\hat{\theta}) = H(u) = H(y)$ if $\hat{u}$ is a function of $u$ and hence $y$. If $\hat{\theta}$ is an even function of $\hat{u}$, $H(\hat{u}) = H(u)$ is an even function of a symmetric error $u$, then

$$E\left(\hat{\beta} - \beta\right) = E\left[H\left(u\right)u\right] = 0 \tag{5.10}$$

because $H(u)u$ is an odd function of symmetric error. Thus, $\hat{\beta}$ is exactly an unbiased estimator of $\beta$.

Now considering $u \sim N(0, \Omega)$, where $\Omega = \Omega(\theta)$, the ML estimator of $\beta$ and $\theta$ can be obtained by Maxlog $L(\theta, \beta)$ with respect to $\beta$ and $\theta$. This is

$$\log L\left(\theta, \beta\right) = -\frac{n}{2}\log 2\pi - \frac{1}{2}\log |\Omega| - \frac{1}{2}(y - X\beta)'\Omega^{-1}(y - X\beta), \tag{5.11}$$

which gives

$$\hat{\beta}^{\mathrm{ML}} = \left(X'\Omega^{-1}X\right)^{-1} X'\Omega^{-1} y,$$

$$-\frac{\partial}{\partial\theta}\log |\Omega| - (y - X\beta)'\left(\frac{\partial\Omega^{-1}(\theta)}{\partial\theta}\right)(y - X\beta) = 0. \tag{5.12}$$

Thus, $\hat{\theta}$ obtained from above clearly satisfies $\hat{\theta}$ to be an even function of $u$, $\hat{\theta}(-\hat{u}) = \hat{\theta}(\hat{u})$, where $\hat{u} = y - X\hat{\beta}^{\mathrm{ML}} = [I - X\left(X'\Omega^{-1}X\right)^{-1}X'\Omega^{-1}]u$. Thus, the ML estimator $\hat{\beta}^{\mathrm{ML}}$ is also unbiased whenever $E\hat{\beta}^{\mathrm{ML}}$ exists.

There is no explicit expression available for the variance of $\hat{\beta}$ for a general $\hat{\theta}$, even when $\hat{\theta}$ is an even function of $u$. However, it is interesting to note the following result.

If $\hat{\theta}$ is an even function of $u$ and does not depend on $\beta$, then $\hat{\beta} - \bar{\beta}$ is distributed symmetrically about the origin and independently of $\bar{\beta}$. Further,

$$V\left(\hat{\beta}\right) - V\left(\bar{\beta}\right) = \text{a positive definite matrix.} \tag{5.13}$$

This result follows by writing

$$\hat{\beta} - \beta = \bar{\beta} - \beta + \hat{\beta} - \bar{\beta},$$

$$= \left( X'\Omega^{-1}X \right)^{-1} X'\Omega^{-1}u + \left[ X'\Omega^{-1}\left(\hat{\theta}\right) X \right]^{-1} X'\Omega^{-1}\left(\hat{\theta}\right) M^* u,$$

$$= H_1 u + H_2 (u) u, \tag{5.14}$$

where $M^* = I - X[X'\Omega^{-1}(\theta)X]^{-1}X'\Omega^{-1}(\theta)$ is an idempotent matrix, and the definition of $H_1$ and $H_2$ is obvious. For given $\theta$, $\bar{\beta}$ is a complete sufficient statistic for $\beta$. Hence, both $\hat{\theta}$ and $\hat{\beta} - \bar{\beta}$ are distributed independently of $\bar{\beta}$ by Basu's Theorem (see Lehmann 1983: 46), which says that any statistic whose distribution does not depend on $\beta$ must be distributed independently of $\bar{\beta}$. Thus,

$$E\left(\hat{\beta} - \beta\right)\left(\hat{\beta} - \beta\right)' = E\left(\bar{\beta} - \beta\right)\left(\bar{\beta} - \beta\right)' + E\left(\hat{\beta} - \bar{\beta}\right)\left(\hat{\beta} - \bar{\beta}\right)' \tag{5.15}$$

or $V(\hat{\beta}) - V(\bar{\beta})$ = a positive definite matrix. Thus, the variance of $\hat{\beta}$ will be larger than its asymptotic variance.

Now we look at a sufficient condition for the existence of the second moment of a class of estimators:

$$\tilde{\beta} = H\left(\hat{u}\right) y, \tag{5.16}$$

where $H\left(\hat{u}\right)$ is such that $H(\hat{u})X = I$ and $H(\hat{u})$ is an even function. For $H\left(\hat{u}\right) = (X'\Omega^{-1}(\hat{\theta})X)^{-1}X'\Omega^{-1}(\hat{\theta})$, we have $\tilde{\beta} = \hat{\beta}$. If $H\left(\hat{u}\right)$ is continuous and scale invariant $(H\left(\hat{u}\right) = H\left(a\hat{u}\right), a > 0)$, then $H\left(\hat{u}\right) = H\left(\hat{u}/\hat{u}'\hat{u}\right)$ and $H\left(\hat{u}\right)$ is bounded by, say, $B_0$. This implies

$$E\tilde{\beta}'\tilde{\beta} = E\left[y'H\left(\hat{u}\right)'H\left(\hat{u}\right)y\right] \le B_0^2 Ey'y,$$

$$= B_0^2 \left[\beta'X'X\beta + \text{tr}\Omega\right] < \infty. \tag{5.17}$$

As noted above, while the operational GLS estimator is unbiased, its exact covariance matrix is not known except that it will be bigger than the covariance matrix of $\bar{\beta}$. The exact distribution of $\hat{\beta}$ is also not available. In view of this we now look at the approximate distribution of $\hat{\beta}$.

## 5.2.2  Approximate Distribution and Moments

First let us consider the approximate distributions of the vector $\hat{\beta}$ and the scalar $c'\hat{\beta}$, where $c$ is a $k \times 1$ vector of constants. Under the assumption of $u \sim N\left(0, \Omega\right)$, the standardized statistic:

$$Z_n = \sqrt{n}A^{1/2}\left(\bar{\beta} - \beta\right) \sim N\left(0, I\right), \quad A = \left(\frac{X'\Omega^{-1}X}{n}\right). \tag{5.18}$$

Further, if $Z_n^* = \sqrt{n}A^{1/2}(\hat{\beta} - \bar{\beta})$ converges in probability to zero, then as $n \longrightarrow \infty$

$$T_n = \sqrt{n}A^{1/2}\left(\hat{\beta} - \beta\right) \sim N\left(0, I\right). \tag{5.19}$$

For obtaining the Edgeworth expansion of $\hat{\beta}$, we write by using Taylor series expansion

$$\sqrt{n}\left(\hat{\beta} - \beta\right) = \left[\frac{1}{n}X'\Omega^{-1}\left(\hat{\theta}\right)X\right]^{-1}\frac{1}{\sqrt{n}}X'\Omega^{-1}\left(\hat{\theta}\right)u,$$

$$= \xi_0 + \xi_{-1/2} + \xi_{-1} + O_p\left(n^{-3/2}\right), \tag{5.20}$$

where

$$\xi_0 = \frac{1}{\sqrt{n}}A^{-1}X'\Omega^{-1}u, \qquad \xi_{-1/2} = \frac{1}{\sqrt{n}}\sum_j A^{-1}P_j u d_j, \tag{5.21}$$

$$\xi_{-1} = \frac{1}{n}\sum_i\sum_j A^{-1}P_{ij}u d_i d_j,$$

in which $d = \sqrt{n}(\hat{\theta} - \theta)$ and

$$P_j = \frac{1}{\sqrt{n}}\left(X'\Omega_j - A_j A^{-1}X'\Omega^{-1}\right), \tag{5.22}$$

$$P_{ij} = \frac{1}{\sqrt{n}}\left(X'\Omega_{ij} - 2A_i A^{-1}X'\Omega_j\right.$$

$$\left. + 2A_i A^{-1}A_j A^{-1}X'\Omega^{-1} - A_{ij}A^{-1}X'\Omega^{-1}\right),$$

$$\Omega_j = \partial\Omega^{-1}/\partial\theta_j, \quad \Omega_{ij} = \partial^2\Omega^{-1}\left(\theta\right)/\partial\theta_i\partial\theta_j,$$

$$A_j = X'\Omega_j X/n, \quad A_{ij} = X'\Omega_{ij}X/n.$$

We note that

$$P_j X = P_{ij}X = 0, \qquad P_i\Omega P_j' = Q_{ij}, \tag{5.23}$$

where

$$Q_{ij} = \frac{1}{n}X'\Omega_i\Omega\Omega_j X - A_i A^{-1}A_j. \tag{5.24}$$

The Edgeworth density function of $T_n = \sqrt{n}A^{1/2}(\hat{\beta} - \beta)$, up to $O\left(n^{-1}\right)$, is then obtained by following the technique in Chapter 3, also see Rothenberg (1984b). This is

$$f\left(t\right) = \phi\left(t\right)\left[1 - \frac{1}{2n}\text{tr}\left(A^{-1/2}\left(\sum_i\sum_j Q_{ij}\lambda_{ij}\right)A^{-1/2}\left(I_K - tt'\right)\right)\right], \tag{5.25}$$

where $\phi(t)$ is the standard normal density and $\lambda_{ij}$ is the $i, j$th element of $\wedge$ which is the asymptotic covariance of a consistent estimator $\hat{\theta}$ such that $d = \sqrt{n}(\hat{\theta} - \theta) \sim N(0, \wedge)$. Further, the distribution, up to $O(n^{-1})$, is a normal distribution:

$$F(t) = P\left[V^{-1/2}T_n\right] = P\left[\sqrt{n}V^{-1/2}A^{1/2}\left(\hat{\beta} - \beta\right)\right] = \Phi(t), \qquad (5.26)$$

where $\Phi(t)$ is the cumulative distribution of a standard normal variable and

$$V = I_k + \frac{1}{n}A^{-1/2}\left(\sum_i^p \sum_j^p Q_{ij}\lambda_{ij}\right)A^{-1/2} \qquad (5.27)$$

is the covariance matrix of $\sqrt{n}A^{1/2}(\hat{\beta} - \beta) = T_n$.

The bias vector, up to $O(n^{-1})$, and mean square error (MSE) matrix of $\hat{\beta}$, to $O(n^{-2})$, is

$$E\left(\hat{\beta} - \beta\right) = 0, \qquad (5.28)$$

$$E\left(\hat{\beta} - \beta\right)\left(\hat{\beta} - \beta\right)' = \frac{1}{n}A^{-1/2}VA^{-1/2}.$$

The approximate distributions of the scalar $c'\hat{\beta}$ follow from the above results. In this case, up to $O(n^{-1})$,

$$P\left[\frac{c'\left(\hat{\beta} - \beta\right)}{\sigma_n} \leq t\right] = \Phi(t), \qquad (5.29)$$

where $\sigma_n^2 = c'A^{-1/2}VA^{-1/2}c/n = c'\left(X'\Omega^{-1}X\right)^{-1}c\,[1 + (\text{tr}\,\wedge B)/n]$, up to $O(n^{-2})$, where $B$ is a $p \times p$ matrix of

$$b_{ij} = \frac{c'\left(X'\Omega^{-1}X\right)^{-1}X'\Omega_i M^*\Omega^{-1}M^{*'}\Omega_j X\left(X'\Omega^{-1}X\right)^{-1}c}{c'\left(X'\Omega^{-1}X\right)^{-1}c}. \qquad (5.30)$$

Also, the bias to $O(n^{-1})$ and variance to $O(n^{-2})$ are

$$Ec'\left(\hat{\beta} - \beta\right) = 0,$$

$$V\left(c'\left(\hat{\beta} - \beta\right)\right) = c'\left(X'\Omega^{-1}X\right)^{-1}c\left[1 + \text{tr}\,\frac{\wedge B}{n}\right]. \qquad (5.31)$$

The above distribution can be extended up to $O(n^{-3/2})$. This is given by

$$P\left[\frac{c'\left(\hat{\beta} - \beta\right)}{\sigma_n} \leq t\right] = \Phi\left(t - \frac{t^2 - 3t}{24n^2}a_n\right), \qquad (5.32)$$

where

$$\sigma_n^2 = c' \left(X'\Omega^{-1}X\right)^{-1} c \left[1 + \text{tr}\, \frac{V(A_n)}{n}\right],$$

$$= \left(X'\Omega^{-1}X\right)^{-1} c \left[1 + \frac{\text{tr}(\wedge B)}{n} + O\left(\frac{1}{n^2}\right)\right] \tag{5.33}$$

and $a_n$ is the fourth cumulant of $A_n$ given by

$$a_n = 6\text{tr}\,(\wedge B \wedge B) + O(1/n); \tag{5.34}$$

the element $A_n$ appears in the following expansion:

$$Z_n^* = \frac{c'\left(\hat{\beta} - \bar{\beta}\right)}{\sqrt{c'\left(X'\Omega^{-1}X\right)^{-1}c}} = \frac{\sqrt{n}c'\left(\hat{\beta} - \bar{\beta}\right)}{\sqrt{c'A^{-1}c}}, \tag{5.35}$$

$$= \frac{A_n}{\sqrt{n}} + \frac{R_n}{n^2\sqrt{n}},$$

where

$$A_n = \sum_j c'A^{-1}P_j ud_j / \sqrt{c'A^{-1}c} = \sqrt{n}c'\xi_{-1/2}/\sqrt{c'A^{-1}c}$$

and $R_n$ is stochastically bounded with $P[|R_n| > (\log n)^\ell] = o\left(n^{-2}\right)$ for some $\ell$, see Rothenberg (1984b).

To use the above distribution of $c'(\hat{\beta} - \beta)$ we need to have the $O\left(n^{-2}\right)$ term in $\sigma_n^2$. But this is usually difficult to obtain except for the cases where we know the specific forms of $\hat{\theta}$. In practice, therefore, it is easier to use the simple normal approximation up to $O(n^{-1})$ in (5.29).

We summarize the results discussed above. First the error introduced by using the estimated covariance matrix has no effect on the limiting distribution of regression estimators and test statistics, but only modifies second- and higher-order terms in the asymptotic expansions of their distribution functions. In fact, the effect is small even to second order in the sense that there is no effect on the approximate distribution of $\hat{\beta}$, which is still normal, except that estimating covariance matrix increases the variance. These results hold under the fact that $\hat{\theta}$ based on the LS regression residuals $\hat{u}$ are distributed independently of $\bar{\beta}$. However, when the errors are nonnormal, this independence does not necessarily hold. Cavanagh and Rothenberg (1983) show that the results under normality go through for nonnormal cases under the weaker condition that $\hat{\theta}$ are asymptotically uncorrelated with $\hat{\beta}$. This is usually not satisfied in the models with heteroskedasticity, but hold in time series models. Thus, even under nonnormality, the shape of the distribution of $\hat{\beta}$ will be similar to that of $\bar{\beta}$, but they may not be normal.

## 5.2.3   Hypothesis Testing

Now we consider the problem of testing that $\beta$ satisfies the $q$ linear restrictions

$$H_0: R\beta = r,$$
$$H_1: R\beta \neq r, \tag{5.36}$$

where $R$ is a $q \times k$ matrix of constants of rank $q$ and $r$ is a $q \times 1$ vector of constants. Under the assumption of normality of the errors, the log likelihood function is

$$\log L\,(\beta, \theta) = -\frac{n}{2}\log(2\pi) - \frac{1}{2}\log|\Omega| - \frac{1}{2}(y - X\beta)'\Omega^{-1}(y - X\beta). \tag{5.37}$$

Let $(\hat{\beta}, \hat{\theta})$ be the unconstrained ML estimates under $H_1$ and let $(\tilde{\beta}, \tilde{\theta})$ be the constrained ML estimators under $H_0$. Then, $\hat{\beta} = (X'\hat{\Omega}^{-1}X)^{-1}X'\hat{\Omega}^{-1}y$, where $\hat{\Omega} = \Omega(\hat{\theta})$ is as before and

$$\tilde{\beta} = \left(X'\tilde{\Omega}^{-1}X\right)^{-1}X'\tilde{\Omega}^{-1}y - \left(X'\tilde{\Omega}^{-1}X\right)^{-1}$$
$$\times R'\left[R\left(X'\tilde{\Omega}^{-1}X\right)^{-1}R'\right]^{-1}\left[R\left(X'\tilde{\Omega}^{-1}X\right)^{-1}X'\tilde{\Omega}^{-1}y - r\right], \tag{5.38}$$

where $\tilde{\Omega} = \Omega(\tilde{\theta})$.

The Wald ($W$), Rao Score (RS), and the likelihood ratio (LR) test statistics are given as

$$W = \left(R\hat{\beta} - r\right)'\left[R\left(X'\hat{\Omega}^{-1}X\right)^{-1}R'\right]^{-1}\left(R\hat{\beta} - r\right),$$

$$\mathrm{RS} = \left(R\tilde{\beta}_0 - r\right)'\left[R\left(X'\tilde{\Omega}^{-1}X\right)^{-1}R'\right]^{-1}\left(R\tilde{\beta}_0 - r\right), \tag{5.39}$$

$$\mathrm{LR} = -2\left[\log L\left(\tilde{\beta}, \hat{\theta}\right) - \log L\left(\hat{\beta}, \hat{\theta}\right)\right],$$

where $\tilde{\beta}_0 = (X'\tilde{\Omega}^{-1}X)^{-1}X'\tilde{\Omega}^{-1}y$.

Under suitable regularity conditions, it is well known that each of these statistics is asymptotically $\chi^2$ with $q$ degrees of freedom (d.f.) under the null hypothesis. Let $z_\alpha$ be the initial point corresponding to the upper $\alpha$-percentage point of a $\chi^2_q$ distribution. Then the asymptotic tests W, RS, and LR reject the null hypothesis if $W > z_\alpha, RS > z_\alpha$, and $\mathrm{LR} > z_\alpha$, provided $n$ goes to infinity. But for small or moderately large samples, the probabilities of rejections (critical regions) may not be $\alpha$-percentage for any of these tests. Therefore, as in Chapter 4, we need to look at the Edgeworth-type expansions for the probability distributions of each of these tests which can provide their accurate critical regions. We can then also compare the approximate local power functions of three size-corrected tests.

The Edgeworth expansion of the distributions of W, RS, and LR can be obtained by first obtaining the approximate characteristic function (moment generating function) and then using the inversion theorem (Chapter 3 and Rothenberg (1984c)). This gives, up to $O(1/n)$,

$$
\begin{aligned}
P(W > z) = F(z) + \frac{1}{2n} \Big[ & (a + b - 2\delta' B_1 \delta) f_2(z) \\
& + (c + 2\delta'(B_1 + D - C)) \, \delta f_4(z) \\
& + \left( 2\delta' c\delta - \frac{1}{2}\Delta \right) f_6(z) + \frac{1}{2}\Delta f_8(z) \Big],
\end{aligned}
\tag{5.40}
$$

$$
\begin{aligned}
P(\mathrm{LR} > z) = F(z) + \frac{1}{2n} \Big[ & (a - 2\delta' B_1 \delta) f_2(z) + 2\delta'(D - C)\,\delta f_4(z) \\
& - \frac{1}{2}\Delta f_6(z) \Big],
\end{aligned}
$$

$$
\begin{aligned}
P(\mathrm{RS} > z) = F(z) + \frac{1}{2n} \Big[ & (a - b - 2\delta' B_1 \delta) f_2(z) \\
& - (c + 2\delta'(B_1 + C - D)\,\delta) f_4(z) \\
& - \left( 2\delta' c\delta + \frac{1}{2}\Delta \right) f_6(z) - \frac{1}{2}\Delta f_8(z) \Big],
\end{aligned}
$$

where $F(z) = P(\chi_q^2(\delta'\delta) > z)$, $\chi_q^2(\delta'\delta)$ is a noncentral $\chi^2$ with the noncentrality parameter $\delta'\delta$, $\delta = [R(X'\Omega^{-1}X)^{-1}R']^{-1/2}(R\beta - r)$, $a = \mathrm{tr}\,(2D - C)$, $b = 2\mathrm{tr}\,B_1$, $c = \mathrm{tr}\,C$, $f_r(z)$ is the noncentral $\chi^2$ with $q + r$ d.f., and

$$
B_1 = \sum_i \sum_j \lambda_{ij} P'\Omega_i \left[ \Omega - X\left(X'\Omega^{-1}X\right)^{-1} X' \right] \Omega_j,
\tag{5.41}
$$

$$
C = \sum_i \sum_j \lambda_{ij} \left( C_i C_j + \frac{1}{2} C_i \mathrm{tr} C_j \right),
$$

$$
D = \sum_i C_i \mu_i + \sum_i \sum_j \lambda_{ij} \left( C_i C_j + \frac{1}{2} D_{ij} \right),
$$

$$
\Delta = \sum_i \sum_j \lambda_{ij} \frac{\delta' C_i \delta}{(\delta'\delta)^2} \delta' C_j \delta,
$$

$$
P = X\left(X'\Omega^{-1}X\right)^{-1} R' \left[ R\left(X'\Omega^{-1}X\right)^{-1} R' \right]^{-1/2},
$$

$$
C_i = P'\Omega_i P,
$$

$$
D_{ij} = P'[\Omega_{ij} - \Omega_i X\left(X'\Omega^{-1}X\right)^{-1} X'\Omega_j - \Omega_j X\left(X'\Omega^{-1}X\right)^{-1} X'\Omega_i]P.
$$

Further, $\wedge = ((\lambda_{ij}))$, $\Omega_i$ and $\Omega_{ij}$ are given above, and as before $d = \sqrt{n}(\hat{\theta} - \theta) \sim N(0, \wedge)$ as $n \longrightarrow \infty$, where

$$\wedge^{-1} = ((\lambda^{ij})) = \left[ \lim \frac{1}{2n} \text{tr} \ \Omega^{-1}\Omega_i\Omega^{-1}\Omega_j \right]. \tag{5.42}$$

Under $H_0$ we have $\delta = 0$, which gives the Edgeworth-corrected critical values, up to $O\left(n^{-1}\right)$, for the three tests as

$$z_{\text{LR}} = z_\alpha \left( 1 + \frac{\hat{a}}{2qn} \right),$$

$$z_{\text{W}} = z_\alpha \left( 1 + \frac{(q+2)\left(\hat{a} + \hat{b}\right) + \hat{c}z_\alpha}{2q(q+2)n} \right), \tag{5.43}$$

$$z_{\text{RS}} = z_\alpha \left( 1 + \frac{(q+2)\left(\hat{a} - \hat{b}\right) - \hat{c}z_\alpha}{2q(q+2)n} \right),$$

where $\hat{a} = \text{tr}(2\hat{D} - \hat{c})$, $\hat{b} = 2\text{tr} \ \hat{B}$, $\hat{c} = \text{tr} \ \hat{C}$ and we use $zf(z) = qf_2(z) + \delta'\delta f_4(z)$. This gives, under $H_0$, the critical region LR $> z_{\text{LR}}$, W $> z_{\text{W}}$, and RS $> z_{\text{RS}}$ of size $\alpha$ upto a second order of approximation.

Under the local alternatives, the approximate power function of the size-adjusted LR, W and RS statistics can be written as

$$P(\text{LR} > z_{\text{LR}}) \simeq F(z_\alpha) - \frac{\delta'\delta}{n} \left[ \gamma_1 f_2(z_\alpha) + \gamma_2 f_4(z_\alpha) + \gamma_3\delta'\delta f_6(z_\alpha) \right], \tag{5.44}$$

$$P(W > z_{\text{W}}) \simeq P(\text{LR} > z_{\text{LR}}) - \xi,$$

$$P(\text{RS} > z_{\text{RS}}) \simeq P(\text{LR} > z_{\text{LR}}) + \xi,$$

where

$$\xi = \frac{\delta'\delta}{n} \left( w_1 f_4(z_\alpha) + w_2 f_6(z_\alpha) + w_3\delta'\delta f_8(z_\alpha) \right), \tag{5.45}$$

$$w_1 = \frac{\text{tr} \ B_1}{q} - \frac{\delta' B_1 \delta}{\delta'\delta}, \qquad w_2 = \frac{\text{tr} \ C}{q} - \frac{\delta' C \delta}{\delta'\delta}, \qquad w_3 = \frac{\text{tr} \ C}{2q(q+2)} - \frac{\Delta}{4}.$$

When $q = 1$, $w_1$ to $w_3$ are zero and so these three tests have the same approximate power function. When $q > 1$, even after correcting for the size, the tests do not have the same power function. There exists a possibility of conflicting results, partly due to the fact that three tests are not functions of each other. For example, $\text{LR} = (W + \text{RS})/2 + O_p\left(n^{-1}\right)$ (see Rothenberg 1984$c$). Thus, while the conflicting results based on the asymptotic test can be avoided by doing size adjusted tests for small samples in the regression with scalar covariance matrix (Chapter 4), this is not the case in the nonscalar covariance matrix case. This is because in the scalar covariance matrix case, the tests are monotonic functions of $F$ statistic.

The Edgeworth expansions of the test statistics above are based on some regularity conditions (Rothenberg 1984$c$). These are

$A_1'$: The matrices $X'\Omega_i X/n$, $X'\Omega_{ij}X/n$, and $X'\Omega_i\Omega\Omega_j X/n$ tend to a finite limit, and $X'\Omega^{-1}X/n$ tends to a positive definite matrix as $n \longrightarrow \infty$.

$A_2'$: The matrices $X'(\hat{\Omega}^{-1} - \Omega^{-1})X/n$, $X'(\hat{\Omega}_i - \Omega_i)X/n$, $X'(\hat{\Omega}^{-1} - \Omega^{-1})u/\sqrt{n}$, $X'(\hat{\Omega}_i - \Omega_i)u/\sqrt{n}$ converge to zero in probability. The same applies if $\hat{\Omega}$ is replaced by $\tilde{\Omega}$.

$A_3'$: The matrix $\partial^2 \log L/\partial\theta_i\partial\theta_j$, evaluated at the true parameter value and at the constrained and unconstrained parameter estimators, converges to $-\wedge^{-1}$.

$A_4'$: The third partial derivatives of $\log L$, evaluated at the true values and estimated values, converge to constants in probability.

In addition, the derivatives up to the third order of $\Omega^{-1}$ with $\theta$ are assumed to hold. Further, the derivatives of the average $\log L$ should behave well as $n \longrightarrow \infty$.

## 5.3 Specialized Models

### 5.3.1 Heteroskedasticity

When the regression disturbances have variances which are not constant across observations, the disturbances are said to have the problem of conditional heteroskedasticity. It arises both in the time series and cross-sections data. In this case, for $i = 1, \ldots, n$,

$$V\left(u_i \mid x_i\right) = \sigma_i^2, \tag{5.46}$$

which gives the conditional covariance matrix as

$$Euu' = \Omega = \begin{bmatrix} \sigma_1^2 & 0 & \cdots & 0 \\ 0 & \sigma_2^2 & & \vdots \\ \vdots & & \ddots & \vdots \\ 0 & 0 & \cdots & \sigma_n^2 \end{bmatrix}. \tag{5.47}$$

If we do not have any a priori assumption about $\sigma_i^2$, then it is the heteroskedasticity of unknown form. On the other hand, in many applications, $\sigma_i^2$ is assumed to be a parametric function of $x_i$ or some other variable not in the regression model (5.1) with regressors $x$. For example, in many studies on household consumptions, the variance across household consumption expenditure is assumed to increase as income increases. This is formulated as

$$\sigma_i^2 = \sigma^2 x_i, \tag{5.48}$$

where $x_i$ is the income variable. If this parametric form is not consistent with the data, then this misspecification may affect the statistical quality of econometric analysis. A solution to this problem is to use the nonparametric method to determine the data-based specification, see Pagan and Ullah (1999, chapter 5). Another example of parametrically specified heteroskedasticity is the autoregressive conditional heteroskedastic (ARCH) model or generalized ARCH (GARCH) often observed in the time series data on exchange rate, inflation, and stock return; see Engle (1982) and Bollerslev (1986). In this case,

$$u_i = \epsilon_i \sqrt{\alpha_0 + \alpha_1 u_{i-1}^2}, \tag{5.49}$$

where $\epsilon_i$ has a distribution with zero mean and unit variance. We assume that $\text{Cov}(x_i, u_j) = 0$, for all $i$ and $j = 1, \ldots, n$ so the model (5.1) is still a classical regression model with $E(u_i \mid u_{i-1}) = Eu_i = 0$. But,

$$\sigma_i^2 = V(u_i \mid u_{i-1}) = E(u_i^2 \mid u_{i-1}) = \alpha_0 + \alpha_1 u_{i-1}^2. \tag{5.50}$$

Therefore, conditional on $u_{i-1}$, $u_i$ is heteroskedastic. The unconditional variance, however, is

$$V(u_i) = E[V(u_i \mid u_{i-1})] = \alpha_0 + \alpha_1 V(u_{i-1}) = \frac{\alpha_0}{1 - \alpha_1} \tag{5.51}$$

by assuming that the unconditional variance does not change over time. For examples of heteroskedasticity due to varying regression parameters, see Raj and Ullah (1981).

Let us consider the estimation of $\beta$. The LS estimator is $b = (X'X)^{-1} X'y$ and the variance of $b$ is $V(b) = (X'X)^{-1} X'\Omega X (X'X)^{-1}$. The usual formula $\sigma^2 (X'X)^{-1}$ is not the correct variance if $\Omega \neq \sigma^2 I$. We note that, for $\Omega^* = \Omega/\sigma^2$,

$$\Delta = \sigma^2 (X'X)^{-1} - \sigma^2 (X'X)^{-1} X'\Omega^* X (X'X)^{-1},$$
$$= \sigma^2 (X'X)^{-1} X' (I - \Omega^*) X (X'X)^{-1} \tag{5.52}$$

is a positive semidefinite matrix if $I - \Omega^*$ is a positive definite matrix. This will depend upon the eigenvalues of $I - \Omega^*$. Thus, the standard error based on $\sigma^2 (X'X)^{-1}$ can be an underestimate or overestimate of the true covariance matrix.

To estimate the $V(b)$, we need to estimate $\Omega$ which involves estimating $n$ unknown parameters along with $k$ parameters in $\beta$ based on $n$ observations. Estimating $n + k$ parameters with $n$ observation is a difficult task. Instead, we observe that

$$\frac{1}{n} X'\Omega X = \frac{1}{n} \sum_1^n x_i{'} x_i \sigma_i^2 = E\left[\frac{1}{n} \sum_1^n x_i{'} x_i u_i^2\right], \tag{5.53}$$

where $x_i$ is a row vector of $k$ regressors. Thus, a consistent estimator of $X'\Omega X/n$ is

$$\frac{1}{n} \sum_1^n x_i{'} x_i \hat{u}_i^2 = \frac{X'\hat{\Omega}X}{n}, \tag{5.54}$$

where $\hat{u}_i = y_i - x_i b$ is the LS residual; see White (1980). Thus, while the estimator $\hat{\Omega}$, where $\hat{\sigma}_i^2 = \hat{u}_i^2$, is not a consistent estimator of $\Omega$, it still helps to obtain a consistent estimator of $X'\Omega X/n$ by $X'\hat{\Omega}X/n$. The estimated standard error of $b$ can then be calculated by

$$\hat{V}(b) = (X'X)^{-1} X'\hat{\Omega}X (X'X)^{-1} = \frac{1}{n} \left(\frac{X'X}{n}\right)^{-1} \frac{X'\hat{\Omega}X}{n} \left(\frac{X'X}{n}\right)^{-1}. \tag{5.55}$$

In general, if the heteroskedasticity $(u_i^2)$ is not correlated with the variables $x_i (x_i^2)$ in the model, then at least in large samples, the $V(b) = \sigma^2 (X'X)^{-1}$ may not be misleading. But if $u_i^2$ is correlated with $x_i^2$, then it will be useful to use the correct $V(b)$ given above.

Now we consider the properties of the estimated $V(b)$. Taking expectations, we have

$$E\left(\hat{V}(b)\right) = (X'X)^{-1} X' \left(E\hat{\Omega}\right) X (X'X)^{-1}, \tag{5.56}$$

where $E(\hat{\Omega})$ can be obtained by obtaining $E\hat{u}_i^2$. This can be evaluated by writing

$$\hat{u} = Mu, \quad M = \begin{bmatrix} m_1 \\ \vdots \\ m_n \end{bmatrix} \tag{5.57}$$

so that

$$\hat{u}_i = m_i u, \tag{5.58}$$

where $m_i$ is a $1 \times n$ $i$th vector of $M$. Then,

$$E\hat{u}\hat{u}' = M\Omega M, \tag{5.59}$$

and collecting the diagonal elements on both sides

$$E\left(\hat{u}\right) = \dot{M}\,\sigma, \tag{5.60}$$

where $\sigma = \left(\sigma_1^2, \ldots, \sigma_n^2\right)'$, $\hat{u} = \left(\hat{u}_1^2, \ldots, \hat{u}_n^2\right)' = \hat{u} * \hat{u}$, and $\dot{M}$ is a matrix of the squared elements of $M$ so that

$$\dot{M} = \begin{bmatrix} \dot{m}_1 \\ \vdots \\ \dot{m}_n \end{bmatrix} = \begin{bmatrix} m_{11}^2 & \cdots & m_{1n}^2 \\ \vdots & & \vdots \\ m_{n1}^2 & \cdots & m_{nn}^2 \end{bmatrix} = M * M, \tag{5.61}$$

where $*$ is the Hadamard product. Thus, $E\hat{u}_i^2 = \dot{m}_i\,\sigma$. Alternatively, $E\hat{u}_i^2 = E\left(m_i u\right)^2 = m_i \Omega m_i' = \sum_j m_{ij}^2 \sigma_j^2 = \dot{m}_i\,\sigma$. Further,

$$E\left(\hat{V}\left(b\right)\right) - V\left(b\right) = \left(X'X\right)^{-1} X'\Omega_0 X \left(X'X\right)^{-1}, \tag{5.62}$$

where

$$\Omega_0 = \begin{pmatrix} \left(\dot{m}_1 - \iota_1\right)\sigma & \cdots & 0 \\ \vdots & \ddots & \vdots \\ 0 & \cdots & \left(\dot{m}_n - \iota_n\right)\sigma \end{pmatrix}, \tag{5.63}$$

where $\iota_i$ is a $1 \times n$ vector with unity at the $i$th place and $n-1$ zeros elsewhere. Since

$$M = I - H, \quad H = X\left(X'X\right)^{-1} X' = \left(\left(h_{ij}\right)\right) = O\left(\frac{1}{n}\right), \tag{5.64}$$

we can see that

$$\left(\dot{m}_i - \iota_i\right)\sigma = -2h_{ij}\sigma_i^2 + \sum_{j=1}^{n} \sigma_j^2 h_{ij}^2,$$

$$= -2h_{ij}\sigma_i^2 + \dot{h}_j\,\sigma \tag{5.65}$$

and

$$\Omega_0 = -2H * \Omega + \dot{D}, \tag{5.66}$$

where $\dot{D}$ is the diagonal matrix $\left(\dot{h}_1\,\sigma, \ldots, \dot{h}_n\,\sigma\right)$. Although $H$ is idempotent and $0 \le h_{ij} \le 1$, the matrix $\Omega_0$ can be positive semidefinite or negative semidefinite. Thus, $\hat{V}(b)$ can be an under- or overestimate of $V(b)$.

An alternative estimator of $\sigma$ can be obtained by writing

$$\hat{u} = \dot{M}\,\sigma + \eta, \tag{5.67}$$

where $\eta = \hat{u} - E\hat{u}$. Thus, the LS estimator of $\sigma$ is

$$\tilde{\sigma} = \left(\dot{M}\,'\,\dot{M}\right)^{-1} \dot{M}\,'\hat{u} = \left(\dot{M}\right)^{-1}\hat{u}, \tag{5.68}$$

which is Rao's (1970) minimum norm quadratic unbiased estimator (MINQUE) of $\sigma$, $E\tilde{\sigma} = \sigma$. This estimator is defined when $\dot{M}$ is nonsingular (see Mallela 1972) for these conditions. Alternatively, if $\dot{M}$ is singular we can write $\tilde{\sigma} = \dot{M}^{+}\hat{u}$ where $\dot{M}^{+}$ is a generalized inverse of $\dot{M}$. Again $\tilde{\sigma}$ is not a consistent estimator of $\sigma$ but $X'\Omega X/n$ can be consistently estimated by $X'\tilde{\Omega}X/n$.

Notice that $M = I - H = I + O(1/n)$. Thus, for large $n$, $M \simeq I$ and hence $\dot{M} \simeq I$. In this case, $\tilde{\sigma}$ reduces to $\hat{u} = \hat{\sigma}$ and $X'\tilde{\Omega}X/n$ reduces to $X'\hat{\Omega}X/n$.

An advantage of using $X'\tilde{\Omega}X/n$ is that it provides

$$\tilde{V}(b) = (X'X)^{-1}X'\tilde{\Omega}X(X'X)^{-1}, \tag{5.69}$$

which is unbiased, that is

$$E\left(\tilde{V}(b)\right) - V(b) = 0. \tag{5.70}$$

Now we look into the efficient estimation of $\beta$. For known heteroskedasticity $\Omega$, the GLS estimator $\bar{\beta}$ is BLUE. For unknown $\Omega$, the operational GLS can be used for the parametrically specified heteroskedasticity given above; see other specifications in Johnston and DiNardo (1997). One can also determine $\sigma_i^2 = \sigma^2(z_i)$ by nonparametric kernel estimators, where the vector $z_i$ can also include $x_i$. This is given by

$$\hat{\sigma}_i^2 = \hat{\sigma}^2(z_i) = \frac{\sum_{j=1}^{n} \hat{u}_j^2 K((z_j - z_i)/h)}{\sum_{j=1}^{n} K((z_j - z_i)/h)}, \tag{5.71}$$

where $K$ is the weight (kernel) and $h$ is the window width around the point $z_i$. Essentially $\hat{\sigma}^2(z_i)$ is an estimator of $E(u_i^2 \mid z_i)$ by data points which are in the interval $h$ around $z_i$. The kernel $K$ is chosen so that it gives low weight to the data on $z$ which are far away from $z_i$ and high weight to the data which are close to $z_i$. Using this nonparametric estimator of $\sigma^2(z_i)$, we can get the operational or feasible GLS estimator $\hat{\beta}$, which is known as the semiparametric GLS estimator, see Pagan and Ullah (1999, chapter 5). This estimator is useful in practice since obtaining the operational GLS estimator is not available when $\sigma_i^2$ is unknown. This is because while $X'\hat{\Omega}X/n$ is a consistent estimator of $X'\Omega X/n$, the estimator $X'\hat{\Omega}^{-1}X/n$ is not a consistent estimator of $X'\Omega^{-1}X/n$.

Since $\hat{\sigma}^2(z_i)$ is an even function of $\hat{u}$ or $u$, the semiparametric GLS estimator, conditional on $x$ and $z$, is unbiased, see Section 5.2.1. Also see Linton (1992, 1996) for Edgeworth expansions.

Now we turn to the time series regression model with the ARCH errors. In this case, the estimation of the parameters $\beta$, $\alpha_0$, $\alpha_1$ are done by the ML estimation. The log likelihood function is

$$\log L = -\frac{n}{2} \log(2\pi) - \frac{1}{2} \sum_{2}^{n} \log \left(\alpha_0 + \alpha_1 u_{i-1}^2\right) - \frac{1}{2} \sum_{2}^{n} \frac{u_i^2}{\alpha_0 + \alpha_1 u_{i-1}^2}, \qquad (5.72)$$

where $u_i = y_i - x_i\beta$. The score function is

$$S(\theta) = \frac{\partial \log L}{\partial \theta} = 0, \qquad ES(\theta) = 0, \qquad (5.73)$$

where $\theta = (\beta', \alpha_0, \alpha_1)'$. The iterative ML estimation is obtained by using

$$\hat{\theta} = \theta_0 - [H(\theta_0)]^{-1} S(\theta_0), \qquad (5.74)$$

where $H()$ is the Hessian matrix of $\log L$, also see Engle (1982) for a simpler four-step procedure. The finite sample bias, up to $O(n^{-1})$, and MSE, up to $O(n^{-2})$, of this follows from the results in Chapter 2. This follows by noting that the estimator of $\theta$ is a solution from $ES(\theta) = 0$; also see Bao and Ullah (2002), and Iglesias and Phillips (2001).

## 5.3.2   Heteroskedasticity Testing

Let us now consider a test statistic for testing heteroskedasticity, $V(u_i) = \sigma_i^2 = h(z_i\alpha)$, where the first element of $1 \times q$ vector $z_i$ is unity and $\alpha = (\alpha_1, \alpha_2, \dots, \alpha_q)'$. Thus, testing for heteroskedasticity implies testing for

$$H_0\colon \alpha_2 = \alpha_3 \cdots = \alpha_q = 0. \qquad (5.75)$$

The test statistic is half of the regression sum of squares in the regression of $n\hat{u}_i^2/\hat{u}'\hat{u}$ on $z_i$, which is

$$Q = \frac{n^2}{2} \frac{\hat{u}'PZ(Z'PZ)^{-1} Z'P\hat{u}}{(\hat{u}'\hat{u})^2}, \qquad P = I - \frac{1}{n}\iota\iota' \qquad (5.76)$$

and it follows $x_{q-1}^2$ as $n \longrightarrow \infty$; $\iota$ is an $n \times 1$ vector of unit elements. Our aim is to see the effect on the null distribution of $Q$ under nonnormality of $u$ in the regression $y = X\beta + u$.

Under $H_0$, $u \sim (0, \sigma^2)$, where $\sigma^2 = h(\alpha_1)$. Also,

$$\frac{\hat{u}'\hat{u}}{n} = \sigma^2 + \left(\frac{1}{n}u'u - \sigma^2\right) - \frac{1}{n}u'X(X'X)^{-1} X'u, \qquad (5.77)$$

$$= \xi_0 + \xi_{-1/2} + \xi_{-1}.$$

Thus, one can write
$$Q = Q_0 + Q_{-1/2} + Q_{-1}, \tag{5.78}$$

where

$$Q_0 = \frac{1}{2\sigma^4} \hat{u}' P_0 \hat{u}, \quad P_0 = PZ (Z'PZ)^{-1} Z'P, \tag{5.79}$$

$$Q_{-1/2} = -\frac{1}{\sigma^4} \hat{u}' P_0 \hat{u} \left( \frac{1}{n\sigma^2} u'u - 1 \right),$$

$$Q_{-1} = \frac{1}{2\sigma^4} \hat{u}' P_0 \hat{u} \left( \frac{2}{n\sigma^2} u'X (X'X)^{-1} X'u + 3 \left( \frac{1}{n\sigma^2} u'u - 1 \right)^2 \right).$$

Under nonnormality, from Section A.6 in the Appendix,

$$E \left( \hat{u}' P_0 \hat{u} \right) = \sigma^4 \left[ \gamma_2 \mathrm{tr} P_0 \dot{M}^2 + 2\mathrm{tr}\, P_0\, \dot{M} + \iota'\, \dot{M}\, P_0 \dot{M}\, \iota \right], \tag{5.80}$$

where $\gamma_2$ represents excess in kurtosis (kurtosis $-3$). When, for large $n$, $\dot{M} \simeq I$ we get

$$E \left( \hat{u}' P_0 \hat{u} \right) \simeq \sigma^4 (\gamma_2 + 2) \mathrm{tr}\, P_0 = \sigma^4 (\gamma_2 + 2) (q - 1). \tag{5.81}$$

Thus,

$$E (Q_0) \simeq \frac{\gamma_2 + 2}{2} (q - 1). \tag{5.82}$$

Under normality, $\gamma_2 = 0$ and $EQ_0 = q - 1$. This is consistent with the asymptotic distribution result that $Q$, under $H_0$, is a $\chi^2$ with $q - 1$ d.f. Under nonnormality, the $Q$ test will be biased by the term $(\gamma_2 + 2)/2$. A modified robust test statistic of heteroskedasticity should be adjusted for this bias and it is given by

$$Q^* = \frac{2}{(\gamma_2 + 2)} Q, \tag{5.83}$$

which is asymptotically distributed as a $\chi^2$ at $q - 1$ d.f. (see Koenker 1981). For the hypothesis testing work related to grouped heteroskedasticity, see Sharma and Giaccotto (1991) and Bekker (2002).

## 5.3.3   Model with Autocorrelation

Consider the regression model (5.1) where the errors are a stationary AR(1) process:

$$u_i = \rho u_{i-1} + \epsilon_i, \quad |\rho| < 1, \tag{5.84}$$

where $\epsilon_i$ is independent identically distributed (i.i.d.) $\sim N (0, \sigma_\epsilon^2)$. Thus, $u \sim N (0, \sigma^2 \Omega)$, where $\sigma^2 = \sigma_\epsilon^2 / (1 - \rho^2)$ and $\Omega = \Omega (\rho) = ((w_{ij}))$, where $w_{ij} = \rho^{j-i}$ for $j \geq i$.

The estimator of $\rho$ is

$$\hat{\rho} = \frac{\sum_1^{n-1} \hat{u}_i \hat{u}_{i+1}}{\sum_1^n \hat{u}_i^2}, \tag{5.85}$$

where $\hat{u}_i$ are the LS residuals. There are other estimators of $\rho$ such as by Theil (1971) as $[(n-k)/(n-1)]\hat{\rho}$ and Durbin–Watson (DW) as $1 - \frac{1}{2}d$, where $d = \sum_2^n (\hat{u}_i - \hat{u}_{i-1})^2 / \sum_1^n \hat{u}_i^2$. But these do not change the approximate results given below.

The GLS estimator $\hat{\beta}$ with $\hat{\rho}$ given above is known as the Prais–Winsten (PW) two-stage estimator. Iterating this estimator with respect to $\hat{\rho}$ based on the new estimator of $\beta$ gives the iterative Prais–Winsten estimator. The iterative ML estimator of $\beta$ is given by

$$\hat{\beta}^{\mathrm{ML}} = \left(X'\Omega^{-1}\left(\tilde{\rho}\right)X\right)^{-1}X'\hat{\Omega}^{-1}\left(\tilde{\rho}\right)y, \tag{5.86}$$

$$\tilde{\rho}^3 + a\tilde{\rho}^2 + b\tilde{\rho} + c = 0,$$

where, denoting $d_0 = (n-1)\left(\sum \hat{u}_{i-1}^2 - \hat{u}_1^2\right)$,

$$a = -(n-2)\sum \hat{u}_i \hat{u}_{i-1}/d_0, \tag{5.87}$$

$$b = \left((n-1)\hat{u}_1^2 - n\sum \hat{u}_{i-1}^2 - \sum \hat{u}_i^2\right)/d_0,$$

$$c = n\sum \hat{u}_i \hat{u}_{i-1}/d_0,$$

and summation is from 2 to $n$, see Beach and Mackinnon (1978).

Since $\hat{\rho}$ is an even function of $\hat{u}$, the above estimators of $\beta$ are unbiased. Magee et al. (1983) show that the MSE estimator of $\hat{\beta}$, up to $O\left(n^{-2}\right)$, remains the same for different choices of $\hat{\rho}$. Further, Magee (1985) shows that the MSEs of $\hat{\beta}$, iterative Prais–Winsten and ML estimator, up to $O\left(n^{-2}\right)$, are shown to be the same. This is given by

$$V\left(\hat{\beta}\right) = \sigma^2\left(X'\Omega^{-1}X\right)^{-1} + \sigma^2\frac{\left(1-\rho^2\right)}{n\rho^2}\left(X'\Omega^{-1}X\right)^{-1}X'FX\left(X'\Omega^{-1}X\right)^{-1}, \tag{5.88}$$

where $F = \Omega - X\left(X'\Omega^{-1}X\right)^{-1}X'$. The readers can attempt to develop this result alternatively by using the result in Section 2.5.3. It is simple to verify that

$$V\left(\hat{\beta}\right) - V\left(\bar{\beta}\right) = \text{positive semidefinite matrix}$$

because $F$ is a positive semidefinite matrix. Thus, the variance of $\hat{\beta}$ is more compared to $\bar{\beta}$ due to estimation of $\hat{\rho}$.

An estimator which is used extensively in applied work is the Cochrane–Orcutt (CO, 1949) estimator which is based on $n - 1$ observations. This is given by

$$\hat{\beta}_{CO} = \left( X^{*'} X^* \right)^{-1} X^{*'} y^*,$$

$$= \left( X' \hat{P}' C' C \hat{P} X \right)^{-1} X' \hat{P}' C' C \hat{P} y, \tag{5.89}$$

where $X^*$ is the matrix of $x_i - \hat{\rho} x_{i-1}$, $y^*$ is the vector of $y_i - \hat{\rho} y_{i-1}$, $\hat{P}$ is a matrix such that $\hat{\Omega}^{-1} = \hat{P}' \hat{P}$, and $C = [0: I_{n-1}]$ is an $n-1 \times n$ constant matrix. Then,

$$V\left( \hat{\beta}_{CO} \right) = V\left( \hat{\beta} \right) + \sigma^2 \left( X' \Omega^{-1} X \right)^{-1} X' D X \left( X' \Omega^{-1} X \right)^{-1}, \tag{5.90}$$

where $D$ is a diagonal matrix with a first element of 1 and the other diagonal elements equal to zero; hence $D$ is a positive semidefinite matrix. Thus,

$$V\left( \hat{\beta}_{CO} \right) - V\left( \hat{\beta} \right) = \text{positive definite matrix},$$

which implies that the CO estimator is inefficient compared to PW or ML estimator for small samples.

The variance (MSE) approximation given above also follows (5.28), and it also gives the $V(c'\hat{\beta})$, which can be written from (5.31), up to $O\left(n^{-2}\right)$, as

$$V\left( c'\left( \hat{\beta} - \beta \right) \right) = c' \left( X' \Omega^{-1} X \right)^{-1} c \left[ 1 + \frac{\lambda b}{n} \right], \tag{5.91}$$

where $\lambda = 1 - \rho^2$ and $b$ is as in (5.30) with $\Omega_i$ and $\Omega_j$ replaced by $\Omega(\rho)$. It can also be shown that the variance of $c\hat{\beta}$ is bounded by $c' \left( X' \Omega^{-1} X \right)^{-1} c [1 + (4/n)((1 + |\rho|)/(1 - |\rho|))]$. This shows that the approximate variance is not negligible when $|\rho|$ is close to 1. In fact the approximate $V(\hat{\beta})$ given above is invalid for $|\rho| = 1$, and they are least accurate for large $|\rho|$. This is also consistent with the simulation studies of Beach and Mackinnon (1978) that the MSE of the iterative PW and ML are very similar but differ most when $|\rho| = 1$.

The numerical calculations of the determinant and trace of $V(b)$, $V(\hat{\beta})$, and $V(\bar{\beta})$ in Magee, Ullah, and Srivastava (1987) and Magee (1985) suggest that the efficiency of these estimators is affected by the values of $\rho$ and the nature of $x$. The results are consistent with the theoretical results discussed above. In addition, they show that the LS estimator is better than $\hat{\beta}$ for small $\rho$ in $0 < \rho \leq 0.3$. However, $\hat{\beta}$ is better than the LS estimator for large $\rho$. Also LS is particularly bad for large $\rho$ values when there is an intercept and/or trend in the model. Further, CO estimator also performs worse with intercept and trend model. We note that the $O(1/n^2)$ terms of the MSE of PW and ML estimators of $\hat{\beta}$ are the same and the simulation studies also indicate this similarity. To see the differences in the MSE of iterative PW and ML and different choices of $\hat{\rho}$, one may need to analyze higher-order approximation than $O\left(1/n^2\right)$.

The Edgeworth expansion of the distribution of $\hat{\beta}$ with $\hat{\Omega} = \Omega\left(\hat{\rho}\right)$ is normal from (5.26) with the variance given by (5.27).

Ullah and Zinde-Walsh (1984, 1985, 1987), Vinod and Ullah (1981), and Dufour (1984) have explored the numerical and inferential robustness of the exact F, LR, RS, and W tests, for testing $H_0$: $R\beta = r$ against $H_1$: $R\beta \neq r$, by comparing the numerical values and distributions, respectively, under the assumptions of spherical normality with mean zero and variance $\sigma^2 I$ and elliptical normal against the general class of elliptical error distributions (zero mean and covariance matrix $\Omega$). They show that for autoregressive moving average models (ARMA) and/or heteroskedastic structures numerical robustness is rare in the sense that the usual test statistics for $\sigma^2 I$ cases are not identical with those under $\Omega \neq I$ cases. For inferential robustness they explore bounds for critical values of these tests which will ensure that the conclusions based on the usual tests are not affected against a particular class of elliptical distributions.

Finally, we note that the exact distributions of $\hat{\rho}$ and DW, which are the ratio of quadratic forms in $y$ or $u$, have been extensively studied in Koerts and Abrahamse (1969) and Farebrother (1984, 2002), King (1980), and others. Ali and Sharma (1993) derived first four moments of the null distribution of DW, up to $O\left(1/n^3\right)$, when the errors are nonnormal and find that nonnormality has an insignificant effect on the mean and the fourth central moment of the distribution. The test tends to be deflated (inflated) if the distribution is long tailed (short tailed). Further, the test is relatively robust for moderate nonnormality and large $n$.

## 5.3.4    Seemingly Unrelated Regressions

We consider here the multi-regression (seemingly unrelated regression equations, SURE) model developed by Zellner (1962). Such a model is needed when we wish to analyze a set of demand equations of different commodities or a set of investment functions for various industries. The temporal cross-section models (including panel data) which contain a number of cross-sectional units observed over time and the random coefficient model of Swamy (1970, 1971) can also belong to a multi-regression model.

Let us postulate the following SURE model of M equations:

$$y_i = X_i\beta_i + u_i, \quad i = 1, 2, \ldots, M, \tag{5.92}$$

where $y_i$ is $n \times 1$, $X_i$ is $n \times k_i$ of full column rank, $\beta_i$ is $k_i \times 1$, and $u_i$ is $n \times 1$. We can write this as

$$y = X\beta + u, \tag{5.93}$$

where

$$y = \begin{bmatrix} y_1 \\ \vdots \\ y_n \end{bmatrix}, \qquad X = \begin{bmatrix} X_1 & 0 & \cdots & 0 \\ 0 & X_2 & \cdots & 0 \\ \vdots & \vdots & \ddots & \vdots \\ 0 & 0 & \cdots & X_M \end{bmatrix}, \qquad \beta = \begin{bmatrix} \beta_1 \\ \vdots \\ \beta_M \end{bmatrix}, \qquad u = \begin{bmatrix} u_1 \\ \vdots \\ u_M \end{bmatrix}.$$

The error vectors $u_i$ and $u_j$, $i, j = 1, \ldots, M$ are assumed to be correlated only at the same time point, and within each equation the disturbance vector is assumed to be homoskedastic. Thus, $E(u_i) = 0$ and $E(u_i u_i') = \sigma_{ij} I_n$ so that

$$Eu = 0 \quad \text{and} \quad E(uu') = \Omega = \Sigma \otimes I_n, \tag{5.94}$$

where $\sigma_{ij}$ is the $(i, j)$th element of the $M \times M$ matrix $\Sigma$.

The operational or feasible GLS estimator $\hat{\beta}$, known as the SURE estimator, is obtained by using the consistent estimator of $\sigma_{ij}$ as

$$\hat{\sigma}_{ij} = \frac{\hat{u}_i' \hat{u}_j}{n} \quad \text{or} \quad \tilde{\sigma}_{ij} = \frac{\tilde{u}_i' \tilde{u}_j}{n}, \tag{5.95}$$

where $\hat{u}_i = y_i - X_i b_i$ is the LS residual vector of the $i$th regression and $\tilde{u}_i = y_i - Z_i b_i^*$, where $Z_i$ is a $n \times k$ matrix on all $k$ distinct regressors in the model. We note that SURE estimators based on $\hat{\sigma}_{ij}$ and $\tilde{\sigma}_{ij}$ are referred to as SURR (RR is restricted residual) and SUUR (UR is unrestricted) estimators.

Since $\hat{\Omega}$ is an even function of $\hat{u}$, the SURR and SUUR estimators $\hat{\beta}$ are again exactly unbiased. The exact covariance matrix of SURR $\hat{\beta}$ is obtained in Hillier and Satchell (1986); see also Srivastava and Giles (1987, chapter 4). Ullah and Rafiquzaman (1977), however, developed first four exact moments of $\hat{\beta}$ for the case of $M = 2$, $X_2$ is a subset of $X_1$ and $u \sim N(0, \Omega)$. Based on the four moments the following results for skewness and kurtosis of $\hat{\beta}_{1k}$, the $k$th element of $\hat{\beta}_1$, are

$$\text{skewness}\left(\hat{\beta}_{1k}\right) = 0, \tag{5.96}$$

$$\text{kurtosis}\left(\hat{\beta}_{1k}\right) = 3 + \Delta, \quad \Delta \geq 0, \tag{}$$

where

$$\Delta = 6\sigma_{11}^2 \left(1 - \rho^2\right)^2 \frac{n_0 - 1}{(n_0 - 2)^2 (n_0 - 4)} \frac{\left(\sum_1^n a_{ki}^2\right)^2}{w^2}, \tag{5.97}$$

where $\rho^2 = \sigma_{12}^2 / \sigma_{11} \sigma_{22}$, $n_0 = n - k_1 > 4$ for the fourth moments to exist, $a_{ki}$ is the $(k, i)$th element of $(X_1' X_1)^{-1} X_1' \left(I - X_2 (X_2' X_2)^{-1} X_2'\right)$ and

$$w^2 = E\left(\hat{\beta}_{1k} - \beta_{1k}\right)^2 = \sigma_{11} \left[\sum_1^n c_{ki}^2 - \left(\rho^2 - \frac{1 - \rho^2}{n - 2}\right) \sum_1^n a_{ki}^2\right], \tag{5.98}$$

where $c_{ki}$ is the element of $(X_1' X_1)^{-1} X_1'$.

As expected, skewness $= 0$ and kurtosis $= 3$ as $n \longrightarrow \infty$, that is, the sampling distribution of SURE estimator is symmetric, but kurtosis $>3$ implies that the distribution is leptokurtic and falls under Pearsonian Type VII family of distribution. Further, when the correlation in the contemporaneous disturbances across equations is close to one $(\rho^2 \longrightarrow 1)$, the exact distribution of $\hat{\beta}$ becomes normal.

Under the normality of $u$, Srivastava (1970), and Srivastava and Upadhyaya (1978) obtained a large-$n$ approximation of the covariance matrix of SURR and SUUR and showed that they are identical upto $O(n^{-2})$. Srivastava and Maekawa (1995) considered the bias and MSE of both SURR and SUUR under nonnormal errors of $u_{it}$ whose first four moments exist such that

$$E\left(u_{it_1}u_{jt_2}u_{et_3}\right) = \sigma_{ije}, \quad \text{if } t_1 = t_2 = t_3,$$

$$= 0, \quad \text{otherwise.} \tag{5.99}$$

$$E\left(u_{it_1}u_{jt_2}u_{et_3}u_{mt_4}\right) = \sigma_{ijem}, \quad \text{if } t_1 = t_2 = t_3 = t_4,$$

$$= \sigma_{ij}\sigma_{em}, \quad \text{if } t_1 = t_2, \quad t_3 = t_4, \quad \text{but } t_1 \neq t_3,$$

$$= \sigma_{ie}\sigma_{jm}, \quad \text{if } t_1 = t_3, \quad t_2 = t_4, \quad \text{but } t_1 \neq t_2,$$

$$= \sigma_{im}\sigma_{je}, \quad \text{if } t_1 = t_4, \quad t_2 = t_3, \quad \text{but } t_1 \neq t_2,$$

$$= 0, \quad \text{otherwise.} \tag{5.100}$$

The bias, up to $O(n^{-1})$, of SURR $\hat{\beta}$ is then given as

$$\text{Bias}\left(\hat{\beta}\right) = E\left(\hat{\beta} - \beta\right) = -\Omega_0 X'\Omega^{-1}\delta, \tag{5.101}$$

where $\Omega_0 = \left(X'\Omega^{-1}X\right)^{-1}$ and $\delta' = (\delta_1', \delta_2', \ldots, \delta_M')$ with

$$\delta_g = \frac{1}{n}\sum_{i,j}^{M}\sigma_{gij}Q_{ji}\,\iota, \qquad Q = \Omega^{-1} - \frac{1}{n}\Omega^{-1}X\Omega_0 X'\Omega^{-1} \quad \text{and} \quad \iota = (1,\ldots,1)'.$$

Further, the MSE of $\hat{\beta}$, up to $O(n^{-2})$, is

$$\text{MSE}\left(\hat{\beta}\right) = \Omega_0 + \Omega_0 X'(N - D)X\Omega_0, \tag{5.102}$$

where $N$ is an $M \times M$ matrix of

$$N_{gh} = \frac{1}{n}\left[Q_{gh} + \sigma^{gh}\sum_{i,j}^{M}\sigma_{ij}Q_{ij}\right],$$

$\sigma^{gh}$ denotes the $(g,h)$th element of $\Sigma^{-1}$, and $D = F + F'$ with $F$ as an $M \times M$ matrix given as

$$F_{gh} = \frac{1}{n}\sum_{i,j,m,e}^{M}\sigma^{gi}\sigma^{jh}\alpha_{ijem}Q_{jm}\left(I_n * \bar{P}_i\bar{P}_j\right),$$

where $P_i = I - X_i (X_i'X_i)^{-1} X_i'$, and for $i, j, e, m = 1, \ldots, M$,

$$\alpha_{ijem} = \sigma_{ijem} - \sigma_{ij}\sigma_{em} - \sigma_{ie}\sigma_{jm} - \sigma_{im}\sigma_{je}.$$

It is easy to see that the third-order moments $(\sigma_{ije})$ vanish under the symmetric errors. Further, all $\alpha_{ijem}$ are zero under the normal errors. Thus, $\sigma_{ije}$ and $\alpha_{ijem}$ provide departures from the normal errors. For the SUUR $\hat{\beta}$, the bias and the MSE are the same as those of SURR except that $\bar{P}_i\bar{P}_j$ in $D$ is replaced by $\bar{P} = I - Z (Z'Z)^{-1} Z'$.

When the errors are symmetric or normal, the bias to $O(1/n)$ becomes zero since $\delta = 0$. Further, if all the M equations contain a constant term, then $QX = 0$ and hence $\delta = 0$, which makes the estimator to be unbiased.

Under nonnormality, the estimators SUUR and SURR, however, have different MSE matrices. For $M = 2$ and $k = 1$, one can see that MSE differences of SURR and SUUR is a function of $r^2 = X_1'X_2/(X_1'X_1)(X_2'X_2)$, which is the square of correlation if $X_i$ is the derivation from its mean. The simulation study in Srivastava and Maekawa (1995) suggests that the biases are generally small and insensitive to a wide range of asymmetric disturbances. But if the disturbances are symmetric, then the two estimators have the identical MSE matrices.

While the MSE of SUUR and SURR are identical, up to $O(1/n^2)$, under the normality, the results of Tracy and Srivastava (1990) show that, up to $O(1/n^3)$, the MSE are different. Thus, higher-order efficiency comparison is useful in this case.

Considering $c' = (c_1', c_2', \ldots, c_M')$ with $c_i'$ of order $1 \times k_i$, Srivastava and Maekawa (1995) provided the large-$n$ Edgeworth expansion of $S_n = \sqrt{n}c'(\hat{\beta} - \beta)$. This is

$$P(S_n < z) = \Phi\left(\frac{z}{\sigma}\right) - \phi\left(\frac{z}{\sigma}\right)\left\{\frac{1}{\sqrt{n}}\frac{h_1}{\sigma} + \frac{1}{6\sqrt{n}}\frac{h_3}{\sigma^3} - \left[\left(\frac{z}{\sigma}\right)^2 - 1\right]\right\}, \quad (5.103)$$

where $\sigma = \sqrt{h_2}$,

$$h_1 = -c'\left(\frac{X'\Omega^{-1}X}{n}\right)^{-1} X'\Omega^{-1}\delta,$$

$$h_2 = c'\left(\frac{X'\Omega^{-1}X}{n}\right)^{-1} c,$$

$$h_3 = \sum_{ijm=1}^{M} \sigma_{ijk}\theta_m'\left(I_n * \frac{1}{n}\theta_i\theta_j'\right) + 3\left(c'\left(\frac{X'\Omega^{-1}X}{n}\right)^{-1} c\right)$$

$$\times c'\left(\frac{X'\Omega^{-1}X}{n}\right)^{-1} X'\Omega^{-1}\delta,$$

where $\theta_j{}' = \sum_{rs}^K \sigma^{sj} c_r{}' w_{rs} X_s{}'$, $w_{rs}$ are the elements of $\left(X'\Omega^{-1}X/n\right)^{-1}$. The asymptotic distributional results for both the SUUR and SURR estimators are the same, up to $O\left(n^{-1/2}\right)$, but the results up to $O\left(n^{-1}\right)$ can be different. Under normality, $h_1 = h_3 = 0$, so the distributions of both the SUUR and SURR estimators become $\Phi\left(z/\sigma\right)$. Maekawa (1985) (also see Phillips 1977c) also shows that this is the case up to $O\left(n^{-1}\right)$ since the approximate distribution did not contain any term up to $O\left(n^{-1}\right)$. Thus, while the distributions of both the estimators converge to the same normal distribution irrespective of the distributional structures of the errors, the nonnormality of errors slows down the convergence rate to $O\left(n^{-1/2}\right)$ under nonnormality and of $O\left(n^{-1}\right)$ under normality. The simulation results in some special cases of two equations in Srivastava and Maekawa suggest that the approximate results are quite accurate for small samples and robust to departures from normality of errors. In general, relying on the normality of errors may give misleading results when the distributions are in fact nonnormal.

## 5.3.5    Limited Dependent Variable Models

Here we consider models which are commonly used in applied work, especially in the labor economics. A popular model is the latent variable decision model in which

$$z_i^* = W_i \gamma + u_i, \quad i = 1, \ldots, n, \tag{5.104}$$

where $z_i^*$ is the unobserved latent variable which is the net utility, cost or profit, $W_i$ is a $k_w \times 1$ vector of explanatory variables, and $u_i$ is the error term with the variance normalized to one. This model is useful for analyzing migration, labor force participation, decision of participating in a program or organization (union), among others. For the estimation of $\gamma$, we observe an indicator variable

$$z_i = 1, \quad \text{if } z_i^* \geq 0,$$
$$= 0 \quad \text{otherwise.}$$

For example, in the labor force participation model, $z_i = 1$ implies the individual taking job if the net benefit $z_i^*$ is positive. Then,

$$E\left(z_i \mid_{W_i\gamma}\right) = E z_i = 1 - P\left(u_i \leq -W_i\gamma\right),$$
$$= 1 - \Phi\left(-W_i\gamma\right),$$
$$= \Phi\left(W_i\gamma\right), \tag{5.105}$$

where $\Phi\left(\right)$ is the cumulative distribution function. Therefore,

$$z_i = \Phi\left(W_i\gamma\right) + e_i, \tag{5.106}$$

where $e_i$ is the error term. The estimation of $\gamma$ is then done by specifying the form of $\Phi$ as a logit or probit specification and using ML procedure. The log likelihood function is

$$L\left(\gamma\right) = \prod_{1}^{n_1} \Phi\left(W_i\gamma\right) \prod_{1}^{n-n_1} \left(1 - \Phi\left(W_i\gamma\right)\right) = \prod_{1}^{n_1} P\left(z_i = 1\right) \prod_{1}^{n-n_1} P\left(z_i = 0\right)$$

(5.107)

and

$$\log L\left(\gamma\right) = \sum_{1}^{n} \left[z_i \log \Phi\left(W_i\gamma\right) + \left(1 - z_i\right) \log\left(1 - \Phi\left(W_i\gamma\right)\right)\right],$$

where $n_1$ is the number of observations for which $z_i = 1$. The score function is

$$S\left(\gamma\right) = \frac{\partial \log L\left(\gamma\right)}{\partial \gamma} = \sum_{1}^{n} S_i\left(\gamma\right) = 0,$$

(5.108)

where

$$S_i\left(\gamma\right) = \left(z_i\lambda_i - \left(1 - z_i\right)\bar{\lambda}_i\right) W_i$$

and

$$\lambda\left(W_i\gamma\right) = \lambda_i = \frac{\phi\left(W_i\gamma\right)}{\Phi\left(W_i\gamma\right)}, \qquad \bar{\lambda}_i = \frac{\phi\left(W_i\gamma\right)}{1 - \Phi\left(W_i\gamma\right)}.$$

(5.109)

The $\lambda_i$ is known as the inverse Mill's ratio. Under the logit assumption, $\Phi\left(W_i\gamma\right) = e^{W_i\gamma}/1 + e^{W_i\gamma}$ and under the probit assumption, $\phi$ and $\Phi$ become the density and cumulative distribution of a standardized normal variable, respectively. The ML estimator of $\gamma$ is then obtained which is known to be consistent and asymptotically normal.

An extension of the above limited dependent variable is the sample selection model. In this case, the equation of interest is

$$y_i = x_i\alpha + v_i,$$

(5.110)

where $y_i$ is observed only if $z_i^* \geq 0$, that is, $z_i = 1$. Due to this, $E\left(v_i \mid z_i = 1\right) \neq 0$ and hence $E\left(y_i \mid_{z_i=1}\right) \neq x_i\alpha$. So the LS regression of $y_i$ on $x_i$ will be asymptotically biased and inconsistent. To correct for this bias we need to know $E\left(y_i \mid z_i = 1\right)$. For this let us consider $u_i$ and $v_i$ to be a joint normal distribution with correlation coefficient $\rho$ and $v_i$ with variance $\sigma_v^2$. Then, conditional on $z_i = 1$, $v_i$ has a truncated normal distribution and $E\left(v_i \mid z_i = 1\right) = \rho\sigma_v\lambda_i$ and so

$$E\left(y_i \mid z_i = 1\right) = x_i\alpha + \rho\sigma_v\lambda\left(W_i\gamma\right)$$

(5.111)

or

$$y_i = x_i\alpha + \eta\lambda\left(W_i\gamma\right) + \epsilon_i,$$

where $\eta = \rho\sigma_v$ and $\lambda_i = \lambda\left(W_i\gamma\right)$. Further, $E\left(\epsilon_i \mid z_i = 1\right) = 0$ and $V\left(\epsilon_i \mid z_i = 1\right) = \sigma_i^2 = \sigma_v^2(1 + \rho^2\lambda_i^{(1)})$, where $\lambda_i^{(1)} = -\lambda_i\left(\lambda_i + W_i\gamma\right)$ is the first derivative of $\lambda_i$ with respect to $\gamma$. This is a model which adjusts for the sample selection bias.

Heckman's (1979) two-step estimator of estimating $k \times 1$ vector $\beta = (\alpha', \eta, \gamma')'$, $k = k_x + k_w + 1$, first estimates $\gamma$ by ML from the decision model. This provides observation on $\lambda_i$ after which the LS estimation of $\alpha$ and $\eta$ are obtained in the above regression model. To obtain the finite sample properties of this two-step estimator, we first write it in terms of the method of moments estimator, which leads to solving the following moments:

$$\frac{1}{n} \sum_{1}^{n} q_i \left( \hat{\beta} \right) = 0, \tag{5.112}$$

where

$$q_i (\beta) = \begin{pmatrix} z_i x_i \epsilon_i (\beta) \\ z_i \lambda (W_i \gamma) \epsilon_i (\beta) \\ S_i (\gamma) \end{pmatrix}.$$

Before analyzing finite sample results, let us consider the known results on the asymptotic results which are helpful in interpreting the finite sample results. Heckman (1979) showed that

$$\sqrt{n} \left( \hat{\beta} - \beta \right) \longrightarrow N (0, \Sigma), \tag{5.113}$$

where

$$\Sigma = [E (\nabla q_i)]^{-1} E (q_i q_i') (E \nabla q_i)^{-1},$$
$$= E d_i d_i',$$

where $d_i = (E (\nabla q_i))^{-1} q_i$ and $\nabla q_i (\beta)$ is the $k \times k$ matrix of the first derivative of $q_i (\beta)$ with respect to $\beta$.

The asymptotic standard errors, by looking at the diagonal elements of $\Sigma$, can be inspected to be large ($E \nabla q_i$ approaches to singularity) when $x_i$ are closely collinear, especially when $\lambda_i$ can be written as a linear combination of the $x$s. This can be a problem when the $w_i$s are a subset of $x_i$ or are highly correlated with them and $\lambda_i$ is approximated by a linear function $w_i \gamma$. By inspection, another situation in which the standard errors can be large is when the degree of simultaneity $\rho$ is large. In many applied studies, it has been found that these two situations of large standard errors are frequently found.

The second-order bias, up to $O (n^{-1})$, can be written from (2.81) as

$$B \left( \hat{\beta} \right) = E \left( \hat{\beta} - \beta \right) = \frac{1}{n} (E \nabla q_i)^{-1} \left( E(V_i d_i) - \frac{1}{2} E (\nabla^2 q_i) E (d_i \otimes d_i) \right), \tag{5.114}$$

where $\nabla^2 q_i$ is the $k \times k^2$ matrix of second-order derivative and $V_i = \nabla q_i - E (\nabla q_i)$. We note that if $e$th row of $\nabla q_i (\beta)$ contains the gradient vector of the $e$th element of $q_i (\beta)$, the $e$th row of $\nabla^2 q_i$ contains the vectorized Hessian matrix of the $e$th element of $q_i (\beta)$.

It is clear that the bias depends on the curvature of the model implied by $\nabla q_i$ and $\nabla^2 q_i$. Further, $E V_i d_i$ is the correlation of $V_i$ and $q_i$, usually small, and $E\left(d_i \otimes d_i\right)$ is the vectorization of the term $E d_i d_i{}'$ in the asymptotic variance. Thus, the factors influencing these are similar to those affecting $\left(E\left(\nabla q_i\right)\right)^{-1}$ and hence asymptotic variance described above, which are near nonidentification (collinearity) and simultaneity. Finally, an estimate of bias can be obtained by calculating sample averages at $\beta = \hat{\beta}$, for example, replacing $E\left(\nabla q_i\right)$ by $\sum_1^n \nabla q_i\left(\hat{\beta}\right)/n$.

The simulations results in Rilstone and Ullah (2002) indicate that in the case of small sizes 50, 100 and for the case of single variables in each of $x$ and $w$, $B\left(\hat{\alpha}\right)$ increases as $\rho$ increases or $\rho_{xw}$(correlation between $x$ and $w$) increases. Further the MSE of $\hat{\alpha}$ also increases with $\rho$ and $\rho_{xw}$. These results are consistent with the analytical results on the bias above. The analytical MSE results can also be written and analyzed from the results in Chapter 2.

## 5.3.6 Panel Data Models

Here we consider the estimation of linear models with the data on $n$ cross-sectional units over $T$ time points. Such a model is known as a panel data model, and such models are used to study the behavior of the cross-sections of groups, regions, countries, and households over time. There is an extensive literature on the theory and applications of these models; see Hsiao (1986) and Baltagi (2001). The possibility of observing variations across both cross-section and time points creates several interesting opportunities in applied econometrics; see Baltagi (2001) and Deaton (1997) for the advantages of panel data models.

A basic difference between the panel data models and the traditional models is the presence of changing (varying) intercepts across cross-sections and across time. These are called as heterogeneity parameters which take care of unobservable variables which change with cross-sectional units but are fixed over time (cross-sectional heterogeneity) and unobservable variables which are fixed over cross-sections but change over time (time series heterogeneity). For example, in a production function management, efficiency variable will qualify for the cross-sectional heterogeneity and technology variable will represent the time heterogeneity. There are two kinds of panel data models. First is the fixed effect panel data model where the heterogeneity parameters are treated as fixed parameters. In this case, the model is estimated by the LS procedure which provides the best linear unbiased estimator under the Gauss–Markov assumptions. Second is the random effect (error components) model in which the heterogeneity parameters are treated as random error along with the equational random error. Such a model is estimated by the GLS method, the small sample properties of which will be discussed below.

Let us consider a random effect panel data model as

$$y_{it} = x_{it}\beta + w_{it}, \quad w_{it} = \alpha_i + u_{it} \left(i = 1, \ldots, n; \quad t = 1, \ldots, T\right), \qquad (5.115)$$

where $y_{it}$ is the dependent variable, $x_{it}$ is a $1 \times k$ vector of regressors, $u_{it}$ is the error term, and the heterogeneity parameter $\alpha_i$ is the cross-sectional random effect, and $u_{it}$ and $\alpha_i$ are independently distributed random variables.

In the matrix notation, we can express the model as

$$y = X\beta + w, \quad w = D\alpha + u, \tag{5.116}$$

where $y$ is $nT \times 1$ vector, $X$ is $nT \times k$ matrix, $w$ is $nT \times 1$ vector, $\alpha$ is $n \times 1$ vector of random effects, and $D = I_n \otimes \iota; \iota = (1, \dots, 1)'$. It is assumed that for all $i$ and $t$,

$$E(\alpha_i) = 0, \quad E(\alpha_i^2) = \sigma_\alpha^2, \quad E(\alpha_i^3) = \sigma_\alpha^3 \gamma_{1\alpha}, \quad E(\alpha_i^4) = \sigma_\alpha^4(\gamma_{2\alpha} + 3),$$

$$E(u_i) = 0, \quad E(u_i^2) = \sigma_u^2, \quad E(u_i^3) = \sigma_u^3 \gamma_{1u}, \quad E(u_i^4) = \sigma_u^4(\gamma_{2u} + 3). \tag{5.117}$$

Note that $\gamma_1$ and $\gamma_2$ represent the skewness and kurtosis measures, respectively. If $\gamma_1 = \gamma_2 = 0$, the $\alpha_i$ and $u_{it}$ have a normal distribution.

The LS estimator of $\beta$ is

$$b = (X'X)^{-1} X'y,$$

which is unbiased. The variance–covariance matrix of $b$ is given by

$$V(b) = (X'X)^{-1} X'\Omega X (X'X)^{-1}, \tag{5.118}$$

where $\Omega = E(ww') = \sigma_u^2 [Q + \lambda^{-1}\bar{Q}]$, $Q = I_{nT} - \bar{Q}$, $\bar{Q} = (1/T)DD'$, $\lambda = \sigma_u^2/(\sigma_u^2 + T\sigma_\alpha^2) = \sigma_u^2/\sigma_\eta^2$, $\sigma_\eta^2 = \sigma_u^2 + T\sigma_\alpha^2$, $\sigma_\alpha^2 = ((1 - \lambda)/\lambda T)\sigma_u^2$. Obviously, $Q$ and $\bar{Q}$ are independent idempotent matrices, thus $Q^2 = Q$, $\bar{Q}^2 = \bar{Q}$, $Q\bar{Q} = 0$. The GLS estimator is given by

$$\tilde{\beta} = (X'\Omega^{-1}X)^{-1} X'\Omega^{-1}y, \tag{5.119}$$

which is unbiased and its variance–covariance matrix is

$$V(\tilde{\beta}) = (X'\Omega^{-1}X)^{-1},$$

where $\sigma_u^2\Omega^{-1} = Q + \lambda\bar{Q} = I_{nT} - (1 - \lambda)\bar{Q}$.

The FGLS of $\beta$ is given by

$$\hat{\beta} = (X'\hat{\Omega}^{-1}X)^{-1} X'\hat{\Omega}^{-1}y, \tag{5.120}$$

where $\hat{\sigma}_u^2\hat{\Omega}^{-1} = Q + \hat{\lambda}\bar{Q} = I_{nT} - (1 - \hat{\lambda})\bar{Q}$, in which $\hat{\lambda} = \hat{\sigma}_u^2/(\hat{\sigma}_u^2 + T\hat{\sigma}_\alpha^2) = \hat{\sigma}_u^2/\hat{\sigma}_\eta^2$,

$$\hat{\sigma}_u^2 = \frac{y'M_zy}{n(T-1) - k} = \frac{u'M_zu}{n(T-1) - k} = \frac{u'\left(Q - QX(X'QX)^{-1}X'Q\right)u}{n(T-1) - k},$$

$\hat{\sigma}_\eta^2 = (w'\bar{Q}w - w'\bar{Q}X(X'\bar{Q}X)^{-1}X'\bar{Q}w)/(n-k)$, and $M_Z = I_{nT} - Z(Z'Z)^{-1}Z'$ and $Z = [X\ D]$.

In addition to the above estimators, one can also obtain the following two independent unbiased estimators of $\beta$. One is the within fixed effect estimator or simply the within estimator of $\beta$. For this we write:

$$y = D\alpha + X\beta + u,$$
$$M_D y = M_D X\beta + M_D u,$$

so that the LS estimator of $\beta$ is

$$\hat{\beta}_w = (X'M_D X)^{-1} X'M_D y, \tag{5.121}$$

where $w$ represents within estimator and $M_D = I - D(D'D)^{-1}D'$ transforms the data into deviation from cross-sectional (time averaged) means. Its $V(\hat{\beta}_w) = \sigma_u^2 (X'M_D X)^{-1}$.

Second, an unbiased estimator is the between estimator represented by $\hat{\beta}_B$. This is given by doing LS in the following regression $(\bar{M}_D = I - M_D)$:

$$\bar{M}_D y = \bar{M}_D X\beta + (\bar{M}_D D\alpha + \bar{M}_D u),$$

which gives

$$\hat{\beta}_B = (X'\bar{M}_D X)^{-1} X'\bar{M}_D y, \tag{5.122}$$

where $\bar{M}_D$ transforms the data grouped by cross-sectional units into time averages for each unit. Its $V(\hat{\beta}_B) = (X'\bar{M}_D X)^{-1} X'(\sigma_\alpha^2 DD' + \sigma_u^2 \bar{M}_D) X(X'\bar{M}_D X)^{-1}$.

Assuming the unobservable to be uncorrelated with the exogenous variables, both $\hat{\beta}_w$ and $\hat{\beta}_B$ are unbiased for $\beta$ and are independent. Further, it can be verified that the GLS estimator $\tilde{\beta}$ is a matrix weighted average of the within and between estimators

$$\tilde{\beta} = \Delta\hat{\beta}_B + (I - \Delta)\hat{\beta}_w, \tag{5.123}$$

where

$$\Delta = \left[\frac{1}{\sigma_u^2 + T\sigma_\alpha^2} X'\bar{M}_D X + \frac{1}{\sigma_u^2} X'M_D X\right]^{-1} \left[\frac{1}{\sigma_u^2 + T\sigma_\alpha^2} X'\bar{M}_D X\right].$$

Of course the FGLS estimator is also $\hat{\beta} = \hat{\Delta}\hat{\beta}_B + (I - \hat{\Delta})\hat{\beta}_w$, where $\hat{\Delta}$ is $\Delta$ with $\sigma_u^2$ and $\sigma_\alpha^2$ replaced by $\hat{\sigma}_u^2$ and $\hat{\sigma}_\alpha^2$ given above.

The GLS estimator $\tilde{\beta}$ is the BLUE estimator. Also, from Lehmann (1983, theorem 1.1, p. 77), $\tilde{\beta}$ is also the uniformly minimum variance unbiased (UMVU) estimator of $\beta$. That is, in the class of unbiased estimators, $\Delta_0\hat{\beta}_B + (I - \Delta_0)\hat{\beta}_w$, the UMVU estimator is for $\Delta_0 = \Delta$. But this result does not hold for the FGLS estimator $\hat{\beta}$.

The FGLS estimator $\hat{\beta}$ is an unbiased estimator of $\beta$ since $\hat{\Omega}$ is an even function of the random errors $\alpha$ and $u$. The exact variance, under normality is developed in Taylor (1980) in terms of hypergeometric infinite series. The numerical calculations there suggest that, for any sample size, the variance of the limiting distribution of $\hat{\beta}$, $(X'\Omega^{-1}X)^{-1}$, understates the true variance by no more than 17 percent, but for small $n - k$, this understatement remains around 12–14 percent for samples of 25 or 50. Thus, the total sample size does not help in the accuracy of the asymptotic moment approximation and that convergence is probably slower. Second, using more efficient estimators of $\sigma_u^2$ and $\sigma_\alpha^2$ do not improve the efficiency of $\hat{\beta}$ much. Next, for the larger cross-sectional units, the estimator $\hat{\beta}$ is more efficient compared to within estimator, but for smaller samples $(n - k \leq 10)$, there is an ambiguity in the selection of estimator. Also, if the relative efficiencies of the between and within estimators are close to one, there are larger sets of sample sizes for which $\hat{\beta}$ is more efficient compared to within estimator.

We now look at the nature of approximate bias, up to $O\left(n^{-1}\right)$, for a general class of nonnormal errors, assuming T to be fixed. This is given by

$$B\left(\hat{\beta}\right) = \frac{\lambda(1 - \lambda)}{n} \left(\frac{\sigma_u \gamma_{1u}}{T} - \sigma_\alpha \gamma_{1\alpha}\right) \left(A^{-1} - \lambda A^{-1} B A^{-1}\right) X'\iota, \qquad (5.124)$$

where

$$A = \frac{X'\Omega^{-1}X}{n}, \quad B = \frac{X'\bar{Q}X}{n}.$$

The following remarks follow from this result.

We observe that the approximate bias in the estimator $\hat{\beta}$ is affected by the skewness coefficients $\gamma_1$ but it does not depend on the measure of kurtosis. Further, for the symmetric distributions of errors $(\gamma_{1\alpha} = \gamma_{1u} = 0)$, the estimator $\hat{\beta}$ becomes unbiased. The bias is also zero if $\lambda$ is 0 or 1. This case implies $\sigma_u^2$ or $\sigma_\alpha^2 = 0$, that is, the random effect errors become the usual errors. Moreover, the bias is zero if $X'\iota = 0$, which is the case if the matrix $X$ contains variables deviated from their means.

Next, the direction of bias depends upon the signs of $\sigma_u \gamma_{1u} - T\sigma_\alpha \gamma_{1\alpha}$ and the average values of the regressors $X$, since $0 < \lambda < 1$ and $A - \lambda B = n^{-1}X'\left(I - \bar{Q}\right)X$, which is positive semidefinite. Assuming that the average value of each regressor is positive,

$$\text{Bias}(\hat{\beta}) > 0, \quad \text{if } \sigma_u \gamma_{1u} > T\sigma_\alpha \gamma_{1\alpha}, \tag{5.125}$$
$$< 0, \quad \text{if } \sigma_u \gamma_{1u} < T\sigma_\alpha \gamma_{1\alpha}.$$

Thus, if $\gamma_{1\alpha} < 0$ and $\gamma_{1u} > 0$, then $\hat{\beta}$ will be positively biased.

The approximate bias expression in (5.124) can be verified using the stochastic expansion in (5.20) and then evaluating it under the nonnormal errors. The result for approximate MSE can be similarly obtained. For the bias analysis in the nonlinear panel models, see Hahn and Newey (2002).

# 6

# Dynamic Time Series Model

## 6.1 Introduction

In this chapter we consider the finite sample analysis of the time series models used in economics and finance. We consider the autoregressive model (AR), AR with regressors, and autoregressive moving average models with regressors (ARMAX). The exact and approximate (Laplace, Large-$n$, and Small-$\sigma$) moments as well as the distributions of the estimators of the lag coefficients and the regression coefficients have been derived and analyzed. Based on these results the bias and mean squared error (MSE) of the one period and $s$-periods ahead forecast errors have been analyzed. Since unit root and cointegration play an important role in the modern time series, these cases are also covered in this chapter.

## 6.2 Model and Least-Squares Estimator

Let us write the general first-order dynamic model as

$$y_i = \alpha y_{i-1} + x_i \beta + u_i, \quad i = 1, \ldots, n, \tag{6.1}$$

where $y_{i-1}$ is a lagged value of the dependent variable with fixed or random startup condition, $x_i$ is the $i$th observation on the $1 \times p$ vector of exogenous variables, $\alpha$ and $\beta$ are parameters, and $u_i$ is the disturbance term. Using recursive substitutions we can write (6.1) as

$$y_i = \alpha^i y_0 + \sum_{r=0}^{i-1} \alpha^s \left( x_{i-r} \beta + u_{i-r} \right) = \mu_i + v_i, \tag{6.2}$$

where

$$\mu_i = \alpha^i y_0 + \sum_{r=0}^{i-1} \alpha^r x_{i-r}\beta, \qquad v_i = \sum_{r=0}^{i-1} \alpha^r u_{i-r}. \tag{6.3}$$

In the matrix notation

$$y = \alpha y_{-1} + X\beta + u, \tag{6.4}$$

where $y = (y_1, \ldots, y_n)'$, $y_{-1} = (y_0, \ldots, y_{n-1})'$, $X$ is a $n \times p$ matrix, and $u$ is an $n \times 1$ vector. We note that

$$y_{-1} = Ly + \iota_1 y_0, \tag{6.5}$$

where $\iota_1 = (1\ 0\ 0\ \text{-}\ \text{-}\ \text{-}\ 0)'$ is an $n \times 1$ vector and $L$ is an $n \times n$ matrix as

$$L = \begin{bmatrix} 0 & 0 & 0 & - & - & - & 0 \\ 1 & 0 & 0 & - & - & - & 0 \\ 0 & 1 & 0 & - & - & - & 0 \\ & & \mathsf{I} & & & & \\ & & \mathsf{I} & & & & \\ 0 & 0 & 0 & - & - & 1 & 0 \end{bmatrix}. \tag{6.6}$$

Substituting (6.5) in (6.4) we get

$$y = \alpha L y + \alpha \iota_1 y_0 + X\beta + u \tag{6.7}$$

or

$$(I - \alpha L)\, y = \alpha \iota_1 y_0 + X\beta + u, \tag{6.8}$$

which gives

$$y = c y_0 + C\,(X\beta + u)$$
$$= \mu + v \tag{6.9}$$

where

$$\mu = c y_0 + C X \beta, \qquad v = C u \tag{6.10}$$

and

$$C = (I - \alpha L)^{-1} = \begin{bmatrix} 1 & 0 & 0 & - & - & - & 0 \\ \alpha & 1 & 0 & - & - & - & 0 \\ \mathsf{I} & & & & & & \\ \mathsf{I} & & & & & & \\ \alpha^{n-1} & \alpha^{n-2} & \alpha^{n-3} & - & - & - & 1 \end{bmatrix}, \tag{6.11}$$

$$c = \alpha\,(I - \alpha L)^{-1}\iota_1 = \left(\alpha, \alpha^2, \ldots, \alpha^n\right)'.$$

Further

$$y_{-1} = L\,(\mu + v) + \iota_1 y_0,$$
$$= L\mu + \iota y_0 + Lv,$$
$$= \mu_{-1} + v_{-1}, \tag{6.12}$$

where $\mu_{-1} = L\mu + \iota_1 y_0 = c^* y_0 + C^* X\beta, v_{-1} = Lv = LCu = C^* u$ and

$$c^* = Lc + \iota_1 = \left(1, \alpha, \ldots, \alpha^{n-1}\right)', \tag{6.13}$$

$$C^* = LC = \begin{bmatrix} 0 & 0 & 0 & - & - & - & 0 \\ 1 & 0 & 0 & - & - & - & 0 \\ \alpha & 1 & 0 & - & - & - & 0 \\ | & & & & & & \\ | & & & & & & \\ \alpha^{n-2} & \alpha^{n-3} & \alpha^{n-4} & - & - & 1 & 0 \end{bmatrix}.$$

We note that the $i$th elements of (6.9) and (6.12) are as in (6.3). Further if $y_0$ is stochastic then it is replaced by $E(y_0)$ in (6.10) and (6.12). Also the random vector $v$ is distributed with $Ev = 0$ and $V(v) = C\Omega C' = \Sigma$ where $\Omega = V(u)$ is an $n \times n$ variance–covariance matrix of $u$. If $V(u) = \sigma_u^2 I$ then $V(v) = \sigma_u^2 CC'$. Thus

$$Ey = \mu \quad \text{and} \quad V(y) = \Sigma. \tag{6.14}$$

The form of $\mu$ and $\Sigma$ will vary depending on the stability conditions and regressor choice in the model. Thus:

(a) Stable Models, $|\alpha| < 1.0$, random startup where $y_i \sim (\mu_i, \sigma_u^2/(1 - \alpha^2))$ for $i = 0$, then $\mu = cE(y_0) + CX\beta$ and the $(i, j)$th element of $\Sigma$ is $\sigma_{ij} = \sigma_u^2 \alpha^{|i-j|}/(1 - \alpha^2)$ for all $i, j \geq 1$. This means that $V(y) = \Sigma = \sigma_u^2 CC'$ where $C$ is as in (6.11) with each element of first column multiplied by $(1 - \alpha^2)^{-1/2}$. If $Ey_0 = 0$ and $\beta = 0$ then the model is stationary.

(b) Nonstationary Models (unit root models), fixed startup $y_0$, then $\mu = cy_0 + CX\beta$ and $\Sigma = \sigma_u^2 CC'$, where $C$ is as given in (6.11). If $|\alpha| < 1.0$ and $\beta = 0$, then the model is stationary asymptotically; for $|\alpha| = 1$, this is a well known random walk model and if $|\alpha| > 1$, the model is explosive.

(c) ARMAX (1, 1) model with the coefficients of both AR and MA are $\alpha$. Then $\mu = cy_0 + CX\beta$ and $\Sigma = \sigma_u^2 I$.

The model in (6.1) or (6.4) is for $i = 1, \ldots, n$, so it involves $y_0$, which is not realized for the estimation of $\alpha$ and $\beta$. Therefore we write the model and its canonical form where the initial observation is the first sample observation. This is

$$y^* = \alpha y_{-1}^* + X^* \beta + u^*, \tag{6.15}$$

where $y_i^* = y_i, u_i^* = u_i$, and $x_i^* = x_i$, $i = 2, \ldots, n$. The least squares (LS) estimators of $\alpha$ and $\beta$ are then given by

$$\hat{\alpha} = \frac{y_{-1}^{*'} M y^*}{y_{-1}^{*'} M y_{-1}^*} = \frac{y' N_1 y}{y' N y} = \frac{z' N_1^* z}{z' N^* z} \tag{6.16}$$

and

$$\hat{\beta} = \left(X^{*'} X^*\right)^{-1} X^{*'} \left(y^* - \hat{\alpha} y_{-1}^*\right), \tag{6.17}$$

where $M = I - X^*(X^{*'}X^*)^{-1}X^{*'}$ is $n - 1 \times n - 1$ and idempotent of rank $n-1-p$, $D_1 y = y^*_{-1}$, and $D_2 y = y^*$, where $D_1 = [I_{n-1} : O]$ and $D_2 = [O : I_{n-1}]$ are $n - 1 \times n$ data transformation matrices. Furthermore,

$$N_1 = \tfrac{1}{2}(D_1' M D_2 + D_2' M D_1), \quad N = D_1' M D_1, \tag{6.18}$$

where $N$ is an idempotent matrix of rank $n-1-p$. The canonical reduced form variables are defined as $z = \Sigma^{-1/2} y$, where $\Sigma^{-1/2} = P \wedge^{-1/2} P'$, $\wedge = $ diagonal $(\lambda_i)$, $i = 1, \ldots, n$, where $\lambda_i$ are eigenvalues of $\Sigma$ and $P$ is the orthogonal matrix of the eigenvectors of $\Sigma$. Thus, $N_1^* = \Sigma^{1/2} N_1 \Sigma^{1/2}, N^* = \Sigma^{1/2} N \Sigma^{1/2}$, and

$$z = \mu_z + \eta, \tag{6.19}$$

where $\mu_z = \Sigma^{-1/2}\mu$ and $\eta = \Sigma^{-1/2}v$ such that $V(\eta) = V(z) = I$ and $z \sim (\mu_z, I)$.

In a special case where $\beta = 0$ so that

$$y_i = \alpha y_{i-1} + u_i, \quad i = 1, \ldots, n \tag{6.20}$$

and $M = I_{n-1}$, the estimator $\hat{\alpha}$ becomes

$$\hat{\alpha} = \frac{y^{*'}_{-1} y^*}{y^{*'}_{-1} y^*_{-1}} = \frac{y' N_1 y}{y' N y}, \tag{6.21}$$

where

$$N_1 = \frac{1}{2}(D_1' D_2 + D_2' D_1) = \frac{1}{2}
\begin{bmatrix}
0 & 1 & 1 & - & - & 0 & 0 \\
1 & 0 & 1 & - & - & 0 & 0 \\
0 & 1 & 0 & - & - & 0 & 0 \\
\mathrm{I} & \mathrm{I} & \mathrm{I} & & & & \\
\mathrm{I} & \mathrm{I} & \mathrm{I} & & & & \\
0 & 0 & 0 & - & - & 0 & 1 \\
0 & 0 & 0 & - & - & 1 & 0
\end{bmatrix} \tag{6.22}$$

and

$$N = D_1' D_1 =
\begin{bmatrix}
1 & 0 & 0 & - & - & 0 & 0 \\
0 & 1 & 0 & - & - & 0 & 0 \\
0 & 0 & 1 & - & - & 0 & 0 \\
\mathrm{I} & \mathrm{I} & \mathrm{I} & & & & \\
\mathrm{I} & \mathrm{I} & \mathrm{I} & & & & \\
0 & 0 & 0 & - & - & 1 & 0 \\
0 & 0 & 0 & - & - & 0 & 0
\end{bmatrix}. \tag{6.23}$$

We now give the forecasts based on (6.1) or (6.4). For example one period ahead forecast is

$$\hat{y}_{n+1} = \hat{\alpha} y_n + x_{n+1}\hat{\beta} = \hat{\alpha}\iota_n' y + x_{n+1}\hat{\beta} \tag{6.24}$$

and its forecast error is

$$\hat{y}_{n+1} - y_{n+1} = (\hat{\alpha} - \alpha)\iota_n' y + x_{n+1}\left(\hat{\beta} - \beta\right) - u_{n+1}, \tag{6.25}$$

where $\iota_n = [0 \ldots 0, 1]$. If $\beta = 0$, then $\hat{y}_{n+1} - y_{n+1} = (\hat{\alpha} - \alpha)\iota_n' y - u_{n+1}$. Similarly $\hat{y}_{n+2} - y_{n+2} = (\hat{\alpha} - \alpha)y_{n+1} - u_{n+2}$.

When we develop forecasts $s$-time periods ahead we use

$$\hat{y}_{n+2} = \hat{\alpha}\hat{y}_{n+1} + x_{n+2}\hat{\beta} = \hat{\alpha}^2 y_n + (x_{n+2} + \hat{\alpha}x_{n+1})\hat{\beta},$$

and

$$\hat{y}_{n+s} = \hat{\alpha}^s y_n + (x_{n+s} + \hat{\alpha}x_{n+s-1} + \hat{\alpha}^{s-1}x_{n+1})\hat{\beta}.$$

Further the forecast error is

$$\hat{y}_{n+s} - y_{n+s} = (\hat{\alpha}^s - \alpha^s)y_n + \sum_{i=0}^{s-1} x_{n+s-i}(\hat{\alpha}^i\hat{\beta} - \alpha^i\beta) + \sum_{i=0}^{s-1} u_{n+s-i}\alpha^i.$$

When $\beta = 0$,

$$\hat{y}_{n+s} - y_{n+s} = (\hat{\alpha}^s - \alpha^s)y_n + \sum_{i=0}^{s-1} u_{n+s-i}\alpha^i.$$

Further if we define $\bar{y}_{n+s} = E(y_{n+s}|y_n) = \alpha^s y_n$, then $\hat{y}_{n+s} - \bar{y}_{n+s} = (\hat{\alpha}^s - \alpha^s)y_n$.

# 6.3 Finite Sample Results for Dynamic Model

## 6.3.1 Review

We consider the AR(1) model in (6.20) and consider the properties of the LS estimator $\hat{\alpha}$ in (6.21). Since this model has been extensively studied in the literature we first provide a brief summary of the results for this model and then present analytical expressions.

Hurwicz (1950) was the first to investigate the small sample bias in this model. He finds that for small samples the bias of LS is as much as 25 percent of the value of $\alpha$. For the case of normally distributed $u$'s he provided a closed form equation for the bias of the LS estimator when $n = 3$ or 4 for the stationary case and for $n = 3$ for the fixed startup case where $y_0 = 0$. For other "$n$" he suggests a Maclaurin series expansion but only demonstrates how the first term of such an expansion would be calculated.

Copas (1966) used Monte Carlo methods to compare the MSE of the LS, and the maximum-likelihood (ML) when the $u$'s are distributed $N(0,1)$ for the stationary case and for the fixed startup case when $y_0 = 1$. Copas found that the ML and LS estimators are on average the best in terms of the MSE and that for the stationary case the ML has a slightly lower MSE in the region $|\alpha| < 0.6$ and LS has a slightly lower MSE in the region $0.6 < |\alpha| < 0.9$. The region considered was $|\alpha| < 0.9$. Copas did not tell us which region each estimator does best for the fixed startup case, but for both the stationary and the fixed startup cases he showed that the ML does slightly better on average over the region considered. For another Monte Carlo study related to AR(1) model, see Thornber (1967).

Sawa (1978) developed the exact moments by using the moment generating function and calculated the exact small sample bias and variance of $\hat{\alpha}$ for $|\alpha| < 1$

in the stationary case with normal error terms. Sawa (1978) also added to Hurwicz (1950) results by recording the bias of $\hat{\alpha}$ for $\alpha = 0.2, 0.4, 0.6$, and 0.8, and $6 < n < 30$ in the stationary case with normal error terms.

Hoque (1985) extended Sawa (1978) by deriving the exact first and second moments of $\hat{\alpha}$ for the case where the $u$'s follow an MA(1) process. Hoque and Peters (1986), and Mercurio (2000) developed the exact moments of the LS estimators of the parameters in the AR models with exogenous variables. For these models, Kiviet and Phillips (1993), Srivastava and Ullah (1995), and Bao and Ullah (2002) analyzed the large-$n$ and small-$\sigma$ approximate moments. The extension to the case of AR $(p)$ models is also considered in Bao and Ullah (2002). Peters (1989) provided the exact moments for the nonnormal error case.

Now we turn to the distribution of $\hat{\alpha}$, which has been studied extensively. Asymptotically, it has a normal distribution (Mann and Wald 1943) if $|\alpha| < 1$. White (1958) found that for $|\alpha| > 1$, $|\alpha|^n (\hat{\alpha} - \alpha)/(\alpha^2 - 1)$ has a Cauchy distribution in the limit when the $u$'s are normally distributed which Anderson (1959) note implied that $(\sum_{i=2}^{n} y_{i-1}^2)^{1/2}(\hat{\alpha} - \alpha)$ has mean zero normal distribution in the limit for $|\alpha| \neq 1$. White (1958, 1959) also showed that the distribution of $\hat{\alpha}$ for $|\alpha| = 1$ was not normal. Anderson (1959) showed that for $|\alpha| > 1$, $\sqrt{n}(\hat{\alpha} - \alpha)$ has a mean zero normal distribution in the limit when the $u$'s are *i.i.d.* Anderson (1959) also builds on the results of White (1958) by showing that the limiting distribution of $\sqrt{n}(\hat{\alpha} - \alpha)$ for $|\alpha| > 1$ depends on the distribution of the $u$'s. White (1961) builds on Hurwicz (1950) by calculating the first three terms on the MacLaurin expansion approximation for the first two moments of $\hat{\alpha}$.

The exact distribution of $\hat{\alpha}$ can be written by using the Imhof (1961) result on the distribution of the quadratic forms, see Chapter 3. It was numerically computed by Phillips (1977a, 1978), Evans and Savin (1981), and Tsui and Ali (1994) for various values of $\alpha$ and $n$. An extensive numerical study of unit root distributions was done by Evans and Savin (1981, 1984), which warned that the conventional tests are not good detectors of unit root behavior since they have low powers in typical sample sizes. In addition several authors (Dickey 1976; Fuller 1976) have done Monte Carlo Studies to tabulate the distribution of $\hat{\alpha}$ for the case of $\alpha = 1$ and $y_0 = 0$, also see bootstrap unit root test by Park (2003). These distributions can be used to test for unit root hypothesis. Nankervis and Savin (1985, 1988) examined how well hypothesis testing on $\alpha$ does with the $t$-statistic when $y_i$ is stationary and for a fixed nonzero $y_0$, also see Dickey and Fuller (1981). They use Monte Carlo methods to estimate the exact distribution of the $t$-statistic and find that the student-$t$ is not a good approximation for small sample sizes.

Phillips (1987a,b,c) extended White's distributional results using ratios of functions of Wiener processes, also see Abadir (1994) for the exact distribution. Phillips (1987c), and Stock (1987) also showed that the LS estimator $\hat{\alpha}$ converges to $\alpha$ faster in the unit root case compared to the stable root ($|\alpha| < 1$) case. Banerjee, Donaldo, Hendry, and Smith (1986) explored this result through a Monte Carlo study and found out that the LS bias did not decline at the expected rate when the sample size was increased. In an important paper Abadir (1993*a*) reconciled the findings of Phillips and Stock with Banerjee, Dolando, Hendry, and Smith by providing a higher order analytical approximate bias of $\hat{\alpha}$ for the case of $\alpha = 1$. This result proves analytically that the bias declines at a rate, which is slower than the consistency rate, thus explaining Banerjee and coworkers simulation findings. He also shows cases of $n$ and nonzero values of $y_0/\sigma$, where the bias increases with the sample size.

In addition to the work on the exact distribution, several authors have attempted to obtain approximations to the distribution of $\hat{\alpha}$. Phillips (1977*a*, 1978), Satchell (1984), Tsui and Ali (1992), Wang (1992), and Lieberman (1994) developed the Edgeworth expansion, Cornish–Fisher type expansion, and saddle point approximations of the distribution for the case of stationary AR(1) model. They indicate that the Edgeworth expansion is unsatisfactory except for smaller values of $\alpha$. In most of these studies the accuracy has been tested for only a few values of $n$ and $\alpha$. Furthermore the approximations have been found to be computationally demanding, especially for large $n$ for the model where $y_0$ is fixed at zero. Phillips (1987*a*), Lieberman (1994*b*), and Nabeya and Taneka (1990) have looked at the limiting distribution of $n(\hat{\alpha} - \alpha)$ under a near-integrated random process, also see Park (2003). Further Perron (1991) has analyzed the approximate distribution of $\hat{\alpha}$ for the case where $y_0$ is fixed at a nonzero constant. Again these studies consider the accuracy at a few selected points of $n$ and $\alpha$. Ali (2002) considered both the cases of stationary and fixed models and provided a uniform asymptotic expansion for the distribution, which is applicable for all the values of $\alpha$. This uniform expansion, however, provides a mixed result on its accuracy.

Now we turn to the works on the properties of forecasts. Box and Jenkins (1970) obtained the asymptotic MSE of the $s > 0$ period ahead forecast for the stationary AR(1) model when LS is applied as:

$$\text{MSE}\left(\hat{y}_{n+s}\right) = \sigma_u^2 \left\{ \sum_{j=0}^{s-1} \alpha^{2j} + n^{-1} s^2 \alpha^{2(s-1)} \right\} + o\left(n^{-1}\right), \tag{6.26}$$

so that for a one period ahead forecast:

$$\text{MSE}\left(\hat{y}_{n+1}\right) = \sigma_u^2 \left(1 + n^{-1}\right) + o\left(n^{-1}\right), \tag{6.27}$$

where the one period ahead forecast for $n$ observations is $\hat{y}_{n+1} = \hat{\alpha} y_n$. Bloomfield (1972) extended this result to a one period ahead stationary AR($p$) model and Yamamoto (1976) extended it further to an "$s$" period ahead stationary AR($p$) model.

Malinvaud (1970) showed that if $y_0$ is a mean zero symmetric random variable then the forecast bias of LS is zero. Phillips (1979) pointed out that this is an *unconditional* forecast error and that what is far more interesting is the forecast bias conditioned on known values of the dependent variable, such as $y_n$. That is to say that since we have observed $y_n$ we should use this information when deciding what the forecast error is. Phillips (1979) develops an approximation to the distribution of the forecast bias conditional on $y_n$ and finds that forecasts are biased toward the origin for almost all values of $y_n$. If $\hat{\alpha}$ and $y_n$ are assumed independent and $y_i$ is stationary then he finds that:

$$E\left(\hat{y}_{n+1} - y_{n+1}|y_n\right) = -\left(2\alpha/n\right)y_n + O\left(n^{-2}\right). \tag{6.28}$$

If, as is usually the case, $\hat{\alpha}$ and $y_n$ are dependent then

$$E\left(\hat{y}_{n+1} - y_{n+1}|y_n\right) = \frac{y_n}{n}\alpha\left(\left(y_n\bigg/\frac{\sigma_u}{(1-\alpha^2)^{1/2}}\right)^2 - 3\right). \tag{6.29}$$

Hoque, Magnus, and Pesaran (1988) give an exact expression for the MSE of the forecast for both the fixed startup and the stationary cases. They find that the MSE decreases as the number of periods into the future of the forecast is increased and that the behavior of the fixed startup and stationary cases are very similar except for $|\alpha|$ near one.

Now we look into the results for the AR(1) with an intercept. Orcutt and Winokur (1969) used Monte Carlo techniques to study the LS estimation of the model $y_i = \gamma + \alpha y_{i-1} + u_i$ in the stationary case, where the $u$'s are normal and *i.i.d.* He finds that LS produced no bias in estimating $\gamma$ and that a Student-$t$ distribution may be used as an approximate sampling distribution for $\gamma$. However, there is a significant bias in the estimation of $\alpha$. He examined the bias correction technique of Marriott and Pope (1954) and found it has lower MSE than LS for higher values of $\alpha$. However, in terms of the estimated Monte Carlo MSE of the forecast the Marriott and Pope (1954) technique did not improve on LS. Sawa (1978) applied a numerical method to the stationary case of the model $y_i = \gamma + \alpha y_{i-1} + u_i$ and finds that in this model $\hat{\alpha}$ is severely biased for $n < 100$ confirming Orcutt and Winokur's (1969) Monte Carlo results. Sawa (1978) also used numerical integration method to calculate the exact small sample bias and variance of $\hat{\alpha}$ for the model $y_i = \gamma + \alpha y_{i-1} + u_i$, where $|\alpha| < 1$ in the stationary case with normal error terms. Hoque (1985) extended this to the case where the $u$'s follow an MA(1) process. Dickey and Fuller (1979) were also able to find the limiting distribution for $\hat{\alpha}$ when $y_0 = 0$ and $|\alpha| = 1$.

As stated above, Orcutt and Winokur (1969) showed that in terms of the estimated Monte Carlo MSE of prediction the Marriott and Pope (1954) technique does not improve on LS. Fuller and Hasza (1980) building on the work of Malinvaud (1970) showed that if $y_i$ is a mean zero symmetric random variable then the forecast bias of LS is zero for the model $y_i = \gamma + \alpha y_{i-1} + u_i$ for the cases: (*a*) $|\alpha| < 1$ and stationary, that is, mean of the process equals $\gamma/(1-\alpha)$, (*b*) $\gamma = 0 = $ mean of process, and (*c*) $\gamma = 0$ and $\alpha = 1$. Dufour (1984) showed the same results of unbiasedness under somewhat weaker conditions. As stated above, it is important to remember that these are *unconditional results* and that the bias or MSE conditioned on the known $y$'s are more interesting statistics from the point of view of the applied researcher. Also these results assume $E\left(y_0\right) = 0$, which may not always be a good assumption. Fuller and Hasza (1981$b$) find that conditional on $y_n$ the MSE is:

$$\text{MSE}\left(\hat{y}_{n+1}\right) = \sigma_u^2 \left(1 + 2/n\right) + O\left(n^{-3/2}\right). \tag{6.30}$$

Hoque (1985) looks at the unconditional forecast bias of the model (6.1) and finds it to be nonzero as opposed to the (6.20) model, which has a zero unconditional forecast bias.

## 6.3.2 Exact Results for AR(1) model

The finite sample behavior of the LS estimator $\hat{\alpha}$ in (6.21) and the forecasts are analyzed for the model (6.20), $y_i = \alpha y_{i-1} + u_i, i = 2, \ldots, n$ with $y_1 = \alpha y_0 + u_1 = \mu_1 + u_1$. Both the stable models with random startup and the nonstationary model with fixed startup will be considered. In the fixed startup we consider the cases where $\mu_1 = \alpha y_0 = 0$ and $\mu_1 \neq 0$. The exact results on the moments are compared with the Monte Carlo results as well as the approximate moments by the Laplace, the large-$n$ and small-$\sigma$ methods.

From (6.21)

$$\hat{\alpha} = \frac{y' N_1 y}{y' N y}, \tag{6.31}$$

where $N_1$ and $N$ are as given in (6.22) and (6.23). Further, assuming $u \sim N(0, \sigma_u^2 I)$ we get $y \sim N(\mu, \Sigma)$ where $\mu = c y_0$ and $\Sigma = \sigma_u^2 C C'$ where $c$ and $C$ are given in (6.11). Therefore the exact mean, $E\hat{\alpha}$ and $E\hat{\alpha}^2$ are as in (2.28). Thus the exact $V(\hat{\alpha}) = E(\hat{\alpha}^2) - (E\hat{\alpha})^2$.

Now we look into the exact moments of the one period ahead forecast

$$\hat{y}_{n+1} = \hat{\alpha} y_n = \hat{\alpha}\left(\iota_n' y\right), \tag{6.32}$$

where $\iota_n = [0, \ldots, 0, 1]'$ is an $n \times 1$ vector. We note that $\hat{\alpha} = h\left(y\right)$ and $\iota_n' = g\left(y\right)$. Thus from Lemma 1 in Chapter 2 we note that

$$E\left(\hat{y}_{n+1}\right) = E\left(\hat{\alpha} \iota_n' y\right) = \iota_n' d E\left(\hat{\alpha}\right), \tag{6.33}$$

$$= \iota_n'\left(\mu + \Sigma \frac{\partial}{\partial \mu}\right) E\left(\hat{\alpha}\right),$$

$$= \left(\left(\iota_n' \mu\right) + \iota_n' \Sigma \frac{\partial}{\partial \mu}\right) E\left(\hat{\alpha}\right),$$

$$= \left(\alpha^n y_0 + \sigma_u^2 \left(\iota_n' C C'\right) \frac{\partial}{\partial \mu}\right) E\left(\hat{\alpha}\right),$$

where $\partial E\left(\hat{\alpha}\right)/\partial\mu$ is the derivative of (2.29) with respect to $\mu$. Further

$$E\left(\hat{y}_{n+1}^2\right) = E\left(\hat{\alpha}^2\left(\iota_n'y\right)^2\right) = \left(\iota_n'd\right)^2 E\hat{\alpha}^2, \tag{6.34}$$

$$= \left(\iota_n'd\right)\left(\iota_n'd\right)E\hat{\alpha}^2,$$

$$= \left(\iota_n'd\right)\left(\left(\iota_n'\mu + \sigma_u^2\left(\iota_n'CC'\right)\frac{\partial}{\partial\mu}\right)E\hat{\alpha}^2\right),$$

$$= \left(\iota_n'\mu + \iota_n'\Sigma\frac{\partial}{\partial\mu}\right)\left(\left(\iota_n'\mu + \sigma_u^2\iota_n'\Sigma\frac{\partial}{\partial\mu}\right)E\hat{\alpha}^2\right),$$

$$= \left(\mu'\iota_n\iota_n'\mu + \iota_n'\Sigma\iota_n\right)E\hat{\alpha}^2 + \sigma_u^2\mu'\iota_n\iota_n'\Sigma\frac{\partial}{\partial\mu}E\hat{\alpha}^2$$

$$+ \sigma_u^2\iota_n'\Sigma\left(\frac{\partial^2}{\partial\mu\partial\mu'}E\hat{\alpha}^2\right)\Sigma\iota,$$

where $\mu'\iota_n\iota_n'\mu = \alpha^{2n}y_0^2$ and $\partial^2/\partial\mu\partial\mu'$ is the second derivative of $E\hat{\alpha}^2$ in (2.29).

Suppose $Ey_0 = 0$ for the random startup or $y_0 = 0$ for the fixed startup so that $\mu_1 = 0$ and hence $\mu = 0$. Further $\partial E\hat{\alpha}/\partial\mu$ is zero for $\mu = 0$. Thus $E\hat{y}_{n+1} = 0 = E\left(y_{n+1}\right)$, and

$$E\left(\hat{y}_{n+1} - y_{n+1}\right) = 0. \tag{6.35}$$

Similarly for $s$th period ahead forecast, $E\left(\hat{y}_{n+s}\right) = E\left(\hat{\alpha}^s y_n\right) = E\left(\hat{\alpha}^s\iota_n'y\right) = \left(\iota_n'\mu + \iota_n'\Sigma\partial/\partial\mu\right)E\hat{\alpha}^s = 0$ for $\mu = 0$ because $\partial E\hat{\alpha}^s/\partial\mu = 0$ for $\mu = 0$ follows by writing $E\hat{\alpha}^s$ from (2.28) or (2.32). Thus for $\mu_1 = 0$, the forecast bias $E\left(\hat{y}_{n+s} - y_{n+s}\right)$ is zero. This compares with the results of Malinvaud (1970), Fuller and Hasza (1980), and Dufour (1984). Hoque, Magnus, and Pesaran (1988) also provided the result that $E\left(\hat{y}_{n+s} - y_{n+s}\right)$ exists when $1 \le s \le n-2$. When $\mu_1 \ne 0$ we note that the bias will not be zero and it is given by (6.33).

Regarding the MSE of the forecast error we note that

$$E\left(\hat{y}_{n+s} - y_{n+s}\right)^2 = \sigma_u^2\alpha^{2s}\iota_n'\Sigma\iota_n + E\left(\hat{\alpha}^{2s}\left(\iota_n'y\right)^2\right) \tag{6.36}$$

$$- 2\alpha^s E\left(\hat{\alpha}^s\left(\iota_n'y\right)^2\right) + \sigma_u^2\sum_{j=0}^{s-1}\alpha^{2j}$$

$$= \sigma_u^2\alpha^{2s}\iota_n'\Sigma\iota_n + \left(\iota_n'd\right)^2\left(E\hat{\alpha}^{2s} - 2\alpha^s E\hat{\alpha}^s\right) + \sigma_u^2\sum_{j=0}^{s-1}\alpha^{2j},$$

and for one period forecast error

$$E\left(\hat{y}_{n+1} - y_{n+1}\right)^2 = \sigma_u^2\left(1 + \alpha^2\iota_n'\Sigma\iota_n\right) + \left(\iota_n'd\right)^2\left(E\hat{\alpha}^2 - 2\alpha E\hat{\alpha}\right) \tag{6.37}$$

$$= \sigma_u^2\left(1 + \alpha^2\iota_n'\Sigma\iota_n\right) + E\hat{y}_{n+1}^2 - 2\alpha\left(\iota_n'd\right)E\hat{y}_{n+1}.$$

It is easy to verify that, at $\mu = 0$,

$$\left(\iota_n'd\right)^2 E\hat{\alpha} = \left(\iota_n'd\right)E\hat{y}_{n+1} = \int_0^\infty |N_0|^{-1/2}\left[\iota_n'\Sigma\iota_n\mathrm{tr}\left(N_1N_2\right)\right.$$

$$\left. + 2\iota_n'N_2N_1N_2\iota_n\right]dt, \tag{6.38}$$

where $N_2$ and $N_0$ are as in (2.29) and Lemma 2 of Chapter 2. Similarly, at $\mu = 0, (\iota_n' d)^2 E\hat{\alpha}^2 = E\hat{y}_{n+1}^2$ follows from (6.34).

**Numerical Evaluation** The integrals given above are calculated numerically using the Mathematica© software package and are then used to generate the exact bias and MSE of $\hat{y}_{n+1}$. The exact forecast bias and MSE of $\hat{y}_{n+1}$ are presented for parameter values $\alpha = 0.2, 0.4, 0.7$, and $0.9$; $n = 10$ and $20$; and $\mu_1 = \alpha y_0 = 0$ and 10 in Tables 6.1 and 6.2. Also the results for $\mu_1 = 0$ in Table 6.2 match the results of Hoque, Magnus, and Pesaran (1988: 338).

If $\alpha = 0.2$, $\mu_1 = 10$, and $n = 10$, Table 6.1 shows that MSE $(\hat{y}_{10+1}) = 1.00936$ and forecast bias $(\hat{y}_{10+1}) = 1.7811 \times 10^{-6}$. If instead $\mu_1 = 0$, Table 6.2 shows that MSE $(\hat{y}_{10+1}) = 1.1279$ and forecast bias $(\hat{y}_{10+1}) = 0$, so that, as noted earlier, the LS estimator is unbiased in the case where $\mu_1 = 0$ but for $\mu_1 = 10$ LS is positively biased but has smaller MSE. Mercurio (2000) plots the bias of the LS forecast versus $\mu_1$ for $\alpha = 0.4$. He finds that the bias is zero for $\mu_1 = 0$, reaches a maximum at about $\mu_1 = 4.83$, then asymptotically ($\mu_1 \to \infty$) approaches zero. Further, he plots the bias as a function of $\mu_1$ and $\alpha$, showing the bias appears to be a quasi-concave function of $\mu_1$ and $\alpha$ and reaching a maximum at about $\mu_1 = 2.5$ and $\alpha = 0.95$.

We can also notice from comparing Tables 6.1 and 6.2 that the MSE is lower for $\mu_1 = 10$ than for $\mu_1 = 0$. Mercurio (2000) shows that for $\alpha = 0.4$, the MSE of the forecast starts at 1.13498 and then seems to asymptotically ($\mu_1 \to \infty$) approach one. Further, he plots the MSE as a function of $\mu_1$ and $\alpha$, which shows that the MSE appears to be a quasi-convex function in the given range. The MSE reaches a maximum in the range plotted at $\mu_1 = 0$ and $\alpha = 1$. It is also interesting to note that (again using numerical methods) $\lim_{\mu_1 \to \infty} \text{bias}(\hat{\alpha}) = 0$ and $\lim_{\mu_1 \to \infty} \text{MSE}(\hat{\alpha}) = 0$ so $\lim_{\mu_1 \to \infty} \text{Var}(\hat{\alpha}) = 0$. Upon reflection, this is what we would expect intuitively. As $\mu_1$ tends toward infinity, the relative size of the nonstochastic part of (6.9) begins to overwhelm the randomness generated by $u_j$ so that it becomes increasingly easy for LS to estimate the value of $\alpha$. In general we observe from Tables 6.1 and 6.2 that $\hat{\alpha}$ is negatively biased and its MSE is a decreasing function of $\alpha$.

When $\alpha = 1$ for the AR(1) model, $y_i = \alpha y_{i-1} + u_i$, it is said to have a unit root or be integrated of order one, I(1). It is useful to look at the small sample behavior of the bias and MSE of $\hat{\alpha}$ and forecast at or near $\alpha = 1$ for a number of different values of the parameters $\mu_1$ and $n$. For the one period ahead forecast, see this analysis in Mercurio (2000).

### 6.3.3 Approximate Methods

This section will discuss three approximations to the bias and MSE of $\hat{\alpha}$ and forecast and examine how well they do in estimating the true bias and MSE

Table 6.1

Model: $y_j = \alpha y_{j-1} + u_j$, $\hat{y}_{j+1} = \hat{\alpha} y_j$, $\mu_1 = 10$, $\sigma_u^2 = 1$

| $n$ | $\alpha$ | $E(\hat{\alpha})$ | $E(\hat{\alpha}^2)$ | Bias$(\hat{\alpha})$ | MSE$(\hat{\alpha})$ | $E(\hat{y}_{n+1}^2)$ | $E(\hat{\alpha}y_n^2)$ | $E(\hat{y}_{n+1})$ | $E(y_{n+1})$ | Bias$(\hat{y}_{n+1})$ | MSE$(\hat{y}_{n+1})$ |
|---|---|---|---|---|---|---|---|---|---|---|---|
| 10 | 0.2 | 0.196371 | 0.04738 | $-0.00362$ | 0.00883993 | 0.051067 | 0.208446 | $2.8051\times10^{-6}$ | $1.024\times10^{-6}$ | $1.7811\times10^{-6}$ | 1.00936 |
| 10 | 0.4 | 0.392742 | 0.16206 | $-0.0072576$ | 0.00786964 | 0.200107 | 0.476488 | 0.00143832 | 0.00104858 | $3.8974\times10^{-4}$ | 1.00939 |
| 10 | 0.7 | 0.687411 | 0.47759 | $-0.0125891$ | 0.00522083 | 1.0733 | 1.50135 | 0.300812 | 0.282475 | 0.018337 | 1.01121 |
| 10 | 0.9 | 0.886858 | 0.78917 | $-0.0131416$ | 0.00283256 | 16.6956 | 18.0876 | 3.52422 | 3.48678 | 0.0374565 | 1.0404 |
| 10 | 0.99 | 0.980009 | 0.96219 | $-0.0099905$ | 0.00167824 | 92.8213 | 92.6691 | 9.06282 | 9.04382 | 0.0190018 | 1.09561 |
| 20 | 0.2 | 0.196677 | 0.04675 | $-0.0033230$ | 0.00808355 | 0.0502464 | 0.208428 | $4.1522\times10^{-13}$ | $1.049\times10^{-13}$ | $3.104\times10^{-13}$ | 1.00854 |
| 20 | 0.4 | 0.393354 | 0.16186 | $-0.0066456$ | 0.00718581 | 0.199246 | 0.476435 | $1.8055\times10^{-7}$ | $1.100\times10^{-7}$ | $7.0595\times10^{-8}$ | 1.00857 |
| 20 | 0.7 | 0.688376 | 0.47844 | $-0.0116243$ | 0.00471764 | 0.971176 | 1.37377 | 0.0089512 | 0.00797923 | 0.00097198 | 1.00874 |
| 20 | 0.9 | 0.885528 | 0.786311 | $-0.014472$ | 0.00236074 | 5.84414 | 6.39379 | 1.24371 | 1.21577 | 0.0279445 | 1.01356 |

Table 6.2

Model: $y_j = \alpha y_{j-1} + u_j$, $\hat{y}_{j+1} = \hat{\alpha} y_j$, $\mu_1 = 0$, $\sigma_u^2 = 1$

| $n$ | $\alpha$ | $E(\hat{\alpha})$ | $E(\hat{\alpha}^2)$ | Bias$(\hat{\alpha})$ | MSE$(\hat{\alpha})$ | $E(\hat{y}_{n+1}^2)$ | $E(\hat{\alpha}y_n^2)$ | $E(\hat{y}_{n+1})$ | $E(y_{n+1})$ | Bias$(\hat{y}_{n+1})$ | MSE$(\hat{y}_{n+1})$ |
|---|---|---|---|---|---|---|---|---|---|---|---|
| 10 | 0.2 | 0.167721 | 0.123324 | −0.0322787 | 0.0962353 | 0.176726 | 0.221205 | 0 | 0 | 0 | 1.12991 |
| 10 | 0.4 | 0.335771 | 0.203709 | −0.0642286 | 0.0950921 | 0.350499 | 0.507427 | 0 | 0 | 0 | 1.13503 |
| 10 | 0.7 | 0.5900 | 0.4264 | −0.1100 | 0.0908 | 1.26758 | 1.47869 | 0 | 0 | 0 | 1.15743 |
| 10 | 0.9 | 0.886858 | 0.660127 | −0.0131416 | 0.0891476 | 4.54895 | 4.49514 | 0 | 0 | 0 | 1.20255 |
| 20 | 0.2 | 0.181963 | 0.0800941 | −0.0180373 | 0.047309 | 0.0976839 | 0.21158 | 0 | 0 | 0 | 1.05473 |
| 20 | 0.4 | 0.363986 | 0.175815 | −0.0360137 | 0.0446258 | 0.252839 | 0.48428 | 0 | 0 | 0 | 1.05589 |
| 20 | 0.7 | 0.637552 | 0.439875 | −0.0624482 | 0.037303 | 1.0668 | 1.40437 | 0 | 0 | 0 | 1.06147 |
| 20 | 0.9 | 0.822529 | 0.700908 | −0.0774711 | 0.0303558 | 4.56271 | 4.82463 | 0 | 0 | 0 | 1.07853 |

when LS is used. Since we know from above that the exact bias and MSE are

$$E\left(\hat{y}_{n+1} - y_{n+1}\right) = E\left(\left(\iota'_n y\right)\left(\hat{\alpha} - \alpha\right)\right) = \iota'_n dE\left(\hat{\alpha} - \alpha\right) \tag{6.39}$$

and

$$E\left(\hat{y}_{n+1} - y_{n+1}\right)^2 = E\left[\left(\iota'_n y\right)\left(\hat{\alpha} - \alpha\right) - u_{n+1}\right]^2, \tag{6.40}$$

$$= E\left[\left(\iota'_n y\right)^2\left(\hat{\alpha} - \alpha\right)^2\right] + \sigma_u^2,$$

$$= \left(\iota'_n d\right)^2 E\left(\hat{\alpha} - \alpha\right)^2 + \sigma_u^2,$$

where $d = \mu + \Sigma\partial/\partial\mu$. Thus we first find approximations to $E\left(\hat{\alpha}\right)$ and $E\hat{\alpha}^2$ and from these calculate the approximations of the bias and MSE of the forecast error.

**The Laplace Approximation**  Denote the Laplace approximation to $E\left(\hat{\alpha}\right)$ by $E_L\left(\hat{\alpha}\right)$. Through the use of the Laplace method discussed in Chapter 2 we obtain

$$E_L\left(\hat{\alpha}\right) = \frac{E\left(y' N_1 y\right)}{E\left(y' N y\right)} = \frac{\mu' N_1 \mu + \operatorname{tr}\left(\Sigma N_1\right)}{\mu' N \mu + \operatorname{tr}\left(\Sigma N\right)}. \tag{6.41}$$

Similarly

$$E_L\left(\hat{\alpha}^2\right) = \frac{E\left(y' N_1 y\right)^2}{\left(E\left(y' N y\right)\right)^2}, \tag{6.42}$$

where

$$E\left(y' N_1 y\right)^2 = \left(\mu' N_1 \mu\right)\left(\mu' N_1 \mu + \operatorname{tr}\Sigma N_1\right) + 4\mu' N_1 \Sigma N_1 \mu$$

$$+ \operatorname{tr}\left[\left(N_1 \Sigma\right)\left\{\left(\mu' N_1 \mu\right) + \operatorname{tr}\Sigma N_1 + 2 N_1 \Sigma\right\}\right]$$

from (2.17). Thus,

$$E_L\left(\hat{y}_{n+1}\right) = \left(\iota'_n d\right) E_L\left(\hat{\alpha}\right) = \iota'_n\left(\mu + \Sigma\frac{\delta}{\delta\mu}\right) E_L\left(\hat{\alpha}\right), \tag{6.43}$$

$$= \iota'_n \mu E_L\left(\hat{\alpha}\right) + \iota'_n \Sigma\frac{\partial}{\partial\mu} E_L\left(\hat{\alpha}\right),$$

where

$$\frac{\partial}{\partial\mu} E_L\left(\hat{\alpha}\right) = \frac{\partial}{\partial\mu}\left[\frac{\mu' N_1 \mu + \operatorname{tr}\left(\Sigma N_1\right)}{\mu' N \mu + \operatorname{tr}\left(\Sigma N\right)}\right]$$

$$= \frac{2 N_1 \mu}{\mu' N \mu + \operatorname{tr}\left(\Sigma N\right)} - \frac{2 N \mu\left(\mu' N_1 \mu + \operatorname{tr}\left(\Sigma N_1\right)\right)}{\left(\mu' N \mu + \operatorname{tr}\left(\Sigma N\right)\right)^2}.$$

Further,

$$\operatorname{MSE}_L\left(\hat{y}_{T+1}\right) = \left(\iota'_n d\right)^2\left(E\left(\hat{\alpha}^2\right) - 2\alpha E_L\left(\hat{\alpha}\right) + \alpha^2\right) + \sigma^2, \tag{6.44}$$

where

$$\left(\iota_n' d\right)^2 E_{\mathrm{L}}\left(\hat{\alpha}\right) = \left(\iota_n' d\right)\left(\iota_n' d\right) E_{\mathrm{L}}\left(\hat{\alpha}\right)$$

$$= \left(\iota_n' \mu + \iota_n' \Sigma \frac{\partial}{\partial \mu}\right)\left(\iota_n' \mu E_{\mathrm{L}}\left(\hat{\alpha}\right) + \iota_n' \Sigma \frac{\partial}{\partial \mu} E_{\mathrm{L}}\left(\hat{\alpha}\right)\right)$$

$$= \left(\iota_n' \mu\right)^2 E_{\mathrm{L}}\left(\hat{\alpha}\right) + \left(\iota_n' \mu\right)\iota_n' \Sigma \frac{\partial}{\partial \mu} E_{\mathrm{L}}\left(\hat{\alpha}\right)$$

$$+ \iota_n' \Sigma \frac{\partial}{\partial \mu}\left(\iota_n' \mu E_{\mathrm{L}}\left(\hat{\alpha}\right)\right) + \left(\iota_n' \Sigma \left(\frac{\partial^2}{\partial \mu \, \partial \mu'} E_{\mathrm{L}}\left(\hat{\alpha}\right)\right)\Sigma \iota_n\right).$$

Similarly $(\iota_n' d)^2 E_{\mathrm{L}}(\hat{\alpha}^2)$ and $(\iota_n' d)^2 \alpha^2$ are the same with $E_{\mathrm{L}}(\hat{\alpha})$ replaced by $E_{\mathrm{L}}(\hat{\alpha}^2)$ and $\alpha^2$. The derivatives of $E_{\mathrm{L}}(\hat{\alpha})$ and $E_{\mathrm{L}}(\hat{\alpha}^2)$ with respect to $\mu$ are straightforward to obtain.

**Small-$\sigma$ Expansion**   The results for the bias and MSE of $\hat{\alpha}$, based on small-$\sigma$ expansion, follow from the results in Chapter 2. First we make the assumption that

$$\mu_{-1} = c^* y_0 \neq 0.$$

Note that if $\beta = 0$ and $y_0 = 0$ then $y = v = Cu$ or $\sigma_u Cu$ if $V(u) = I$ and $\hat{\alpha}$ becomes invariant to $\sigma_u$ and so the small-$\sigma$ expansion does not exist. Same is true if $y_0$ in the random startup has $Ey_0 = 0$.

The bias of $\hat{\alpha}$, to $O(\sigma^2)$, is

$$E_s\left(\hat{\alpha} - \alpha\right) = \frac{\sigma_u^2}{\mu_{-1}' \mu_{-1}}\left[\mathrm{tr}\left(C^*\right) - 2\frac{\mu_{-1}' C^* \mu_{-1}}{\mu_{-1}' \mu_{-1}}\right] \qquad (6.45)$$

$$= -\frac{2\sigma_u^2}{\left(\mu_{-1}' \mu_{-1}\right)^2}\mu_{-1}' C^* \mu_{-1}.$$

Similarly, the MSE is as in 6.3.5 with $M = I$. The result on the bias is also in Kiviet and Phillips (1993), and Srivastava and Ullah (1995), and the MSE is in Srivastava and Ullah (1995).

Using the bias and MSE of $\hat{\alpha}$ we get

$$E_s\left(\hat{y}_{n+1}\right) = \iota_n' d\left(E_s\left(\hat{\alpha}\right)\right),$$
$$E_s\left(\hat{y}_{n+1} - y_{n+1}\right)^2 = \left(\iota_n' d\right)^2 E_s\left(\hat{\alpha} - \alpha\right)^2 + \sigma^2, \qquad (6.46)$$

where $\iota_n' d = (\iota_n' \mu + \iota_n' \Sigma \partial/\partial \mu)$. The derivatives are straightforward and they are left as an exercise.

**Large-$n$ approximation**   The large-$n$ approximations can be obtained from the results (2.101) and (2.102) in Chapter 2 and the results of Kiviet and

Phillips (1993). First we note that

$$\bar{D} = E\left(y'Ny\right) = \mu'N\mu + \sigma_u^2 \operatorname{tr}\left(N\Sigma\right),$$

$$= \mu'_{-1}\mu_{-1} + \sigma_u^2 \operatorname{tr}\left(NCC'\right),$$

$$= \mu'_{-1}\mu_{-1} + \sigma_u^2 \operatorname{tr} C^{*'}C^{*}, \tag{6.47}$$

where $\mu_{-1}$ and $C^*$ are given above. Then, using $\alpha < 1$,

$$E_n\left(\hat{\alpha} - \alpha\right) = \frac{\sigma_u^2}{\bar{D}}\left[\operatorname{tr}\left(C^*\right) - \frac{2}{\bar{D}}\left[\mu'_{-1}C^*\mu_{-1} + \sigma_u^2 \operatorname{tr}\left(C^{*'}C^{*2}\right)\right]\right] \tag{6.48}$$

$$= -\frac{2\sigma_u^2}{\bar{D}}\left[\frac{\alpha}{1-\alpha^2} + \frac{2}{\bar{D}}\left(\mu'_{-1}C^*\mu_{-1} - \frac{\alpha}{1-\alpha^2}\mu'_{-1}\mu_{-1}\right)\right].$$

When $\mu_{-1} = 0, E_n\left(\hat{\alpha} - \alpha\right) = -2\alpha/n$, also see White (1961: 89–90). As before the bias of the one period ahead forecast is

$$E_n\left(\hat{y}_{n+1} - y_{n+1}\right) = \iota'_n dE_n\left(\hat{\alpha} - \alpha\right).$$

Similarly the MSE of $\hat{\alpha}$ can be obtained from (2.102), which will give the MSE of $\hat{y}_{n+1}$.

We can make some comparisons between the small-$\sigma$ bias $B_s(\hat{\alpha})$ with the large-$n$ $B_n(\hat{\alpha})$. The $O(n^{-1})$ approximation $B_n(\hat{\alpha})$ is a nonlinear function of $\sigma_u^2$ whereas the small-$\sigma$ bias is a linear function of $\sigma_u^2$. Second the $B_s(\hat{\alpha})$ does not exist if $\beta = 0$ and $y_0$ or $Ey_0 = 0$ but this is not the case for $B_n(\hat{\alpha})$. In fact $O(n^{-1})$ bias approximations are essentially the same whether or not we condition on $y_0$, since $\mu'_{-1}\mu_{-1} = y_0^2 c^{*'}c^* = O(1)$.

It is easy to note that $B_n(\hat{\alpha}) - B_s(\hat{\alpha}) = O(\sigma_u^4)$ and $(B_n(\hat{\alpha}) - B_s(\hat{\alpha})/\sigma_u^4 = O(n^{-1}))$. Thus the large-$n$ bias contains all the terms of small-$\sigma$ expansion, whereas small-$\sigma$ expansion does not contain all the terms of large-$n$. Thus, for the AR(1) model, large-$n$ approximation may be more accurate than the small-$\sigma$ approximation, except when $\sigma$ is small.

The approximate one period ahead LS forecast bias using the Laplace, large-$n$, and small-$\sigma$ methods, is compared with the exact one period ahead LS forecast bias for various parameter values in Mercurio (2000). From these results, it appears no one approximation method dominates over all parameter values. When sigma is very small, the small-$\sigma$ method dominates for all values of $\alpha$ and $\mu_1$. For larger sigma and intermediate values of $\alpha$, the Laplace method seems to give the best approximation. For larger values of sigma and larger values of alpha, the large-$n$ approximation does the best.

The above approximations do not work for $\alpha = 1$. Abadir (1993a) provides a useful result on the approximate bias of $\hat{\alpha}$ for $|\alpha| = 1$ when $y_0 = 0$ and $\beta = 0$. Let us write

$$B_n\left(\hat{\alpha}\right) = E\left(\hat{\alpha} - \alpha\right) = \frac{\sqrt{2}}{n}E\left(\hat{\alpha}^*\right), \tag{6.49}$$

where $\hat{\alpha}^* = n(\hat{\alpha} - \alpha)/\sqrt{2} = y'N_1^* y/y'Ny$; $N_1^* = n(N_1 - \alpha N)/\sqrt{2}$. Then from (2.30) in Chapter 2

$$E(\hat{\alpha}^*) = \int_0^\infty \frac{\partial M(U, -V)}{\partial U}|_{U=0}\, dV. \tag{6.50}$$

Abadir (1993a) then uses an innovative expansion of the moment generating function $M(U, -V)$ to obtain the bias result as an asymptotic expansion in $1/n$. The first term in this asymptotic expansion for $B_n(\hat{\alpha})$ can be shown to be $\alpha B_n(\hat{\alpha}) \simeq -1.7814/n$, derived earlier by Shenton and Johnson (1965), and LeBreton and Pham (1989).

Abadir has looked into the accuracy of the asymptotic expansion with the exact results, also see Evans and Savin (1981). His results suggest that the approximate bias of $\alpha E(\hat{\alpha}_n)$ is an overestimate of less than 0.8 percent of true value for $n = 50$. He also indicates that his approximate bias result is more accurate compared with Tsui and Ali (1989), which have provided series expansion of $E\hat{\alpha}$ for $\alpha \leq 1$.

Numerical results in Abadir suggest that for small $n$, $E\hat{\alpha}^*$ is a nonlinear function of $n$. Based on the behavior of $E\hat{\alpha}^*$, Abadir shows that the relative bias is of order lower than $1/n$. This is consistent with the super-consistency rate of $1/n$, and the simulation results of Banerjee, Donaldo, Hendry, and Smith (1986). Abadir also considers the case where $y_0$ is not zero and shows that a higher $y_0/\sigma_u$ reduces the bias for any given $n$, but the bias may even increase with $n$ in finite samples. Thus the large samples do not necessarily reduce biases under $\alpha = 1$.

Finally we note that a corrected LS estimator can be obtained as

$$\widetilde{\alpha} = \hat{\alpha} - \hat{B}_n(\hat{\alpha}), \tag{6.51}$$

where $\hat{B}$ is the value of bias above with $\alpha$ and $\sigma_u^2$ replaced by $\hat{\alpha}$ and $\hat{\sigma}_u^2 = \sum \hat{u}_i^2/n - 1$, $\hat{u}_i = y_i - \hat{\alpha} y_{i-1}$. Kiviet and Phillips (1993) have shown that $\widetilde{\alpha}$, for $\alpha < 1$, is unbiased up to $O(n^{-1})$ and its Monte Carlo MSE are generally smaller than those of $\hat{\alpha}$.

### 6.3.4 Probability Distributions

We now look at the probability distributions of $\hat{\alpha}$ and the forecasts. First, the exact distribution of $\hat{\alpha}$, which is the ratio of quadratic forms, can be analyzed by the Imhof result in Chapter 3, see the contributions by Phillips (1977a, 1978), Tsui and Ali (1994), and Evans and Savin (1981). Further, from Phillips (1979), the approximate distribution, conditional on $y_n$, is

$$
\begin{aligned}
P\left(\sqrt{n}(\hat{\alpha} - \alpha) \leq z|y_n\right) &= \Phi(z^*) + \frac{1}{\sqrt{n}} \frac{\alpha}{(1 - \alpha^2)^{1/2}} \phi(z^*) \\
&\times \left[1 + z^{*2} + 1 - \left(\frac{y_n}{\sigma_y}\right)^2\right] + O(n^{-1}), \tag{6.52}
\end{aligned}
$$

where $z^* = z/(1-\alpha^2)^{1/2}$ and $\sigma_y^2 = \sigma_u^2/(1-\alpha^2)$. Deleting the term $1 - (y_n/\sigma_y)^2$ gives the unconditional distribution $P(\sqrt{n}\,(\hat\alpha - \alpha) \leq z)$, see Phillips (1977$a$, 1978), and Lieberman (1994$b$). Thus for the conditional distribution, the skewness of the unconditional distribution is accentuated when $|y_n| \leq \sigma_y$. However, if $y_n$ is an outlier the skewness of the conditional distribution is less marked.

The approximation to the $t$-ratio statistic $t = (\hat\alpha - \alpha)/s_\alpha$, where $s_\alpha^2 = \hat\alpha_u^2/y'Ny$ and $\hat\sigma_u^2$ is based on the LS residuals, is given by

$$P\left(t \leq z\right) = \Phi\left(z^*\right) + \left[\alpha\left(1 - \alpha^2\right)^{-1/2}\right]\frac{\phi\left(z^*\right)}{\sqrt{n}} + O\left(n^{-1}\right), \qquad (6.53)$$

see Phillips (1977$a$). Also see Phillips (1978) for the saddle point approximation. These and the approximate distributions given above are usually not very satisfactory in the tails for small $n$ and large $|\alpha|$ values. Given the approximate distributions one can also obtain the bias and MSE of $\hat\alpha$.

From the above result one can also deduce the approximation to the conditional distribution of $\hat y_{n+1} - \bar y_{n+1}$ given $y_n$, where $\bar y_{n+1} = E\left(y_{n+1}|y_n\right)$. This is

$$P\left(\sqrt{n}\,(\hat y_{n+1} - \bar y_{n+1}) \leq z|y_n\right) = \Phi\left(\frac{z^*}{y_n}\right) + \frac{1}{\sqrt{n}}\frac{\alpha}{(1-\alpha^2)^{1/2}}\phi\left(\frac{z^*}{y_n}\right)$$

$$\times \left\{2 + \frac{z^{*2}}{y_n^2} - \left(\frac{y_n}{\sigma_y}\right)^2\right\} + O\left(\frac{1}{n}\right) \qquad (6.54)$$

when $y_n > 0$, and when $y_n < 0$

$$= \Phi\left(\frac{-z^*}{y_n}\right) - \frac{1}{\sqrt{n}}\frac{\alpha}{(1-\alpha^2)^{1/2}}\phi\left(\frac{z^*}{y_n}\right)\left\{2 + \frac{z^{*2}}{y_n^2} - \left(\frac{y_n}{\sigma_y}\right)^2\right\} + O\left(\frac{1}{n}\right).$$

Deleting $(y_n/\sigma_y)^2$ we get the distributions when $\hat\alpha$ and $y_n$ are independent. Thus the dependence of $\hat\alpha$ and $y_n$ can accentuate the skewness toward the origin.

Phillips (1979) also provides the distribution of forecast error $\hat y_{n+1} - y_{n+1}$. This is up to $O\left(n^{-2}\right)$

$$P\left(\hat y_{n+1} - y_{n+1} \leq z|y_n\right) = \Phi\left(\frac{z}{\sigma_u}\right) + \phi\left(\frac{z}{\sigma_u}\right) \times \left[\frac{1}{n}\frac{\alpha}{(1-\alpha^2)^{1/2}}\right.$$

$$\left.\times \left(\frac{y_n}{\sigma_y}\right)\left(3 - \left(\frac{y_n}{\sigma_y}\right)^2\right) - \frac{1}{2n}\left(\frac{y_n}{\sigma_y}\right)^2\left(\frac{z}{n^2}\right)\right].$$

$$(6.55)$$

When $\hat{\alpha}$ and $y_n$ are independent the term $3 - (y_n/\sigma_y)^2$ is dropped. The conditional distribution of $\hat{y}_{n+1} - y_{n+1}$ is negatively/positively skewed when $y_n > 0/y_n < 0$. Further the conditional distribution is accentuated when $|y_n| < \sigma_y$ and $\hat{\alpha}$ and $y_n$ are dependent.

The distribution of the $s$th period ahead forecast error and that of $\hat{\alpha}^s$ are also discussed in Phillips (1979).

## 6.3.5    ARMAX model

Let us consider the AR(1) model with $p$ regressors (ARMAX) given in (6.15). Then the exact moments of $\hat{\alpha}$ are as given in (2.29) with $N_1$ and $N$ matrices given by (6.18). To obtain the results for $\hat{\beta}$ we write

$$\hat{\beta} = \left(X^{*'}X^*\right)^{-1} X^{*'}(D_2 y - D_1 \hat{\alpha} y) = Hh(y)$$

and

$$E\hat{\beta} = H \left(D_2 \mu - D_1 E\left(\hat{\alpha}y\right)\right), \tag{6.56}$$

where $h(y) = D_2 y - D_1 \hat{\alpha} y$, $E(\hat{\alpha}y) = dE\hat{\alpha} = (\mu + \Sigma \partial/\partial \mu)E\hat{\alpha}$, $H = (X^{*'}X^*)^{-1}X^*$ and $\mu$ is as in (6.10). Further

$$E\hat{\beta}\hat{\beta}' = HE\left(h(y)h'(y)\right)H', \tag{6.57}$$

where

$$E\left(h(y)h'(y)\right) = D_2 \left(Eyy'\right) D_2' - D_2(E\hat{\alpha}yy')D_1' - D_1(E\hat{\alpha}yy')D_2'$$
$$+ D_1 \left(E\hat{\alpha}^2 yy'\right) D_1'$$

with

$$Eyy' = \mu\mu' + \sigma_u^2 CC', \quad E\left(\hat{\alpha}yy'\right) = dd'E\hat{\alpha}, \tag{6.58}$$

$$E\hat{\alpha}^2 yy' = dd'E\hat{\alpha}^2. \tag{6.59}$$

The evaluations of $dd'E\hat{\alpha}$ and $dd'E\hat{\alpha}^2$ are as given in 6.3.2.

The approximate results by Laplace, large-$n$ and small-$\sigma$ follow by noting the following results for $\hat{\alpha}$. The Laplace approximations of $E_L\hat{\alpha}$ and $E_L\hat{\alpha}^2$ are as given in 6.3.3 by appropriate substitutions of $N_1$, $N$, and $\mu$. The small-$\sigma$ bias and MSE are given from Srivastava and Ullah (1995) as

$$E_s \left(\hat{\alpha} - \alpha\right) = \frac{\sigma_u^2}{\mu_{-1}' M \mu_{-1}} \left[\operatorname{tr}\left(MC^*\right) - \frac{2\mu_{-1}'\mathrm{MC}^* M \mu_{-1}}{\mu_{-1}' M \mu_{-1}}\right] \tag{6.60}$$

and

$$E_s \left(\hat{\alpha} - \alpha\right)^2 = \frac{\sigma_u^2}{\mu_{-1}' M \mu_{-1}} \left[\operatorname{tr}\left(\mathrm{MC}^*\right) - \frac{2}{\mu_{-1}' M \mu_{-1}}\left(\mu_{-1}'\mathrm{MC}^* M \mu_{-1}\right.\right.$$
$$\left.\left. + \sigma_u^2 \operatorname{tr}\left(C^{*'}\mathrm{MC}^*\mathrm{MC}^*\right)\right)\right]. \tag{6.61}$$

Taking the derivatives of the above approximations we obtain the approximations for the moments of $\hat{\beta}$. The exact and approximate moments of the one period ahead forecast error can then be obtained in the same way as in 6.3.2 and 6.3.3. For this we write

$$\hat{y}_{n+1} - y_{n+1} = (\hat{\alpha} - \alpha) \, \iota'_n y + x_{n+1} \left( \hat{\beta} - \beta \right) - u_{n+1}, \tag{6.62}$$

which gives

$$E \left( \hat{y}_{n+1} - y_{n+1} \right) = (\iota'_n d) \, E \left( \hat{\alpha} - \alpha \right) + x_{n+1} E \left( \hat{\beta} - \beta \right) \tag{6.63}$$

and

$$\begin{aligned}
E \left( \hat{y}_{n+1} - y_{n+1} \right)^2 &= x_{n+1} E \left( \hat{\beta} - \beta \right) \left( \hat{\beta} - \beta \right)' x'_{n+1} \\
&\quad + \left( \iota'_n d \right)^2 E \left( \hat{\alpha} - \alpha \right)^2 + \sigma_u^2 \\
&\quad + 2 x_{n+1} E \left( (\hat{\beta} - \beta) \left( \hat{\alpha} - \alpha \right) \iota'_n y \right),
\end{aligned} \tag{6.64}$$

where

$$\begin{aligned}
E \left( (\hat{\beta} - \beta) \left( \hat{\alpha} - \alpha \right) \iota'_n y \right) &= H \left[ D_2 d \left( \iota'_n d \right) E \left( \hat{\alpha} - \alpha \right) - D_1 dE \hat{\alpha} \left( \hat{\alpha} - \alpha \right) \right] \\
&\quad - \beta \left( \iota'_n d \right) E \left( \hat{\alpha} - \alpha \right).
\end{aligned}$$

Finally we note that Carter and Ullah (1979) and Ullah and Maasoumi (1986) considered the ARMX $(1,1)$ where $u_i$ in (6.1) follows an MA(1) process with the coefficient $\alpha$. In this case $V(y) = \Sigma = \sigma_u^2 I$ and so the integral representation of the exact moments reduces to confluent hypergeometric series, see Chapter 2. Also see Hoque (1985), and Hoque and Peters (1986) for ARMAX models. In another work Dufour and Kiviet (1994) have the ARMAX $(p, 0)$ model and provided the exact tests for the restrictions on the parameters.

## 6.3.6   Nonnormal Case

The exact moments of $\hat{\alpha}$ for the nonnormal case is analyzed in Peters (1989). This is done by developing the joint moment generating of $y' N_1 y$ and $y' N y$ under an Edgeworth–Gram–Charlier type nonnormal family of the error distribution. The exact moments are then obtained by using the results of Sawa (1972) given in Chapter 2. These were evaluated numerically over the space of values of parameters involved in the moments. It appeared that the bias and MSE of $\hat{\alpha}$ in a stationary intercept model are not affected by the direction of skewness and that both are sensitive to leptokurtosis when $\alpha$ gets to the unit circle. At $\alpha = 1$, both the bias and MSE are affected by the skewness direction. In this case the bias is still negative and robust to changes in third ($\kappa_3$) and fourth ($\kappa_4$) cumulants. But the MSE is very sensitive to changes in $\kappa_3$ and $\kappa_4$.

The results for the nontrended model suggest that for low $\alpha$ values MSE is relatively insensitive to $\kappa_3$ and $\kappa_4$ compared to $\alpha$ close to unit root. The bias is generally robust.

Overall, while the bias is relatively insensitive to skewness and kurtosis the MSE is relatively sensitive to both skewness and kurtosis and this sensitivity increases as the signal to noise ratio increases. Therefore the inference based on the assumption of normality of error can be misleading if the true error is nonnormal.

The approximate moments of $\hat{\alpha}$ by the large-$n$, Laplace, and small-$\sigma$ can be written from the results in Chapter 2. These results also suggest that the MSE are sensitive to the changes in skewness and kurtosis. Lieberman (1994$b$) also provides the approximate Laplace distribution of $\hat{\alpha}$.

## 6.3.7   Cointegration Model

Let us consider a simple cointegration model

$$y_i = x_i\alpha + v_{i1}, \tag{6.65}$$
$$x_i = \beta_1 i + \beta y_i + u_i,$$

where $u_i = u_{i-1} + v_{i2}$ and $(v_{i1}, v_{i2})$ is $i.i.d$ normal errors with zero means, $Ev_{i1}^2 = \sigma_1^2$, $Ev_{i2}^2 = \sigma_2^2$, and cov $(v_{i1}, v_{i2}) = 0$. If $\beta_1 = 0$ then there is no linear trend. Assuming $\alpha\beta \neq 1$, the reduced form of the model is

$$x_i = \frac{\beta_1}{1 - \alpha\beta}i + \frac{\beta v_{i1} + u_i}{1 - \alpha\beta}, \tag{6.66}$$

$$y_i = \frac{\alpha\beta_1}{1 - \alpha\beta}i + \frac{v_{i1} + \alpha u_i}{1 - \alpha\beta},$$

which imply that $y_i$ and $x_i$ are random walks with drifts, $\beta_1/(1 - \alpha\beta)$, $\alpha\beta_1/(1 - \alpha\beta)$, respectively. Therefore $x_i$ and $y_i$ are cointegrated with cointegrating coefficient $\alpha$.

Let $\hat{\alpha}$ be the LS estimator of $\alpha$, then

$$\hat{\alpha} - \alpha = \frac{\sum_i x_i v_{i1}}{\sum_i x_i^2}. \tag{6.67}$$

Using $u_i = \sum_{j=1}^{i} v_{j2}$ in the reduced form and doing simplifications $\hat{\alpha} - \alpha$ can be written as a ratio of quadratic forms (Ellison and Satchell 1988, and Fan 1990). Thus

$$\frac{\hat{\alpha} - \alpha}{\delta} = \frac{z'N_1 z}{z'Nz}, \tag{6.68}$$

where $\delta = (1/\beta) - \alpha$, $z = [\epsilon' v']'$ is a $2n \times 1$ vector with the element $z_j = [\epsilon_j v_j]'$ with $\epsilon_j = (\beta_1 + v_{j2})/\sigma_2$ and $v_j = v_{j1}/\sigma_1$, $j = 1, \ldots, n$ and $N_1$ and $N$ are

$2n \times 2n$ nonsymmetric matrices

$$N_1 = \begin{bmatrix} 0 & \lambda P \\ \lambda P' & 4\lambda^2 I_n \end{bmatrix}, \qquad N = \begin{bmatrix} J & 2\lambda P \\ 2\lambda P' & 4\lambda^2 I_n \end{bmatrix} \tag{6.69}$$

in which $\lambda = \beta \sigma_1 / 2\sigma_2$, $J = PP'$ and

$$P = \begin{bmatrix} 1 & 1 & 1 & \cdots & 1 \\ 0 & 1 & 1 & \cdots & 1 \\ \vdots & \vdots & \vdots & & \vdots \\ 0 & 0 & 0 & \cdots & 1 \end{bmatrix}. \tag{6.70}$$

The variable $z \sim N(\mu, I_{2n})$ where

$$\mu = \lambda_0 (\iota' \, 0'), \qquad \lambda_0 = \frac{\beta_1}{\sigma_2} \tag{6.71}$$

and $\iota$ is an $n \times 1$ vector of unit elements.

Given that the LS estimator $\hat{\alpha}$ is a ratio of quadratic forms its moments and distributions immediately follow from the results (2.28) and (2.29) in Chapter 2 and 3.2.1 in Chapter 3. First from the result in 2.2 it can be verified that the LS estimator $\hat{\alpha}$ has finite sample moments up to order $n - 1$ and does not have any other higher order moments. Second the first two moments of $(\hat{\alpha} - \alpha)/\delta$ are given by the results in (2.29). Consider the first moment, which is

$$E\left(\frac{\hat{\alpha} - \alpha}{\delta}\right) = \int_0^\infty |I + 2tN|^{-1/2} \times \left[\left(\mathrm{tr}\left(N_1 (I + 2tN)^{-1}\right)\right)\right.$$

$$+ \mu' (I + 2tN)^{-1} N_1 (I + 2tN)^{-1} \mu\bigg]$$

$$\times \exp\left(-t\mu' N (I + 2tN)^{-1} \mu\right) dt. \tag{6.72}$$

Since $\lambda$ appears in $N$ and $N_1$ and $\lambda_0$ appears in $\mu$ the first moment is a function of $\lambda$ and $\lambda_0$. But for any fixed $\lambda$ and sample size $n$ it can be verified that the function under the integral is a strictly decreasing function of $\lambda_0$. Therefore $E((\hat{\alpha} - \alpha)/\delta)$ is a strictly decreasing function of $\lambda_0$. This also implies that the bias of $\hat{\alpha}$ is always smaller when $\lambda_0 \neq 0$ than when $\lambda_0 = 0$ or $\beta_1 = 0$ (no drift).

The approximate moments of $\hat{\alpha}$ can also be written from the small-$\sigma$ and large-$n$ results in 6.3.3 or from 2.5.1 and 2.5.2.

Next the exact distribution and density of $(\hat{\alpha} - \alpha/\delta)$ follows from the result on the Imhof distribution of the ratio of quadratic forms in Chapter 3. This has been studied in Fan (1990), also see Ellison and Satchell (1988) where $\lambda_0 = 0$.

The density functions of the standardized $\hat{\alpha}$, for fixed $n$ and $\lambda_0$, is skewed to the right for small values of $\lambda$, then becomes less and less skewed as $\lambda$ increases, finally becoming skewed to the left. However, the change of the density function from being positively skewed to negatively skewed appears at much larger $\lambda$ value for $\lambda_0 \neq 0$ compared to the model with no drift ($\lambda_0 = 0$). This implies that the finite sample bias of $\hat{\alpha}$ goes up as $\lambda_0$ decreases. Thus the model with no drift has larger bias compared to the model with a drift.

Next the asymptotic distribution of the standardized $\hat{\alpha}$ in the model with a drift is well known to be normal, that is $n^{3/2}(\hat{\alpha} - \alpha)/\delta \sim N(0, 3(2\lambda/\lambda_0)^2)$, and it depends on $\lambda$ and $\lambda_0$. For a model with no drift, however, the asymptotic distribution is nonnormal with nonzero mean. Comparisons of the asymptotic distribution with the exact distribution reveals that for small $\lambda$ and large $\lambda_0$ the asymptotic distribution provides a good approximation for $n$ as small as 25. But, as $\lambda_0$ decreases or $\lambda$ increases, the asymptotic distribution approximation becomes less and less satisfactory and may lead to misleading inferences in small samples.

Finally as pointed above the bias of $\hat{\alpha}$ declines very quickly for increases in $\lambda_0$. Also the bias of $\hat{\alpha}$ when $\lambda_0 \neq 0$ declines much more quickly than the bias when $\lambda_0 = 0$ for changing $n$, which is consistent with the faster asymptotic convergence of $n^{3/2}$ when $\lambda_0 \neq 0$. Thus for the models with a drift the use of $\hat{\alpha}$ for testing may not be too hazardous, see Banerjee, Donaldo, Hendry, and Smith (1986), Ellison and Satchell (1988), and Fan (1990).

Most of these results have been developed for a simple model and under the assumptions of normality. It will be interesting to use the results of Chapters 2 and 3 to develop the results for nonnormal errors. In this case the approximate moments can be developed and using them an Edgeworth expansion of the distribution can also be developed.

# 6.4   Conclusion

In this chapter we have presented the results on the exact and approximate moments and distribution of the parameters of AR(1) model for both the stable and nonstationary cases. The AR(1) model with exogenous variables is also analyzed. These results show the applications of the procedures in Chapters 2 and 3. A systematic application of the approximate moments results (2.101) and (2.102) is developed in Bao and Ullah (2002) for various time series models. This includes the AR(p) models, MA(1) models, ARMAX models, structural model with AR(1) errors, VAR model, partial adjustment model, and ARCH models. For bias corrections in ARMA models, see Cordeiro and Klein (1994). Phillips (1986, 1987c) explores the asymptotic expansion of the regression coefficients in nonstationary VARs, also see Vahid and Issler (2002) for common cycles features in VAR and Abadir, Hadri and Tzavalis (1999). Kiviet and Dufour (1997) have considered an AR(p) model with regressors and developed the procedures which yield exact inference. For given (up to an unknown scalar factor) distribution of the innovative errors, these include exact tests on the maximum lag length, structural change, and on the presence of unit roots. On the works related to testing in dynamic regression models, also see Dufour and Kiviet (1996), Dufour and King (1991), Dufour (1990), Kiviet and Phillips (1990, 1992), Müller and Elliott (2001), Pesaran and Timmermann (2003), and Rothenberg (2002). The finite sample moments of the ML estimators in ARCH models are analyzed in Iglesias and Phillips (2001). Linton (1997) provides asymptotic expansion of the distribution of the parameters in the GARCH $(1, 1)$. For the dynamic panel data model, see Kiviet (1995). Xiao and Phillips (2002) develop asymptotic expansions for Wald test statistics in time series regressions with integrated processes, also see Xiao and Phillips (1998) for second-order expansions and MSE approximations for efficient frequency domain regression estimators.

# 7

# Simultaneous Equations Model

## 7.1 Introduction

Most of our earlier chapters were related to the finite sample analysis of single equation models. However, it is well known that most of the developments in economics theory are based on the system of several economic relationships, for example, system of demand equations and models of macro economy. The interactions or endogeneity of the economic variables have special implications for the interpretation and statistical inference of part or complete system of the economic models. The implications of simultaneity or enodogeneity for econometric estimation are buried in the works of Working (1926) and Haavelmo (1943) among others. Cowles Commission monographs published in 1950 and 1953 were perhaps the first to deal extensively and exclusively with the problem of identification and estimation of simultaneous equation models. This subject matter of econometrics has grown rapidly over the last five decades, see the text books by Davidson and Mackinnon (1996), Amemiya (1985), and Greene (2000) for details.

Major work on the finite sample analysis in econometrics was initiated and developed for the estimators of the parameters of the simultaneous equations model. This literature can be classified in the areas of exact sampling distributions, exact moments, and approximate moments and distributions of the two-stage least squares (2SLS) and ordinary least-squares (OLS) estimators in a structural equation. Based on the early works by Haavelmo (1947), and Anderson and Rubin (1949) on the confidence regions for structural coefficients, the pioneering works toward the exact sampling distribution were done by Basmann (1961), Bergstrom (1962), and Kabe (1963, 1964), and later on by Richardson (1968), Basmann (1974), Anderson (1984), Anderson and Sawa (1979), Mariano (1982), Phillips (1983), and Cribbett, Lye and Ullah (1989).

The developments in analyzing the exact moments were the outcomes of the works by Richardson (1968), Sawa (1972), Takeuchi (1970), Nagar and Ullah (1973), Ullah and Nagar (1974), and Hillier, Kinal, and Srivastava (1984). A parallel development took place by the pioneering work of Nagar (1959) on the asymptotic expansion giving the large-$n$ approximate moments of the $k$-class estimators. This was followed by the work of Sargan (1974) who explored the validity of Nagar's large-$n$ expansions (Edgeworth expansions) in the light of the questions raised by Srinivasan (1970). Kadane (1971) provided small-$\sigma$ expansion of the k-class estimators. Phillips (1977*b*, 1980), and Sargan (1975, 1976, 1980) provided a major breakthrough by their important contributions to analyze the validity and applications of Edgeworth expansions for econometric estimators and test statistics, also see Arellano and Sargan (1990). For details on the various techniques and details of results in these works see the reviews by Phillips (1983), Mariano (1982), Rothenberg (1984*a*, 1988), and Taylor (1983).

In this chapter we analyze the moments and distribution of the estimators in the simultaneous equations models, by using the techniques in Chapters 2 and 3.

## 7.2    Simultaneous Equations Model

### 7.2.1    Model Specification

Let us write the structural form of a system of $M$ contemporaneous simultaneous equations models as

$$Y^s\Gamma + XB = U, \tag{7.1}$$

where $Y^s = [y_1, \ldots, y_M]$ is a $n \times M$ matrix of $n$ observations of $M$ endogeneous variables, $X = [x_1, \ldots, x_K]$ is a $n \times K$ matrix of $n$ observations of $K$ nonrandom exogeneous variables and $U = [u_1, \ldots, u_M]$ is a $n \times M$ matrix of the structural disturbances of the system. Further the vectors $y_i, u_i$, and $x_l$ for $i = 1, \ldots, M$ and $l = 1, \ldots, K$ are $n \times 1$ vectors. The coefficient matrices $\Gamma(M \times M)$ (assumed to be nonsingular) and $B(K \times M)$ consist of parameters that are to be estimated from the data.

The reduced form of the structural form in (7.1) is

$$Y^s = X\Pi^s + V^s, \tag{7.2}$$

where $\Pi^s = -B\Gamma^{-1}$ and $V^s = U\Gamma^{-1}$ are the matrices of reduced form coefficients and disturbances, respectively.

We will be working with a single structural equation of (7.1). By incorporating the exclusion type restrictions, this can be written in the following form:

$$y_1 = Y_1\gamma + X_1\beta + u, \tag{7.3}$$

or

$$y_1 = Z_1\delta + u, \quad Z_1 = [Y_1\ X_1], \quad \delta' = (\gamma'\ \beta'), \tag{7.4}$$

where $y_1(n \times 1)$ and $Y_1(n \times m_1)$ contain $n$ observations of $m_1 + 1$ included endogenous variables, $X_1$ is a $n \times K_1$ matrix of included exogenous variables and $u$ is the vector of random disturbances on this equation. Also, $\gamma$ and $\beta$ are $m_1 \times 1$ and $K_1 \times 1$ coefficient vectors, respectively, and $\delta$ is a $(m_1 + K_1) \times 1$ vector. Thus, (7.3) represents one equation of the full model (7.1). Further, the reduced form of (7.3) is written as

$$y_1 = X_1\pi_{11} + X_1^*\pi_{12} + v_1.$$
$$Y_1 = X_1\Pi_{21} + X_1^*\Pi_{22} + V_1$$

or

$$Y = X\Pi + V, \tag{7.5}$$

where $Y = [y_1\ \ Y_1]$, $X = [X_1\ \ X_1^*]$, and $X_1^*$ is a $n \times K_1^*$, $K_1^* = K - K_1$, matrix of excluded exogenous variables from (7.3). We also assume that $K_1^* \geq m_1$ and the submatrix $\Pi_{22}(K_1^* \times m_1)$ has full rank $m_1$ so that the structural equation is identified. We note that (7.3) can be obtained by postmultiplication of (7.5) by $(1 - \gamma')'$, which provides

$$\pi_{11} - \Pi_{21}\gamma = \beta, \qquad \pi_{12} - \Pi_{22}\gamma = 0. \tag{7.6}$$

The parameters $K_1^* - m_1 \geq 0$ will be used here as the measure of the degree by which the structural equation (7.3) is over identified. When $K_1^* - m_1 = 0$ we have a just identified equation.

## 7.2.2  Moments of the Single Equation Estimators

We consider the estimation of the complete system in (7.1) by estimating each equation incorporating the identifiability restrictions. These are known as the limited information estimators.

We will begin by considering the instrumental variable (IV) estimator, $\hat{\delta}_{IV} = \hat{\delta}$, of the coefficient vector $\delta$ in (7.4) based on the instrument matrix $W$. $\hat{\delta}_{IV}$ minimizes the function

$$S(\delta) = (y_1 - Z_1\delta)' W(W'W)^{-1}W'(y_1 - Z_1\delta) \tag{7.7}$$

and writing

$$P_W = W(W'W)^{-1}W', \quad \bar{P}_W = I - P_W \tag{7.8}$$

we obtain the following expression for the IV estimator $\delta$ :

$$\hat{\delta} = (Z_1'P_W Z_1)^{-1}Z_1'P_W y_1. \tag{7.9}$$

Further the expressions for the IV estimators of $\gamma$ and $\beta$ can be written as

$$\hat{\gamma} = \left( Y_1' P_W \left( I - X_1 \left( X_1' P_W X_1 \right)^{-1} X_1' \right) P_W Y_1 \right)^{-1}$$

$$\times Y_1' P_W \left( I - X_1 \left( X_1' P_W X_1 \right)^{-1} X_1' \right) P_W y_1 \qquad (7.10)$$

$$\hat{\beta} = (X_1' P_W X_1)^{-1} X_1' P_W (y_1 - Y_1 \hat{\gamma}). \qquad (7.11)$$

In the usual case where $W$ includes $X_1$ as a subset of its instruments and $P_W X_1 = X_1$ we get

$$\hat{\gamma} = (Y_1' N Y_1)^{-1} Y_1' N y_1, \qquad (7.12)$$

$$\hat{\beta} = (X_1' X_1)^{-1} X_1' (y_1 - Y_1 \hat{\gamma}), \qquad (7.13)$$

where

$$N = P_W - P_{X_1}.$$

The ordinary least squares (OLS) and the two-stage least squares (2SLS) estimators can be written as the special cases of the IV estimators, and they differ with respect to $N$ matrices. These are

$$\text{OLS} : N = I - P_{X_1} = \bar{P}_{X_1}, \qquad \text{2SLS} : N = P_X - P_{X_1}. \qquad (7.14)$$

If $N = P_X - P_{X_1} - (K_1^* - 2)/n$ then we get a bias-corrected 2SLS (B2SLS) estimator in Donald and Newey (2001). Also see Nagar (1959), and Sawa (1973a) for other types of bias-corrected estimators.

We also note that the $k$-class estimators of $\gamma$ and $\beta$ can also be written as $\hat{\gamma}$ and $\hat{\beta}$ with

$$k\text{-class} : N = k(P_X - P_{X_1}) + (1 - k)\bar{P}_{X_1}. \qquad (7.15)$$

The values of $k = 0, 1$ provide the OLS and 2SLS estimators, respectively. The limited information maximum likelihood (LIML) estimator is given for the value of $k$ which is the smallest root of the determinantal equation

$$\left| Y' \bar{P}_{X_1} Y - k Y' \bar{P}_X Y \right| = 0. \qquad (7.16)$$

This is the same as the LIML of $\gamma_* = (1 - \gamma')'$, which is the value of $\gamma_*$ for which the ratio $\gamma_*' Y' \bar{P}_{X_1} Y \gamma_* / \gamma_*' Y' \bar{P}_X Y \gamma_*$ is minimum or the concentrated likelihood $L(\gamma_*)$ attains its maximum. We also note here that the OLS/2SLS estimators given above can also be seen as the value of $\gamma$ which minimizes $\gamma_*' Y' \bar{P}_{X_1} Y \gamma_*$ and $\gamma_*' Y' (P_X - P_{X_1}) Y \gamma_*$ with respect to $\gamma_*$.

We note that the single equation estimators given above differ with respect to the matrix $N$ in (7.12). Here we will first analyze the moments of the OLS, 2SLS, LIML, and $k$-class estimators and then consider their distributions in the following Section. We will go into details for the case of 2 endogenous variables and then discuss the results for the general case.

For analyzing the exact moments we consider the structural equation with two endogenous variables. In this case, $Y_1$ is simply a column vector (say, $y_2$) and $\gamma$ is a scalar quantity. So we can write the equation as

$$y_1 = y_2\gamma + X_1\beta + u \tag{7.17}$$

and the *IV* estimator $\hat{\gamma} = c$ of $\gamma$ from (7.12) is

$$c = \frac{y_1' N y_2}{y_2' N y_2} = \frac{y' N_1 y}{y' N_2 y}, \tag{7.18}$$

where

$$y = \begin{bmatrix} y_1 \\ y_2 \end{bmatrix}, \qquad N_1 = \frac{1}{2}\begin{bmatrix} 0 & N \\ N & 0 \end{bmatrix}, \qquad N_2 = \begin{bmatrix} 0 & 0 \\ 0 & N \end{bmatrix}. \tag{7.19}$$

Both $N_1$, and $N_2$ are the symmetric matrices. We assume that the elements of $X$ are nonstochastic and fixed in repeated samples, rank of $X = K < n$, and the vector $u$ is distributed with $Eu = 0$ and $V(u) = \sigma_u^2 I$. Further the vector $y$ is assumed to be a $2n \times 1$ vector distributed as

$$y = \begin{bmatrix} y_1 \\ y_2 \end{bmatrix} \sim N\left[\begin{pmatrix} X\pi_1 \\ X\pi_2 \end{pmatrix}, \; \Omega = \begin{pmatrix} w_{11} & w_{12} \\ w_{21} & w_{22} \end{pmatrix} \otimes I_n\right], \tag{7.20}$$

where $\pi_1 = (\pi_{11}\,\pi_{12})'$ and $\pi_2 = (\pi_{21}\,\pi_{22})'$.

The exact moments of the *IV* estimator $c$ and that of (7.10), for $m_1 = 1$, can then be written from (2.28) and (2.29). These include the results for the OLS, 2SLS, and $k$-class estimators, but not for the LIML for which $k$ is a stochastic variable. However, the matrix $N$ and hence $N_2$ are idempotent matrices of rank $n - K_1$ and $K_1^*$, respectively, for the OLS and 2SLS cases. Therefore the integral representation of the exact moments can be written in terms of the confluent hypergeometric series expressions given in Chapter 2. The results for the 2SLS estimator $\hat{\gamma} = c$ can be written as

$$Ec = \rho + \lambda\gamma^*\theta f_{0,1} = \gamma - (\gamma - \rho)\frac{(K_1^* - 2)}{2}f_{-1,0},$$

$$Ec^2 = \rho^2 + \lambda^2\left[\left(\frac{\theta}{2} + \gamma^{*2}\theta^2\right)f_{0,2} + \frac{1}{2}\left(\frac{K_1^*}{2} + \gamma^{*2}\theta\right)f_{-1,1}\right] + 2\rho\lambda Ec, \tag{7.21}$$

where

$$\rho = w_{12}/w_{22}, \lambda = w_{22}^{-1}\left(w_{11}w_{22} - w_{12}^2\right)^{1/2} = \left(w_{11}w_{22}^{-1} - \rho^2\right)^{1/2}, \gamma^* = \frac{1}{\lambda}(\gamma - \rho),$$

$$f_{\mu,\nu} = \frac{\Gamma(K_1^*/2 + \mu)}{\Gamma(K_1^*/2 + \nu)}e^{-\theta}{}_1F_1\left(K_1^*/2 + \mu; K_1^*/2 + \nu; \theta\right) \tag{7.22}$$

and

$$\boldsymbol{\theta} = \pi_2' X' N X \pi_2 / 2w_{22} \tag{7.23}$$

is a noncentrality parameter of $O(n)$. For the confluent hypergeometric function $_1F_1()$, see Appendix A.9.

We can also develop the third and fourth moments as

$$Ec^3 = \rho^3 + 3\rho^2 \lambda Ec + 3\rho\lambda^2 Ec^2 + \frac{\lambda^3}{4}\theta\gamma^* \left[2\theta\left(3 + 2\theta\gamma^{*2}\right) f_{0,3}\right.$$
$$\left. + 3\left(K_1^* + 2 + 2\theta\gamma^{*2}\right) f_{-1,2}\right] \tag{7.24}$$

and

$$Ec^4 = \rho^4 + 4\rho^3 \lambda Ec + 6\rho^2\lambda^2 Ec^2 + 4\rho\lambda^3 Ec^3$$
$$+ \lambda^4 \left[\frac{\theta^2}{4}\left\{\left(2\theta\gamma^{*2} + 3\right)^2 - 6\right\} f_{0,4} + \frac{3}{4}\theta\left\{4\theta^2\gamma^{*4} + 2(K_1^* + 5)\theta\gamma^{*2}\right.\right.$$
$$\left. + (K_1^* + 2)\right\} f_{-1,3} + \frac{3}{16}\left\{4\theta^2\gamma^{*4} + 4(K_1^* + 2)\theta\gamma^{*2} + K_1^*(K_1^* + 2)\right\} f_{-2,2}\right]. \tag{7.25}$$

See Ullah and Ullah (1976).

Using the asymptotic expansion of the confluent hypergeometric functions from the Appendix A.9.1, the following results can be easily obtained for large $\theta$. Since large $\theta$ could be due to large-$n$ or small $-w_{22}$ the results given below are equivalent to Nagar's (1959) large-$n$ expansions and Kadane's (1971) small-$w_{22}$ expansions. Thus the bias, up to $O(n^{-2})$, and the MSE, up to $O(n^{-2})$, are

$$E(c - \gamma) = (\gamma - \rho)\left[\frac{2 - K_1^*}{2\theta} + \frac{(2 - K_1^*)(4 - K_1^*)}{4\theta^2}\right]$$
$$E(c - \gamma)^2 = \frac{\lambda^2 + (\gamma - \rho)^2}{2\theta} + \frac{(4 - K_1^*)}{4}$$
$$\times \left[\lambda^2 + (4 - K_1^*)(\gamma - \rho)^2\right]\frac{1}{\theta^2}. \tag{7.26}$$

Further the variance and the central third moments, up to $O(n^{-2})$, are

$$E(c - Ec)^2 = \frac{\lambda^2 + (\gamma - \rho)^2}{2\theta}$$
$$+ \left[\frac{(4 - K_1^*)}{4}\lambda^2 + (3 - K_1^*)(\gamma - \rho)^2\right]\frac{1}{\theta^2}$$
$$E(c - Ec)^3 = 3(\gamma - \rho)\frac{\lambda^2 + (\gamma - \rho)^2}{2\theta^2} \tag{7.27}$$

and the central fourth moment, up to $O(n^{-3})$, is

$$E(c - Ec)^4 = \frac{3}{4}\left[\left(\lambda^2 + (\gamma - \rho)^2\right)^2 \frac{1}{\theta^2} + \left(\lambda^2 + (\gamma - \rho)^2\right)\right.$$
$$\left. \times \left(\lambda^2 + 4(\gamma - \rho)^2\right)(6 - K_1^*)\frac{1}{\theta^3}\right]. \tag{7.28}$$

Thus the Pearsonian Skewness and Kurtosis coefficients of the distributions of $c$, up to $O(1/\theta)$ or $O(1/n)$, are

$$\sqrt{\text{Skewness}}(c) = \frac{3\sqrt{2}(\gamma - \rho)}{\sqrt{\lambda^2 + (\gamma - \rho)^2}} \frac{1}{\sqrt{\theta}} \tag{7.29}$$

and

$$\text{Kurtosis}(c) = 3 + 6 \frac{\lambda^2 + 6(\gamma - \rho)^2}{\lambda^2 + (\gamma - \rho)^2} \frac{1}{\theta}. \tag{7.30}$$

It is clear that the 2SLS estimator is unbiased if $\rho = \gamma$. This holds for both the exact and approximate biases. Also the approximate bias shows that it vanishes for $K_1^* = 2$. Further the direction of bias is opposite to the sign of $(\gamma - \rho)$. We also note Skewness $\to 0$ and Kurtosis $\to 3$ as $\theta \to \infty$. In fact it is well known that the limiting distribution of the 2SLS estimator is normal. However, it is interesting to note that the departure from symmetry and mesokurticity depends on the value of $\gamma$. If $\gamma = \rho$, then we have Skewness $= 0$ and Kurtosis $= 3 + 6/\theta$, that is, the distribution of $c$ is symmetrical. However, if $\gamma < \rho$, $c$ is negatively skewed and positively skewed if $\gamma > \rho$, even for small samples. Further, for small samples, the distribution of $c$ is platykurtic.

For $n \to \infty$, we observe that the estimator $c$ is asymptotically unbiased. Further the asymptotic variance is

$$\lim_{n \to \infty} nE(c - Ec)^2 = \frac{\lambda^2 + (\gamma - \rho)^2}{2\bar{\theta}},$$

where $\bar{\theta} = \theta/n$ as $n \to \infty$. The use of this variance for the moderately large sample may provide an underestimation or overestimation of the variance by the magnitude of $O(1/\theta^2)$ term which is

$$\left[ (4 - K_1^*) \lambda^2 + 4 (3 - K_1^*) (\gamma - \rho)^2 \right] / 4\theta^2. \tag{7.31}$$

This term is positive for $K_1^* \leq 3$ which implies the underestimation in using the asymptotic variance. On the other hand if $K_1^* > 4$ then the $O\left(1/\theta^2\right)$ term becomes negative, which implies overestimation in using the asymptotic variance. As discussed below $K_1^* \geq 2$ is needed for the existence of the bias, and $K_1^* \geq 3$ for the MSE.

As mentioned above the moments of IV estimator, which includes $k$-class estimators, is given by the equations (2.28) and (2.29). For the OLS and 2SLS the integral representations can be written in terms of an infinite series represented by confluent hypergeometric function, and this is analyzed for the 2SLS estimator above. Similarly the exact moments of $k$-class estimator, $\hat{\gamma} = c_k$, can be expressed as an infinite series. These are given for $0 \leq k \leq 1$ from Sawa (1972) as

$$Ec_k = \rho + (\gamma - \rho)\theta G\left(k, \theta; \frac{n - K_1}{2}, \frac{n - K}{2}\right) \tag{7.32}$$

and the second moment for $0 \leq k \leq 1$ when $n - K_1 \geq 3$ and for $k = 1$ when $K_1^* \geq 3$ as

$$
\begin{aligned}
Ec_k^2 = {} & \rho^2 + 2\rho(\gamma - \rho)\theta G\left(k, \theta; \frac{n - K_1}{2} + 1, \frac{n - K}{2}\right) \\
& + \left(\theta\lambda^2 + 2(\gamma - \rho)^2\theta^2\right) H\left(k, \theta; \frac{n - K_1}{2} + 1, \frac{n - K}{2}\right) \\
& + \left(\frac{K_1^*}{2}\lambda^2 + (\gamma - \rho)^2\theta\right) H\left(k, \theta; \frac{n - K_1}{2}, \frac{n - K}{2}\right) \\
& + \lambda^2(1 - k)^2\frac{(n - K)}{2} H\left(k, \theta; \frac{n - K_1}{2}, \frac{n - K}{2} + 1\right),
\end{aligned} \tag{7.33}
$$

where

$$
H(k, \theta; p, q) = -\frac{1}{2}\frac{\partial}{\partial\theta}G(k, \theta; p, q), \tag{7.34}
$$

and for $0 \leq k < 1$ and $p > 1$

$$
G = e^{-\theta}\sum_{j=0}^{\infty}\frac{\Gamma(q + j)}{\Gamma(q)}\frac{\Gamma(p - 1)}{\Gamma(p + j)}k_1^j F_1(p - 1; p + j; \theta) \tag{7.35}
$$

and for $k = 1$ and $p - q > 1$

$$
G = e^{-\theta}\frac{\Gamma(p - q - 1)}{\Gamma(p - q)}{}_1F_1(p - q - 1; p - q; \theta). \tag{7.36}
$$

Note that $G$ is an $_1F_1$ function for $k = 0$ also.

It can be seen from the Magnus' Lemma in Chapter 2 that the first two moments of $c_k$ exist for $0 \leq k < 1$, provided $n - K_1 \geq 2$ for bias and $n - K_1 \geq 3$ for the MSE, and when k = 1 provided $K_1^* \geq 2$ for the bias and $K_1^* \geq 3$ for the MSE. It is also true that the moments do not exist for $k > 1$ (Sawa 1972).

It is clear that the $k$-class estimator is unbiased if $\gamma = \rho$. If $\gamma \neq \rho$, then $c_k$ is biased in the same direction for all $0 \leq k \leq 1$, which is opposite to the sign of $(\gamma - \rho)$. Further, the absolute value of the bias is a strictly decreasing and concave function of $k$. This follows by noting that $\partial^s G/\partial k^s > 0$, for $0 \leq k \leq 1$ and $s = 1, 2, \ldots$. For $k = 0, 1$ the results in Richardson and Wu (1971) show that the absolute bias of 2SLS is always the smaller of the OLS estimator. But the 2SLS estimator may have a larger MSE for some values of the parameters $\beta$ and $\theta$, especially for small samples.

To look into the approximate moments of the $k$-class estimators we first write the asymptotic expansion of $G$ function by using the expansion of the

$_1F_1$ function. This can be written, up to $O(1/\theta^4)$, as

$$G(k, \theta; p, q) = \frac{1}{\theta} + (qk - p + 2)\frac{1}{\theta^2} + \Big[q(q+1)k^2 - 2q(p-2)k$$

$$+ (p-2)(p-3)\Big]\frac{1}{\theta^3} + \Big[q(q+1)(q+2)k^3$$

$$- 3q(q+1)(p-2)k^2 + 3q(p-3)k$$

$$- (p-2)(p-3)(p-4)\Big]\frac{1}{\theta^4}. \tag{7.37}$$

This then provides the bias of $c_k$, up to $O(1/\theta)$, for $0 \le k \le 1$ as

$$E(c_k - \gamma) = (\gamma - \rho)\left(\left(\frac{n-K}{2}\right)k - \left(\frac{n-K_1}{2}\right) + 1\right)\frac{1}{\theta}. \tag{7.38}$$

Further the MSE of $c_k$, up to $O(1/\theta^2)$, is

$$E(c_k - \gamma)^2 = \frac{1}{2}\Big[\lambda^2 + (\gamma - \rho)^2\Big]\frac{1}{\theta} + \Big[\Big\{\frac{n-K}{2}\left(\frac{n-K}{2} + 1\right)k^2$$

$$- 2\frac{n-K}{2}\left(\frac{n-K_1}{2} - \frac{3}{2}\right)k + \left(\frac{n-K_1}{2} - 2\right)^2\Big\}$$

$$\times (\gamma - \rho)^2 + \left(\frac{n-K}{2}k^2 - \left(\frac{n-K_1}{2}\right) + 2\right)\frac{\lambda^2}{2}\Big]\frac{1}{\theta^2} \tag{7.39}$$

provided when $0 \le k < 1$ we have $n - K_1 \ge 3$ and when $k = 1$ we have $K_1^* \ge 3$. For $k = 1$ this result reduces to (7.26).

The approximate bias and MSE given above for $0 \le k < 1$ coincide with the large-$n$ approximation of Nagar (1959) and the small-$\sigma$ expansion of Kadane (1971). This is because large-$n$ or small-$w_{22}$, hence small $\sigma_u^2$, imply large $\theta$. For $k = 1$ these results reduce those given for the 2SLS estimator. We note that Kadane's and Nagar's have the same form for all $k$ whereas we notice that the exact moments and hence their approximations do not exist for $k > 1$. This is perhaps because Nagar and Kadane do not look into the conditions of existence of their asymptotic expansions, an issue first raised by Srinivasan (1970) and dealt with by Sargan (1974).

From the above results, we also observe that the optimum value of $k$, for which the MSE of $c_k$ up to $O(1/\theta^2)$ is minimum is $k = (\gamma-\rho)^2(n-K_1-3)/((\gamma-\rho)^2(n-K+2)+\lambda^2)$, provided $K_1^* < 5+\lambda^2/(\gamma-\rho)^2$ and if $K_1^* \ge 5+\lambda^2/(\gamma-\rho)^2$, the optimum is $k = 1$. Thus the OLS estimator ($k = 0$) is efficient compared with other members of $k$-class, if and only if $\gamma = \rho$ or $n - K_1 = 3$. This may hold for many practical small econometric systems. However, in the large systems where $K_1^* > 5 + \lambda^2/(\gamma - \rho)^2$ is likely to be satisfied the 2SLS may be the most efficient. Further it can be easily seen that if the sample size and the predetermined variables are both small and/or the number of included predetermined variables is large so that $n - K_1 + K_1^* \leq 8$ is satisfied then the MSE of OLS estimator is smaller than that of the 2SLS estimator. Furthermore, the larger the variance ratio $w_{11}/w_{22}$ and smaller the correlation $w_{12}/\sqrt{w_{11}w_{22}}$, the closer the optimal value of $k$ is to zero. In the converse case, $k = 1$ is optimal. Thus the nature of the matrix $\Omega$ influences the behavior of $k$-class estimator.

### 7.2.3    Moments of the IV Estimators of $\beta$

Let us write the IV estimator of $\beta$ as

$$\hat{\beta} = (X_1'X_1)^{-1} X_1'(y_1 - \hat{\gamma}y_2) = (X_1'X_1)^{-1}X_1'(D_1 - D_2\hat{\gamma})y, \qquad (7.40)$$

where $D_1 y = y_1$ and $D_2 y = y_2$ with $D_1 = [I_n\ 0]$ and $D_2 = [0\ I_n]$. Thus the moments of $\hat{\beta}$ are

$$E\hat{\beta} = (X_1'X_1)^{-1}X_1' \left(D_1\mu - D_2 dE\hat{\gamma}\right) \qquad (7.41)$$

and

$$E\hat{\beta}\hat{\beta} = (X_1'X_1)^{-1}X_1' \left(D_1 \left(\Omega + \mu\mu'\right) D_1' + D_2 dd' E\hat{\gamma}^2 \right.$$
$$\left. - D_1 dd' E\hat{\gamma} D_2' - D_2 dd' E\hat{\gamma} D_1'\right) X_1 \left(X_1'X_1\right)^{-1},$$

where $\mu = Ey$ is the column of $X\pi_1$ and $X\pi_2$, $V(y) = \Omega$, $E(\hat{\gamma}y) = dE\hat{\gamma}$, and $E(yy'\hat{\gamma}) = dd'E\hat{\gamma}$ from Lemma 1 in Chapter 2 with $d = (\mu + \Omega\partial/\partial\mu)$. These derivatives of $E\hat{\gamma}$ and $E\hat{\gamma}^2$ can be easily written for both the approximate and exact moments of $\hat{\gamma}$, for example when $\hat{\gamma} = c_k$.

### 7.2.4    General Case of $m$ Endogenous Variables

Let the structural equation have $m + 1$, where $m = m_1$ endogenous variables. Then the exact moments of the IV estimators in (7.10) and (7.12) can be developed by using the results in Chapter 2. Considering the case of the IV estimator in (7.12) let us write $\hat{\gamma} = c$ as

$$c = (Y_1'NY_1)^{-1}Y_1'Ny_1,$$
$$= (A'Y'NYA)^{-1}A'Y'NYa,$$
$$= R^{-1}Sa, \qquad (7.42)$$

where $R = A'Y'NYA$, $S = A'Y'NY$, $Y = (y_1\ Y_1)$, $Y_1 = YA$, and $y_1 = Ya$ with the $(m + 1) \times m$ matrix $A = [0\ I_m]'$ and the $(m + 1) \times 1$ vector $a = (1\ 0)'$.
    Then

$$Ec = E(R^{-1}S)a,$$
$$= \left[E\left(S'R^{-1}\right)\right]' a,$$
$$= \left(D'NDAE(R^{-1}\right)' a, \qquad (7.43)$$

Next

$$Ecc' = E\left[R^{-1}Saa'S'R^{-1}\right],$$

$$= E\left[(adj.R)\,Saa'S'(adj.R)\,|R|^{-2}\right],$$

$$= (adj.\bar{R})\bar{S}aa'\bar{S}'(adj.\bar{R})E\,|R|^{-2}, \tag{7.44}$$

where $\bar{R} = A'D'NDA$, $\bar{S} = A'D'ND$, and $E|R|^{-2}$ and the derivative operator $D$ are as given in 2.4.

We note that when $N$ in the OLS and 2SLS estimators are the idempotent matrices then $V = Y'NY$ is a Wishart Matrix. Now if we assume the covariance matrix of $(y_1\,Y_1)$ to be an identity matrix then the values of $E\,|R|^{-1}$ and $E\,|R|^{-2}$ above are given in 2.4.

To use the above results we note that the covariance matrix of $[v_1\,V_1]$ is

$$\frac{1}{n}E\begin{pmatrix}v_1'\\V_1'\end{pmatrix}(v_1\ V_1) = \Omega. \tag{7.45}$$

Therefore we can obtain a nonsingular matrix $P$ such that $\Omega^{-1} = P'P$. Then

$$(y_1\ Y_1)P'P'^{-1}\begin{pmatrix}1\\-\gamma\end{pmatrix} = X_1\beta + u \tag{7.46}$$

so that the transformed endogenous variables are $(y_1^*\ Y_1^*) = (y_1\ Y_1)P'$, and if $a_0$ is the first element of the vector $P'^{-1}\begin{pmatrix}1\\-\gamma\end{pmatrix}$ then

$$\begin{pmatrix}1\\-\gamma^*\end{pmatrix} = \frac{1}{a_0}P^{-1}\begin{pmatrix}1\\-\gamma\end{pmatrix} \tag{7.47}$$

and $\beta^* = \beta/a_0$. Further the covariance matrix of the transformed endogenous variables $(y_1^*\ Y_1^*)$ is a unit matrix, that is,

$$E\begin{pmatrix}(y_1^* - Ey_1^*)'\\(Y_1^* - EY_1^*)'\end{pmatrix}(y_1^* - Ey_1^*\ Y_1^* - EY_1^*) = P\Omega P' = I. \tag{7.48}$$

The relationship between the transformed parameter and the original parameter is (Phillips 1983)

$$\gamma^* = \left(w_{11} - w_{21}'\Omega_{11}^{-1}w_{21}\right)^{-1/2}\Omega_{11}^{1/2}\left(\gamma - \Omega_{11}^{-1}w_{21}\right) \tag{7.49}$$

and its IV estimator is

$$c^* = \left(w_{11} - w_{21}'\Omega_{11}^{-1}w_{21}\right)^{-1/2}\Omega_{11}^{1/2}\left(c - \Omega_{11}^{-1}w_{21}\right), \tag{7.50}$$

where $\Omega_{11} = EV_1'V_1/n$. Thus assuming $\Omega = I$ above implies that we have obtained the moments of $c^*$. The moments of $c$ then follow from the relationship between $c^*$ and $c$. For an alternative approach, see Hillier, Kinal and Srivastava (1984).

## 7.2.5    Approximate Moments

Here we present the large-$n$ approximate moments of the bias and MSE of the $k$-class IV estimators of $\hat{\delta}$ in (7.9), where $k$ is nonstochastic with $k = 1 + a/n$ so that $1 - k = O(1/n)$, $a$ is a real number independent of $n$. From the results of Nagar (1959) the bias up to $O(n^{-1})$, is

$$E(\hat{\delta} - \delta) = [(1 - k)n + L - 1]\bar{Q}\bar{q}, \tag{7.51}$$

where $L = K - (m_1 + K_1)$ is the number of predetermined variables in excess of the number of coefficients estimated and

$$\bar{Q} = (\bar{Z}'_1\bar{Z}_1)^{-1}, \qquad \bar{q} = \begin{pmatrix} \frac{1}{n}EV'_1u \\ 0 \end{pmatrix} \tag{7.52}$$

with $\bar{Z}_1 = (EY_1 \ X_1)$ and $u = v_1 - V_1\gamma$. Further the MSE of $\hat{\delta}$, up to $O(n^{-2})$, is

$$\mathrm{MSE}(\hat{\delta}) = \sigma_u^2\bar{Q}(I + A), \tag{7.53}$$

where $A$ is a matrix of $O(n^{-1})$

$$\begin{aligned} A = &\left[(2(k - 1)n - 2L + 3)\,tr(C_1\bar{Q}) + tr(C_2\bar{Q})\right]I \\ &+ \{((k - 1)n - L + 2)^2 + 2((k - 1)n + 1)\}C_1\bar{Q} \\ &+ (2(k - 1)n - L + 2)C_2\bar{Q} \end{aligned} \tag{7.54}$$

where

$$C_1 = \frac{1}{\sigma_u^2}\bar{q}\bar{q}' \quad \text{and} \quad C_2 = \begin{bmatrix} \frac{1}{n}EW'_1W_1 & 0 \\ 0 & 0 \end{bmatrix},$$

with $V_1 = u\pi' + W_1$, $u$ and $W_1$ are independently distributed and $\pi$ is $m_1 \times 1$.

These results also follow using the results in (2.82) and (2.83). Bao and Ullah (2002) use (2.101) and (2.102) to extend the above results for the case where $u$ follows AR(1) process.

In a special case where $m_1 = 1$ and $K_1 = 0$ the bias and MSE of $\hat{\gamma}$ can be written from the above or (2.82) and (2.83) and these are as given in (7.26). If the instruments matrix $X$ is weak, it implies some elements of $\Pi$ and $|\bar{Z}'_1\bar{Z}_1|$ tend to be small and the bias will be larger. This is the problem of weak instruments analyzed in the papers by Morimune (1983), Bound, Jaeger, and Baker (1995), Hall, Rudebusch, and Wilcox (1996), and Zivot and Wang (1998) where they show that the finite sample properties of estimators and test statistics are sensitive to the quality of instruments. This is discussed in Section 7.3.

## 7.2.6    Nonlinear Simultaneous Equations Model

Let us consider a simple nonlinear structural equation with the one right-hand side endogenous variable as

$$y_1 = f(y_2, \gamma) + u. \tag{7.55}$$

Suppose there is one instrument $x_i$. Then an IV estimator $\hat{\gamma}$ is a solution of

$$\frac{1}{n}\sum(y_{i1} - f_i(\hat{\gamma}))\,x_i = 0, \tag{7.56}$$

where $f_i(\hat{\gamma}) = f(y_{i2}, \hat{\gamma})$. Let us denote $f_i^{(j)}$ as the $j$th derivative of $f(y_{i2}, \gamma)$ with respect to $\gamma$, and

$$f_i^{(j)} = \bar{f}_i^{(j)} + v_{ji}, \tag{7.57}$$

where $\bar{f}_i^{(j)} = E(f_i^{(j)} \mid x_i)$ and put $\rho_j = E(uv_j)$. In a special case when $f(y_{i2}, \gamma)$ is linear $f_i^{(1)} = y_{i2}, \bar{f}_i^{(1)} = \pi x_i$ and $v_{1i} = v_i$.

In the above case the bias to $O(1/n)$ can be written from the general result in (2.81) as

$$E(\hat{\gamma} - \gamma) = -\frac{1}{n}a_1\frac{\rho_1}{\sigma_u^2} - \frac{1}{2n}a_1\frac{E[f^{(2)}x]}{E[f^{(1)}x]}, \tag{7.58}$$

where

$$a_1 = \sigma_u^2\frac{Ex^2}{\left(E[f^{(1)}x]\right)^2}. \tag{7.59}$$

When $x_i$ is nonstochastic we replace $Ex^2$ with $\sum x_i^2/n$ and $E(f^{(2)}x)$ with $\sum f_i^{(2)}x_i/n$. For the linear case, $f(y_{i2}, \gamma) = y_{i2}\gamma$, this bias result reduces to that given above. The MSE is left as an exercise.

The result given above suggests that the bias is affected by the derivatives (curvature) of the function. If $f^{(1)}$ is very small then the bias will tend to be high. In the linear case $f^{(1)}$ became the correlation parameter and hence the measure of the quality of instrument. In the nonlinear case this may not necessarily be the case. For example, assuming $Ex = 0$ and using the approximation $f^{(1)}(y_2) \simeq f^{(1)}(\bar{y}_2) + (y - \bar{y}_2)f^{(2)}(\bar{y}_2)$,

$$E[f^{(1)}x] = f^{(2)}(\bar{y}_2)\mathrm{cov}(x, y_2)$$

$$E[f^{(2)}x] = f^{(3)}(\bar{y}_2)\mathrm{cov}(x, y_2). \tag{7.60}$$

Then

$$E(\hat{\gamma} - \gamma) = -\frac{1}{n}\frac{\sigma_u^2 E(x^2)}{\left(f^{(2)}(\bar{y}_2)\mathrm{cov}(x, y_2)\right)^2}\left[\frac{\rho_1}{\sigma_u^2} + \frac{1}{2}\frac{f^{(3)}(\bar{y}_2)}{f^{(2)}(\bar{y}_2)}\right]. \tag{7.61}$$

This shows that the bias depends on the $f^{(2)}(\bar{y}_2)$, $f^{(3)}(\bar{y}_2)$ of the regression $f(y_2, \gamma)$ at $y_2 = \bar{y}_2 = Ey_2$. These derivatives will depend on the nature of the structural parameters. For example, if $f(y_{i2}, \gamma) = e^{y_2\gamma}$ then $f^{(j)}(\bar{y}_2) = \bar{y}_2^j e^{\bar{y}_2\gamma}$ and

$$E(\hat{\gamma} - \gamma) = -\frac{1}{n}\frac{\sigma_u^2 E(x^2)}{[\bar{y}_2^2 e^{\bar{y}_2\gamma}\mathrm{cov}(y_2, x)]^2}\left[\frac{\rho_1}{\sigma_u^2} + \frac{\bar{y}_2}{2}\right]. \tag{7.62}$$

Thus if $\bar{y}_2$ is close to zero then the bias will be large. Further if $\text{cov}(y_2, x)$ is very small, that is the instrument is weak, then the bias will be large.

## 7.2.7 Density Function of IV Estimator

The IV estimator is a ratio of quadratic forms in the $2n \times 1$ vector $y$, which is $N(\mu, \Omega)$. Therefore the cumulative probability distribution of the IV estimator $\hat{\gamma}$ is given by (3.5) and (3.6) by the appropriate substitutions of the matrices $N_1, N_2$, and $\Omega$. As indicated there the numerical calculations can be done using Koerts and Abrahamse (1969), and Davies (1980). For the calculations we need the eigenvalues and corresponding eigenvectors of the matrix $\Omega^{1/2}(N_1 - qN_2)\Omega^{1/2}$ where $q$ is the point at which the distribution is evaluated. These can be found numerically, and in many specialized IV estimators analytically. For the case of 2SLS estimator Cribbett, Lye, and Ullah (1989) provide the eigenvalues of the matrix $N_1 - qN_2$ as

$$\lambda_1 = -\tfrac{1}{2}\left(q - (1+q^2)^{1/2}\right), \qquad \lambda_2 = -\tfrac{1}{2}\left(q + (1+q^2)^{1/2}\right) \qquad (7.63)$$

both having multiplicity $K_1^*$, and zero with multiplicity $2(n - K_1^*)$. The noncentrality parameters associated with $\lambda_1$ and $\lambda_2$ are

$$\delta_1^2 = \theta\left[1 + \gamma^2 + (2\gamma - q + q\gamma^2)(1+q^2)^{-1/2}\right]$$
$$\delta_2^2 = \theta\left[1 + \gamma^2 - (2\gamma - q + q\gamma^2)\left(1+q^2\right)^{-1/2}\right] \qquad (7.64)$$

This can be used in writing the distribution of 2SLS estimator $\hat{\gamma}$ as

$$P\left(\hat{\gamma} \leq q\right) = P\left(\sum_{r=1}^{2} \lambda_r \chi_r^2\left(K_1^*, \delta_r^2\right) \leq 0\right), \qquad (7.65)$$

where $\chi_r^2$ is a noncentral chi-square with $K_1^*$ degrees of freedom (d.f.) and noncentrality parameter $\delta_r^2$.

There are many ways to obtain the exact density of the IV estimators, including $k$-class and LIML estimators. The expressions are generally in terms of multiple series in hypergeometric functions, unlike the method given above. So they are not presented here except giving an idea of the type of procedures used. For example, Richardson (1968), and Sawa (1969) noted that the joint distribution of the elements, $(y_1'Ny_2, y_2'Ny_2, y_1'Ny_1)$ in the 2SLS estimator is non-central Wishart of order 2. The noncentral Wishart density is then written in closed form and integrating out nuisance variables and simplifying one gets the marginal density of the 2SLS estimator $(y_2'Ny_2)^{-1}y_2'Ny_1$. A similar approach was used by Mariano and Sawa (1972) to obtain the density of the LIML estimator. They also showed that the moments of the LIML estimators do not exist. Phillips (1980, 1986) also explored the densities by contour integration.

For the $k$-class, $0 \leq k \leq 1$, Anderson and Sawa (1973) explored an alternative method to provide the exact density as a fourth-order infinite series. The expressions for the densities of 2SLS and OLS estimators are given in terms of doubly noncentral $F$-distribution. Cribbett, Lye, and Ullah (1989) compared the calculations based on the straightforward Imhof distribution of the 2SLS in (7.65) with the Anderson and Sawa (1973, 1979) expressions. They found that the absolute difference between the results are negligible. The largest absolute difference arose in all cases where Anderson and Sawa (1979) had computational difficulties with their exact density and used the approximate density. We therefore recommend the using of Imhof procedure, which is also useful for a class of other econometric estimators discussed in earlier chapters.

From the extensive calculations in Anderson and Sawa one can observe the following findings. The distribution of 2SLS estimator is asymmetric except when $\gamma = \rho$. This was also earlier reported on the basis of the skewness and kurtosis coefficients in (7.29) and (7.30). Further the LIML estimator tends to have larger dispersion and thicker tails than the 2SLS, perhaps because of the nonexistence of the LIML estimator moments. But the distribution of LIML tends to normality much faster than that of 2SLS, and that in many cases the asymptotic normal theory may be a better approximation to the exact density of LIML but not so in the case of 2SLS.

While we have discussed above the exact density of the IV estimator, Anderson and Sawa (1973) have also provided an asymptotic expansion of the $k$-class estimator. This is done by first obtaining the exact characteristic function of the $k$-class estimator and its normalized form and then expand the logarithm of this characteristic function as a Taylor Series. Then using the inversion theorem an Edgeworth Series expansion of the distribution function is obtained in the form

$$F(q) = \Phi(q) + \phi(q) \sum_{i=1}^{r} \left( \varphi_i(q)/n^{i/2} \right) + O\left( n^{-(r+1)/2} \right),$$

where $\varphi_i(q)$ is a polynomial of finite degree in $q$ and is $O(1)$ and $\Phi(\cdot)$ and $\phi(\cdot)$ denote the cumulative distribution and probability density functions, respectively, of the standard unit normal, see Chapter 3 for details.

To see the application of the Edgeworth expansion for the 2SLS estimator $c$ we consider the distribution of

$$Z_n = \frac{\sqrt{\theta}\,(c - \gamma)}{\sigma_u}. \tag{7.66}$$

Then from the moments of $c - \gamma$ given above we can verify that $EZ_n = c_1/\sqrt{\theta}$ and $V(Z_n) = 1 + (c_2/\theta)$ where $c_1$ and $c_2$ are nonstochastic terms of $O(1)$. Using these results define

$$Z_n^* = \frac{Z_n - EZ_n}{\sqrt{V(Z_n)}}, \tag{7.67}$$

which has zero mean, unit variance, and approximate third and fourth moments as $EZ_n^{*3} = c_3/\sqrt{\theta}$ and $EZ_n^{*4} = 3 + (c_4/\theta)$, where $c_3$ and $c_4$ are of $O(1)$. Then the Edgeworth expansion of $Z_n$ or $Z_n^*$ is as given in (3.33) where $c_1$ to $c_4$ are given from the moments of $(c - \gamma)$ and $(c - Ec)$ above. This expression is an Edgeworth-B (3.30) type expansion. The Edgeworth-A expansion can also be developed from (3.29) by using the moments of $c - \gamma$. This is, up to $O(1/\sqrt{\theta})$,

$$P(Z_n \le z) = \Phi(z) + \frac{w_{12} - \gamma w_{22}}{\sqrt{\theta}} \left( z^2 - (K_1^* - 1) \right) \phi(z). \qquad (7.68)$$

The density of $Z_n$ is then

$$\left\{ 1 - \frac{w_{12} - \gamma w_{22}}{\sqrt{\theta}} \left( z^3 - (K_1^* + 1)z \right) \right\} \phi(z), \qquad (7.69)$$

see also Anderson and Sawa (1973).

Usually, the asymptotic expansions may not perform well in the tails of the distribution. For more details on the quality of asymptotic approximations, see Phillips (1980, 1986), and Holly and Phillips (1979).

## 7.2.8   Further Finite Sample Results

Phillips (1986) has provided a representation of the exact joint density function of IV estimators for $m_1 + 1$ endogenous variable case. It shows that as the number of endogenous variables increases the marginal distributions of IV estimator tend to concentrate more slowly as $n \to \infty$ and it may lead to reduction in the precision of estimation. Further the marginal distribution has more bias if more numbers of instruments are used for the $m_1$ endogenous variables.

There are various attempts in getting improved estimators for structural coefficients. Nagar (1959) provided a class of almost unbiased $k$-class estimators. Sawa (1973$a$, $b$) provided a linear combination of the OLS and 2SLS estimators, which is unbiased up to $O(\sigma^2)$ in the small-$\sigma$ sense. Morimiune (1978) provided a combined estimator based on the LIML and 2SLS which has smaller MSE, up to $O(\sigma^4)$, compared to LIML. But both Morimiune's as well as Sawa's estimators are dominated by the 2SLS for the low degrees of over identification. Fuller (1977) considers a modification of LIML by using $k - \alpha/(n - k)$ with $k$ as defined for the LIML above and $\alpha$ is some arbitrary nonstochastic real number determined under an optimizing criterion. This modified LIML estimator possesses moments, it is approximately unbiased for $\alpha = 1$ and has the minimum approximate MSE for $\alpha = 4$, also see Rothenberg (1978) and Takeuchi and Morimiune (1979) for higher-order efficiency. Ullah and Srivastava (1988) provide a Stein-type shrinkage 2SLS estimator which has smaller MSE compared to 2SLS estimator under certain conditions. Further Zellner (1998) analyzes the finite sample properties of Bayesian method of moments estimators and Kiviet and Phillips (1987) provide bias reduction in a dynamic simultaneous equation model. Gao and Lahiri (2002), and Dwivedi and Srivastava (1984) have analyzed the moments of Nagar's (1962) double $k$-class estimators. The results of Gao and Lahiri (2002) also suggest the superior performance of Zellner's (1998) Bayesian estimators. Tsurumi's (1990) work analyzed the results for MELO estimators, also see Koenker and Machaso (1999) for the GMM estimators.

The finite sample properties of the reduced form coefficients estimators, unrestricted and partially restricted, have been analyzed by many authors, see Goldberger, Nagar, and Odeh (1961), McCarthy (1972), Nagar and Sahay (1978), Knight (1977), and Sargan (1973, 1974). Maasoumi (1978) considered the Stein-type improved estimation of the reduced form coefficients.

The literature on the hypothesis testing is much more limited compared with estimation of structural models. Richardson and Rohr (1971), when $m_1 = 1$, provided the exact distribution of a $t$−test statistic based on the 2SLS estimator:

$$t = \frac{(c - \gamma)}{s_c},$$

where $s_c^2$ is the estimator of the asymptotic covariance from $\sigma_u^2 \bar{Q}$ in (7.53) with

$$\hat{\sigma}_u^2 = (y_1 - Z_1\hat{\delta})'(P_X - P_{X_1})(y_1 - Z_1\hat{\delta})/(K_1^* - 1),$$

which is not the usual large sample estimate of the $\sigma^2$. But this definition of $\hat{\sigma}_u^2$ helps Richardson and Rohr to show that the derived exact distribution, which is in terms of a doubly infinite series of hypergeometric functions, converges to student-$t$ distribution with $K_1^* - 1$ d.f. Maddala (1974), however, shows that the Monte Carlo power calculations of this statistic is smaller compared to the $t$ with $\hat{\sigma}_u^2$ having $\bar{P}_{X_1}$, or $\bar{P}_X$ in place of $P_X - P_{X_1}$ and $K_1^* - 1$ replaced by $n - K$ or $n - K - 1$. Further the test $t$ above is skewed over the parameter space, even for large noncentrality parameter $\theta$. Also, the difference between the exact distribution of $t$ and Student-$t$ with one d.f. may be large, especially for small $\theta$.

Several authors have analyzed the distributions of the identifiability test statistic

$$F_{(k)} = \frac{(y_1 - Z_1\hat{\delta}_k)'(P_X - P_{X_1})(y_1 - Z_1\hat{\delta}_k)}{(y_1 - Z_1\hat{\delta}_k)'\bar{P}_X(y_1 - Z_1\hat{\delta}_k)}$$

based on $k$-class estimators including the LIML estimator. For details see, for example, Basmann (1965, 1966), Richardson (1968), McDonald (1972), Kadane (1974), Rhodes (1981), and Anderson and Rubin (1950). For details on the use of Edgeworth series expansions for econometric test statistics based on $k$-class estimators, see Sargan (1975, 1976, 1980) and Sargan and Mikhail (1971). Further, for the results on the moments and distribution of the residual variance, see Basmann (1974), Basmann and Richardson (1973), Ebbeler and McDonald (1973), and Smith (1994) among others.

## 7.2.9    Summary of Results

Here we look into the main results emerging from the works on the moments and distribution of the $k$-class estimators. These are as follows.

The direction of the bias of estimator, for nonstochastic $0 \leq k \leq 1$, depends on the sign of the $\rho$. If $\rho < 0$ there is a downward bias, and if $\rho > 0$ then we have an upward bias. For $k > 1$ the moments of $k$-class estimators do not exist. This is also the case for the LIML estimator, and the 2SLS estimator for the just identified case. Nonexistence of the moments do not imply that those estimators are bad, instead they simply mean that the quadratic loss function (MSE) is not the suitable way of comparing the efficiency of these estimators. For example, as indicated above and below, LIML estimator is considered to be a well behaved estimator.

The exact MSE of the $k$-class estimators ($0 \leq k \leq 1$) can be shown to be a decreasing function of $\theta$, increasing function of $|\rho|$ and an indefinite function of the degrees of overidentification of OLS, $K_1^* - 1$, or the degree of overidentification of 2SLS, $n - K_1 - 1$. Further an additional observation will decrease the MSE of 2SLS but it has an indefinite effect for other estimators. Also the optimal value of $k$ minimizing MSE is sensitive to changes in the sample size and parameter values.

Regarding the behavior of the members of $k$-class, we note that the absolute bias of the OLS is higher to 2SLS. Also for higher $\rho$ the OLS bias becomes higher relative to 2SLS.

Regarding the MSE for large $\theta$ and large $n$ the 2SLS does much better than OLS because of the inconsistency of OLS. However, in cases such as small value of $\rho$ and $n$ the OLS would dominate 2SLS. Regarding the comparison of LIML with 2SLS we compare the asymptotic MSE, up to $O(n^{-1})$, since the finite sample MSE of LIML estimator does not exist. From Anderson (1974),

$$\mathrm{AMSE}(c_{2\mathrm{SLS}}) - \mathrm{AMSE}(c_{\mathrm{LIML}}) = (K_1^* - 1)[(K_1^* - 7)a^2 - 2]/(\theta b^2),$$

where $a^2 = r^2 \sigma_u^2 w_{22}/(w_{11}w_{22} - w_{12}^2)$, $b^2 = a^2/r^2$, and $r$ is the correlation between $u$ and $v_2$. Thus if $K_1^*$ (degree of overidentification is $K_1^* - 1$) is less than 7 then 2SLS is more efficient. On the other hand for $K_1^* > 7$ and $a^2$ is not too small LIML will be more efficient. Similar results were obtained by Anderson (1974), and Fujikoshi and Veitch (1979) on the basis of the approximate distributions of LIML and 2SLS, up to $O(n^{-1})$. They show by comparing the concentration probabilities, $P(|c - \gamma|)$, that while LIML is favorable for high $K_1^*$, 2SLS is better for small $K_1^*$ and for small $r^2$.

Regarding the distribution of OLS and 2SLS the calculations in Sawa (1969), and Anderson and Sawa (1973, 1979) suggest that while the OLS distribution is almost symmetric the distribution of 2SLS is quite asymmetric. When the $K_1^*$ is large, however, the distribution of OLS and 2SLS tend to be the same. Also the convergence of the distribution of 2SLS to normality is very slow, especially when either $K_1^*$ or $r$ or both are large. In contrast the distribution of LIML converges to normality faster, and is more symmetric but has more spread. Further the approximate LIML distribution, up to $O(n^{-1})$ is median unbiased.

The impact of misspecification, with wrongly omitted variables, on the distributions and moments of the OLS, 2SLS, and LIML estimators have been done by Hale, Mariano, and Ramage (1980), Mariano and Ramage (1978), Mariano and McDonald (1979), Rhodes and Westbrook (1981), and Maasonmi and Phillips (1982), among others. These works suggest that under the misspecification the nonstochastic $k$-class estimators are dominated by both OLS and 2SLS estimators. Further OLS is generally relatively insensitive to specification error and when the error of misspecification is more severe compared with degree of simultaneity OLS is preferable to 2SLS. The effect of multi-collinearity on the properties of estimators is also analyzed. The results here suggest that unlike in the regression models, higher multicollinearity can increase or decrease the MSE of estimators depending upon the values of the parameters in $\theta$ and the values of exogenous variables.

Based on the above discussions we summarize that OLS and 2SLS estimators show similar statistical patterns for a medium to large econometric model where $K_1^*$ is usually large and d.f. is low. If, in addition, $\rho$ is high the LIML may be more preferable. Next, for $K_1^* < 7$ 2SLS is better than LIML and preferred over OLS in the presence of moderate to strong $\rho$ (simultaneity). Further, in the case of a very small sample, very week $\rho$, or strong presence of misspecifications OLS would be a fine estimator, for more details see Mariano (1982).

# 7.3   Analysis of Weak Instruments

## 7.3.1   Effects on the Moments and Distribution

Here we consider the effect of the quality of instruments and the degree of endogeneity on the bias and MSE and the distribution of the IV estimators. The quality of instruments is judged by the correlation of the instrument with the endogenous variables and the lack of association with the structural error or with the outcome of study. In general the $F$ statistic or goodness of fit $R^2$ of the first stage reduced form regression of the right hand endogenous variables on the instruments will indicate the quality of instruments. A small $F$ or small goodness of fit $R^2$ is referred to as the weak instruments. Similarly the degree of endogenity is measured by the correlations of the right hand endogenous variables with the structural error.

When regressors are endogenous, OLS is a biased and inconsistent estimator. But, under the assumptions that the instruments are correlated with the endogenous regressor but uncorrelated with the outcome variable, the IV estimator is a consistent estimator, see Bowden and Turkington (1984). Note that the MSE of the IV estimator given above goes to zero as $n$ tends to infinity.

However, it is often the case that the IV's are weak instruments in which case several problems may arise. First, even with a weak endogeneity, the IV can have a large inconsistency, see Bound, Jaeger, and Baker (1995), and Staiger and Stock (1997). Second, in finite samples, IV estimates are biased in the same direction as the OLS estimator, with the magnitude of the bias approaching that of OLS as the first stage $R^2$ approaching to 0. Third, the IV estimators may have large standard errors. These problems can produce misleading results in empirical work. For example, in Angrist and Krueger (AK 1991) a large sample of U.S. census data is used to estimate wage equations with quarter of birth used as an instrument for educational attainment. This instrument was chosen because of the evidence of its association with the educational attainment, for example the individuals born during the first quarter start school later, have lower educational attainment, and earn less than those born in the other quarters. Furthermore the quarter of birth is unlikely to have a strong correlation with wages. AK argued that the compulsory school attendance laws lead to the correlation between quarter of birth and education. However, Bound, Jarger, and Baker (1995) find the quarter of birth to be a weak instrument, since $R^2$ in the first stage of regression of quarter of birth on educational attainment to be 0.0001 and 0.0002 in their samples. Given this they find significantly different numerical values of the estimates compared to AK estimates, and report significant finite sample bias in some of AK estimates. Based on these results they conclude that quarter of birth does not give much usable information regarding the effect of education on earnings. They further conclude that even those working with the large cross sectional samples should be careful with having weak instruments. To see these findings we look at the following analytical results.

Consider a special case of (7.17) where

$$y_1 = \gamma y_2 + u$$
$$y_2 = X\pi + v. \tag{7.70}$$

Thus there is no exogenous variable in the structural equation and total number of instruments are $K$ variables in $X$. Then it is easy to show that

$$p \lim c_0 = \gamma + \frac{\text{cov}(y_2, u)}{V(y_2)} \tag{7.71}$$

and

$$p \lim c_1 = \gamma + \frac{\text{cov}(\hat{y}_2, u)}{V(\hat{y}_2)},$$

where $\hat{y}_2 = X\hat{\pi} = X(X'X)^{-1}X'y_2$, $c_0$ is the OLS estimator and $c_1$ is the 2SLS (IV) estimator. It is clear that the OLS will be consistent if $V(y_2) = \sigma^2 \neq 0$ and $y_2$ must be uncorrelated with $u$. Similarly the IV estimator will be consistent if $V(\hat{y}_2)$ is nonzero, that is $X$ must be correlated with $y_2$, and $\text{cor}(\hat{y}_2, u) = 0$, which means that $X$ is uncorrelated with $u$ and hence $y_1$ (outcome variable).

From above the relative asymptotic bias is

$$\frac{\text{Abias}(c_1)}{\text{Abias}(c_0)} = \frac{\lambda_0}{\rho_0^2}, \lambda_0 = \frac{\text{cor}(\hat{y}_2, u)}{\text{cor}(y_2, u)}, \tag{7.72}$$

where $\rho_0^2 = V(\hat{y}_2)/V(y_2)$ is the population goodness of fit in the regression of $y_2$ on $X_1^*$. If both the structural and reduced forms have the matrix $X_1$ then $\rho_0^2$ will be replaced by the partial $\rho_0^2$ in the regression of $y_2 - X_1\hat{\pi}_{21}$ on $X_1^*$. Further, when $K = 1$, $\lambda_0/\rho_0^2$ can be written as $\rho_{x,u}/(\rho_{y_2,u} \times \rho_{y_2,x})$, where $\rho$ is the correlation coefficient.

It is clear from above that in the case of having a weak instrument ($\rho_0^2$ or $\rho_{y_2,x}$ small), even a weak endogeneity (small correlation $\rho_{y_2,u}$) can produce a larger inconsistency in the IV estimator than in the OLS estimator.

We note that Staiger and Stock (1997) consider the case that $\pi = \pi_0/\sqrt{n}$, where $\pi_0$ is a matrix of constants. They refer to this as the case of weak instruments. In this case the $\rho_0^2$ is of $O(n^{-1})$, and condition of a good instrument that $W'Z_1/n$ converges in probability to a nonrandom matrix fails. They show that, under the weak instruments, $c_{\text{IV}} - \gamma$ converges to a nonrandom variable and the nonzero mean of the $c_{\text{IV}} - \gamma$ (asymptotic bias) is in the same direction as the bias of OLS as indicated above. Han and Schmidt (2001) consider the case of irrelevant instruments where $\pi_0 = 0$ so that $\pi = 0$ in the reduced form for all $n$. They show that the mean of the asymptotic distribution of $c_{\text{IV}} - \gamma$ is the same as $(p \lim c_0 - \gamma)$, the asymptotic bias of the OLS estimator.

As indicated above Staiger and Stock (1997) considered the case of weak instruments in the local to zero sense at the rate of $1/\sqrt{n}$. They showed that both the LIML and 2SLS estimators become inconsistent and their asymptotic distributions are nonstandard. An explanation for this is that as $n$ tending to infinity the concentration (noncentrality) parameter does not increase and is of $O(1)$ as long as the number of instruments $K$ remains fixed. Chao and Swanson (2002) have considered a more general case where the weak instruments are in a general sense of local to zero at an unspecified rate of $1/b_n$, consider the $k$-class estimators along with the Jacknife IV estimator of Angrist, Imbens, and Kreuger (1999) and assume the number of instruments $K$ and hence the noncentrality parameters increasing with the sample size. Under this scenario they show that the above estimators are consistent and the use of many weak instruments in empirical applications may be beneficial. They also explore the connection between their approach and the asymptotic analysis based on the taking of infinite instruments by Morimiune (1983), Bekker (1994), Hahn (1997), Hahn and Inoue (2000), and Hahn, Hausman, and Kuersteiner (2001).

To see the effect of weak instruments on the finite sample bias let us write the bias, up to $O(n^{-1})$, from (7.26) as

$$\text{Bias}(c) = \frac{\text{cov}(u, v)}{\pi' X' X \pi}(K - 2) = \frac{\text{cov}(u, v)}{\sigma_v^2} \frac{(K - 2)}{2\theta}, \tag{7.73}$$

where $(\text{cov}(u, v)/\sigma_v^2)$ is approximately the Abias$(c_0)$ when $X$ explains very little variation in $y_2$ and $\theta = (\pi' X' X \pi / 2\sigma_v^2)$. This result suggests the finite sample approximate bias of the IV relative to the asymptotic OLS bias is inversely related to $\theta/K$, which is population analog of the $F$ statistics in the reduced form regression ($F$ value on the excluded instruments $X_1^*$ when $X_1$ is present in both equations). Generally sample $F$ tends to overestimate $\theta/K$ in the same way as the sample $R^2$ tends to have an upward bias of $\rho_0^2$, see Chapter 4. Thus the examination of the $F$ or $R^2$ statistic on the excluded instruments in the reduced form regression is useful in judging the quality of instruments and their impact on the finite sample behavior of the IV estimator.

While the above result on the finite sample bias is based on the approximate bias, a similar result holds on the basis of the exact expressions, which is from (7.21)

$$E(c_k - \gamma) = (\gamma - \rho) \left[ \frac{2\theta}{n_k} {}_1F_1 \left( 1, \frac{n_k + 2}{2}; -\theta \right) - 1 \right], \qquad (7.74)$$

where $k = 0$ for the OLS and $k = 1$ for the 2SLS(IV), and $n_k = n - 1$, for $k = 0$ and it is $K$ for $k = 1$. Note that $\theta/n - 1$ is the population $\rho_0^2$ in the regression $y_2$ on $X$. Numerical results in Bound, Jaeger and Baker (1995) suggest that the bias of the IV relative to the bias of LS depends on $\theta/K$ as was in the case of approximate bias.

Woglom (2001) considers the model with $m_1 = 1$, $K_1 = 0$, and $K_1^* = K = 1$, and analyzed the distribution of the IV estimator with moderately weak instruments ($R^2 \simeq 1/n$), very weak instruments, and various degrees of endogeneity. He finds that in the case of moderately weak instruments the distribution will be much more peaked than the asymptotic distribution with a mode somewhere between the true value and the $p$ lim of OLS estimators. In the case of very weak instruments ($R^2 \simeq 0$), the distribution approaches a student $t$ with a mode at the $p$ lim of OLS in the totally unidentified case. Further, as the degree of endogeneity increases, the distribution becomes more peaked and the mode moves away from the true value. When the degree of endogeneity is very high with moderate first stage $R^2$ the distribution can have an important second mode. Finally when the instruments are very weak ($R^2 \simeq 0$) the $t$ statistic based on $c_{IV} - \gamma$ will concentrate around the number greater than 1, with moderate or high endogeneity.

The above discussion emphasizes that under the weak instruments the inference based on IV estimators and asymptotic standard errors is generally misleading in finite samples. This is because the IV estimator is strongly biased and the estimated standard error is too small, with the result that the true null hypothesis is rejected much too often. Traditional confidence intervals based on IV estimation and asymptotic standard errors provide a valid approach in the sense of producing confidence regions that cover the true value with the stated probability when the system is well identified and have large sample. But when the instruments are weak and the endogeneity is strong, this traditional approach produces confidence regions that are highly misleading. Zivot, Startz, and Nelson (1997) provide the examples where the size of Wald(W) Test is 100 percent. Staiger and Stock (1997) show that under the weak instruments the asymptotic distribution of W-test for linear restrictions on $\delta$ is not $\chi^2$ under the null hypothesis. Zivot, Startz, and Nelson (1997) provide alternative confidence regions based on inverting Rao score test, likelihood ratio, and Anderson-Rubin statistics, which are easy to compute and provide better size and power properties. Zivot, Startz, and Nelson show that W-based confidence intervals provide better probability of rejecting the null than their nominal size, also see Hall, Rudebusch, and Wilcox (1996). This is partly because of the bias of IV estimator, leading to an underestimate of the variance of the estimator. This set of results is important since weak instruments are often the case, see AK (1991, 1992). Furthermore, see Moore, Fuhrer, and Sehuh (1995), Hall (1988), McClellan et al. (1994), and Koenker and Machaso (1999) among others.

## 7.3.2 Issue of Optimal Instruments

Donald and Newey (2001) considered the model in (7.3) and (7.5) and have looked into the issue of determining the optimal choice of the number of instruments $K$ for 2SLS, LIML, and bias-corrected 2SLS (B2SLS) estimators given in 7.2.1. The procedure of selecting the instruments is based on minimizing the approximate MSE of a linear combination of the IV estimator $\hat{\delta}$. For the MSE of $\hat{\delta}$ they considered Nagar (1959) type expansion for $K$ and $n$ such that $K^2/n \rightarrow 0$ for the case of 2SLS and $K/n \rightarrow 0$ for LIML and B2SLS. As $n$ and $K$ increase they indicate that the MSE of LIML and B2SLS are smaller compared with 2SLS, and LIML is best among them for large $K$, also see Morimune (1983). In general the MSE for LIML is smaller than that of B2SLS for all $K$. The comparison between LIML and 2SLS depends on the size of the simultaneity (endogeneity) $\sigma_{uv_1}$. For $\sigma_{uv_1} = 0$, 2SLS has smaller MSE than LIML for all $K$ and optimal choice of K would be large leading to OLS for $K = n$, the optimal estimator under no endogeneity. For the case of endogeneity, $\sigma_{uv_1} \neq 0$, the LIML may perform better than 2SLS for various values of $n, K$.

Let us consider again the empirical equation of AK(1991), which deals with log weekly wage equation with the explanatory variables as education (number of years of schooling), intercept, nine year of birth dummies and 50 state dummies (AK, table VII). The quarter of birth was used as instruments. The sample was from 1980 U.S. census and consisted of 329,500 men born in 1930–39. The OLS estimate on schooling was 0.0673 and its standard error was 0.0003.

For the model under consideration, $y_1 = \log$ wage, $y_2 = $ education, $X_1$ is a set of 60 $(1 + 9 + 50)$ explanatory variables. In the reduced form for $y_2$ the IV matrices $W^K = [X_1 \, X_2]$ considered are

$$K = 63, X_2 = Q = 3 \text{ quarter of birth dummies}$$
$$K = 90, X_2 = [Q, Q * Y],$$

$$K = 213, X_2 = [Q, Q * S],$$
$$K = 240, X_2 = [Q, Q * S, Q * Y],$$
$$K = 72, X_2 = [Q, Q * R_4],$$
$$K = 99, X_2 = [Q, Q * Y, Q * R_4],$$
$$K = 87, X_2 = [Q, Q * R_9],$$
$$K = 114, X_2 = [Q, Q * Y, Q * R_9],$$

where $Q * Y$ is interaction of quarter of birth dummies with the 9 year of birth dummies, $S$ is state dummies, $R_4$ is three region dummies, $R_9$ is nine region dummies. Note that $X_2$ is like $X_1^*$ in 7.2.1.

Using the above sets of instruments the first stage reduced form regressions gave largest set of instruments; $K = 240$, as the best cross validated Mallows' (1973) goodness of fit. Also Wald test was significant and partial $R^2 = 0.0014$. Based on $K = 240$ the IV estimates can be obtained. This is the usual practice in applied work, also see AK (1991). Instead of this Donald and Newey (2001) determined optimal $K$ for 2SLS, LIML, and B2SLS by evaluating their estimated MSE for different sets of instruments given above. For 2SLS and B2SLS the MSE criteria suggest that one should use the minimal number of instruments 63, that is using the set of quarter of birth dummy variables. But for the LIML its MSE is smallest for the largest instrument set, 240, which is optimal for first-stage regression.

Estimates of the returns to education for different instruments sets can be obtained for three estimators. These estimates and their standard errors are similar for LIML and B2SLS, but those of 2SLS are smaller than LIML and B2SLS even though the point estimates for the optimal $K = 63$ for 2SLS and B2SLS and $K = 240$ for the LIML are similar, although the standard error for LIML is smaller. AK (1991) used 2SLS based on $K = 240$ instruments and got the point estimate of 0.0928 and a standard error of 0.0093. Compared to this the estimates using the MSE based optimal number of instruments are larger with a standard error that is 50 percent larger when using LIML and 100 percent larger when using 2SLS or B2SLS.

The above example indicates that for 2SLS, choosing instruments to minimize MSE avoids cases where asymptotic interness are bad due to the bias (discussed above due to weak instruments) being large relative to the standard deviation. For AK data this produces a 2SLS estimate that uses smallest number of instruments and is similar to LIML, which is known to have less bias. For LIML and B2SLS the optimum number of instruments helps avoid under estimated variances.

We note that the above is the choice of optimum number of instruments from a large set of valid instruments. This is different than searching for the largest set of valid instruments in Andrews (1999). The results discussed here may be sensitive when the errors $(u, v_1)$ are not assumed to be homoskedastic and/or they are nonnormally distributed.

There are also some studies which look into the effect of weak instruments and endogeneity on the distribution of IV estimators and the tests based on them.

Under the weak instruments ($R^2 < 1/n$), Nelson and Startz (1990$a$, $b$) exposed to the substantial differences between the exact distribution of the IV estimator with its asymptotic distribution in following ways: ($a$) The IV estimates will concentrate around a value more than the $p$ lim of the OLS estimate and the ratio of the IV to OLS biases will fall as the degree of endogeneity rises, also see above. ($b$) The $t$-statistic based on the asymptotic standard errors will tend to be around a value greater than 1, and this increases with the degree of endogeneity. ($c$) The true distribution is bimodal and the density is zero at a point between the modes, and hence the true distribution is quite different compared with asymptotic distribution. Maddala and Jeong (1992), however, point out that the distribution of the IV estimator is not bimodal except when the correlation between $u$ and $v$, $\rho_{uv}$, is very high, thus the bimodality of Nelson and Startz are not due to instrument quality but due to the assumption of $\rho_{uv} = 1$.

Phillips (1989) pioneered the study of the distribution of IV in the totally unidentified case, where the population correlation between the instrument and the instrument is zero. For the case of one right hand endogenous variable he showed that the exact distribution of the IV estimator is equal to the $p$ lim of OLS estimate plus a unimodal $t$-distribution. In this case of totally unidentified equation Zivot, Startz, and Nelson (1997), and Zivot and Wang (1998) showed that, with no endogeneity, ($\rho_{uv} = 0$), the exact unimodal distribution is concentrated with a median error of zero. But when the degree of endogeneity approaches to 1, the distribution collapses at a spike at the $p$ lim of OLS. In this case the asymptotic result is a biased approximation for the exact distribution.

# Appendix A

# Statistical Methods

The finite sample theories of econometrics heavily depend on several statistical concepts. These include moments, distributions, and asymptotic expansions. Accordingly, the objective here is to present results that are useful for the finite sample results covered in this book. In doing so it is assumed that the reader has a basic knowledge of probability and statistics.

## A.1 Moments and Cumulants

The characteristic function of a random variable $y$ is

$$\psi(t) = Ee^{ity},$$

$$= 1 + itEy + (it)^2 \frac{Ey^2}{2!} + \frac{(it)^3 Ey^3}{3!} + \cdots,$$

$$= \sum_{r=0}^{\infty} \frac{(it)^r}{r!} \mu'_r,$$

$$= \sum_{r=0}^{\infty} \frac{(it)^r}{r!} \frac{\psi^{(r)}(0)}{i^r}, \tag{A.1}$$

where $\mu'_r = Ey^r$ and the last equality is the expansion of $\psi(t)$ around zero. Then the $r$th moment around zero of $y$ is

$$Ey^r = \mu'_r = \frac{1}{i^r} \psi^{(r)}(0), \tag{A.2}$$

where $\psi^{(r)}(0)$ is the $r$th derivative of $\psi(t)$ with respect to $t$ and evaluated at $t = 0$.

The cumulant function is defined by

$$K(t) = \log \psi(t). \tag{A.3}$$

Using the expansion of $K(t)$ around 0

$$K(t) = K(0) + tK^{(1)}(0) + \frac{t^2}{2!}K^{(2)}(0) + \cdots,$$

$$= \sum_{r=1}^{\infty} \frac{(it)^r}{r!}\kappa_r, \tag{A.4}$$

where

$$\kappa_r = \frac{1}{i^r}K^{(r)}(0) \tag{A.5}$$

is the $r$th cumulant of $y$.

It is easy to verify that $\kappa_1 = \mu'_1, \kappa_2 = \mu_2, \kappa_3 = \mu_3, \kappa_4 = \mu_4 - 3\mu_2^2, \kappa_5 = \mu_5 - 10\mu_3\mu_2, \kappa_6 = \mu_6 - 15\mu_4\mu_2 - 10\mu_3^2 + 30\mu_2^3$, where $\mu_r = E(y - Ey)^r$ is the $r$th central moment around mean.

## A.2  Gram–Charlier and Edgeworth Series

Gram (1879), and Charlier (1905) series represent the density of a standardized variable $y$ as a linear combination of the standardized normal density $\phi(y)$ and its derivatives. That is

$$f(y) = \sum_{j=0}^{\infty} c_j \phi^{(j)}(y), \tag{A.6}$$

where the $c_j$ are constants and

$$\phi^{(j)}(y) = \frac{d^j \phi(y)}{dy^j} = (-1)^j H_j(y)\phi(y); \tag{A.7}$$

$H_j(y)$ is a polynomial in $y$ of degree $j$, which is the coefficient of $t^j/j!$ in $\exp\left(ty - \frac{1}{2}t^2\right)$, for example $H_0(y) = 1$, $H_1(y) = y$, $H_2(y) = y^2 - 1$, $H_3(y) = y^3 - 3y$, and $H_4(y) = y^4 - 6y^2 + 3$. These $H_j(y)$ form an orthogonal set of polynomials (Hermite Polynomials) with respect to normal density $\phi(y)$, that is

$$\int_{-\infty}^{\infty} H_j(y)H_e(y)\phi(y)dy = j!, \quad \text{when } j = e,$$

$$= 0 \quad \text{otherwise.} \tag{A.8}$$

Because of this, multiplying $f(y)$ by $H_j(y)$ and integrating term by term we get

$$c_j = (-1)^j \frac{1}{j!} \int_{-\infty}^{\infty} H_j(y)f(y)dy. \tag{A.9}$$

These $c_j$ can be obtained in terms of the moments of $y$, and these are

$$c_0 = 1, c_1 = c_2 = 0, c_3 = -\frac{\kappa_3}{3!}, c_4 = \frac{\kappa_4}{4!}, c_5 = -\frac{\kappa_5}{5!}, c_6 = \frac{1}{6!}\left(\kappa_6 + 10\kappa_3^2\right).$$

$$\tag{A.10}$$

Then the Gram–Charlier series of Type A can be written as

$$f(y) = \phi(y) \left[ 1 + \frac{1}{3!}\kappa_3 H_3 + \frac{1}{4!}\kappa_4 H_4 + \cdots \right]$$

$$= \phi(y) - \frac{\kappa_3}{3!}\phi^{(3)}(y) + \frac{\kappa_4}{4!}\phi^{(4)}(y) + \cdots . \qquad (A.11)$$

Using this

$$F(y) = \Phi(y) - \phi(y) \left[ \frac{\kappa_3}{3!}H_2(y) + \frac{\kappa_4}{4!}H_3(y) + \cdots \right].$$

If $y$ is not a standardized variable then

$$c_j = (-1)^j \frac{1}{j!} \left[ \mu'_j - \frac{(j)_2}{2!}\mu'_{j-2} + \frac{(j)_4}{2^2 2!}\mu'_{j-4} + \cdots \right], \qquad (A.12)$$

where $(j)_r = j(j-1)\cdots(j-r+1)$. Then

$$c_0 = 1, \quad c_1 = 0, \quad c_2 = \frac{1}{2!}(\mu_2 - 1), \quad c_3 = -\frac{1}{3!}\mu_3$$

$$c_4 = \frac{1}{4!}(\mu_4 - 6\mu_2 + 3), \quad c_5 = -\frac{1}{5!}(\mu_5 - 10\mu_3)$$

$$c_6 = \frac{1}{6!}(\mu_6 - 15\mu_4 + 45\mu_2 - 15).$$

In this case

$$f(y) = \phi(y) \left[ 1 + \frac{1}{2!}(\mu_2 - 1)H_2 + \frac{1}{3!}\mu_3 H_3 \right.$$

$$\left. + \frac{1}{4!}(\mu_6 - 6\mu_2 + 3)H_4 + \cdots \right]. \qquad (A.13)$$

The Edgeworth Type A (1905) series is closely related to Gram–Charlier series. For this we obtain the characteristic function around the normal distribution and then use inversion theorem to obtain the series expansion of the density. Let us write

$$\psi(t) = e^{-(1/2)t^2} \int e^{[ity - (1/2)(it)^2]} f(y)dy$$

$$= e^{-(1/2)t^2} \int \sum_{j=0}^{\infty} \frac{(it)^j}{j!} H_j(y)f(y)dy$$

$$= e^{-(1/2)t^2} \sum_{j=0}^{\infty} (-it)^j c_j, \qquad (A.14)$$

where $c_j$ is given by (A.10). Alternatively, (A.14) can be obtained by using (A.4) as

$$\psi(t) = \exp[K(t)] = e^{-(1/2)t^2} \exp\left[\sum_{j=3}^{\infty} \frac{(it)^j}{j!} \kappa_j\right]$$

$$= e^{-(1/2)t^2} \sum_{j=0}^{\infty} \frac{(-it)^j}{j!} c_j.$$

Now using the inversion theorem

$$f(y) = \frac{1}{2\pi} \int_{-\infty}^{\infty} e^{-ity} \psi(t) dt$$

and the fact that if $f$ has the characteristic function $\psi(t)$ the $f^{(j)}$ has the characteristic function $(-it)^j \psi(t)$, which gives

$$\frac{1}{2\pi} \int_{-\infty}^{\infty} e^{-ity} e^{-(1/2)t^2} (-it)^j dt = \phi^{(j)}(y),$$

we obtain the Gram–Charlier type series expansion in (A.11). If we collect the terms containing elements not higher than $H_6$ we can write

$$f(y) = \phi(y) \left(1 + \frac{\kappa_3}{3!} H_3 + \frac{\kappa_4}{4!} H_4 + \frac{\kappa_5}{5!} H_5 + \frac{\kappa_6 + 10\kappa_3^2}{6!} H_6\right). \tag{A.15}$$

This is often called the Edgeworth form of the Type A series, see Kendall and Stuart (1977). Further, if cumulants above the fourth are neglected the Edgeworth series reduces to

$$f(y) = \phi(y) \left[1 + \frac{\kappa_3}{3!} H_3 + \frac{\kappa_4}{4!} H_4 + \frac{10\kappa_3^2}{6!} H_6\right]. \tag{A.16}$$

We note that the above series can also be written as

$$f(y) = \exp\left(-\kappa_3 \frac{D^3}{3!} + \kappa_4 \frac{D^4}{4!} - \cdots\right) \phi(y),$$

where $D = d/dy$. This is the form originally suggested by Edgeworth (1905), also see Kendall and Stuart (1977). The idea behind these series goes back to Chebyshev (1890), also see Cramér (1925, 1928) for the historical details.

## A.3 Asymptotic Expansion and Asymptotic Approximation

For large values of nonstochastic $x$, consider

$$f(x) = A_0 + \frac{A_1}{x} + \frac{A_2}{x^2} + \cdots + \frac{A_n}{x^n} + \cdots \tag{A.17}$$

is the asymptotic expansion of a function $f(x)$ if the coefficients are determined as follows:

$$A_0 = \lim_{|x| \longrightarrow \infty} f(x)$$

$$A_1 = \lim_{|x| \longrightarrow \infty} x(f(x) - A_0)$$

$$A_2 = \lim_{|x| \longrightarrow \infty} x^2 \left( f(x) - A_0 - \frac{A_1}{x} \right)$$

$$\vdots$$

$$A_n = \lim_{|x| \longrightarrow \infty} x^n \left( f(x) - A_0 - \frac{A_1}{x} - \cdots - \frac{A_{n-1}}{x^{n-1}} \right).$$

The series on the right, viz.,

$$A_0 + \frac{A_1}{x} + \frac{A_2}{x^2} + \cdots$$

may be convergent for large values of $x$ or divergent for all values of $x$.

However, it should be noted that the difference between $f(x)$ and the sum of the $n$ terms of its asymptotic expansion:

$$f(x) - \left( A_0 + \frac{A_1}{x} + \cdots + \frac{A_{n-1}}{x^{n-1}} \right) \tag{A.18}$$

is of the same order as the $(n+1)$th term when $|x|$ is large. Then the asymptotic expansion may be considered more suitable for approximate numerical computation than a convergent series.

Let us illustrate this point with the help of the following example, from Whittaker and Watson (1965: 150–151).

Consider the function

$$f(x) = \int_x^{\infty} \frac{1}{t} e^{x-t} \, dt,$$

where $x$ is real and positive. By repeated integration by parts, we get

$$f(x) = \frac{1}{x} - \frac{1}{x^2} + \frac{2!}{x^3} + \cdots + (-1)^{n-1} \frac{(n-1)!}{x^n} + \cdots .$$

We observe that the absolute value of the ratio of the $(m+1)$th term to the $m$th term is equal to

$$\frac{m}{x},$$

which tends to $\infty$ as $m \longrightarrow \infty$ for all values of $x$. It follows that the series expansion of $f(x)$ is, in fact, divergent for all values of $x$. In spite of this, however, the series can be used for the calculation of $f(x)$. This may be seen as follows:
Write

$$S_n(x) = \frac{1}{x} - \frac{1}{x^2} + \frac{2!}{x^3} + \cdots + (-1)^n \frac{n!}{x^{n+1}}$$

and

$$R_n(x) = (-1)^{n+1}(n+1)! \int_x^\infty \frac{e^{x-t}}{t^{n+2}} dt$$

such that

$$f(x) = S_n(x) + R_n(x).$$

Then, because $e^{|x-t|} < 1$

$$|f(x) - S_n(x)| = (n+1)! \int_x^\infty \frac{e^{x-t}}{t^{n+2}} dt$$
$$< (n+1)! \int_x^\infty \frac{dt}{t^{n+2}} = \frac{n!}{x^{n+1}}.$$

This is very small (for any value of $n$) for sufficiently large values of $x$. It follows, therefore, that the value of the function $f(x)$ can be calculated with great accuracy for *large values of* $x$. Even for small values of $x$ and $n$

$$S_5(10) = 0.09152$$

and

$$0 < f(10) - S_5(10) < 0.00012.$$

It has also been shown by Whittaker and Watson (1965: 153, section 8.31), that it is permissible to integrate an asymptotic expansion term by term, the resulting series being the asymptotic expansion of the integral of the function represented by original series. It has also been stated that a given series can be an asymptotic expansion of several distinct functions; however, a given function cannot be represented by more than one asymptotic expansion, see Copson (1967), Kendall and Stuart (1977), and Srinivasan (1970).

## A.3.1   Asymptotic Expansion (Stochastic)

Now we consider the case of stochastic asymptotic expansion. Most econometric estimators and test statistics can be expanded in a power series in $n^{-1/2}$ with coefficients that are well behaved random variables. Suppose, for example,

$Z_n$ is an estimator or test statistic whose stochastic expansion is

$$Z_n = T_n + \frac{A_n}{\sqrt{n}} + \frac{B_n}{n} + \frac{R_n}{n\sqrt{n}}$$

$$= \xi_0 + \xi_{-1/2} + \xi_{-1} + O_p(n^{-3/2}), \qquad (A.19)$$

where $\xi_{-j} = O_p(n^{-j})$ and $T_n$, $A_n$, and $B_n$ are sequences of random variables with limiting distribution as $n$ tends to infinity. If $R_n$ is stochastically bounded, that is, $P\left[|R_n| > c\right] < \epsilon$ as $n \longrightarrow \infty$ for every $\epsilon > 0$ and a constant $c$, then the limiting distribution of $\sqrt{n}(Z_n - \xi_0)$ is the same as the limiting distribution of $A_n$. Then expansion in (A.19) is the asymptotic expansion of $Z_n$, see Chapter 3 for examples.

## A.4    Moments of the Quadratic Forms Under Normality

Let $N_i$, for $i = 1, 2, 3, 4$, be the symmetric matrices. Further consider a $n \times 1$ vector $y$, which is distributed as a normal distribution with the mean vector $Ey = \mu$ and variance matrix as $V(y) = \Sigma$. Then the following results can be verified from the result of Lemma 1 and Exercises 2 and 4 in Chapter 2.

To write these results we first introduce the notations as given below:

$$\begin{aligned}
a_p &= \operatorname{tr}(N_p\Sigma), & a_{pq} &= \operatorname{tr}(N_p\Sigma N_q\Sigma), \\
a_{pqr} &= \operatorname{tr}(N_p\Sigma N_q\Sigma N_r\Sigma), & a_{pqrs} &= \operatorname{tr}(N_p\Sigma N_q\Sigma N_r\Sigma N_s\Sigma), \\
\theta_p &= \mu' N_p\mu, & \theta_{pq} &= \mu' N_p\Sigma N_q\mu, \\
\theta_{pqr} &= \mu' N_p\Sigma N_q\Sigma N_r\Sigma\mu, & \theta_{pqrs} &= \mu' N_p\Sigma N_q\Sigma N_r\Sigma N_s\mu,
\end{aligned} \qquad (A.20)$$

where tr represents the trace of a matrix. Then

$$E(y'N_1y) = a_1 + \theta_1, \qquad (A.21)$$

$$E(y'N_1y)(y'N_2y) = \prod_{p=1}^{2}(a_p + \theta_p) + \sum_{p=1}^{2}\sum_{\substack{q=1\\q\neq p}}^{2}(a_{pq} + 2\theta_{pq})$$

$$E\left(y'N_1y\right)\left(y'N_2y\right)\left(y'N_3y\right) = \prod_{p=1}^{3}(a_p + \theta_p) + \sum_{p=1}^{3}\sum_{\substack{q=1\\p\neq q\neq r}}^{3}\sum_{r=1}^{3}\left(a_p a_{qr}\right.$$

$$\left. + 2(a_p + \theta_p)\theta_{qr} + a_{pq}\theta_r + \tfrac{4}{3}a_{pqr} + 4\theta_{pqr}\right),$$

$$E\left(y' N_1 y\right)\left(y' N_2 y\right)\left(y' N_3 y\right)\left(y' N_4 y\right)$$

$$= \prod_{p=1}^{4}\left(a_p + \theta_p\right) + \sum_{p=1}^{4}\sum_{\substack{q=1 \\ p\neq q\neq r\neq s}}^{4}\sum_{r=1}^{4}\sum_{s=1}^{4}\left[\tfrac{4}{3} a_p a_{qrs} + a_{rs}\left(a_p a_q + a_{pq}\right)\right.$$

$$+ \theta_{rs}(2a_p\left(\theta_q + a_q\right) + 2a_{pq} + \theta_p\theta_q + 4\theta_{pq})$$

$$\left. + \theta_s\left(a_p a_{qr} + a_{pqr} + \tfrac{1}{2} a_{pq}\theta_r\right) + \tfrac{4}{3}\theta_{qrs}\left(\theta_p + a_p\right) + \tfrac{2}{3} a_{pqrs} + 8\theta_{pqrs}\right].$$

The above results can also be developed from Mathai and Provost (1992) where the moment generating functions approach is used.

In the special case where $\mu = 0$, $y \sim N\left(0, \Sigma\right)$, the above results reduce to the following results.

$$E\left(y' N_1 y\right) = a_1 \tag{A.22}$$

$$E\left(y' N_1 y\right)\left(y' N_2 y\right) = a_1 a_2 + 2a_{12}$$

$$E\left(y' N_1 y\right)\left(y' N_2 y\right)\left(y' N_3 y\right) = a_1 a_2 a_3 + 2\left[a_1 a_{23} + a_2 a_{13} + a_3 a_{12}\right] + 8a_{123}$$

$$E\left(y' N_1 y\right)\left(y' N_2 y\right)\left(y' N_3 y\right)\left(y' N_4 y\right)$$

$$= a_1 a_2 a_3 a_4 + 8\left[a_1 a_{234} + a_2 a_{134} + a_3 a_{124} + a_4 a_{123}\right] + 4\left[a_{12} a_{34} + a_{13} a_{24}\right.$$

$$\left. + a_{14} a_{23}\right] + 2[a_1 a_2 a_{34} + a_1 a_3 a_{24} + a_1 a_4 a_{23} + a_2 a_3 a_{14} + a_2 a_4 a_{13} + a_3 a_4 a_{12}]$$

$$+ 16\left[a_{1234} + a_{1243} + a_{1324}\right].$$

When $y \sim N\left(0, I\right)$ then these results in (A.22 ) remain the same except that $\Sigma = I$ in all the terms. For the alternative derivations of these results see Magnus (1978, 1979), Srivastava and Tiwari (1976), and Mathai and Provost (1992).

In another special case where $y \sim N\left(0, I\right)$ and $N_1$ is an idempotent matrix of rank $m$ then $y' N_1 y$ is distributed as a central $\chi^2$ at $m$ d.f. In this case $\operatorname{tr}\left(N_1^i\right) = m$ for $i \geq 1$, and

$$E\left(y' N_1 y\right) = m, \qquad E\left(y' N_1 y\right)^2 = m\left(m + 2\right)$$

$$E\left(y' N_1 y\right)^3 = m\left(m + 2\right)\left(m + 4\right), \qquad E\left(y' N_1 y\right)^4 = m\left(m + 2\right)$$

$$\times\left(m + 4\right)(m + 6),$$

which generalizes to

$$E\left(y' N_1 y\right)^r = 2^r\frac{\Gamma\left(\left(m/2\right) + r\right)}{\Gamma\left(m/2\right)}, \quad r \geq 1. \tag{A.23}$$

This is the $r$th moment of a central $\chi^2$ distribution.

When the matrix $N_1$ is not a symmetric matrix then we can write $y' N_1 y = y'((N_1 + N_1')/2)y$ where $((N_1 + N_1')/2)$ is always a symmetric matrix. Thus the above results also go through when the matrices $N_1$ to $N_4$ are not symmetric.

# A.5 Moments of Quadratic Forms Under Nonnormality

Let $y = (y_1, \ldots, y_n)'$ to be an $n \times 1$ vector of i.i.d. elements with

$$
\begin{aligned}
Ey_i &= 0,\, Ey_i^2 = \sigma^2,\, Ey_i^3 = \sigma^3 \gamma_1, \\
Ey_i^4 &= \sigma^4 \left(\gamma_2 + 3\right),\, Ey_i^5 = \sigma^5 \left(\gamma_3 + 10\gamma_1\right) \\
Ey_i^6 &= \sigma^6 \left(\gamma_4 + 10\gamma_1^2 + 15\gamma_2 + 15\right)
\end{aligned}
\tag{A.24}
$$

for $i = 1, \ldots, n$, where $\gamma_1$ and $\gamma_2$ are the Pearson's measures of skewness and kurtosis of the distribution and these and $\gamma_3$ and $\gamma_4$ can be regarded as measures for deviation from normality. For normal distributions, the parameters $\gamma_1, \gamma_2, \gamma_3$, and $\gamma_4$ are zero while for symmetrical distributions, only $\gamma_1$ and $\gamma_3$ are zero. These $\gamma's$ can also be expressed as cumulants, for example, $\gamma_1$ and $\gamma_2$ represent the third and fourth cumulants, see Section A.1.

Under the above assumptions the following results follow, where $N_1$ and $N_2$ matrices are not assumed to be symmetric, $\iota$ is an $n \times 1$ vector of unit elements and $*$ represents the Hadamard product:

$$
\frac{1}{\sigma^2} E\left(y'N_1 y\right) = \mathrm{tr}\left(N_1\right),
\tag{A.25}
$$

$$
\frac{1}{\sigma^3} E\left(y'N_1 y.y\right) = \gamma_1 \left(I_n * N_1\right) \iota,
$$

$$
\frac{1}{\sigma^4} E\left(y'N_1 y.yy'\right) = \gamma_2 \left(I_n * N_1\right) + \left(\mathrm{tr}\, N_1\right) I_n + N_1 + N_1',
$$

$$
\begin{aligned}
\frac{1}{\sigma^5} \left(y'N_1 y.y'N_2 y.y\right) = {}& \gamma_3 \left(I_n * N_1 * N_2\right) \iota + \gamma_1 \left[\left(\left(\mathrm{tr}\, N_1\right) I_n + N_1 + N_1'\right) \left(I_n * N_2\right)\right. \\
& + \left(\left(\mathrm{tr}\, N_2\right) I_n + N_2 + N_2'\right) \left(I_n * N_1\right) + \left(I_n * N_1' N_2\right) \\
& \left. + \left(I_n * N_1 N_2'\right) + \left(I_n * N_1' N_2'\right) + \left(I_n * N_1 N_2\right)\right] \iota,
\end{aligned}
$$

$$
\begin{aligned}
\frac{1}{\sigma^6} E\left(y'N_1 y.y'N_2 y.yy'\right) = {}& \gamma_4 \left(N_1 * N_2\right) + \gamma_2[\mathrm{tr}\left(N_1 * N_2\right) I_n + \left(\mathrm{tr}\, N_1\right)\left(I_n * N_2\right) \\
& + \left(\mathrm{tr}\, N_2\right)\left(I_n * N_1\right) + \{I_n * \left(N_1(N_2 + N_2')\right. \\
& + N_2(N_1' + N_1))\} + \left(N_1 + N_1'\right)\left(I_n * N_2\right) \\
& + \left(N_2 + N_2'\right)\left(I_n * N_1\right) + \left(I_n * N_2\right)\left(N_1 + N_1'\right) \\
& + \left(I_n * N_1\right)\left(N_2 + N_2'\right)] + \gamma_1^2[\left(N_1 + N_1'\right) * \left(N_2 + N_2'\right) \\
& + \left(I_n * N_1\right) \iota' \left(I_n * N_2\right) + \left(I_n * N_2\right) \iota' \left(I_n * N_1\right) \\
& + I_n * \{\left(N_1 + N_1'\right)\left(I_n * N_2\right)\}\iota' \\
& + I_n * \{\left(N_2 + N_2'\right)\left(I_n * N_1\right)\}\iota'] \\
& + \left[\left(\mathrm{tr}\, N_1\right) I_n + N_1 + N_1'\right](N_2 + N_2')
\end{aligned}
$$

$$+ \left[ (\operatorname{tr} N_2) I_n + N_2 + N_2' \right] (N_1 + N_1')$$

$$+ \left[ (\operatorname{tr} N_1 N_2) + (\operatorname{tr} N_1 N_2') + (\operatorname{tr} N_1) (\operatorname{tr} N_2) \right] I_n.$$

Setting $\gamma_1, \gamma_2, \gamma_3$, and $\gamma_4$ equal to zero, we obtain the results for normally distributed disturbances given above. For derivations and applications, see Chandra (1983) and Ullah, Srivastava, and Chandra (1983).

We also note that $E(y'N_1y.yy')$ above gives the result for $E((y'N_1y)$ $(y'N_2y)) = \operatorname{tr}[N_2 E(y'N_1y.yy')]$ . Similarly $E[(y'N_1y)(y'N_2y)yy']$ gives the result for $E((y'N_1y)(y'N_2y)(y'N_3y)) = \operatorname{tr}[N_3 E(y'N_1y.y'N_2y.yy')]$. Further the results for the case where the mean of $y$ is a vector $Ey = \mu$ the above results can be extended by writing, say, $y'N_1y = (y - \mu + \mu)' N_1 (y - \mu + \mu) = (y - \mu)' \times N_1 (y - \mu) + \mu'N_1\mu + 2(y - \mu)' N_1\mu$. Then $E(y'N_1y) = E((y - \mu)' N_1 (y - \mu)) + \mu'N_1\mu = \sigma^2 \operatorname{tr}(N_1) + \mu'N_1\mu$.

Now consider the case where the elements $y_i$ are non i.i.d. such that

$$Ey_i = 0, \qquad Ey_iy_j = \sigma_{ij}$$
$$E(y_iy_jy_k) = \sigma_{ijk}, \qquad E(y_iy_jy_ky_l) = \sigma_{ijkl} \tag{A.26}$$

for $i, j, k, l = 1, \ldots, n$. Define a $n \times n$ matrix $\Theta_k = ((\sigma_{ijk}))$ and another $n \times n$ matrix $\Delta_{kl} = ((\sigma_{ijkl}))$ for $i, j = 1, \ldots, n$. Further denote

$$\theta = \begin{bmatrix} \operatorname{tr}(N_1'\Theta_1) \\ \vdots \\ \operatorname{tr}(N_1'\Theta_n) \end{bmatrix}, \qquad \Delta = \begin{bmatrix} \operatorname{tr}(N_1'\Delta_1) & \cdots & \operatorname{tr}(N_1'\Delta_{1n}) \\ \vdots & & \\ \operatorname{tr}(N_1'\Delta_{n1}) & \cdots & \operatorname{tr}(N_1'\Delta_{nn}) \end{bmatrix}.$$

Then

$$E(y'N_1y.y') = \theta',$$
$$E(y'N_1y.yy') = \Delta. \tag{A.27}$$

## A.6  Moment of Quadratic Form of a Vector of Squared Nonnormal Random Variables

Consider an $n \times 1$ random vector

$$e = My, \tag{A.28}$$

where $y$ is an $n \times 1$ random vector with $Ey = 0$, $V(y) = \sigma^2 I_n$, and $M$ is an $n \times n$ idempotent matrix of rank $r$.

Let us write $e = (e_1, \ldots, e_n)'$, where $e_i = m_iy$ and $m_i$ is a $1 \times n$ $i$th vector element of the matrix

$$M = \begin{bmatrix} m_1 \\ \vdots \\ m_n \end{bmatrix} = ((m_{ij})),$$

$i, j = 1, \ldots, n$. Further denote $\dot{e} = \left(e_1^2, \ldots, e_n^2\right)'$ as an $n \times 1$ vector of squares of $e_i$ and $\dot{M} = ((m_{ij}^2))$ as an $n \times n$ matrix of the squares of the elements of $M$. Then, for a matrix $N = ((n_{ij}))$

$$E\left(\dot{e}'N\dot{e}\right) = \sigma^4 \left[\gamma_2 \operatorname{tr}\left(N\dot{M}^2\right) + 2\operatorname{tr}\left(N\dot{M}\right) + \iota'\dot{M}N\dot{M}\iota\right] \qquad (A.29)$$

and when $\dot{M} \simeq I_n$.

$$E\left(\dot{e}'N\dot{e}\right) \simeq \sigma^4 \left[(\gamma_2 + 2)\operatorname{tr}N + \iota'N\iota\right].$$

For the proof of this write

$$E\left(\dot{e}'N\dot{e}\right) = \sum_i \sum_j n_{ij} E\left(e_i^2 e_j^2\right),$$

$$= \sum_i \sum_j n_{ij} E\left(y'm_i'm_i y y' m_j' m_j y\right).$$

Then using the results in (A.25) we get the result in (A.29).

When $y \sim N\left(0, \sigma^2 I\right)$ then

$$E\left(\dot{e}'N\dot{e}\right) = \sigma^4 \left[\iota'\dot{M}N\dot{M}\iota + 2\operatorname{tr}\left(N\dot{M}\right)\right]. \qquad (A.30)$$

An application of this result can occur in the linear regression model $y = X\beta + u$ where $X$ is an $n \times k$ matrix. In this case $e = My = Mu$ where $M = I - X\left(X'X\right)^{-1} X'$ is an idempotent matrix of rank $n - k$. Several tests of heteroskedasticity are expressible as a quadratic form of $\dot{e}$, see Chapter 5.

## A.7 Moments of Quadratic Forms in Random Matrices

Let us consider a stochastic $n \times M$ matrix $Y = ((y_{it})) = (y_1, \ldots, y_M)$, where $t = 1, \ldots, n, i = 1, \ldots, M$ and $y_i$ is a $n \times 1$ vector. We assume that, for all $i$ and $t$,

$$Ey_{it} = 0, \qquad (A.31)$$

$$E\left(y_{it}y_{jt'}\right) = \sigma_{ij}, \quad \text{if } t = t',$$

$$= 0, \qquad \text{otherwise,}$$

$$E\left(y_{it}y_{jt'}y_{kt''}\right) = \sigma_{ijk}, \quad \text{if } t = t' = t'',$$

$$= 0, \qquad \text{otherwise,}$$

$$E\left(y_{it}y_{jt'}y_{kt''}y_{et'''}\right) = \sigma_{ijke}, \qquad \text{if } t = t' = t'' = t''',$$

$$= \sigma_{ij}\sigma_{ke}, \quad \text{if } t = t', t'' = t''', \text{ but } t \neq t'',$$

$$= \sigma_{ik}\sigma_{je}, \quad \text{if } t = t'', \ t' = t''', \text{ but } t \neq t',$$

$$= \sigma_{ie}\sigma_{jk}, \quad \text{if } t = t', t'' = t''', \text{ but } t \neq t',$$

$$= 0, \quad \text{otherwise,}$$

where $j, k, e = 1, \ldots, M$.

Define
$$\gamma_{ijke} = \sigma_{ijke} - \sigma_{ie}\sigma_{ke} - \sigma_{ik}\sigma_{je} - \sigma_{ie}\sigma_{jk} \tag{A.32}$$
so that $\sigma_{ijk}$ and $\gamma_{ijke}$ are 0 for normally distributed disturbances.

If $N_1$ is any nonstochastic matrix, we have
$$E\left(y_i' N_1 y_j\right) = \sigma_{ij}\operatorname{tr}(N_1)$$
$$E\left(y_i' N_1 y_j . y_k\right) = \sigma_{ijk}\left(I * N_1\right)\iota$$
$$E\left(y_i' N_1 y_j . y_k y_e'\right) = \gamma_{ijke}\left(I * N_1\right) + \sigma_{ij}\sigma_{ke}\left(\operatorname{tr} N_1\right) I$$
$$+ \sigma_{ik}\sigma_{je} N_1 + \sigma_{ie}\sigma_{jk} N_1'. \tag{A.33}$$
Further denoting $(1/n)E\left(Y'Y\right) = \Sigma = ((\sigma_{ij}))$ and considering $N_1$ of appropriate dimensions we have
$$E\left(Y' N_1 Y\right) = \left(\operatorname{tr} N_1\right)\Sigma, E\left(Y N_1 Y'\right) = \left(\operatorname{tr} N_1\Sigma\right) I_n \tag{A.34}$$
$$E\left(Y N_1 Y\right) = N_1'\Sigma.$$
Now introducing the following notations:
$$\sigma_{(ij)} = \left(\sigma_{ij1}\ldots\sigma_{ijM}\right)'; \quad \Delta_{(h)} = \begin{pmatrix} \sigma_{11h} & \cdots & \sigma_{1Mh} \\ & & \\ \sigma_{M1h} & \cdots & \sigma_{MMh} \end{pmatrix}$$
and considering $N_1$ and $N_2$ are of appropriate dimensions we have
$$E\left(Y' N_1 Y N_2 Y\right) = \left(\left(\sigma_{(hg)}' N_2\left(I * N_1\right)\iota\right)\right), \tag{A.35}$$
$$E\left(Y N_1 Y' N_2 Y\right) = \left[\left(\operatorname{tr} N_1\Delta_{(1)},\ldots,\operatorname{tr} N_1\Delta_{(M)}\right)\otimes\left(I * N_2\right)\iota\right],$$
$$E\left(Y' N_1 Y' N_2 Y\right) = \left(\left(\sigma_{(hg)}' N_1'\left(I * N_2\right)\iota\right)\right),$$
$$E\left(Y N_1 Y N_2 Y\right) = \left(\left(I * N_1'\Delta_{(1)} N_2\right)\iota,\ldots,\left(I * N_1'\Delta_{(M)} N_2\right)\iota\right),$$
$$E\left(Y' N_1 Y N_2 Y'\right) = \begin{pmatrix} \operatorname{tr} N_2'\Delta_{(1)} \\ \vdots \\ \operatorname{tr} N_2'\Delta_{(M)} \end{pmatrix}\otimes\iota'\left(I * N_1\right),$$
$$E\left(Y N_1 Y' N_2 Y'\right) = N_2\begin{pmatrix} \operatorname{tr} N_1\Delta_{(1)} \\ \vdots \\ \operatorname{tr} N_1\Delta_{(M)} \end{pmatrix}\iota',$$
$$E\left(Y' N_1 Y' N_2 Y'\right) = \begin{pmatrix} \iota'\left(I * N_2\Delta_{(1)} N_1'\right) \\ \vdots \\ \iota'\left(I * N_2\Delta_{(M)} N_1'\right) \end{pmatrix},$$
$$E\left(Y N_1 Y N_2 Y'\right) = \iota\left(\operatorname{tr} N_2'\Delta_{(1)},\ldots,\operatorname{tr} N_2'\Delta_{(M)}\right) N_1.$$

For the following results we introduce additional matrix representations:

$$
\lceil_{(ij)} = ((\gamma_{ijke})), \quad N_1 = \begin{pmatrix} n_{11} \\ \vdots \\ n_{1M} \end{pmatrix} \tag{A.36}
$$

$$
N_2 = \begin{pmatrix} n_{21} \\ \vdots \\ n_{2M} \end{pmatrix}, \quad N_3 = \begin{pmatrix} n_{31} \\ \vdots \\ n_{3M} \end{pmatrix}
$$

where $n_{1i}, n_{2i},$ and $n_{3i}$ are now vectors for $i = 1, \ldots, M$. We also use $N_1 = ((n_{1ij})),$ $N_2 = ((n_{2ij}))$ and $N_3 = ((n_{3ij})).$ Then

$$
E\left(YN_1YN_2YN_3Y\right) = \sum_i \sum_j N_3' \lceil_{(ij)} (I * n_{1i}'n_{2j}) + N_3'\Sigma N_2 N_1'\Sigma \tag{A.37}
$$
$$
+ N_1'\Sigma N_2 N_3'\Sigma + (\operatorname{tr} N_3'\Sigma N_1) N_2'\Sigma,
$$

$$
E\left(YN_1YN_2Y'N_3Y\right) = (I * N_3) \sum_i \sum_j n_{2ij} N_1' \lceil_{(ij)} + (\operatorname{tr} N_2) N_1'\Sigma N_2\Sigma
$$
$$
+ N_3 N_1'\Sigma N_2'\Sigma + (\operatorname{tr} N_2\Sigma) N_3' N_1'\Sigma,
$$

$$
E\left(YN_1YN_2YN_3Y'\right) = \sum_i \sum_j \left(\operatorname{tr} N_3 \lceil_{(ij)}\right) (I * n_{1i}'n_{2j}) + (\operatorname{tr} N_1'\Sigma N_3'\Sigma N_2) I_n
$$
$$
+ (\operatorname{tr} N_3\Sigma) N_1'\Sigma N_2 + N_2'\Sigma N_3'\Sigma N_1,
$$

$$
E\left(YN_1YN_2Y'N_3Y'\right) = \sum_i \sum_j \left(\operatorname{tr} N_2 \lceil_{(ij)}\right) (I * n_{3j}'n_{1i}) + (\operatorname{tr} N_3\Sigma N_1)
$$
$$
\times (\operatorname{tr} N_2\Sigma) I_n + N_3\Sigma N_2\Sigma N_1 + N_1'\Sigma N_2\Sigma N_3',
$$

$$
E\left(Y'N_1YN_2YN_3Y\right) = M_1 + (\operatorname{tr} N_1) \Sigma N_2 N_3'\Sigma + \Sigma N_3 N_1' N_2'\Sigma
$$
$$
+ (\operatorname{tr} \Sigma N_2 N_1' N_3') \Sigma,
$$

$$
E\left(Y'N_1YN_2Y'N_3Y\right) = M_2 + (\operatorname{tr} N_1) (\operatorname{tr} N_3) \Sigma N_2\Sigma + (\operatorname{tr} N_1 N_3) (\operatorname{tr} N_2\Sigma) \Sigma
$$
$$
+ (\operatorname{tr} N_1' N_3) \Sigma N_2'\Sigma,
$$

$$
E\left(Y'N_1YN_2YN_3Y'\right) = M_3 N_3 (I * N_1) + (\operatorname{tr} N_1) (\operatorname{tr} \Sigma N_3) \Sigma N_2
$$
$$
+ \Sigma N_3 \Sigma N_2 N_1 + \Sigma N_3' \Sigma N_2 N_1,
$$

$$
E\left(Y'N_1YN_2Y'N_3Y'\right) = M_4 N_3' (I * N_1) + (\operatorname{tr} N_1) \Sigma N_2 \Sigma N_3'
$$
$$
+ \Sigma N_2' \Sigma N_3' N_1 + (\operatorname{tr} \Sigma N_2) \Sigma N_3' N_1',
$$

$$
E\left(YN_1Y'N_2YN_3Y\right) = (I * N_2) N_3' M_5 + (\operatorname{tr} N_2) N_3'\Sigma N_1'\Sigma
$$
$$
+ (\operatorname{tr} N_1\Sigma) N_2 N_3'\Sigma + N_2'N_3'\Sigma N_1\Sigma,
$$

$$E\left(YN_1Y'N_2Y'N_3Y\right) = \left(I * N_3\right) N_2 M_5 + \left(\operatorname{tr} N_3\right)\left(\operatorname{tr}\Sigma N_1\right) N_2\Sigma$$
$$+ N_3 N_2\Sigma\left(N_1 + N_1'\right)\Sigma,$$

$$E\left(YN_1Y'N_2YN_3Y'\right) = \left(\operatorname{tr} N_3 M_5\right)\left(I * N_2\right) + \left(\operatorname{tr} N_1\Sigma N_3'\Sigma\right) N_2$$
$$+ \left(\operatorname{tr} N_1\Sigma\right)\left(\operatorname{tr} N_3\Sigma\right) N_2 + \left(\operatorname{tr} N_1\Sigma N_3'\Sigma\right) N_2'$$

$$E\left(YN_1Y'N_2Y'N_3Y'\right) = \sum_i\sum_j\left(\operatorname{tr} N_1\Gamma_{(ij)}\right)\left(I * n_{3i}'n_{2j}\right) + \left(\operatorname{tr} N_3\Sigma N_1\Sigma N_2'\right) I_n$$
$$+ \left(\operatorname{tr} N_1\Sigma\right) N_2\Sigma N_3' + N_3\Sigma N_1'\Sigma N_2',$$

$$E\left(Y'N_1Y'N_2YN_3Y\right) = M_6 + \left(\operatorname{tr} N_3'\Sigma N_1'N_2\right)\Sigma + \Sigma N_1'N_2'N_3'\Sigma$$
$$+ \Sigma N_3 N_2'N_1\Sigma,$$

$$E\left(Y'N_1Y'N_2Y'N_3Y\right) = M_7 + \left(\operatorname{tr} N_3\right)\Sigma N_1'N_2\Sigma + \Sigma N_2'N_3'N_1\Sigma$$
$$+ \left(\operatorname{tr}\Sigma N_2'N_3 N_1\right)\Sigma,$$

$$E\left(Y'N_1Y'N_2YN_3Y'\right) = M_8 N_1'\left(I * N_2\right) + \left(\operatorname{tr} N_2\right)\Sigma N_3'\Sigma N_1'$$
$$+ \left(\operatorname{tr} N_3\Sigma\right)\Sigma N_1'N_2 + \Sigma N_3\Sigma N_1'N_2',$$

$$E\left(Y'N_1Y'N_2Y'N_3Y'\right) = \sum_i\sum_j\left(I * n_{3i}'n_{2j}\right)\Gamma_{(ij)}\iota N_1' + \Sigma N_3'N_2\Sigma N_1'$$
$$+ \Sigma N_1'N_2\Sigma N_3' + \left(\operatorname{tr} N_1\Sigma N_3'\right)\Sigma N_2'$$

where $M = ((m_{ij}))$ and $m_{ij}$ for $M_1$ to $M_8$ are, respectively,

$$\operatorname{tr}\left(\Gamma_{(ij)}N_2\left(I * N_1\right) N_3'\right), \left(\operatorname{tr}(I * N_1) N_3\right)\left(\operatorname{tr} N_2\Gamma_{(ij)}\right), \operatorname{tr}\left(\Gamma_{(ij)}N_3\right), \operatorname{tr}\left(\Gamma_{(ij)}N_2\right),$$
$$\operatorname{tr}\left(\Gamma_{(ij)}N_1\right), \operatorname{tr}\left(N_1\Gamma_{(ij)}N_3\left(I * N_2\right)\right), \operatorname{tr}\left(\Gamma_{(ij)}N_2'\left(I * N_3'\right) N_1\right), \text{ and } \operatorname{tr}\left(\Gamma_{(ij)}N_3'\right).$$

The above results simplify for the normal distribution by using $\sigma_{ijk} = 0$ and $\gamma_{ijke} = 0$. For the applications, see Ullah and Srivastava (1994), Ullah (2002), Srivastava and Maekawa (1995), among others. These results are useful in developing the moments of various econometric statistics under nonnormal errors, also see Lieberman (1997).

# A.8   Distribution of Quadratic Forms

Let $y \sim N\left(\mu, \Sigma\right)$ be an $n \times 1$ normal vector with $Ey = \mu$ and $V(y) = \Sigma$. Further consider $N$ to be an $n \times n$ nonstochastic matrix and $b$ and $c$ to be constants. Then

$$y^* = y'Ny + 2b'y + c \sim \chi_r^2\left(\theta\right) \tag{A.38}$$

if and only if $r = \operatorname{Rank}\left(N\Sigma\right)$, $\Sigma N\Sigma N\Sigma = \Sigma N\Sigma$, $\Sigma\left(b + N\mu\right) = \Sigma N\Sigma\left(b + N\mu\right)$ and $\theta = c + 2b'\mu + \mu'N\mu$. The $\chi_r^2\left(\theta\right)$ represents the noncentral chi-square distribution with the d.f. $r$ and the noncentrality parameter $\theta$. For $\theta = 0$,

$\chi_r^2(\theta) = \chi_r^2$ becomes a central chi-square with the d.f. $r$, see Srivastava and Khatri (1979: 64), Rao (1973), and Mathai and Provost (1992).

A necessary and sufficient condition for

$$y^* = y'Ny \sim \chi_r^2(\theta) \tag{A.39}$$

is that $\Sigma N \Sigma N \Sigma = \Sigma N \Sigma$ with d.f. $= r = $ Rank of $N\Sigma$, and $\theta = \mu' N \mu$. For $\mu = \theta = 0$, $y^* \sim \chi_r^2$, which is a central chi-square.

If $|\Sigma| \neq 0$ then the above necessary and sufficient condition becomes $N\Sigma N = N$ with the d.f. $r = $ Rank of $N\Sigma$. This implies the condition that $N\Sigma$ or $\Sigma^{1/2} N \Sigma^{1/2}$ is an idempotent matrix of rank $r$, where $\Sigma = \Sigma^{1/2}\Sigma^{1/2}$, see Rao (1973: 188) and Srivastava and Khatri (1979: 64).

A necessary and sufficient condition that the vector $N_1 y$ and the quadratic form $(y - \mu)' N (y - \mu)$ are statistically independent is $\Sigma N \Sigma N_1 = 0$, or $N\Sigma N_1 = 0$ if $|\Sigma| \neq 0$, where $N_1$ is an $n \times n$ nonstochastic matrix. Similarly $(y - \mu)' N_1 (y - \mu)$ and $(y - \mu)' N (y - \mu)$ are independent if $\Sigma N_1 \Sigma N \Sigma = 0$, or $N_1 \Sigma N = 0$ if $|\Sigma| \neq 0$.

## A.8.1 Density and Moments of a Noncentral Chi-square Variable

Let $y \sim N(\mu, \Sigma)$. Then

$$y^* = y' \Sigma^{-1/2} N \Sigma^{-1/2} y \sim \chi_r^2(\theta), \tag{A.40}$$

where $N$ is assumed to be an idempotent matrix of rank $r$, $\theta = (1/2)\mu' \Sigma^{-1/2} N \Sigma^{-1/2} \mu$ and $\Sigma^{-1/2} y \sim N(\Sigma^{-1/2}\mu, I)$. The density function of the noncentral $\chi^2$ variable $y^*$ is

$$f(y^*) = e^{-\theta} \sum_{i=0}^{\infty} \frac{\theta^i}{i!} \frac{y^{*((r+2i)/2)-1}e^{-y^*/2}}{2^{((r+2i)/2)}\Gamma((r+2i)/2)}. \tag{A.41}$$

Further the $s$th inverse moment of $y^*$ is

$$E(y^*)^{-s} = \int_0^{\infty} (y^*)^{-s} f(y^*) \, dy^*,$$

which gives, for $s = 1, 2, \ldots,$

$$E(y^*)^{-s} = 2^{-s} \frac{\Gamma((r/2) - s)}{\Gamma(r/2)} e^{-\theta} {}_1F_1\left(\frac{r}{2} - s; \frac{r}{2}; \theta\right), \tag{A.42}$$

see Ullah (1974).

Using the derivatives of the confluent hypergeometric function in Slater (1960: 15, eq. 2.1.8) we have

$$\frac{d^m E\,(y^*)^{-s}}{d\theta^m} = 2^{-s}\,(-1)^s\,\frac{\Gamma\,(s+m)}{\Gamma\,(s)}\,\frac{\Gamma\,((r/2)-s)}{\Gamma\,((r/2)+m)}\,e^{-\theta}\,{}_1F_1\Big(\frac{r}{2}-s;\frac{r}{2}+m;\theta\Big)$$

(A.43)

for $m = 1, 2, \ldots$.

When $\mu = 0$ so that $\theta = 0$, the density of $y^*$ given above reduces to the density of a central $\chi_r^2$. Further

$$E\,(y^*)^{-s} = 2^{-s}\frac{\Gamma\,((r/2)-s)}{\Gamma\,(r/2)}.$$

(A.44)

We note that the distribution of $y'Ny = y'\Sigma^{-1/2}\left(\Sigma^{1/2}N\Sigma^{1/2}\right)\Sigma^{-1/2}y$ is not a noncentral $\chi^2$ distribution unless $\Sigma^{1/2}N\Sigma^{1/2}$ is idempotent. If $\Sigma^{1/2}N\Sigma^{1/2}$ is not idempotent the $s$th inverse moment of $y'Ny$ is as given in Chapter 2.

## A.8.2   Moment Generating Function and Characteristic Function

Let $y \sim N\,(\mu, \Sigma)$, where $\Sigma = PP'$. Let Let $N_1, N_2, \ldots, N_m$ be $m$ symmetric $n \times n$ matrices. Then the joint moment generating function of $y'N_1y, \ldots, y'N_my$ is

$$M\,(t_1, \ldots, t_m) = E\,\exp\,(t_1 y'N_1 y + \cdots + t_m y'N_m y),$$

$$= \left|I - 2C\right|^{-1/2}\exp\left\{-\tfrac{1}{2}\mu_0'\mu_0\right\}\exp\left\{-\tfrac{1}{2}\mu_0'\,(I-2C)^{-1}\,\mu_0\right\},$$

(A.45)

where $C = P'\,(t_1 N_1 + \cdots + t_m N_m)\,P$ and $\mu_0 = P^{-1}\mu$, see Magnus (1986), and Mathai and Provost (1992). For $m = 2$ this result is given in Chapter 2 and it has been used in Sawa (1972), Magnus (1986), and Mathai and Provost (1992) to obtain the moments of the product and ratio of quadratic forms. For example, if $y_1^* = y'N_1 y$ and $y_2^* = y'N_2 y$, then

$$E\,((y_1^*)^{s_1}\,(y_2^*)^{s_2}) = \frac{\partial^{s_1+s_2} M\,(t_1, t_2)}{\partial t_1^{s_1}\,\partial t_2^{s_2}}\,|_{t_1=0,\,t_2=0}.$$

(A.46)

For the moments of the ratio of $y_1^*/y_2^*$, see Chapter 2.

Now we consider the vector $y$ distributed nonnormally with $Ey = \mu$ and $V(y) = \Sigma$, which is a diagonal matrix of $\sigma_i^2$, $i = 1, \ldots, n$. If we let $\phi\left(y_i\,|_{\mu_i, \sigma_i^2}\right)$ be a normal density with mean $\mu_i$ and variance $\sigma_i^2$ then the Edgeworth or Gram–Charlier series expansion of the density for $f\,(y_i)$ in Section A.2 can be written as (Davis 1976)

$$f(y_i) = \exp\left[\sum_{r=3}^{\infty} c_r \phi^{(r)}\left(y_i \mid_{\mu_i, \sigma_i^2}\right)\right],$$

$$= E_{z_i}\left[\phi\left(y_i \mid_{\mu_i + z_i, \sigma_i^2}\right)\right] \tag{A.47}$$

where $E_{z_i}(z_i^r) = (-1)^r r! c_r$ and $c_r$ is as in (A.10).

Since $y \mid_z \sim N(\mu + z, \Sigma)$, therefore using the Davis (1976) technique the characteristic (c.f.) or moment generating function (m.g.f.) under the Edgeworth density can be obtained in two steps. First find the c.f. for the normal case. Second consider the expectation of this c.f. with respect to $z$. With this approach Knight (1985) provided the c.f. of a linear form $a'y$ and the quadratic form $y'Ny$ with corrections for skewness and kurtosis, that is the first four terms of the Edgeworth expansion.

These results on the c.f. and m.g.f. provide the moments of the products and ratio of quadratic forms under the Edgeworth density of $y$. For applications, see Knight (1985, 1986) for the moments and distribution of the 2SLS estimator and Peters (1989) for the moments of the LS estimator in a dynamic regression model.

## A.8.3 Density Function Based on Characteristic Function

When the absolute value of the c.f. $\psi(t) = \psi(t_1, \ldots, t_n)$ is integrable then the density function $f(y)$ exists and is continuous for all $y$, and it is given by

$$f(y) = \frac{1}{(2\pi)^n} \int_{-\infty}^{\infty} e^{-it'y} \psi(t) dt. \tag{A.48}$$

This is known as the uniqueness theorem or inversion theorem for the c.f., see Cramér (1946).

Next consider the variable $q$, which is the ratio of two random variables $Y$ and $X$, $q = Y/X$. Let $\psi(t_1, t_2)$ be the c.f. of $(Y, X)$. Then the density of $q$ is given by

$$f(q) = \frac{1}{2\pi i} \int_{-\infty}^{\infty} \left[\frac{\partial \psi(t_1, t_2)}{\partial t_2}\right] \frac{dt_1}{t_2 = -qt_1}, \tag{A.49}$$

see Cramér (1946). Phillips (1985) generalizes this result to matrix quotients $Q = X^{-1}Y$ where $X$ is a $k \times k$ positive definite matrix whose expectation of the determinant exists and $Y$ is a $k \times l$ matrix. As an application of this result Phillips (1985) shows that the LS regression coefficient matrix for multivariate normal sample is a matrix $t$-distribution.

## A.9   Hypergeometric Functions

Here we present well known power series, which are used in the text.

A power series

$$
_1F_1(a; c; x) = \frac{\Gamma(c)}{\Gamma(a)} \sum_{i=0}^{\infty} \frac{\Gamma(a+i)}{\Gamma(c+i)} \frac{x^i}{i!}, \quad c > 0, \quad |x| < \infty \tag{A.50}
$$

$$
= 1 + \frac{a}{c}x + \frac{a(a+1)}{c(c+1)} \frac{x^2}{2} + \cdots
$$

is known as the confluent hypergeometric function or Kummer's series, see Slater (1960: 2). It has been used extensively in finite sample econometrics, see Ullah (1974), Sawa (1972), and Phillips (1983), among others. Also, see Abadir (1999) for an introduction to hypergeometric function for economists.

Another power series, hypergeometric functions, is written as

$$
_2F_1(a, b; c; x) = \frac{\Gamma(c)}{\Gamma(a)\Gamma(b)} \sum_{i=0}^{\infty} \frac{\Gamma(a+i)\Gamma(b+i)}{\Gamma(c+i)} \frac{x^i}{i!} \tag{A.51}
$$

for $|c| > 0$ and $|x| < 1$, see Slater (1960), and Ullah and Nagar (1974).

Now we consider the integral of a function, which has a power series expansion in terms of hypergeometric functions, see Sawa (1972). This is, for $0 \le k < 1$ and $p > 1$

$$
G(k, \theta; p, q) = \int_{-\infty}^{0} g(x; k, \theta, p, q)\, dx,
$$

$$
= e^{-\theta} \frac{\Gamma(p-1)}{\Gamma(q)} \sum_{j=0}^{\infty} \frac{\Gamma(q+j)}{\Gamma(p+j)} k^j {}_1F_1(p-1; p+j; \theta),
$$

where

$$
g(x; k, \theta, p, q) = \frac{2}{(1-2x)^{p-q}[1 - 2(1-k)x]^q} \exp\left[-\theta + \frac{\theta}{1-2x}\right]. \tag{A.52}
$$

For $k = 1$ and $p - q > 1$

$$
G(1, \theta; p, q) = e^{-\theta} \frac{\Gamma(p-q-1)}{\Gamma(p-q)} {}_1F_1(p-q-1; p-q; \theta). \tag{A.53}
$$

To derive the above result we can first use the following change of variable transformation $t = 1/(1-2x)$. Then

$$
G(k, \theta; p, q) = e^{-\theta} \int_0^1 t^{p-2}[1 - k(1-t)]^{-q} e^{\theta t}\, dt. \tag{A.54}
$$

Then using the binomial expansion of $[1 - k(1-t)]^{-q}$ and doing term by term integration gives the above result, Sawa (1972).

## A.9.1   Asymptotic Expansion

For $a, c > 0$, and $x > 0$ we have

$$
{}_1F_1\left(a; c; x\right) = \frac{\Gamma(c)e^x x^{-(c-a)}}{\Gamma(a)\,\Gamma(c-a)\,\Gamma(1-a)}
$$

$$
\times \left[ \sum_{j=0}^{r-1} \frac{\Gamma(c-a+j)\,\Gamma(1-a+j)}{j!\,x^j} + O\left(x^{-r}\right) \right], \qquad (A.55)
$$

see Copson (1948: 265), Erdelyi (1956), Slater (1960), and Sawa (1972). For large $x$ this gives the asymptotic expansion up to $O\left(x^{-(r-1)}\right)$. Using this in the $G$ function we get the asymptotic expansion, up to $O\left(\theta^{-4}\right)$, as

$$
G\left(k, \theta; p, q\right) = \frac{1}{\theta} + (qk - p + 2)\,\frac{1}{\theta^2} + [q\,(q+1)\,k^2 - 2q\,(p-2)\,k
$$

$$
+ (p-2)\,(p-3)\,]\frac{1}{\theta^3} + [q\,(q+1)\,(q+2)\,k^3
$$

$$
- 3q\,(q+1)\,(p-2)\,k^2 + 3q\,(p-2)\,(p-3)\,k
$$

$$
- (p-2)\,(p-3)\,(p-4)\,]\frac{1}{\theta^4}. \qquad (A.56)
$$

## A.10   Order of Magnitudes (Small o and Large O)

Here we decide the measure of the order of magnitude of a particular sequence, say, $\{X_n\}$. The magnitude is defined by looking into the behavior of $X_n$ for large $n$.

**Definition 1**   The sequence $\{X_n\}$ of real numbers is said to be at most of order $n^k$ and is denoted by

$$
X_n = O\left(n^k\right), \quad \text{if} \quad \frac{X_n}{n^k} \longrightarrow c
$$

as $n \longrightarrow \infty$, for some constant $c > 0$. Further if $\{X_n\}$ is a sequence of random variables then it is said to be at most of order $n^k$ in probability,

$$
X_n = O_p\left(n^k\right)
$$

if, as $n \longrightarrow \infty$,

$$
\frac{X_n}{n^k} - c_n \longrightarrow 0 \text{ in prob,}
$$

where $c_n$ is a nonstochastic sequence.

**Definition 2**    The sequence $\{X_n\}$ of real numbers is said to be of smaller order than $n^k$ and is denoted by

$$X_n = o\left(n^k\right), \quad \text{if} \quad \frac{X_n}{n^k} \longrightarrow 0$$

as $n \longrightarrow \infty$. Further if $\{X_n\}$ is stochastic then

$$X_n = o_p\left(n^k\right)$$

if

$$\frac{X_n}{n^k} \longrightarrow 0 \text{ in prob.}$$

In the above definitions $k$ can take any real value (positive or negative). Also the order of magnitude is almost sure if the convergence of the sequence is almost sure.

As an example, consider a stochastic sequence

$$X_n = \sqrt{n}\frac{\left(\overline{X} - \mu\right)}{\sigma} = \frac{1}{\sqrt{n}}\sum_{i=1}^{n}\frac{(X_i - \mu)}{\sigma},$$

where $EX_i = \mu$ and $V\left(X_i\right) = \sigma^2$. Then using Chebychev's inequality, the sequence $X_n$ is bounded in probability in the sense that $P\left[|X_n| > \epsilon\right] \leq 1/\epsilon^2$ as $n \longrightarrow \infty$. Thus $X_n = O_p(1)$ and $\overline{X} - \mu = O_p\left(n^{-1/2}\right)$.

The order of magnitudes satisfy the following properties.

If $X_n = O\left(n^k\right)$ and $Y_n = O\left(n^l\right)$ then

1. $X_n Y_n = O\left(n^{k+l}\right)$.

2. $X_n^r = O\left(n^{rk}\right)$.

3. $X_n + Y_n = O\left(n^{l_0}\right), \quad l_0 = \text{Max}(k, l)$.

The same results for small $o$ in place of capital $O$. Further, if $X_n = O\left(n^k\right)$ and $Y_n = o\left(n^l\right)$, then

1. $X_n + Y_n = O\left(n^k\right)$.

2. $X_n Y_n = o\left(n^{k+l}\right)$.

# References

Abadir, K. M. (1993*a*). 'OLS Bias in a Nonstationary Autoregression', *Econometric Theory*, 9:81–93.

——(1993*b*). 'The Limiting Distribution of the Autocorrelation Coefficient Under a Unit Root', *The Annals of Statistics*, 212:1058–70.

——(1994). 'The Joint Density of Two Functionals of Brownian Motion', Discussion Paper 94-03, University of Exeter.

——(1999). 'An Introduction to Hypergeometric Functions for Economists', *Econometric Reviews*, 18:287–330.

—— Hadri, K., and Tzavalis, E. (1999). 'The Influence of VAR Dimensions on Estimator Biases', *Econometrica*, 67:163–82.

Akahira, M. and Takeuchi, K. (1981). *Asymptotic Efficiency of Statistical Estimators: Concepts and Higher Order Asymptotic Efficiency* (New York: Springer-Verlag).

Ali, M. M. (2002). 'Distribution of the Least Squares Estimator in a First-Order Autoregressive Model', *Econometric Reviews*, 21(1):89–119.

—— and Sharma, S. C. (1993). 'Robustness to Nonnormality of Durbin–Watson Test for Autocorrelation', *Journal of Econometrics*, 57:117–36.

————(1996). 'Robustness to Non-Normality of Regression F-tests', *Journal of Econometrics*, 71:175–205.

Amemiya, T. (1985). *Advanced Econometrics*, 1st edition (Cambridge: Harvard University Press).

Anderson, T. W. (1959). 'On Asymptotic Distribution of Estimates of Parameters of Stochastic Difference Equations', *The Annals of Mathematical Statistics*, 30:676–87.

——(1974). 'An Asymptotic Expansion of the Distribution of the Limited Information Maximum Likelihood Estimate of a Coefficient in a Simultaneous Equation System', *Journal of the American Statistical Association*, 69:565–73.

Anderson, T. W. (1982). 'Some Recent Developments on the Distributions of Single-Equation Estimators', in R. L. Basmann and G. F. Rhodes, Jr. (eds.), *Advances in Econometrics* (Cambridge University Press).

——(1984). *An Introduction to Multivariate Statistical Analysis* (New York: Wiley).

—— and Fang, K. T. (1987). 'Cochran's Theorem for Elliptically Contoured Distributions', *Sankhya*, 49:305–15.

—— and Rubin, H. (1949). 'Estimation of the Parameters of a Single Equation in a Complete System of Stochastic Equation', *The Annals of Mathematical Statistics*, 20:46–63.

————(1950). 'The Asymptotic Properties of Estimates of the Parameters of a Single Equation in a Complete System of Stochastic Equations', *The Annals of Mathematical Statistics*, 21:570–82.

—— and Sawa, T. (1973). 'Distributions of Estimator of Coefficients of a Single Equation in a Simultaneous System and their Asymptotic Expansions', *Econometrica*, 41:683–714.

————(1979). 'Evaluation of the Distribution Function of the Two-Stage Least Squares Estimate', *Econometrica*, 47:163–82.

Andrews, D. W. K. (1999). 'Consistent Moment Selection Procedures for Generalized Method of Moments Estimation', *Econometrica*, 67:543–64.

Angrist, J. D. and Kreuger, A. B. (1991). 'Does Compulsory School Attendance Affect Schooling and Earnings?', *Quarterly Journal of Econometrics*, 106:979–1014.

————(1992). 'The Effect of Age at School Entry on Educational Attainment: An Application of Instrumental Variables with Moments from Two Samples', *Journal of the American Statistical Association*, 87:328–336.

—— Imbens, G. W., and Kreuger, A. B. (1999). 'Jackknife Instrumental Variable Estimation', *Journal of Applied Econometrics*, 14:57–67.

Arellano, M. and Sargan, J. D. (1990). 'Imhof Approximations to Econometric Estimators', *Review of Economic Studies*, 57:627–46.

Avram, F. (1988). 'On Bilinear Forms in Gaussian Random Variables and Toeplitz Matrices', *Probability Theory and Related Fields*, 79:37–45.

Baltagi, B. H. (2001). *Econometric Analysis of Panel Data* (New York: John Wiley).

Banerjee, A., Dolando, J. J., Hendry, D. F., and Smith, G. W. (1986). 'Exploring Equilibrium Relationships in Economics Through Static Models: Some

Monte Carlo Evidence', *Oxford Bulletin of Economics and Statistics*, 48:253–77.

Bao, Y. and Ullah, A. (2002). 'The Second-Order Bias and Mean Squared Error of Nonlinear Estimators in Time Series', Manuscript, University of California, Riverside.

Baranchik, A. J. (1964). 'Multiple Regression and Estimation of the Mean of a Multivariate Normal Distribution', Technical Report 51, Department of Statistics, Stanford University, Stanford.

Barndorff-Nielsen, O. E. and Cox, D. R. (1979). 'Edgeworth and Saddle-Point Approximations with Statistical Applications', *Journal of the Royal Statistical Society*, 41:279–312.

———— (1989). *Asymptotic Techniques for Use in Statistics* (New York, NY: Chapman and Hall).

Basmann, R. L. (1961). 'Note on the Exact Finite Sample Frequence Functions of Generalized Classical Linear Estimators in Two Leading Overidentified Cases', *Journal of the American Statistical Association*, 56:619–36.

—— (1965). 'On the Application of the Identifiability Test Statistic in Predictive Testing of Explanatory Economic Models', *Econometric Annual of the Indian Economic Journal*, 13:387–423.

—— (1966). 'On the Application of the Indentifiability Test Statistics Predictive Testing of Explanatory Economic Models', *The Econometric Annual of the Indian Economic Journal*, 13:387–423; Part II, *idem* 14, 233–52.

—— (1974). 'Exact Finite Sample Distribution for Some Econometric Estimators and Test Statistics: A Survey and Appraisal', in M. D. Intriligator and D. A. Kendrick (eds.), *Frontiers of Quantitative Economics*, vol. 2 (Amsterdam: North Holland).

—— and Richardson, D. H. (1973). 'The Exact Finite Sample Distribution of a Non-Consistent Structural Variance Estimator', *Econometrica*, 41: 41–58.

Beach, C. M. and Mackinon, J. G. (1978). 'A Maximum Likelihood Procedure for Regression and Autocorrelated Errors', *Econometrica*, 46:51–8.

Bekker, P. A. (1994). 'Alternative Approximations to the Distributions of Instrumental Variable Estimators', *Econometrica*, 62:657–81.

—— (2002). 'Exact Inference for the Linear Model With Groupwise Heteroscedastic Spherical Disturbances', *Journal of Econometrics*, 111: 285–302.

Bera, A. K. and Ullah, A. (1991). 'Rao's Score Test in Econometrics', *Journal of Quantitative Economics*, 7:189–220.

Beran, R. (1975). 'Tail Probabilities of Non-Central Quadratic Forms', *The Annals of Statistics*, 3:969–74.

Bergstrom, A. R. (1962). 'The Exact Sampling Distributions at Least Squares and Maximum Likelihood Estimators of the Marginal Propensity to Consume', *Econometrica*, 30:480–90.

Berndt, E. and Savin, N. E. (1977). 'Conflict Among Criteria for Testing Hypotheses in the Multivariate Linear Regression Model', *Econometrica*, 45:1263–77.

Berry, A. C. (1941). 'The Accuracy of the Gaussian Approximation to the Sum of Independent Variates', *Transactions of the American Mathematical Society*, 48:122–36.

Bhattacharya, R. N. (1975). 'On Errors of Normal Approximation', *The Annals of Probability*, 3:815–28.

——— and Ghosh, J. K. (1978). 'On the Validity of the Formal Edgeworth Expansion', *The Annals of Statistics*, 6:434–51.

Bloomfield, P. (1972). 'On the Error of Prediction of Time-Series', *Biometrika*, 59:501–08.

Bollerslev, T. (1986). 'Generalized Autoregressive Conditional Heteroskedasticity', *Journal of Econometrics*, 31:307–327.

Bound, J., Jaeger, D. A., and Baker, R. (1995). 'Problems with Instrumental Variables Estimation when the Correlation Between the Instruments and the Endogenous Exlanatory Variables is Weak', *Journal of the American Statistical Association*, 90:443–50.

Bowden, R. J. and Turkington, D. A. (1984). *Instrumental Variables* (Cambridge: Cambridge University Press).

Box, G. E. P. and Jenkins, G. M. (1970). *Time-Series Analysis: Forecasting and Control* (San Francisco: Holden Day).

Breusch, T. S., Robertson, J. C., and Welsh, A. H. (1993). 'The Multivariate Student t Model in Robust Inference and Data Analysis', Working Paper No. 259, the Australian National University, Australia.

Burman, P. (1987). 'Central Limit Theorem for Quadratic Forms for Sparse Tables', *Journal of Multivariate Statistics*, 22:258–77.

Buse, A. (1982). 'The Likelihood Ratio, Wald and Lagrange Multiplier Tests: An Expository Note', *American Statistician*, 36:153–57.

Carter, R. A. L. and Ullah, A. (1979). 'The Finite Sample Properties of OLS and IV Estimators in Special Rational Distributed Lag Models', *Sankhya*, 41:1–18.

—— Srivastava, M. S., Srivastava, V. K., and Ullah, A. (1990). 'Unbiased Estimation of the MSE Matrix of Stein-Rule Estimators, Confidence Ellipsoids and Hypothesis Testing', *Econometric Theory*, 6:63–74.

Cavanagh, C. L. and Rothenberg, T. J. (1983). 'The Second-Order Inefficiency of the Efficient Score Test', Working Paper, Institute of Business and Economic Research, University of California, Berkeley.

Chandra, R. (1983). 'Estimation of Econometric Models when Disturbances are not Necessarily Normal', Ph.D. Thesis, Department of Statistics, Lucknow University.

Chao, J. C. and Swanson, N. R. (2002). 'Consistent Estimation with a Large Number of Weak Instruments', Working Paper, Deparment of Economics, University of Maryland.

Charlier, C. V. L. (1905). 'Uber Das Fehlergesetz', Ark. Mat. Astr. Fiz., 2, No. 8.

Chaturvedi, A. and Shukla, G. (1990). 'Stein Rule Estimation in Linear Model with Nonscalar Error Covariance Matrix', *Sankhya B*, 52:293–303.

—— Hoa, T. V., and Lal, R. (1992). 'Improved Estimation of the Linear Regression Model with Autocorrelated Errors', *Journal of Quantitative Economics*, 8:347–52.

Chaubey, Y. P. and Nur Enayet Talukdev, A. B. M. (1983). 'Exact Moments of a Ratio of Two Positive Quadratic Forms in Normal Variables', *Communications in Statistics-Theory and Methods*, 12:675–79.

Chebyshev, P. L. (1890). 'Sur Deux Theorems Relatifs Aux Probabilités', *Acta Mathematica*, 14:305–15.

Chibishov, D. M. (1980). 'An Asymptotic Expansion for the Distribution of a Statistic Admitting an Asymptotic Expansion', *Theory of Probability and Its Applications*, 25:732–44.

Cochrane, D. and Orcutt, G. H. (1949). 'Application of Least Squares Regressions to Relationships Containing Autocorrelated Error Terms', *Journal of the American Statistical Association*, 44:32–61.

Constantine, A. G. (1963). 'Some Noncentral Distribution Problems in Multivariate Analysis', *The Annals of Mathematical Statistics*, 34: 1270–85.

Copas, J. B. (1966). 'Monte Carlo Results for Estimation in a Stable Markov Time Series', *Journal of the Royal Statistical Society*, 129:110–16.

Copson, E. T. (1967). *Asymptotic Expansions* (Cambridge: Cambridge University Press).

Copson, E. T. (1948). Theory of Functions of a Complex Variable (London: Oxford University Press).

Cordeiro, G. M. and Klien, R. (1994). 'Bias Correction in ARMA Models', *Statistics and Probabilities Letters*, 19:169–796.

Cramér, H. (1925). 'On Some Classes of Series Used in Mathematical Statistics', *Proceedings of the Sixth Scandinavian Congress of Mathematicians*, Copenhagen, 399–425.

—— (1928). 'On the Composition of Elementary Errors', *Skand. Aktnarietidskrift*, 11:13–74, 141–80.

—— (1946). *Mathematical Methods of Statistics* (Princeton: Princeton University Press).

Cramér, J. S. (1987). 'Mean and Variance of R2 in Small and Moderate Samples', *Journal of Econometrics*, 35:253–66.

Cribbett, P., Lye, J. N., and Ullah, A. (1989). 'Evaluation of the 2SLS Distribution Function by Imhof's Procedure', *Journal of Quantitative Economics*, 5(1):91–96.

Daniels, H. E. (1954). 'Saddlepoint Approximations in Statistics', *Biometrika*, 59:204–7.

—— (1956). 'The Approximate Distribution of Serial Correlation Coefficients', *Biometrika*, 43:169–85.

Davidson, R. and MacKinnon, J. G. (1988). 'Monte Carlo Experiments', Manuscript, Queen's University, Ontario.

———— (1996). *The Size Distortion of Bootstrap Tests*, (Kingston, Ontario, Canada: Queen's University).

Davis, A. W. (1976). 'Statistical Distributions in Univariate and Multivariate Edgeworth Populations', *Biometrika*, 63:661–70.

Davies, R. B. (1973). 'Numerical Inversion of a Characteristic Function', *Biometrika*, 60:415–17.

—— (1980). 'The Distribution of a Linear Contribution of $\chi^2$ Random Variables', *Applied Statistics*, 29:323–33.

Deaton, A. (1997). '*The Analysis of Household Surveys: Microeconomic Analysis for Development Policy*', (Maryland: John Hopkins University Press).

De Bruijn, N. G. (1958). *Asymptotic Methods in Analysis* (Amsterdam: North Holland).

—— (1961). *Asymptotic Methods in Analysis* (Amsterdam: North Holland).

Dickey, D. A. (1976). 'Estimation and Hypothesis Testing for Nonstationary Time Series', Ph.D. Dissertation, Iowa State, Ames.

—— and Fuller, W. A. (1979). 'Distribution of the Autoregressive Time Series with a Unit Root', *Journal of the American Statistical Association*, 74:427–31.

———— (1981). 'Likelihood Ratio Statistics for Autoregressive Time Series with a Unit Root', *Econometrica*, 49:1057–72.

Donald, S. G. and Newey, W. K. (2001). 'Choosing the Number of Instruments', *Econometrica*, 69:1161–91.

Dufour, J.-M. (1984). 'Unbiasedness of Predictions from Estimated Autoregressions when the True Order is Unknown', *Econometrica*, 52:209–16.

—— (1990). 'Exact Tests and Confidence Sets in Linear Regressions with Autocorrelated Errors', *Econometrica*, 58:479–94.

—— and King, M. L. (1991). 'Optimal Invariant Test for Both Autocorrelation Coefficient in Linear Regressions with Stationary or Nonstationary AR(1) Errors', *Journal of Econometrics*, 47:115–43.

—— and Kiviet, J. F. (1994). 'Exact Inference Methods for First-Order Autoregressive Distributed Lag Models', Technical Report, C. R. D. E., Université de Montréal and Tinbergen Institute, University of Amsterdam.

———— (1996). 'Exact Tests for Structural Change in First Order Dynamic Models', *Journal of Econometrics*, 70:39–68.

Durbin, J. (1979). 'Discussion of the Paper by Barndorff-Nielsen and Cox', *Journal of the Royal Statistical Society*, 41:301–2.

Dwivedi, T. D. and Chaubey, Y. P. (1981). 'Moments of a Ratio of Two Positive Quadratic Forms in Normal Variables', *Communication in Statistics*, 10:503–16.

—— and Srivastava, V. K. (1984). 'Exact Finite Sample Properties of Double $k$-class Estimators in Simultaneous Equations', *Journal of Econometrics*, 25:263–83.

Ebbeler, D. H. and McDonald, J. B. (1973). 'An Analysis of the Properties of the Exact Finite Sample Distribution of a Nonconsistent GCL Structural Variance Estimator', *Econometrica*, 41:59–65.

Edgeworth, F. Y. (1896). 'The Asymmetrical Probability Curve', *Philosophical Magazine*, 41:90–9.

—— (1905). 'The Law of Error', *Transactions of the Cambridge Philosophical Society*, 20:36–65, 113–41.

Efron, B. (1979). 'Bootstrap Methods: Another Look at the Jacknife', *Annals of Statistics*, 7:1–26.

—— (1982). *The Jackknife, the Bootstrap and Other Resampling Plans* (Philadelphia: SIAM).

Ellison, G. and Satchell, S. E. (1988). *Finite Sample Properties of a Co-integration Model.* (Cambridge: Cambridge University).

Engle, R. F. (1982). 'Autoregressive Conditional Heteroskedasticity with Estimates of the Variance United Kingdom Inflation', *Econometrica*, 50:987–1007.

Erdelyi, A. (1956). *Asymptotic Expansions* (Dover, New York).

Esseen, C.-G. (1945). 'Fourier Analysis of Distribution Functions. A Mathematical Study of the Laplace–Gaussian Law', *Acta Mathematica*, 77:1–125.

Evans, G. B. A. and Savin, N. E. (1981). 'Testing Unit Roots: 1', *Econometrica*, 49:753–79.

—— —— (1982). 'Conflict Among the Criteria Revisited: The W, LR and LM Tests', *Econometrica*, 50:737–48.

—— —— (1984). 'Testing for Unit Roots: 2', *Econometrica*, 50:1241–89.

Fan, Y. (1990). 'Properties of OLS Estimator in Models with Integrated and Polynomial Trend Regressors', Manuscript, University of Windsor, Ontario.

Farebrother, R. W. (1984). 'The Distribution of a Linear Combination of $\chi^2$ Random Variables', *Applied Statistics*, 33:366–9.

—— (2002). 'Computing the Distribution as a Quadratic Form in Normal Variables', in A. Ullah, A. Wan, and A. Chaturvedi (eds.), *Handbook of Applied Economics and Statistical Inference*, (Marcel Dekker), pp. 231–50.

Feller, W. (1971). *An Introduction to Probability Theory and its Applications*, vol. 2 (New York: Wiley).

Fisher, R. A. (1921). 'On the Probable Error of a Coefficient of Correlation Deduced from a Small Sample', *Metron*, 1:1–32.

—— (1922). 'The Goodness of Fit of Regression Formulae and the Distribution of Regression Coefficients', *Journal of the Royal Statistical Society*, 85:597–612.

—— (1928). 'The General Sampling Distribution of the Multiple Correlation Coefficient', *Proceedings of the Royal Statistical Society*, 121:654–73.

—— (1935). 'The Mathematical Distributions Used in the Common Tests of Significance', *Econometrica*, 3:353–65.

Forchini, G. (2002). 'The Exact Cumulative Distribution Function of a Ratio of Quadratic Forms in Normal Variables, with Applications to the AR(1) Model', *Econometric Theory*, 18:823–52.

Fujikoshi, Y. and Veitch, L. G. (1979). 'Estimation of Dimensionality in Canonical Correlation Analysis', *Biometrika*, 66:345–51.

Fuller, W. (1977). 'Some Properties of a Modification of the Limited Information Estimator', *Econometrica*, 45:939–53.

Fuller, W. A. (1976). *Introduction to Statistical Time Series* (New York: Wiley).

—— and Hasza, D. P. (1980). 'Predictors for the First-Order Autoregressive Process', *Journal of Econometrics*, 13:139–57.

———— (1981*a*). 'Corrigenda: Properties of Predictors for Autoregressive Time Series', *Journal of the American Statistical Association*, 76:1023.

———— (1981*b*). 'Properties of Predictors for Autoregressive Time Series', *Journal of the American Statistical Association*, 76:155–61.

Gao, C. and Lahiri, K. (2002). 'A Note on the Double $k$-class Estimator in Simultaneous Equations', *Journal of Econometrics*, 108:101–11.

Gil-Pelaez, J. (1951). 'Note On the Inversion Theorem', *Biometrika*, 38:481–2.

Goldberger, A. S., Nagar, A. L., and Odeh, H. S. (1961). 'The Covariance Matrices of Reduced Form Coefficients and Forecasts for a Structural Econometric Model', *Econometrica*, 29:556–73.

Gram, J. P. (1879). Om Raekkeudviklinger bestempte ved Hjaelp av de mindste Kvadraters Methode (Kobenhavn).

Granger, C. W. J. and Newbold, P. (1974). 'Spurious Regressions in Econometrics', *Journal of Econometrics*, 2:111–20.

Greene, W. H. (2000). *Econometric Analysis* (Upper Saddle River, NJ: Prentice Hall).

Grenader, U. and Szego, G. (1958). *Toeplitz Forms and Their Applications* (Berkeley: University of California).

Gurland, J. (1948). 'Inversion Formulae for the Distribution of Ratios', *The Annals of Mathematical Statistics*, 19:228–37.

—— (1955). 'Distribution of Definite and Indefinite Quadratic Forms', *The Annals of Mathematical Statistics*, 26:122–7.

Gurland, J. (1956). 'Quadratic Forms in Normally Distributed Random Variables', *Sankhya*, 17:37–50.

Haavelmo, T. (1943). 'The Statistical Implications of a System of Simultaneous Equations', *Econometrica*, 11:1–12.

—— (1947). 'Methods of Measuring the Marginal Propensity to Consume', *Journal of the American Statistical Association*, 42:105–22.

Hahn, J. (1997). 'Optimal Inference with Many Instruments', Working Paper, Department of Economics, University of Pennsylvania.

—— and Inoue, A. (2000). 'A Monte Carlo Comparison of Various Asymptotic Approximations to the Distribution of Instrumental Variable Estimators', Working Paper, Department of Economics, Brown University.

—— and Newey, W. (2002). 'Jacknife and Analytical Bias Reduction for Nonlinear Panel Models', manuscript, MIT, Massachusetts.

—— Hausman, J., and Kuersteiner, G. (2001). 'Higher Order MSE of Jackknife 2SLS', Working Paper, Department of Economics, MIT.

Hale, C., Mariano, R. S., and Ramage, J. G. (1980). 'Finite Sample Analysis of Misspecification in Simultaneous Equation Models', *Journal of the American Statistical Association*, 75:418–27.

Hall, P. (1988). 'Theoretical Comparison of Bootstrap Confidence Intervals', *The Annals of Statistics*, 16:927–53.

—— (1992). *The Bootstrap and Edgeworth Expansion* (New York: Springer-Verlag).

Hall, A. R., Rudebusch, G. D., and Wilcox, D. W. (1996). 'Judging Instrument Relevance in Instrumental Variables Estimation', *International Economic Review*, 37:283–98.

Han, C. and Schmidt, P. (2001). 'The Asymptotic Distribution of the Instrumental Variable Estimators when the Instruments are not Correlated with the Regressors', *Economics Letters*, 74:61–6.

Heckman, J. J. (1979). 'Sample Selection Bias as a Specification Error', *Econometrica*, 47:153–61.

Helstom, C. W. (1983). 'Comment. Distribution of Quadratic Forms in Normal Random Variables—Evaluation by Numerical Integration', *SIAM Journal on Scientific and Statistical Computing*, 4:353–56.

Hendry, D. F. (1984). 'The Monte Carlo Experimentation in Econometrics', in M. D. Intriligator and Z. Griliches (eds.), *Handbook of Econometrics*, vol. 2 (Amsterdam: North Holland).

Hillier, G. (2001). 'The Density of a Quadratic Form in a Vector Uniformly Distributed on the n-Sphere', *Econometric Theory*, 17:1–28.

—— Kinal, T., and Srivastava, V. K. (1984). 'On the Moments of Ordinary Least Squares and Instrumental Variable Estimators in a General Structural Equation', *Econometrica*, 52:185–202.

Hillier, G. H. and Satchell, S. E. (1986). 'Finite Sample Properties of a Two-Stage Single Equation Estimator in the SUR Model', *Econometric Theory*, 2:66–74.

Holly, A. and Phillips, P. C. B. (1979). 'A Saddlepoint Approximation to the Distribution of the k-Class Estimator of a Coefficient in a Simultaneous System', *Econometrica*, 47:1527–47.

Hoque, A. (1985). 'The Exact Moments of Forecast Error in the General Dynamic Models', *Sankhya*, 47:128–43.

—— and Peters, T. (1986). 'Finite Sample Analysis of the ARMAX Models', *Sankhya: The Indian Journal of Statistics*, 48:266–83.

—— Magnus, J. R., and Pesaran, B. (1988). 'The Exact Multi-Period Mean-Square Forecast Error for the First-Order Autoregressive Model', *Journal of Econometrics*, 39:327–46.

Horowitz, J. L. (2001). 'The Bootstrap in Econometrics', in J. J. Heckman and E. Leamer (eds.), *Handbook of Econometrics*, vol. 5 (Amsterdam: North Holland).

Hsiao, C. (1986). *Analysis of Panel Data* (Cambridge: Cambridge University Press).

Hurwicz, L. (1950). 'Least Squares Bias in Time Series', in T. C. Koopmans (ed.), *Statistical Inference in Dynamic Economic Models*, (New York: Wiley).

Iglesias, E. and Phillips, G. D. A. (2001). 'Small Sample Properties of ML Estimators in AR-ARCH Models', Mimeo, Cardiff Business School, Cardiff University, Cardiff, Wales, UK.

Imhof, P. J. (1961). 'Computing the Distribution of Quadratic Form in Normal Variables', *Biometrika*, 48:419–26.

James, A. T. (1964). 'Distributions of Matrix Variates and Latent Roots Derived from Normal Samples', *The Annals of Mathematical Statistics*, 35:450–75.

Jensen, D. R. and Solomon, H. (1972). 'A Gaussian Approximation to the Distribution of a Definite Quadratic Form', *Journal of the American Statistical Association*, 67:898–902.

Jeong, J. and Maddala, G. S. (1993). 'A Perspective on Application of Bootstrap Methods in Econometrics', in G. S. Maddala, C. R. Rao, and H. D. Vinod (eds.), *Handbook of Statistics*, vol. 11, pp. 573–610, (New York: North Holland).

Johnston, J. and DiNardo, J. (1997). *Econometric Methods*, 4th edition (New York: McGraw Hill).

Kabe, D. G. (1963). 'A Note on the Exact Distributions of the GCL Estimators in Two-Leading Overidentified Cases', *Journal of the American Statistical Association*, 58:535–7.

—— (1964). 'On the Exact Distributions of the GCL Estimators in a Leading Three-Equation', *Journal of the American Statistical Association*, 58:881–94.

Kadane, J. (1971). 'Comparison of k-Class Estimators when the Disturbances are Small', *Econometrica*, 39:723–37.

—— (1974). 'Testing a Subset of the Overidentifying Restrictions', *Econometrica*, 42:853–67.

Kadane, J. B. (1970). 'Testing Overidentifying Restrictions when the Disturbances are Small', *Journal of the American Statistical Association*, 65:182–5.

Kendall, M. and Stuart, A. (1977). *The Advanced Theory of Statistics*, (New York: Macmillan Publishing).

Khatri, C. G. (1987). 'Quadratic Forms and Null Robustness for Elliptical Distributions', *Proceedings of the Second International Tampere Conference in Statistics*, Tempere, Finland, 177–203.

King, M. L. (1980). 'Robust Tests for Spherical Symmetry and Their Application to Least Squares Regression', *The Annals of Statistics*, 8: 1265–71.

Kiviet, J. F. (1995). 'On Bias, Inconsistency and Efficiency of Various Estimators in Dynamic Panel Data Models', *Journal of Econometrics*, 68:53–78.

—— and Durfour, J. M. (1997). 'Exact Tests in Single Equation Autoregressive Distributed Lag Models', *Journal of Econometrics*, 80:325–53.

—— and Phillips, G. D. A. (1987). 'Bias Reduction in Dynamic Simultaneous Equation Models', Discussion Paper #ES193, Deparment of Econometric and Social Statistics, University of Manchester.

—— —— (1990). 'Exact Similar Tests for the Root of a First Order Autoregressive Regression Model', University of Amsterdam, AE Report, 12/90, Paper presented at ESWM'90, Barcelona.

—— and Phillips, G. D. A. (1992). 'Exact Similar Tests for Unit Roots and Cointegration', *Oxford Bulletin of Economics and Statistics*, 54: 349–67.

————(1993). 'Alternative Bias Approximations in Regressions with a Lagged Dependent Variable', *Econometric Theory*, 9:62–80.

Knight, J. L. (1977). 'On the Existence of Moments of the Partially Restricted Reduced-Form Estimators from a Simultaneous-Equation Model', *Journal of Econometrics*, 5:315–21.

——(1985). 'The Moments of OLS and 2SLS when the Disturbances are Non-Normal', *Journal of Econometrics*, 27:39–60.

——(1986). 'Non-Normal Errors and the Distribution of OLS and 2SLS Structural Estimators', *Econometric Theory*, 2:75–102.

Koenker, R. (1981). 'A Note On Studentizing a Test for Heteroscedasticity', *Journal of Econometrics*, 17:107–12.

—— and Machaso, J. A. F. (1999). 'GMM Inference when the Number of Moment Conditions is Large', *Journal of Econometrics*, 93: 327–44.

Koerts, J. and Abrahamse, A. P. J. (1969). *On the Theory and Application of the General Linear Model* (Rotterdam: Rotterdam University Press).

Konishi, S., Niki, N., and Gupta, A. K. (1988). 'Asymptotic Expansions for the Distribution of Quadratic Forms in Normal Variables', *The Annals of the Institute of Statistical Mathematics*, 40:279–96.

Kwapien, S. and Woyczynski, W. A. (1987). 'Double Stochastic Integrals, Random Quadratic Forms and Random Series in Orlicz Spaces', *The Annals of Probability*, 15:1072–96.

LeBreton, A. and Pham, D. T. (1989). 'On the Bias of the Least Squares Estimator for the First-Order Autoregression Process', *The Annals of the Institute of Statistical Mathematics*, 41:555–63.

Lehmann, E. L. (1983). *Testing Statistical Hypotheses*, 1st edition (New York: John Wiley & Sons).

Li, H. and Maddala, G. S. (1996). 'Bootstrapping Time Series Models', *Econometric Reviews*, 15:115–58.

Lieberman, O. (1994*a*). 'A Laplace Approximation to the Moments of a Ratio of Quadratic Forms', *Biometrika*, 81(4):681–90.

——(1994*b*). 'Saddlepoint Approximations for the Least Squares Estimator in First-Order Autoregression', *Biometrika*, 81(4):807–11.

Lieberman, O. (1994*c*). 'Saddlepoint Approximation for the Distribution of a Ratio of Quadratic Form in Normal Variables', *Journal of American Statistical Association*, 89:924–8.

—— (1997). 'The Effect of Nonnormality', *Econometric Theory*, 13:52–78.

Linton, O. (1992). 'Small Sample Properties of Adaptive GLS Estimators', Discussion Papers in Economics No. 75: Nuffield College, Oxford.

—— (1996). 'Second Order Approximation in a Linear Regression with Heteroscedasticity of Unknown Form', *Econometric Theory*, 15:1–32.

—— (1997). 'An Asymptotic Expansion In the GARCH(1,1) Model', *Econometric Theory*, 13, 558–81.

Luigannini, R. and Rice, S. (1980). 'Saddle Point Approximation for the Distribution of the Sum of Independent Random Variables', *Advanced Applied Probability*, 12:475–90.

———— (1984). 'Distribution of the Ratio of Quadratic Forms in Normal Variables—Numerical Methods', *SIAM Journal on Scientific and Statistical Computing*, 5:476–88.

Lye, J. N. (1987). 'Some Further Results on the Distribution of Double k-Class Estimators', Manuscript, University of Canterbury.

—— (1988). 'On the Exact Distribution of a Ratio of Bilinear to Quadratic Form in Normal Variables with Econometric Applications', Manuscript, University of Canterbury.

Maasoumi, E. (1978). 'A Modified Stein-Like Estimator for the Reduced Form Coefficients of Simultaneous Equations', *Econometrica*, 46:695–703.

—— (1988). *Contributions to Econometrics*, vol. 2 (Cambridge: Cambridge University Press).

—— and Phillips, P. C. B. (1982). 'On the Behavior of Inconsistent Instrumental Variable Estimators', *Journal of Econometrics*, 19:183–201.

MacKinnon, J. G. and Smith, A. A. Jr. (1998). 'Approximate Bias Correction in Econometrics', *Journal of Econometrics*, 85:205–30.

Maddala, G. S. (1974). 'Some Small Sample Evidence on Tests of Significance in Simultaneous Equations Models', *Econometrica*, 42:841–51.

—— and Jeong, J. (1992). 'On the Exact Small Sample Distribution of the Instrumental Variable Estimator', *Econometrica*, 60:181–3.

Maekawa, K. (1985). 'Asymptotic Theory in Regression Analysis', Hiroshima University Monograph series, Hiroshima University, Hiroshima (in Japanese).

Magee, L. (1985). 'Efficiency of Iterative Estimators in the Regression Model with AR(1) Disturbances', *Journal of Econometrics*, 29:275–87.

—— Ullah, A., and Srivastava, V. K. (1987). 'Efficiency of Estimators in the Regression Model with First Order Autoregressive Errors', in M. L. King and D. E. A. Giles (eds.), Specification Analysis in the Linear Model, pp. 81–98, (Routledge and Kegan Paul, New York).

Magnus, J. R. (1978). 'The Moments of Products of Quadratic Forms in Normal Variables', *Statistica Neerlandica*, 32:201–10.

——(1979). 'The Expectation of Products of Quadratic Forms in Normal Variables: The Practice', *Statistica Neerlandica*, 331:131–6.

——(1986). 'The Exact Moments of a Ratio of Quadratic Forms in Normal Variable', *Annals d'Economie et de Statistique*, 4:95–109.

Malinvaud, E. (1970). *Statistical Methods of Econometrics*, 2nd edition (Amsterdam: North Holland).

Mallela, P. (1972). 'Necessary and Sufficient Conditions for MINQU-Estimation of Heteroskedastic Variances in Linear Models', *Journal of the American Statistical Association*, 67:486–7.

Mallows, C. L. (1973). 'Some Comments On CP', *Technometrics*, 15: 661–75.

Mann, H. B. and Wald, A. (1943). 'On the Statistical Treatment of Linear Stochastic Difference Equations', *Econometrica*, 11:173–220.

Mariano, R. S. (1982). 'Analytical Small-Sample Distribution Theory in Econometrics: The Simultaneous-Equations Case', *International Economic Review*, 23:503–33.

—— and McDonald, J. (1979). 'A Note on the Distribution Functions of LIML and 2SLS Coefficient Estimators in the Exactly Defined Case', *Journal of the American Statistical Association*, 74:847–8.

—— and Ramage, J. G. (1978). 'Ordinary Least Squares Versus Other Single Equation Estimators: A Return Bout Under Misspecification in Simultaneous Systems', Discussion Paper No. 400, University of Pennsylvania.

—— and Sawa, T. (1972). 'The Exact Finite Sample Distribution of the Limited Information Maximum Likelihood Estimator in the Case of Two Included Endogenous Variables', *Journal of the American Statistical Association*, 67:159–63.

Marriot, F. and Pope, J. (1954). 'Bias in the Estimation of Autocorrelation', *Biometrika*, 41:390–402.

Martynov, G. V. (1977). 'A Generalization of Smirnov's formula for the Distribution Functions of Quadratic Forms', *Theory of Probability and its Applications*, 22:602–7.

Mathai, A. M. and Provost, S. B. (1992). *Quadratic Forms in Random Variables* (New York: Marcel Dekker, Inc.).

McCarthy, M. D. (1972). 'A Note on the Forecasting Properties of 2SLS Restricted Reduced Forms', *International Economic Review*, 13: 757–61.

McClellan, M., McNeil, B. J., and Newhouse, J. P. (1994). 'Does More Intensive Treatment of Acute Myocardial Infarction in the Elderly Reduce Mortality? Analysis Using Instrumental Variables', *Journal of the American Medical Association*, 272:859–66.

McDonald, J. B. (1972). 'The Exact Finite Sample Distribution Function of the Limited Information Maximum Likelihood Identifiability Test Statistic', *Econometrica*, 40:1109–19.

Menzefricke, U. (1981). 'On Positive Definite Quadratic Forms in Correlated t Variables', *The Annals of the Institute of Statistical Mathematics*, 33:385–90.

Mercurio, M. (2000). 'Econometric Analysis of Forecasts in Dynamic and Panel Data Models', Ph.D. Dissertation, University of California, Riverside.

Moore, G. R., Fuhrer, J. C., and Schuh, S. D. (1995). 'Estimating the Linear-Quadratic Inventory Model: Maximum Likelihood Versus Generalized Method of Moments', *Journal of Monetary Economics*, 35: 115–57.

Morimune, K. (1978). 'Improving the Limited Information Maximum Likelihood Estimator when the Disturbances are Small', *Journal of the American Statistical Association*, 73:867–71.

—— (1983). 'Approximate Distributions of k-Class Estimators when the Degree of Overidentifiability is Large Compared with Sample Size', *Econometrica*, 57:1341–60.

Morin-Wahhab, D. (1985). 'Moments of Ratios of Quadratic Forms', *Communications in Statistics-Theory and Methods*, 14:499–508.

Moschopoulos, P. (1983). 'On a New Transformation to Normality', *Communications in Statistics*, 12:1873–5.

Müller, U. K. and Elliott, G. (2001). 'Tests for Unit Roots and the Initial Observation', Manuscript, University of California, San Diego.

Nabeya, S. and Tanaka, K. (1990). 'A General Approach to the Limiting Distribution for Estimators in Time Series Regression with Nonstable Autoregressive Errors', *Econometrica*, 58:145–63.

Nagar, A. L. (1959). 'The Bias and Moments Matrix of the General k-Class Estimators of the Parameters in Structural Equations', *Econometrica*, 27:575–95.

—— (1962). 'Double *k*-class Estimators of Parameters in Simultaneous Equations and Their Small Sample Properties', *Internal Economic Review*, 3:168–88.

—— and Sahay, S. N. (1978). 'The Bias and Mean Squared Error of Forecasts from Partially Restricted Reduced Form', *Journal of Econometrics*, 7:227–43.

—— and Ullah, A. (1973). 'Note on Approximate Skewness and Kurtosis of the Two Stage Least Squares Estimator', *Indian Economic Review*, 7:70–80.

Nankervis, J. S. and Savin, N. E. (1985). 'Testing the Autoregressive Parameter with the t-Statistics', *Journal of Econometrics*, 27:143–62.

—— —— (1988). 'The Student's-t Approximation in a Stationary First-Order Autoregressive Model', *Econometrica*, 56:119–45.

Nelson, C. R. and Startz, R. (1990a). 'The Distribution of the Instrumental Variable Estimator and its t-Ratio when the Instrument is a Poor One', *Journal of Business*, 63:125–40.

—— —— (1990b). 'Some Further Results on the Exact Small Properties of the Instrumental Variable Estimator', *Econometrica*, 58:967–76.

Neumann, von J. (1941). 'Distribution of the Ratio of the Mean Square Successive Difference to the Variance', *The Annals of Mathematical Statistics*, 12:367–95.

Ohtani, K. and Hasegawa, H. (1993). 'On the Small Sample Properties of R2 in a Linear Regression Model with Multivariate t Errors and Proxy Variables', *Econometric Theory*, 9:504–15.

Okamoto, M. (1960). 'An Inequality for the Weighted Sum of c2 Variates', *Bulletin of Mathematical Statistics*, 9:69–70.

Olver, F. W. J. (1974). *Asymptotics and Special Functions* (New York: Academic Press).

Oman, S. D. and Zacks, S. (1981). 'A Mixture Approximation to the Distribution of a Weighted Sum of Chi-Squared Variables', *Journal of Statistical Computation and Simulation*, 13:215–24.

Orcutt, G. H. and Winokur, H. S. (1969). 'First Order Autoregression: Inference Estimation and Prediction', *Econometrica*, 37:1–14.

Pagan, A., and Ullah, A. (1999). *Nonparametric Econometrics*, (New York: Cambridge University Press).

Palm, F. C. and Sneek, J. M. (1984). 'Significance Tests and Spurious Correlation in Regression Models with Autocorrelated Errors', *Statistische Hefte*, L5:87–105.

Park, J. Y. (2003). 'Bootstrap Unit Root Tests', *Econometrica*, 71:1845–95.

Patnaik, P. B. (1949). 'The Non-Central c2 and F-Distributions and their Applications', *Biometrika*, 36:202–32.

Pearson, E. S. (1959). 'Note on the Approximation to the Distribution of Non-Central $\chi^2$', *Biometrika*, 46:364.

Perron, P. A. (1991). 'A Continuous Time Approximation to the Unstable First-Order Autoregressive Process: The Case Without an Intercept', *Econometrica*, 59(1), 211–36.

Pesaran, M. and Timmermann, A. (2003). 'Small Sample Properties of Forecasts from Autoregressive Models Under Structural Breaks', Manuscript, University of Cambridge, Cambridge.

Peters, T. A. (1989). 'The Exact Moments of OLS in Dynamic Regression Models with Non-Normal Errors', *Journal of Econometrics*, 40:279–305.

Petrov, V. V. (1975). *Sums of Independent Random Variables* (Berlin: Springer-Verlag).

Pfanzagl, J. and Wefelmeyer, W. (1978). 'An Asymptotically Complete Class of Tests', *Zeitschrift fur Wahrscheinlichkeitstheorie*, 45:49–72.

Phillips, P. C. B. (1977a). 'Approximations to Some Finite Sample Distributions Associated with a First-Order Stochastic Difference Equation', *Econometrica*, 45:463–85.

—— (1977b). 'A General Theorem in the Theory of Asymptotic Expansions as Approximations to the Finite Sample Distributions of Econometric Estimators', *Econometrica*, 45b: 1517–34.

—— (1977c). 'An Approximation to the Finite Sample Distribution of Zellner's Seemingly Unrelated Regression Estimator', *Journal of Econometrics*, 6:147–64.

—— (1978). 'Edgeworth and Saddlepoint Approximations in the First-Order Non Circular Autoregression', *Biometrika*, 65:91–8.

——(1979). 'The Sampling Distribution of Forecasts from a First-Order Autoregression', *Journal of Econometrics*, 9:241–61.

——(1980). 'Finite Sample Theory and the Distributions of Alternative Estimators of the Marginal Propensity to Consume', *Review of Economic Studies*, 47:183–224.

——(1983). 'Exact Small Sample Theory in Simultaneous Equations Models', in M. D. Intriligator and Z. Griliches (eds.), *Handbook of Econometrics*, vol. 1 (Amsterdam: North Holland).

——(1985). 'The Distribution of Matrix Quotients', *Journal of Multivariate Analysis*, 16:157–61.

——(1986). 'The Exact Distribution of the Wald Statistic', *Econometrica*, 54:881–95.

——(1987*a*). 'Time Series Regression with a Unit Root', *Econometrica*, 55:277–301.

——(1987*b*). 'Towards a Unified Asymptotic Theory for Autoregression', *Biometrika*, 74:535–47.

——(1987*c*). 'Asymptotic Expansions in Nonstationary Vector Autoregression', *Econometric Theory*, 3:45–68.

——(1987*d*). 'Fractional Matrix Calculus and the Distribution of Multivariate Tests', in I. MacNeill and G. Umphrey (eds.), *Time Series and Econometric Modelling* (Reidell Press, Holland).

——(1989). 'Partially Identified Econometric Models', *Econometric Theory*, 5:181–240.

—— and Park, J. Y. (1987). 'On the Formulation of Wald Tests of Nonlinear Restrictions', *Econometrica*, 55:1065–84.

Press, S. J. (1966). 'Linear Combinations of Non-Central Chi-Squared Variates', *The Annals of Mathematical Statistics*, 37: 480–7.

Provost, S. B. (1989*a*). 'On Sums of Independent Gamma Variables', *Statistics*, 20:1–8.

Provost, S. B. (1989*b*). 'The Distribution Function of Some Ratios of Quadratic Forms', in *Recent Developments in Statistical and Actuarial Science*, 143–54 (SCI-TEX publications, London, Canada).

——(1989*c*). 'On the Distribution of the Ratio of Powers of Sums of Gamma Random Variables', *The Pakistan Journal of Statistics*, 5:157–73.

Provost, S. B. and Rudnik, E. (1991). 'Some Distributional Aspects of Ratios of Quadratic Forms', Technical Report 91-01, Department of Statistical and Actuarial Sciences, U. W. O., London, Canada.

Raj, B. and Ullah, A. (1981). *Econometrics: A Random Coefficient Approach* (England: Croom Helm).

Rao, C. R. (1970). 'Estimation of Heteroskedastic Variances in Linear Models', *Journal of the American Statistical Association*, 65:161–72.

—— (1973). *Linear Statistical Inference and Its Applications* (New York: John Wiley & Sons).

Rhodes, G. F. (1981). 'Exact Density Functions and Approximate Critical Regions for Likelihood Ratio Identifiability Test Statistics', *Econometrica*, 49:1035–56.

—— and Westbrook, M. D. (1981). 'A Study of Estimator Densities and Performance Under Misspecification', *Journal of Econometrics*, 16:311–37.

Rice, S. O. (1980). 'Distribution of Quadratic Forms in Normal Variables— Evaluation by Numerical Integration', *SIAM Journal on Scientific and Statistical Computing*, 1:438–48.

Richardson, D. H. (1968). 'The Exact Distributions of a Structural Coefficient Estimator', *Journal of the American Statistical Association*, 63: 1214–26.

—— and Rohr, R. J. (1971). 'The Distribution of a Structural t-Statistic for the Case of Two Included Endogenous Variables', *Journal of the American Statistical Association*, 66:375–82.

—— and Wu, D. M. (1971). 'A Note on the Comparison of Ordinary and Two Stage Least Squares Estimators', *Econometrica*, 39:973–81.

Rilstone, P. and Ullah, A. (2002). 'The Second-Order Bias of Heckman's Sample Bias Estimator', Manuscript, in Y. P. Chaubey (ed.), *Recent Advances in Statistical Methods* (New Jersey: World Scientific Publishing).

—— Srivatsava, V. K., and Ullah, A. (1996). 'The Second Order Bias and MSE of Nonlinear Estimators', *Journal of Econometrics*, 75:239–395.

Robbins, H. E. and Pitman, E. J. G. (1949). 'Application of the Method of Mixtures to Quadratic Forms in Normal Variates', *The Annals of Mathematical Statistics*, 20:552–60.

Rothenberg, T. J. (1978). 'Multivariate Asymptotic Expansions for Structural Coefficient Estimators', Mimeo, University of California, Berkeley.

—— (1984a). 'Approximating the Distribution of Econometric Estimators and Test Statistics', in M. D. Intriligator and Z. Griliches (eds.), *Handbook of Econometrics*, vol. 2 (Amsterdam: North Holland).

——(1984*b*). 'Approximate Normality of Generalised Squares Estimates', *Econometrica*, 52:811–25.

——(1984*c*). 'Hypothesis Testing in the Linear Model when the Error Covariance Matrix is Nonscalar', *Econometrica*, 52:827–42.

——(1988). 'Approximate Power Functions for Some Robust Tests of Regression Coefficients', *Econometrica*, 56:997–1019.

——(2002). 'Some Elementary Distribution Theory for an Autoregression Fitted to a Random Walk', *Journal of Econometrics*, 111:355–61.

Sargan, J. D. (1973). 'The Bias of the FIML Estimates of the Reduced Form Coefficients', unpublished.

——(1974). 'The Validity of Nagar's expansion for the Moments of Econometric Estimators', *Econometrica*, 42:169–76.

——(1975). 'Gram–Charlier Approximations Applied to t-Ratios of k-Class Estimators', *Econometrica*, 43:326–46.

——(1976). 'Econometric Estimators and the Edgeworth Approximation', *Econometrica*, 44:421–48.

——(1980). 'Some Approximations to the Distribution of Econometric Criteria which are Asymptotically Distributed as Chi-Squared', *Econometrica*, 48:1107–38.

—— and Mikhail, W. N. (1971). 'A General Approximation to the Distribution of Instrumental Variable Estimates', *Econometrica*, 39:131–69.

Satchell, S. E. (1984). 'Approximations to the Finite Sample Distributions for Non-Stable First Order Difference Equations', *Econometrica*, 52:1271–88.

Sawa, T. (1969). 'The Exact Sampling Distributions of Ordinary Least Squares and Two Stage Least Squares Estimates', *Journal of the American Statistical Association*, 64:923–80.

——(1972). 'Finite Sample Properties of k-Class Estimators', *Econometrica*, 40:653–80.

——(1973*a*). 'Almost Unbiased Estimator in Simultaneous Equations Systems', *International Economic Review*, 14:97–106.

——(1973*b*). 'The Mean Square Error of a Combined Estimator and Numerical Comparison with the TSLS Estimator', *Journal of Econometrics*, 1:115–32.

——(1978). 'The Exact Moments of the Least Squares Estimator for the Autoregressive Model', *Journal of Econometrics*, 8:159–72.

Shah, B. K. (1963). 'Distribution of Definite and of Indefinite Quadratic Forms from a Non-Central Normal Distribution', *The Annals of Mathematical Statistics*, 34:186–90.

Sharma, S. C. and Giaccotto, C. (1991). 'Power and Robustness of Jacknife and Likelihood Ratio Tests for Grouped Heteroscedasticity', *Journal of Econometrics*, 49:343–72.

Shenton, L. R. and Johnson, W. I. (1965). 'Moments of a Serial Correlation Coefficient', *Journal of the Royal Statistical Society*, 27:308–20.

Siddiqui, M. M. (1965). 'Approximations to the Distribution of Quadratic Forms', *The Annals of Mathematical Statistics*, 36:677–82.

Siotani, M. (1964). 'Tolerance Regions for a Multivariate Normal Population', *The Annals of the Institute of Statistical Mathematics*, 16:135–53.

Slater, L. J. (1960). *Confluent Hypergeometric Functions* (Cambridge: University Press).

Smith, M. D. (1988). 'Convergent Series Expressions for Inverse Moments of Quadratic Forms in Normal Variables', *The Australian Journal of Statistics*, 30:245–6.

——(1989). 'On the Expectation of a Ratio of Quadratic Forms in Normal Variables', *Journal of Multivariate Analysis*, 31:244–57.

——(1994). 'Exact Densities for Variance Estimators of the Structural Disturbances in Simultaneous Equation Models', *Journal of Econometrics*, 60:157–80.

——(1996). 'Comparing Approximations to the Expectation of a Ratio of Quadratic Forms in Normal Variables', *Econometric Reviews*, 15:81–95.

Solomon, H. and Stephens, M. A. (1977). 'Distribution of a Sum of Weighted Chi-Square Variables', *Journal of the American Statistical Association*, 72:881–5.

——— (1978). 'Approximations to Density Functions Using Pearson Curves', *Journal of the American Statistical Association*, 73: 153–160.

Srinivasan, T. N. (1970). 'Approximation to Finite Sample Moments of Estimators Where Exact Sampling Distributions are Unknown', *Econometrica*, 38:533–41.

Srivastava, M. S. and Khatri, C. G. (1979). *An Introduction to Multivariate Statistics* (New York: North Holland).

Srivastava, V. K. (1970). 'The Efficiency of Estimating Seemingly Unrelated Regression Equations', *The Annals of the Institute of Statistical Mathematics*, 22:483–93.

—— and Giles, D. E. A. (1987). *Seemingly Unrelated Regression Equations Model* (New York: Marcel Dekker).

—— and Maekawa, K. (1995). 'Efficiency Properties of Feasible Generalized Least Squares Estimators in SURE Models Under Non-Normal Disturbances', *Journal of Econometrics*, 66:99–121.

—— and Tiwari, R. (1976). 'Evaluation of Expectations of Products of Stochastic Matrices', *Scandanivian Journal of Statistics*, 3:135–8.

—— and Ullah, A. (1995). 'Stein-rule estimation in models with a lagged-dependent variable', *Communications in Statistics. Theory Methods*, 24:1343–1353.

—— and Upadhyaya, S. (1978). 'Large-Sample Approximations in Seemingly Unrelated Regression Equations', *The Annals of the Institute of Statistical Mathematics*, 30:89–96.

—— Srivastava, A. K., and Ullah, A. (1995). 'The Coefficient of Determination and its Adjusted Version in Linear Regression Models', *Econometric Reviews*, 14:229–40.

Staiger, D. and Stock, J. H. (1997). 'Instrumental Variables Regression with Weak Instruments', *Econometrica*, 65:557–86.

Stock, J. H. (1987). 'Asymptotic Properties of Least Squares Estimators of Cointegrating Vectors', *Econometrica*, 55:1035–56.

Swamy, P. A. V. B. (1970). 'Efficient Inference in a Random Coefficient Regression Model', *Econometrica*, 38:311–23.

—— (1971). *Statistical Inference in Random Coefficient Regression Models* (New York: Springer-Verlag).

Szego, G. (1939). *Orthogonal Polynomials*, American Mathematical Society Colliquium publication 23 (New York: American Mathematical Society) p. 370.

Takeuchi, K. (1970). 'Exact Sampling Moments of Ordinary Least Squares, Instrumental Variable and Two-Stage Least Squares Estimators', *International Economic Review*, 11:1–12.

—— and Morimune, K. (1979). 'Asymptotic Completeness of the Extended Maximum Likelihood Estimators in Simultaneous Equations System', unpublished.

Taneja, V. S. (1976). 'Approximations to the Distribution of Indefinite Quadratic Forms in Non-Central Normal Variables', *Metron*, 34:255–68.

Taylor, W. E. (1980). 'Small Sample Considerations in Estimation from Panel Data', *Journal of Econometrics*, 13:203–23.

Taylor, W. E. (1983). 'On the Relevance of Finite Sample Distribution Theory', *Econometric Reviews*, 2:1–39.

Theil, H. (1971). *Principles of Econometrics* (New York: Wiley).

Thornber, H. (1967). 'Finite Sample Monte Carlo Studies: An Autoregressive Illustration', *Journal of the American Statistical Association*, 62:801–18.

Tracy, D. S. and Srivastava, A. K. (1990). 'Third Order Comparison of Seemingly Unrelated Regression Estimators', *Journal of Quantitative Economics*, 6:351–65.

Tsui, A. K. and Ali, M. M. (1989). 'Exact Moments of the Least Squares Estimator in a First-Order Nonstationary Autoregressive Model', *Proceedings of the American Statistical Association*, 220–5.

——— (1992). 'Approximations to the Distribution of the Least Squares Estimator in a First Order Stationary Autoregressive Model', *Communications in Statistics-Simulation*, 21(2):463–84.

——— (1994). 'Exact Distributions, Density Functions and Moments of the Least Squares Estimator in a First-Order Autoregressive Model', *Computational Statistics and Data Analysis*, 17:433–54.

Tsurumi, H. (1990). 'Comparing Bayesian and Non-Bayesian Limited Information Estimators', in S. Geisser, J. S. Hodges, S. J. Press and A. Zellner (eds.), *Bayesian and Likelihood Methods in Statistics and Econometrics* (Amsterdam: North-Holland).

Ullah, A. (1974). 'On the Sampling Distribution of Improved Estimators for Coefficients in Linear Regression,' *Journal of Econometrics*, 2: 143–50.

—— (1982). 'The Approximate Distribution of the Stein-Rule Estimator', *Economics Letters*, 10:305–8.

—— (1990). 'Finite Sample Econometrics: A Unified Approach', in R. A. L. Carter, J. Dutta and A. Ullah (eds.), *Contributions to Econometric Theory and Application, Volume in Honor of A. L. Nagar* pp. 242–92 (New York: Springer-Verlag).

—— (2002). 'Uses of Entropy and Divergence Measures for Evaluating Econometric Approximations and Inference', *Journal of Econometrics*, 107:313–26.

—— and Maasoumi, E. (1986). 'Moments of OLS Estimators in an Autoregressive Moving Average Model with Explanatory Variables', *Economics Letters*, 21:265–9.

—— and Nagar, A. L. (1974). 'The Exact Mean of the Two Stage Least Squares Estimator of the Structural Parameters in the Equation Having Three Endogenous Variables', *Econometrica*, 42:749–58.

—— and Phillips, P. C. B. (1986). 'Distribution of the F-Ratio', *Econometric Theory*, 2:449–52.

—— and Srivastava, V. K. (1994). 'Moments of the Ratio of Quadratic Forms in Non-Normal Variables with Econometric Examples', *Journal of Econometrics*, 62:129–41.

———— (1988). 'On the Improved Estimation of Structural Coefficients', *Sankhya, Series B*, 50:111–18.

—— and Ullah, S. (1976). 'On the Sampling Distribution of the Two-Stage Least Squares Estimator of the Coefficients of Explanatory Variables', Manuscript, Department of Economics, University of Western Ontario.

———— (1978). 'Double k-Class Estimators of Coefficients in Linear Regression', *Econometrica*, 46:705–22.

—— and Zinde-Walsh, V. (1984). 'On the Robustness of LM, LR and W Tests in Regression Models', *Econometrica*, 52:1055–66.

———— (1985). 'Estimation and Testing in a Regression Model with Spherically Symmetric Errors', *Economics Letters*, 17:127–32.

———— (1987). 'On Robustness of Tests in Linear Models with Elliptical Error Distribution', in I. MacNeill and G. Umphrey (eds.), *Time Series and Econometric Modelling*, (Reidell Press, Holland).

—— Carter, R. A. L., and Srivastava, V. K. (1984). 'The Sampling Distribution of Shrinkage Estimators and their F-Ratios in the Regression Model', *Journal of Econometrics*, 25:109–22.

—— Srivastava, V. K., and Chandra, R. (1983). 'Properties of Shrinkage Estimators when the Disturbances are not Normal', *Journal of Econometrics*, 21:389–402.

———— and Roy, N. (1995). 'Moments of the Function of Non-Normal Random Vector with Applications to Econometric Estimators and Test Statistics', *Econometric Reviews*, 4:459–71.

Vahid, F. and Issler, J. V. (2002). 'The Importance of Common Cyclical Features in VAR Analysis: A Monte-Carlo Study', *Journal of Econometrics*, 109(2), 341–63.

Vinod, H. D. (1993). 'Bootstrap Methods: Applications In Econometrics', in G. S. Maddala, C. R. Rao, and H. D. Vinod (eds.), *Handbook of Statistics: Econometrics*, vol. 11, pp. 629–61 (New York: North Holland).

—— and Ullah, A. (1981). *Recent Advances in Regression Methods* (New York: Marcel Dekker).

Wallace, D. L. (1958). 'Asymptotic Approximations to Distributions', *The Annals of Mathematical Statistics*, 29:635–54.

Wang, S. (1992). 'Tail Probability Approximations in the First-Order Noncircular Autoregression', *Biometrika*, 79:431–4.

White, H. (1980). 'A Heteroskedasticity-Consistent Covariance Matrix and a Direct Test for Heteroskedasticity', *Econometrica*, 48:817–38.

White, J. S. (1957). 'Approximation Moments for the Serial Correlation Coefficients', *The Annals of Mathematical Statistics*, 28:798–803.

—— (1958). 'The Limiting Distribution of the Serial Correlation Coefficient in the Explosive Case', *The Annals of Mathematical Statistics*, 29:1188–97.

—— (1959). 'The Limiting Distribution of the Serial Correlation Coefficient in the Explosive Case II', *The Annals of Mathematical Statistics*, 30:831–34.

—— (1961). 'Asymptotic Expansions for the Mean and Variance of the Serial Correlation Coefficient', *Biometrika*, 48:85–94.

Whittaker, E. T. and Watson, G. N. (1965). *A Course of Modern Analysis* (Cambridge: Cambridge University Press).

Whittle, P. (1964). 'On the Convergence to Normality of Quadratic Forms in Independent Variables', *Teoriya Veroyatnostei i ee Primeneniya*, 9:113–18.

Wilson, E. B. and Hilferty, M. M. (1931). 'The Distribution of Chi-Square', *Proceedings of the National Academy of Sciences*, 17:684–8.

Working, H. (1926). 'Bank Deposits as a Forecaster of the General Wholesale Price Level', *The Review of Economic Statistics*, 8:120–33.

Woglom, G. (2001). 'More Results on the Exact Small Sample Properties of the Instrumental Variable Estimator', *Econometrica*, 69: 1381–89.

Xiao, Z. and Phillips, P. C. B. (1998). 'Higher Order Approximations for Frequency Domain Time Series Regression', *Journal of Econometrics*, 86:297–336.

———— (2002). 'Higher Order Approximation for Wald Statistics in Time Series Regression with Integrated Process', *Journal of Econometrics*, 108(1):157–97.

Yamamoto, T. (1976). 'Asymptotic Mean Square Prediction Error for an Autoregressive Model with Estimated Coefficients', *Applied Statistics*, 25:123–7.

Zellner, A. (1962). 'An Efficiency Method of Estimating Seemingly Unrelated Regression Equations and Tests for Aggregation Bias', *Journal of the American Statistical Association*, 57:348–68.

—— (1971). *An Introduction to Bayesian Inference in Econometrics* (New York: Wiley).

—— (1976). 'Bayesian and Non-Bayesian Analysis of the Regression Model with Multivariate Student t Error Terms', *Journal of the American Statistical Association*, 71:400–5.

—— (1998). 'The Finite Sample Properties of Simutaneous Equations' Estimates and Estimators: Bayesian and Non-Bayesian Approaches', *Journal of Econometrics*, 83:185–212.

Zivot, E. and Wang, J. (1998). 'Inference on Structural Parameters in Instrumental Variables Regressions with Weak Instruments', *Econometrica*, 66:1389–404.

—— Startz, R., and Nelson, C. R. (1997). *Valid Confidence Intervals and Inference in the Presence of Weak Instruments*, (Seattle: University of Washington).

# Index